MASTERLESS MISTRESSES

Sor Antonia de S[...]
[...]nica Ramos Nació el
[...]de S[...]. Vistió el ábito de
[...]osa Ursulina, en la Nueva
[...] el año de 1779, y el de 180[...]
[...]a esta Ciudad, con diez y seis
[...]osas; y fue fundadora de[...]
[...]Conv.to la q.e se realizó en S[...]
[...]m.e de 182[...] haviendo ejer[...]
[...] la Prelacia 27 años y
[...]atro meses.

masterless Mistresses

THE NEW ORLEANS URSULINES

AND THE DEVELOPMENT OF A

NEW WORLD SOCIETY, 1727–1834

EMILY CLARK

Published for the
Omohundro Institute of
Early American History and Culture,
Williamsburg, Virginia,
by the
University of North Carolina Press,
Chapel Hill

The Omohundro Institute of Early American History
and Culture is sponsored jointly by the College of William
and Mary and the Colonial Williamsburg Foundation. On
November 15, 1996, the Institute adopted the present name
in honor of a bequest from Malvern H. Omohundro, Jr.

Set in Cycles type by Tseng Information Systems, Inc.
Manufactured in the United States of America

Library of Congress Cataloging-in-Publication Data
Clark, Emily, 1954–
Masterless mistresses : the New Orleans Ursulines and the
development of a new world society, 1727–1834 / Emily Clark.
    p. cm.
Includes bibliographical references and index.
ISBN 978-0-8078-3122-9 (cloth : alk. paper) —
ISBN 978-0-8078-5822-6 (pbk. : alk. paper)
1. Ursulines of New Orleans (New Orleans, La.) 2. Ursulines—
Louisiana—New Orleans—History. 3. New Orleans (La.)—
Church history. I. Title.
BX4543.U6C53 2007
271'.974076335—dc22

                                        2006033612

The paper in this book meets the guidelines for permanence
and durability of the Committee on Production Guidelines
for Book Longevity of the Council on Library Resources.

This volume received indirect support from an unrestricted
book publication grant awarded to the Institute by the
L. J. Skaggs and Mary C. Skaggs Foundation of Oakland,
California.

cloth   11 10 09 08 07   5 4 3 2 1
paper   11 10 09 08 07   5 4 3 2 1

For Ron, and in memory of Alice, with love

ACKNOWLEDGMENTS

The manuscript for this book left my office in New Orleans to go into production a week before the first anniversary of Hurricane Katrina. Historians know that no book is written without the support and assistance of a large community of colleagues and friends who read drafts, share ideas and sources, preserve us from errors, reassure us, feed us, humor us, house us, and assure us that someday the book really will appear in print. Historians in New Orleans in the summer of 2006 know that we are indebted, too, to thousands of men and women whose names we will never know who made it possible for us to come back to the city six weeks after the storm and pick up our lives and our work again. I am especially grateful to the glazier who years ago installed the window in my office so expertly that neither wind nor water penetrated beyond it to disturb my files.

There would have been no files to protect if I had not had the good fortune and privilege to study early American history and write my dissertation under Sylvia Frey, whose rigor and relentlessly daunting expectations were always balanced by her intellectual passion and the boundlessness of her generosity as a teacher and a friend. She taught me the joys and responsibilities of scholarship and the importance of finding my own voice. I owe her a debt that can never be repaid. James Boyden and Linda Pollock introduced me to early modern Europe when I was a student and continue to keep me honest in my attempts to write Atlantic history now that we are colleagues. Tulane University colleagues Marline Otte, Lawrence Powell, and Justin Wolfe are always ready to listen and talk and take my historical thinking in new and profitable directions.

Between finishing my studies at Tulane University and returning to teach there, I had the good fortune to work at three other fine institutions filled with generous colleagues. At the University of Cambridge, the principal and fellows of Newnham College, especially Onora O'Neill, Tessa Stone, Gillian Sutherland, and Sheila Watts, helped create an idyll of intellectual collegiality. Betty Wood, Mary Laven, and Martin Daunton made Cambridge's Faculty of History a welcoming and productive workplace. Ruth and Tony Badger, along with Chris and Nick, made my husband and me at home in Cambridge in every way, and they continue to be a source of professional and personal support. Marjorie Spruill, who never let me forget that women's history did not end in 1800, stood out among a cadre of great colleagues at the University of Southern Mississippi. Jane Hunter, Robert Kugler, and Rachel Wheeler helped me find my way in the liberal arts at Lewis and Clark College. Their perspectives and the opportunities they gave me to teach outside my early American box helped make this a better book.

Many people read all or part of the manuscript at various stages in its development. Susan Juster, Daniel Usner, Jr., and James Horn read an early draft and provided comments that helped me understand better the story I was trying to tell and what I needed to do to tell it well. Sylvia Frey read the full manuscript more than once, and more than once helped me push through the thicket to clarity. Virginia Gould, Gwendolyn Midlo Hall, the late Kimberly Hanger, Peter Kastor, Mary Laven, Jennifer Spear, Cécile Vidal, François Weil, and Sophie White read parts of the manuscript or essays that became part of or grew out of it and asked tough questions, provided some answers, and helped solve research problems in the process. Others, including Patricia Bonomi, Patricia Brady, Catherine Brekus, Charles Cohen, Laurent Dubois, Alicia Long, Donald Matthews, Stephen Ochs, Sue Peabody, Sarah Pearsall, Jon Sensbach, Randy Sparks, and James Walvin heard and commented on papers that eventually became part of this book. These readers and auditors gave unstintingly of their expertise and knowledge to help me, and I am grateful to them all, even though, as they will see, I did not always act on their good counsel.

When the Ursuline community of New Orleans agreed to break with tradition and give me unrestricted access to their private archives, writing this book became a possibility. Convent archivist Sister Joan Marie Aycock opened the door to a vault full of eighteenth-century records for a historian who had never met a nun, let alone written about one, without ever knowing what the outcome would be. I thank her and her sisters in religion for taking that leap of faith, though I know now that in supporting my scholarly endeavor they were simply being faithful to the rule that brought them to New Orleans nearly three hundred years ago. Charles Nolan, Archivist for the Archdiocese of New Orleans, and Dorenda Dupont helped me navigate the riches of the colonial sacramental registers in their care. The staffs of the Louisiana Collection in the Howard-Tilton Memorial Library at Tulane, the New Orleans Notarial Archives, the Historic New Orleans Collection, the Louisiana Division of the New Orleans Public Library, and the Archives Départementales de la Seine-Maritime in Rouen all gave generously of their time and expertise.

Financial support at the dissertation stage came in the form of fellowships and grants from Tulane University, the Pew Program in Religion and American History, the Louisiana chapter of the Colonial Dames of America, and the Newcomb College Center for Research on Women. Later the Mellon Postdoctoral Fellowship in American History at the University of Cambridge provided crucial support.

Earlier versions of portions of this book and its arguments have appeared previously in other publications. " 'By All the Conduct of Their Lives': A Laywomen's Confraternity in New Orleans, 1730-1744," *William and Mary Quarterly*, 3d Ser., LIV (1997), 769-794, and "The Feminine Face of Afro-Catholicism in New Orleans, 1727-1852," with Virginia M. Gould, *WMQ*, 3d Ser., LIX (2002), 409-448, describe the Ursuline role in the evangelization of enslaved Africans. Much of Chapter 6 is an elaboration of two essays published previously as "Patrimony without Pater: The New Orleans Ursulines and the Creation of a Material Legacy," in Bradley G. Bond, ed., *French Colonial Louisiana and the Atlantic World* (Baton Rouge, La., 2005), 95-110, and "Peculiar Professionals: The Financial Strategies of the New Orleans Ursulines, 1777-1825," in Michele Gillespie and Susana Delfino, eds., *Neither Lady, Nor Slave: Working Women of the Old South* (Chapel Hill, N.C., 2002), 198-220.

The Omohundro Institute of Early American History and Culture has guided the development of this book and supported the historian who wrote it in many ways. Michael McGiffert edited my first article for the *William and Mary Quarterly* and gave me a preview of the demanding road that lay ahead. Philip Morgan continued the tutelage. Sally Mason and Ronald Hoffman showed interest in my project from the first and made publication with the Institute seem possible. Fredrika J. Teute, editor of publications for the Institute, brought her peerless experience to bear on my manuscript and prodded it into its final form. Virginia Montijo copyedited the manuscript and so much more with grace and good cheer.

Friends Jay and Rockie Beaman, Michelle Haberland, Rosalind Hinton, Michael Kane, Joan Kay, Tamara Kreinin, Susan Millemann, Diana Pinckley, John Pope, Paul and Susan Sorensen, Cathy Travis, Fran and Jeff Turner, Marianne Wafer, and Alison Zehr kept me going with food, music, laughter, and insight. My sister and brother-in-law, Judith and Don Woodman, and their daughter Jessie have long sustained me with Sunday dinners, scary movies, and love. My sister, Barbara Clark, came to live with us after Hurricane Katrina destroyed the building where she lived. She has taught me much about flexibility, accepting one's limits, and the unexpected gifts of family. My mother, Alice Fite Clark, was a *femme forte* who wanted me to find a way to become a historian but did not live to see it happen. My husband, Ron Biava, made sure that it did. He bore my decision to change careers and reduce our circumstances with fortitude and love and never once let me think of giving up. I owe this book to Alice and Ron, and I dedicate it to them with love.

CONTENTS

ILLUSTRATIONS

TABLES

ABBREVIATIONS

AANO	Archives of the Archdiocese of New Orleans
AC, C13A	Archives des Colonies, Archives nationales de France, Centre des archives d'outre mer, Aix-en-Provence, France, Series B57, B59, C11A, C12A, C13A
ADSM	Archives départementales de la Seine-Maritime, Rouen, France
AGI, PC	Archivo General de Indias, Papeles Procedentes de la Isla de Cuba, Seville, Spain, microfilm copy, Historic New Orleans Collection, New Orleans
AGI, SD	Archivo General de Indias, Audiencia de Santo Domingo, Seville, Spain, microfilm copy, Historic New Orleans Collection, New Orleans
HTML	Howard-Tilton Memorial Library, Tulane University, New Orleans
LHQ	*Louisiana Historical Quarterly*
MPA	*Mississippi Provincial Archives: French Dominion*, I–III, ed. Dunbar Rowland and Albert Godfrey Sanders (Jackson, Miss., 1929–1932)
NANO	Notarial Archives of New Orleans, New Orleans
RSC	Records of the Louisiana Superior Council, Louisiana Historical Center, Louisiana State Museum, New Orleans
SLC-B1	Saint Louis Cathedral Baptisms, I, 1731–1733, AANO
SLC-B2	Saint Louis Cathedral Baptisms, II, 1744–1753, AANO
SLC-B3	Saint Louis Cathedral Baptisms, III, 1753–1759, AANO
SLC-B4	Saint Louis Cathedral Baptisms and Marriages, IV, 1759–1762, AANO
SLC-B5	Saint Louis Cathedral Baptisms and Marriages, V, 1763–1766, AANO
SLC-B6	Saint Louis Cathedral Baptisms and Marriages, 1767–1771, AANO
SLC-B7	Saint Louis Cathedral Baptisms, VII, 1772–1776, AANO
SLC-B8	"Libro donde se asientan las partidas de baptismos de negros esclavos y mulattos que se han celebr[a]do en esta Iglesia parroquial de Sr. San Luis de la ciudad de la Nueva

Orleans desde el dia 1 de enero de 1777 que empezo hasta el ano de 1781 que es el corriente," 1777–1783, AANO

SLC-B10 "Libre donde se asientan las partidas de bautismos de negros y mulatos libres o esclavos el que dió principio en 17 de junio de 1783 para el Isso de esta parroquial de San Luis de Nueva Orleans en la provincia de la Luisiana," AANO

SLC-B12 "Libro de bautizados de negros y mulatos," 1786–1792, AANO

SLC-B13 "Libro quinto de bautizados negros y mulatos de la parroquia de sn. Luis de esta ciudad de la Nueva Orleans: Contiene doscientos trienta y siete folios útiles, y da principio de primero de octubre de mil setecientos noventa y dos, y acaba [en 1798]," AANO

SLC-B15 Saint Louis Cathedral Baptism of Negroes, 1798–1801, AANO

SLC-F3 "Libro de diffuntos . . . d[e negros y] mu[latos . . .]," 1790–1796, AANO

SLC-M1 Saint Louis Cathedral Marriages, 1720–1730, AANO

SLC-M2 Saint Louis Cathedral Marriages, 1764–1774, AANO

SLC-M3 "Libro primero de matrimonios de negros y mulatos de la parroquia de Sn. Luis de la Nueva Orleans; en 137 folios; da principio en 20 de enero de 1777 y acaba en 1830"

SLC-M4 Saint Louis Cathedral Marriages, 1777–1784, AANO

SLC-M5 "Libro de matrimonies celebrados en esta Iglesia parroq.l de San Luis de Nueva Orleans, provincia de la Luisiana, el que da principio en el mes de abril del año de mil setecientos ochenta y quarto en adelante," AANO

UCANO Ursuline Convent Archives, New Orleans

INTRODUCTION

In 1596, a handful of women in southern France organized under the rule of the Company of Saint Ursula to teach Christian doctrine. A century later, more than three hundred Ursuline schools throughout France taught girls reading, writing, and arithmetic along with the elements of the Catholic faith. In 1727, twelve Ursuline nuns arrived in New Orleans, where they founded an enterprise that educated women and girls of European, Indian, and African descent, enslaved and free, throughout Louisiana's colonial period. After the Louisiana Purchase of 1803, the nuns remained in the city and continued their apostolate. In the first instance, this book is the history of this intrepid community of women. Theirs is a story worth telling in its own right, richly rewarding in its revelation of Old World institutions and conventions of gender and religion negotiating rites of passage and adaptation in the Americas. A study so framed would satisfy the demands of Atlantic history, but it would leave the Ursulines, New Orleans, and Louisiana on the periphery of American history and bless the continuation of the parallel colonial narratives of early America that rise like silos on the scholarly landscape. The Ursulines themselves make such a study impossible. When they crossed the divide of the Louisiana Purchase and chose to remain in New Orleans, the nuns made their history part of early America's not simply as a retrospective addendum but as a living force. Embedded in the Ursulines' colonial legacy at the intersection of gender, class, religion, and race were elements that were at odds with the normative culture of British North America that prevailed in the young Republic.[1]

1. Alan Taylor's virtuosic *America Colonies* (New York, 2002), takes a "half step toward a more global (and less national) sensibility for our place in time" (xiv), but the national imperial boundaries of France, Spain, the Netherlands, and Britain structure his account.

Historians of French colonial America in general, and those of Louisiana in particular, have been as guilty as British colonial American specialists of the perpetuation of this failure to relate to one another the multiple colonial pasts of the continent to forge a well-integrated early American history. Scholars who have explored the social and cultural past of Louisiana have often succumbed to teleology. Reading the contemporary distinctiveness of New Orleans backward, they emphasize and romanticize Louisiana's differences from British colonial America. See, for example, Arnold R. Hirsch and Joseph Logsdon, eds., *Creole New Orleans: Race and*

Christianity bound together the European women who participated in making the early modern Atlantic, but the religious reformations of the sixteenth century divided them and endowed them with distinct traditions that molded their New World experience. The roots of the Ursulines' mission to New Orleans lay in the Catholic Counter-Reformation, which produced a vigorous female religious movement unique to seventeenth-century France. There, religious fervor and social conditions allowed women to surmount traditional hostility to organized female piety and to revolutionize female monasticism in the process. Women flocked by the thousands to more than a dozen new orders and congregations that replaced cloistered contemplation with various forms of apostolic activism that aimed to suppress Protestantism and make France a model Catholic society.[2]

Female education was the exclusive focus of the Ursuline order, one of the earliest and largest of the new organizations to emerge from the movement. The spiritual underpinnings of the Ursuline educational project lay in a reimagining of the place of Mary in the celestial hierarchy and an expansion of the basis and scope of women's authority and action within the formal structures of French Catholicism. The distinctive female piety that legitimated and animated the nuns' ambitious educational apostolate had practical effects for what amounted to a revolutionary rethinking of women's place in the spiritual universe and had implications for women's place in the earthly realm as well.

During the era of French colonial rule in Louisiana, from 1727 through

---

Americanization (Baton Rouge, La., 1992), and, to a lesser extent, Gwendolyn Midlo Hall, *Africans in Colonial Louisiana: The Development of Afro-Creole Culture in the Eighteenth Century* (Baton Rouge, La., 1992). Kimberly S. Hanger, *Bounded Lives, Bounded Places: Free Black Society in Colonial New Orleans, 1769–1803* (Durham, N.C., 1997); and Daniel H. Usner, Jr., *Indians, Settlers, and Slaves in a Frontier Exchange Economy: The Lower Mississippi Valley before 1783* (Chapel Hill, N.C., 1992), achieve more measured interpretations of early Louisiana's divergence from British colonial patterns. Guillaume Aubert, "'Français, Nègres, et Sauvages': Constructing Race in Colonial Louisiana" (Ph.D. diss., Tulane University, 2002), and Thomas N. Ingersoll, *Mammon and Manon in Early New Orleans: The First Slave Society in the Deep South, 1718–1819* (Knoxville, Tenn., 1999), contest, to varying degrees, the distinctiveness of colonial Louisiana's ideology of race and race relations.

2. For an excellent study of the flowering of female religious life in seventeenth-century France, see Elizabeth Rapley, *The Dévotes: Women and Church in Seventeenth-Century France* (Montreal, 1990).

1767, Ursulines transplanted France's distinctive female religious tradition to New Orleans. There, the Ursulines struggled to negotiate for a missionary field in the colony in the face of official responses that ranged from indifference and neglect to open hostility. Although religious women were an accepted part of French society, these international missionary endeavors did not enjoy unanimous official support, and the nuns' introduction into Louisiana was neither automatic nor easily sustained. But the Ursulines were tenacious, and colonial officials needed the social services they provided. Once they gained a foothold in New Orleans, the nuns quickly established themselves as a focal point for female community. In addition to their free and boarding schools, which offered free women in the city instruction in literacy and numeracy, they sponsored a laywomen's confraternity that mounted a sweeping program of catechesis among the enslaved. By the end of the French period, the Ursulines' influence revealed itself in high female literacy rates and a vibrant Afro-Catholic community. When the last third of the eighteenth century brought a recalibration of the contours of colonial society, the nuns' program to enlist all women in the propagation of the faith made the convent a setting where colliding categories of nationality, race, and class were mediated.

The French Ursuline tradition and practice matured and adapted, along with the New Orleans community, during the era of Spanish rule, from 1767 until 1803. The Spanish colonial women who joined French sisters at the convent in the late eighteenth century forced a reconsideration of the gender and racial identities forged decades earlier. Spanish colonial nuns and ecclesiastics practiced an established choreography of racial demarcation at odds with the slippery categories that evolved in the French colonial church and convent. The Ursulines' convent economy and their modified observance of cloister affronted Spanish religious gender sensibilities, further exacerbating relations within the community. In the 1780s and 1790s, the tension between French and Spanish expectations erupted in fractious convent politics. Yet the Spanish era also brought real prosperity to the convent and the extension of its educational program to an unprecedented number of colonial women and girls. At the end of the eighteenth century, the Ursulines were more financially secure and less susceptible to interference from male authorities of church and state than they had ever been.

Louisiana's incorporation into the American Republic and its maturation as a slave society presented the Ursulines with a new set of challenges. Never able to rely on unconditional support from colonial male authorities, their relationship with the social and political leaders of the emerging slave society in New Orleans deteriorated during the first decades of the American era. With the Louisiana Purchase of 1803, the Ursulines found themselves increasingly under attack for a succession of perceived infractions against the interests of the city's planter elite. And in the 1820s, the nuns of New Orleans became the objects of a public political assault that foreshadowed the more familiar antebellum offensive against nuns that played out in convent captivity narratives and the riotous mob that burned down the Ursuline convent of Charlestown, Massachusetts, in 1834.

On the one hand, the New Orleans Ursulines demonstrate the clear continuity of a distinctive European legacy and illustrate the enduring effect of Reformation-era formulations of spirituality for women. At the same time, the nuns were profoundly shaped by the colonial experience. This they held in common with Protestant women elsewhere in colonial America. There are commonalities, too, in the arc of their histories. Like Anglo-American Protestant women, the Ursulines encountered and responded to the opportunities for self-assertion afforded by the flexibility of a fluid colonial society and later found themselves constrained by the political culture of the young Republic that pursued broader equality for white men through the exclusion of women and men of color. And, like Protestant women elsewhere in colonial and early national America, the New Orleans Ursulines negotiated the confines of gender prescriptions to participate in shaping the polity of which they were a part.

These elements of shared history mark the Ursulines as American, yet their experience in the years following the Louisiana Purchase reveals that this identity was neither assumed nor easily ascribed to them when New Orleans became part of the United States. The confessional divide of the Reformation remained a formidable barrier. The Protestant Reformation did away with nuns, but Catholic women retained access to a religiously approved feminine ideal that allowed them to act without the appearance of submission that the married state signaled. The Ursulines' inability to project even the semblance of economic and legal dependence occasionally brought them into conflict with Louisiana's colonial authorities, but French and Spanish officials and inhabitants accepted the religious context from which nuns' independence sprang and relied on the sisters' social services. The same was not true for the Protestant Anglophones who poured into New Orleans after the Louisiana Purchase. In their view, the Ursulines, and other nuns in nineteenth-century America, stood glaringly outside the domestic civic partnership that had been crafted by husbands and wives in the young Republic. Nuns' highly visible, self-supported, self-directed enterprises made obvious the lack of an equality between the sexes beyond the enlightened confines of middle-class companionate marriage and the commonwealth of the household. The anti-Catholicism that erupted in nineteenth-century America had roots in class and economic tensions, but it sprang as well from the nun's affront to the Protestant construction of femininity and the potential of the convent to highlight its limits.[3]

Nuns everywhere in antebellum America posed a threat to the precarious balance of gender relations, but, in the slave South of which New Orleans was a part, the Ursulines found themselves on the wrong side on matters of race as well. Their application of their order's apostolic mandate in Louisiana turned them into missionaries to the enslaved. The nuns played a crucial role in the formation of an Afro-creole majority in the Catholic Church of New Orleans. Instead of serving as the undisputed stage for the performance of white male authority and control, the church in the colonial and early national eras was a site physically dominated by people of African descent who used its sacraments and ceremonies to forge community and exert leadership. The nuns maintained racial integration in their elite boarding school after the turn of the nineteenth century, confounding the strict racial hierarchy planter elites tried to impose in the wake of Louisiana's rapid development of a plantation economy in the 1790s. Their own status as slaveholders rendered the Ursulines doubly confounding. Unconstrained by a husband's authority, these mistresses without masters privileged the imperatives of a religious tradition forged in seventeenth-century France over the obligations dictated by their race in nineteenth-century America.

Even from the vantage point of America beyond the slave South, the nun was an ideological outlaw. She drew on her religious tradition to reject the dependent state of marriage that was ideally prescribed for Protestant women, and by her overt example she made manifest what was possible

3. For Catholic women in France, see Joan B. Landes, *Women and the Public Sphere in the Age of the French Revolution* (Ithaca, N.Y., 1988); and Dena Goodman, "Public Sphere and Private Life: Toward a Synthesis of Current Historiographical Approaches to the Old Regime," *History and Theory*, XXXI (1992), 1–20. Catherine Allgor, *Parlor Politics: In Which Ladies of Washington Help Build a City and a Government* (Charlottesville, Va., 2000); Susan Branson, *These Fiery Frenchified Dames: Women and Political Culture in Early National Pennsylvania* (Philadelphia, 2001); Linda Sturtz, *Within Her Power: Propertied Women in Colonial Virginia* (New York, 2002); and Karin Wulf, *Not All Wives: Women of Colonial Philadelphia* (Ithaca, N.Y, 2000), discuss the experience of Anglo-American Protestant women.

for women not obliged to defer publicly to a husband. Antebellum Protestant women were already employing female education, benevolence, and the politics of reform and antislavery to challenge the exclusive nature of the American polity. Making the married state normative for Protestant femininity preserved the illusion that autonomy of will and the financial self-sufficiency to pursue it were effectively beyond the reach of women. The Ursulines in New Orleans and nuns elsewhere in antebellum America proved otherwise, drawing aside the ideological veil of domesticity to reveal the capacity and ambition of American women. Not surprisingly, one of the most dramatic eruptions of violence in antebellum America, outside those related to slavery, was the burning of the Ursuline convent in Charlestown, Massachusetts, in 1834. Gender, as much as race and class, gnawed at the fragile foundations of unified American identity. Weaving the Ursulines into the fabric of American history tellingly reveals that to us.

prelude

In August 1727, twelve French Ursuline nuns disembarked the ship
that had carried them across a treacherous Atlantic, dodging pirates and
sandbars to land them safely on the southern coast of the colony of Louisiana. Driven by missionary enthusiasm, they had made the voyage to establish a convent in the capital of the French colony of Louisiana. Life aboard
the oceangoing *Gironde* had been uncomfortable, but now the women encountered the novel adversities and dangers of colonial life. Shallow, rough-
hewn pirogues waited to carry them from the mouth of the Mississippi to
the settlement of New Orleans, small boats dwarfed by the mighty, muddy
torrent that spread out before them. Hiking up heavy black serge habits,
they scrambled onto precariously balanced mounds of luggage and bedding and commenced a steamy six-day paddle upriver. At dusk, the labori-
ous task of making camp on the riverbank began. "To make the sleeping
place," the young missionary Marie Madeleine Hachard reported to her
father in Rouen, "our sailors put cane in the form of a cradle around a mat-
tress and enclosed us two by two in our tents where we lay down all fully
dressed." The palisades successfully deflected the alligators and snakes that
roamed the hot, damp Louisiana nights, but the subtler perils of the swamp
took their toll. Summer torrents and swarming insects mocked the limitations of the nuns' strange New World cells, and they passed five sleepless
nights of tormented swatting and scratching in sodden habits. The women
caught cold, their mosquito bites festered, their faces and legs swelled.
Marie Hachard's youthful candor overrode religious solemnity when she
reported to her father that "these little troubles bothered us at the time,"
but she recaptured the proper missionary spirit when she averred that "the
ardent desire that we had to arrive at this promised land made us endure
our trials with joy."[1]

1. [Marie Madeleine Hachard], *De Rouen à la Louisiane: Voyage d'une Ursuline en 1727*
(Rouen, 1988), 59–60 (author's translation). A new English translation of Hachard's

The women embraced the dangers and discomfort of colonial Louisiana as the missionary's due, a welcome signal that their longed-for colonial adventure in the name of God had finally begun. The longing that brought these twelve women to New Orleans was at once linked to the colonial enterprises that followed the opening of the Atlantic world and to a cluster of other historical processes rooted in Europe. The French Ursuline missionaries of 1727 were the immediate products of a novel variant of female monasticism that emerged in early-seventeenth-century France, but they were also shaped by more ancient religious traditions, the cyclical history of revival and decline in medieval conventual life, and the situation of women generally in early modern Europe. The women's decision to come to Louisiana, as well as the work they undertook after they arrived, were directed to a large degree by this constellation of Old World legacies.

The limitations of medieval sources make it easiest to trace the pre-Reformation rhythms of female religious life by following the fortunes of the nun and women who otherwise embraced an exclusively religious life rather than those of pious laywomen: nuns produced more sources and are more visible than laywomen in sources produced by others. Simply described, nuns were women who chose to lead lives whose primary object was to worship and serve the Christian God, a goal they pursued by adopting a distinctive mode of life that set them apart from other women. The nun came to Western Europe in the fifth century, carrying with her the classic features of monastic life that were first worked out in primitive communities in Egypt. The monastery was a community of individuals who were perpetually vowed to lives of poverty, chastity, and obedience and whose days were dedicated to prayer and spiritual contemplation. The community lived, worked, and worshipped in a space that maintained physical separation from the outside world. Both the place and the mode of life maintained within it came to be known as the cloister. By practicing chastity, living communally in a self-governed, single-sex environment, and managing their own financial affairs, nuns abjured some of the features that defined their gender in the world beyond the cloister.[2]

letters will be published in 2007. Because the same religious name was taken by a number of New Orleans Ursulines over the colonial period, to avoid confusion the nuns are identified whenever possible by their given and family names rather than by their religious names.

2. Lina Eckenstein, *Woman under Monasticism: Chapters on Saint-Lore and Convent Life between A.D. 500 and A.D. 1500* (Cambridge, 1896), remains a reliable comprehen-

The nun's failure to fulfill the primary social and cultural functions assigned to her sex—procreation through childbearing and inculturation of the young through parenting—often made her position in society tenuous. Social approval of a woman's withdrawal from these activities, and therefore general acceptance of female religious life, was contingent on the personal circumstances and location of individual women, but also it reflected broader historical forces. Accordingly, female religious life did not experience a progressive linear development from the modest beginnings of early medieval monasticism to the heyday of teaching and nursing nuns in the early to middle twentieth century. There were, instead, episodes of growth, decline, and suppression, a history that helps make sense of the Ursuline mission in Louisiana.

In its earliest years, female monasticism enjoyed a strong position, and before the tenth century there were a number of double monasteries comprising communities of monks and nuns under the leadership of powerful abbesses. Monastic life generally declined in the ninth and tenth centuries, suffering from the disruption provoked by Viking raiding and settlement. It then experienced a period of revitalization between the late eleventh and early twelfth centuries that perhaps represents the cloister's golden age. Western Christianity in general was stirred in the eleventh century by the Cluniac movement, a program of monastic reform whose hallmarks were a rejection of material wealth accompanied by a return to rigorous spiritual observance. Peripatetic preachers infused with the spirit of the movement carried it into the lay community, where it drew female adherents in large numbers.[3] These women entered vowed religious life and founded

---

sive history of European female monasticism. More recent general studies include Jo Ann Kay McNamara, *Sisters in Arms: Catholic Nuns through Two Millennia* (Cambridge, Mass., 1996); and Patricia Ranft, *Women and the Religious Life in Premodern Europe* (New York, 1996). The word "cloister," the English equivalent of the Latin *clausura*, can refer to both the physical space of religious seclusion and the act of sequestering religious persons, especially nuns. The terms "enclosure" and "clasura" are commonly used interchangeably with "cloister" when referring to the formally recognized and enforced sequestered living arrangements of religious women.

3. Carolyn Walker Bynum, "Religious Women in the Later Middle Ages," in Jill Raitt, ed., *Christian Spirituality: High Middle Ages and Reformation* (New York, 1988), 122; and C. H. Lawrence, *Medieval Monasticism: Forms of Religious Life in Western Europe in the Middle Ages* (New York, 1984), 179, note the role of wandering preachers in the growth of female monasticism. Bruce L. Venarde, *Women's Monasticism and Medieval Society: Nunneries in France and England, 890–1215* (Ithaca, N.Y., 1997), 132, cites a cli-

a rash of monasteries in the European countryside that were fortuitously well adapted to the agrarian economy of the era. These religious communities thrived under the patronage of wealthy aristocratic women who commanded the resources and respect needed to support the new institutions.[4]

Ironically, the Cluniac movement also sowed the seeds of a program of clerical reform that pushed women to the margins of religious life by the end of the twelfth century. Pope Gregory VII (reigned 1073–1085) promoted policies that aimed to clearly distinguish the laity from religious personnel. The priesthood was carefully differentiated as the leading mode of religious life, which in turn restricted to men access to the most acceptable form of religious life. Monks could choose to become priests; nuns could not and so found themselves in limbo between the clergy and the laity.[5]

This blow to the status of women religious occurred in concert with the commercial development that began in the late eleventh century. Shifting the locus of economic activity and wealth to towns and away from the rural areas where nunneries were located, this economic change robbed female religious houses of their traditional sources of support among the minor aristocracy of the countryside. In the later Middle Ages, female monasticism provided no essential service to either the religious establishment or the economy. From the point of view of both the church and society, there was no reason to support convents and the women who inhabited them. Nunneries became fewer, smaller, and more socially exclusive as they struggled to survive. At the threshold of the thirteenth century, female monasticism was all but moribund.[6]

The revival movement inspired by Francis of Assisi (1181/2–1226) and Dominic (circa 1170–1221) spawned a new wave of ardent female piety and produced something of a reprieve for female religious life, though not for the cloistered convent. Ecclesiastical and economic circumstances conspired to suppress the demand for traditional nuns and convents, but the

---

mate of religious enthusiasm and creativity that was supported by the ecclesiastical hierarchy.

4. Venarde, *Women's Monasticism*, 91–92, 104–114, explains the expansion primarily in terms of demographic developments that created a "matrimonial crisis" among aristocratic women that made the growth of monasteries attractive and a robust, socially distributed rural agrarian economy that provided financial underpinnings for new foundations.

5. Penelope D. Johnson, *Equal in Monastic Profession: Religious Women in Medieval France* (Chicago, 1991), 257.

6. Venarde, *Women's Monasticism*, 8, 141–152, and fig. 2.

Franciscan and Dominican revivals swelled the ranks of women who believed they had a vocation for the religious life. Devout women unable to gain admittance to the dwindling number of viable monasteries pursued alternative forms of religious life to satisfy their continuing desire to lead a distinctive life dedicated to God. The thirteenth and early fourteenth centuries saw the growth of communities or associations of nonvowed religious women who did not live in a cloister. The beguines of northern Europe, the tertiaries of Italy, and the beatas of Spain were devout, primarily urban women who chose a life of worship, poverty, chastity, and service to the poor without benefit of cloister or solemn vows. The beguines and beatas pursued their activities without official support, sanction, or supervision of the clergy, living on charity. Neither wives nor nuns, none of these three variants occupied either of the authorized niches for medieval women.[7]

The prospect of so many women who defied the categories that came fully under one of two patriarchal institutions was ultimately intolerable. In 1312, the Council of Vienne outlawed beguinage. By the fourteenth and fifteenth centuries, "holy women were . . . more likely to be lay and married," though beatas continued to survive in Spain into the seventeenth century, when they were finally effectively suppressed by the Inquisition. As the early modern period began, opportunities were few for women who wanted to withdraw literally and figuratively from the world to serve God.[8]

7. A "vowed" religious woman is one who has entered a recognized religious order and taken solemn vows of poverty, chastity, and obedience publicly in the presence of a cleric. "Non-vowed" religious women might take private vows along similar or identical lines, but there is no binding authority on their vows, and they are not considered "vowed" religious or nuns. Ernest W. McDonnell, *The Beguines and Beghards in Medieval Culture, with Special Emphasis on the Belgian Scene* (New York, 1969), is the most extensive full-length study of one of the new forms of female religious life. Lawrence, *Medieval Monasticism,* 186–190; and Bynum, "Religious Women," in Raitt, ed., *Christian Spirituality,* 123–127, discuss beguines less extensively.

8. Lawrence, *Medieval Monasticism,* 189; Bynum, "Religious Women," in Raitt, ed., *Christian Spirituality,* 129. On Spanish beatas, see Mary Elizabeth Perry, *Gender and Disorder in Early Modern Seville* (Princeton, N.J., 1990), 97–117. Franciscan tertiaries also survived in Spain and its colonies long after beguines had disappeared. The reforming Cardinal Francisco Jimenez founded a convent for female Franciscan tertiaries in Illescas, Spain, in 1500, and Franciscan tertiaries were also represented in Spanish colonial America. See Manuel de Castro, "El Monasterio de Franciscanas, de Illescas, Fundación del Cardenal Cisneros," *Archivo Ibero-Americano,* XLIX (1989), 403–411; and

The bumpy path that medieval religious women traveled illustrates two aspects of the setting from which the Ursulines sprang. First, women were enthusiastic participants in larger religious movements such as the Cluniac and Franciscan revivals. The contagion of religious revival could not be confined to men: large numbers of women responded to historic surges of general religious vitality by seeking to enter religious life. Second, gender ideology made the place of women in organized religious life precarious except when they were perceived to serve a positive cultural, social, or economic function. When circumstances were right, authorities tolerated female religious communities that eschewed the otherwise vital functions of procreation and childrearing. When they posed more problems than they solved, they lost support, and their numbers diminished.[9]

On the eve of the Reformation, female religious life lay in a state of stagnation after several centuries of steady decline, mirroring in its own way the more general malaise that plagued the institutional church. This life was soon to experience yet another renaissance tied to broader currents of religious change. As with the Cluniac and Franciscan movements, the sixteenth-century paroxysm of religious revitalization sparked by the Lutheran revolt triggered a surge of organized female religiosity. Although Protestantism abolished religious orders for women, its threatening presence paradoxically fueled the Catholic revival of female religious life by providing it with a new, urgent mission. At the same time, social and economic factors prevailing in early modern Europe acted both to draw women into religious life and to win acceptance for their activities. Two factors were particularly important: changes in the role of women and the growing challenge of the permanently poor.

A preference for social arrangements that favored men in the division of authority was well established at the close of the Middle Ages, but patriarchy received an ideological boost from Renaissance rationalists who breathed new life into the Aristotelian sexual dichotomies that fixed women's inferiority. Aristotle's dualistic philosophy cast men and women and the qualities they possessed in opposite terms. Man was active and complete; woman was not. Women were necessary to the achievement of human perfection because they bore children, but they could not achieve

Brian C. Belanger, "Between the Cloister and the World: The Franciscan Third Order of Colonial Querétaro," *Americas*, XLIX (1992), 157–177.

9. Patricia Wittberg, *The Rise and Decline of Catholic Religious Orders: A Social Movement Perspective* (Albany, N.Y., 1994), 55–174.

perfection themselves. The proper role for a woman was not to develop and rule the polity; it was to people it.[10]

Legal, political, and economic change brought this ideology and day-to-day practice into closer accord. From the thirteenth century, Roman law reshaped European legal structures in ways that diminished women's role in the deployment of family wealth even as it strengthened male economic authority. By the end of the Middle Ages, the ideology of patriarchy was well established and buttressed with a legal apparatus that made it difficult for women to exert power in either the economic or political realms. The evolution of political structures in the early modern period mirrored the family power structure, relying on the ideology of patriarchy to support the emergence of absolutist national monarchs and centralized governments. By the turn of the seventeenth century, women found their range of direct authority diminished nearly to the vanishing point.[11]

Changes in the economy also worked against women. Although the idealized gender hierarchy of medieval and early modern Europe theoretically gave men authority over women, in practice the economy of pre-capitalist Europe created a form of functional equity because women shared equally with men in sustaining household units of subsistence production. The subsequent evolution of a market economy in which women's participation

10. Marilyn J. Boxer and Jean H. Quataert, "Women in the Age of Religious Upheaval and Political Centralization," in Boxer and Quataert, eds., *Connecting Spheres: Women in the Western World, 1500 to the Present* (New York, 1987), 23–24. Some Renaissance humanists advocated female education as a path to piety and private virtue, but they were generally dismayed when their educated daughters used their learning to argue for women's intellectual equality and the right to help shape civic virtue. The "querelle des femmes" that these educated daughters of the Renaissance inaugurated would continue for generations, but their position never dominated.

11. Ibid., 35–36. French laws regulating marriage were particularly supportive of patriarchal control. The age of majority was raised in France, and clandestine marriage was outlawed, making it virtually impossible for young people of any means to make their own marital choices. Patriarchs thus had a free hand in building dynasties, arranging matches that advanced family fortunes and male careers in the minor nobility of the developing French state. See Sarah Hanley, "Family and State in Early Modern France: The Marriage Pact," ibid., 55–57, 62–63. Women's choices were further constrained by an increase in the effective price of dowries. Girls from families of limited means might find themselves forced into unattractive matches or spinsterhood. See Olwen Hufton, *The Prospect before Her: A History of Women in Western Europe*, I, *1500–1800* (New York, 1996), 67–69.

was unnecessary and made inconvenient by the requirements of mother-hood deprived women of their qualitatively different but quantitatively equal role in the success of the household economy.[12] At the same time, women were increasingly excluded from trade guilds as competition for jobs and cash mounted, and their work, when assigned a value in the emerging cash economy, was consistently rewarded at a level well below that of men. Women's functional position in the economy began to mirror the patriarchal ideal.[13]

Early modern women thus had compelling personal incentives inclining them toward life in female communities that sidestepped direct male

12. The first to develop this argument was Alice Clark, *Working Life of Women in the Seventeenth Century*, with an introduction by Miranda Chaytor and Jane Lewis (1919; rpt. London, 1982), 290, 295–300. Although the theory of a "golden age" for pre-capitalist women has been contested since, some scholarship, notably that of Martha Howell, has revived and refined Clark's thesis. Howell and others suggest that the villain was not the emerging market economy, which created increased opportunities for women to engage in trade and manufacture. Rather, the problem lay in patriarchal society's reaction to the potential of women's participation in this new range of activities. Production and commercial transactions became significant sources of wealth and power, bypassing traditional feudal arrangements and creating a new class that no longer had compelling practical reasons to practice deference and submit to the authority of a lord. There was an obvious danger that women engaged in the new economic activities would lay claim to power in their own right as well. As a result, women were increasingly shut out of guilds that had previously accorded them a role in professional self-government and a voice in civic affairs. See Martha C. Howell, *Women, Production, and Patriarchy in Late Medieval Cities* (Chicago, 1986). Merry E. Wiesner, "Women's Work in the Changing City Economy, 1500–1650," in Boxer and Quataert, eds., *Connecting Spheres*, 64–74, emphasizes the expanding opportunities for women to do different kinds of work in the new economy and suggests that multiple factors, including female life-cycle constraints and the trend toward professionalization, in addition to patriarchal reaction combined to limit women's economic autonomy and status during this period. For a revision of this classic interpretation, see Robert B. Shoemaker, *Gender in English Society, 1650–1850: The Emergence of Separate Spheres?* (London, 1998), who detects a qualitative narrowing of women's range of action and authority but argues that the degree of change and its negative nature have been overestimated.

13. Cynthia M. Truant, "The Guildswomen of Paris: Gender, Power, and Sociability in the Old Regime," *Proceedings of the Sixth Annual Meeting of the Western Society for French History*, XV (1988), 130–138; Wiesner, "Women's Work," in Boxer and Quataert, eds., *Connecting Spheres*, 67.

control. Such a life would take them beyond the tightening ligatures of law and custom that constrained their choices and diminished their ability to earn and keep rewards for their talents and efforts. Religious communities offered a way to satisfy the aspiration for more autonomy, but they posed a threat to the progress of patriarchal control. Ironically, the growth of permanent poverty and the Catholic Reformation, two developments that intensified desire for social control and hierarchical authority, gave women an opening to live outside the shrinking domain allocated for their gender.

Poverty and ideas about it changed in early modern Europe. By the middle of the sixteenth century, an expanding population was straining the limits of agriculture, and the lame, blind, diseased, and elderly begging on the cathedral steps were sharing space with young men unable to find work and families laid low by periodic famines and the shortage of land. As the seventeenth century dawned, poverty was no longer the occasional anomaly wearing the pitiable face of the frail. It was constant, vigorous, and frightening. Masterless young men wandered the countryside looking for work, loitered at the town square, and got drunk at village fetes. They were suitable subjects, not for alms, but for exclusion, control, or confinement. Young women, unable to earn the nest egg they needed to set up housekeeping, bore children to young men with no prospects. Bridal pregnancy was common and tolerated, but bastardry was a burden to the community, eroding a social order that demanded a patriarch to rule and support each household. These young men and women were the most alarming contingent among the swollen ranks of the poor, but the growing number of impoverished and dissolute families was a worry as well. Nervous town fathers wanted everyone to be industrious and sober. Productivity, prosperity, and order came from work, right behavior, and religious observance. The sick, too, were a drain on resources and a threat to the healthy workforce. They should be kept from infecting the well and cared for so they could return to their work as soon as possible.[14]

The apparatus of medieval charity was ill equipped to meet the challenges of endemic impoverishment and social displacement. England re-

14. On the crises of demography and poverty in early modern Europe, see Olwen Hufton, *The Poor of Eighteenth-Century France, 1750–1789* (New York, 1974); Emmanuel Le Roy Ladurie, *The Peasants of Languedoc*, trans. John Day (Urbana, Ill., 1974); and Robert Jütte, *Poverty and Deviance in Early Modern Europe* (Cambridge, 1994). A. L. Beier, *Masterless Men: The Vagrancy Problem in England, 1560–1640* (New York, 1985), is especially good on describing middle-class perceptions of the poor.

sponded with the Elizabethan Poor Laws of 1563, 1598, and 1601, instituting a system of "outdoor relief" that provided cash payments to the poor through a church-based but lay-administered system. France developed a system of "indoor relief" that relied on institutions that housed and regulated such problem populations as foundling children, vagabonds, debtors, "fallen women," the chronically ill, and the aged and sick poor. This elaborate network of institutions called for a large labor force from a new source. Religious women were a logical choice.[15]

In addition to social factors, certain currents within the larger movement for religious reform played a crucial part in creating an environment conducive to the renaissance of female religious life. Conventionally, the sixteenth-century religious revival is described as two separate and successive movements: a Protestant Reformation followed by a Catholic Counter-Reformation. The phenomenon is more properly understood, however, as a general revival that wore two confessional faces, one Protestant, the other Catholic, and followed two tracks, one addressing popular devotional concerns and the other focusing on institutional matters. Among the features common to both the Catholic and Protestant reformations was a new emphasis on personal, rather than communal, piety. Movement toward a more individually oriented Christian piety began in the late Middle Ages.[16] The modes of piety available to lay men and women of the later Middle Ages did not give them what they craved: assurance that they were making progress on their quest for salvation. They sought forms of prayer designed to bring them personally closer to God to supplement or replace the incompre-

15. The best studies in English of the development of the early modern French system of indoor relief are Cissie C. Fairchilds, *Poverty and Charity in Aix-en-Provence, 1640–1789* (Baltimore, 1976); and Colin Jones, *The Charitable Imperative: Hospitals and Nursing in Ancien Regime and Revolutionary France* (New York, 1989).

16. John Bossy charts the transition from religious practices that focused on community and unity to those that fed a preoccupation with the pursuit of personal salvation (Bossy, *Christianity in the West, 1400–1700* [New York, 1985]). The roots of this development might have lain in the emergence of market economies that weakened old communal values in favor of individual gain, in the shifting depths of theological developments that refined soteriology and elevated it to the forefront of Christian discourse, or in some combination of these developments. Bossy links the religious developments to socioeconomic change. A. D. Wright, *The Counter-Reformation: Catholic Europe and the Non-Christian World* (New York, 1982), suggests that a renewed interest in the Augustinian struggle to define the nature of grace and salvation was central to the individualist aspects of the reform impulse.

hensible, impersonal Latin Mass. They wanted maps to salvation drawn by individuals who had studied the route to heaven, or perhaps had been given a glimpse of it, people who knew which were the best roads, where the obstacles lay, what the milestones were, and how sweet the rewards might be.[17]

Protestants responded to these yearnings with a soteriology that rejected the efficacy of works in favor of the doctrine of grace and placed the word at the center of their devotional practice, with a vernacular liturgy, Bible reading, and interpretive preaching as featured elements. Catholics reaffirmed the importance of works to salvation and underlined the importance of charity in that respect. Inspired by the spiritual virtuosity of the Spanish mystic Teresa of Avila (1515–1582) and the spiritual methods and preaching of the founder of the Society of Jesus, Ignatius of Loyola (1491–1556), they also promoted the tools of self-examination, confession, meditation, and prayer.[18]

The popular contribution to the age of religious reform was this impulse toward a more satisfying form of personal piety and the laity's enthusiasm for participation in new kinds of religious activities. The institutional wing of the movement focused on the distribution and operation of authority. As Protestants experimented with forms of church governance like Presbyterianism and congregationalism that distributed power away from the center and flattened hierarchies, Catholicism reasserted its centralized, transnational structure of parish priests, bishops, and pontiff. The Council of Trent (1545–1563) clarified and pruned the Catholic Church's lines of authority and ordained a campaign of orthodoxy in religious practice. Local religion, with its array of patron saints attuned to community rhythms and the politics of neighborhood, guild, and family, was suppressed. Religious celebrations that gave exuberant expression to lay piety but did not put the priest and his sacramental repertoire at center stage were discouraged. Instead, Catholic reformers promoted a religious program built around priests, the

17. This sketch of the devotional desires of individuals in the era of reform draws on Jean Delumeau, *Catholicism between Luther and Voltaire: A New View of the Counter-Reformation*, trans. Jeremy Moiser (London, 1977); H. Outram Evennett, *The Spirit of the Counter-Reformation: The Birkbeck Lectures in Ecclesiastical History Given in the University of Cambridge in May 1951*, ed. John Bossy (Cambridge, 1968); and Wright, *The Counter-Reformation*.

18. Evennett, *Spirit of the Counter-Reformation;* John W. O'Malley, *The First Jesuits* (Cambridge, Mass., 1993); Jodi Bilinkoff, *The Avila of Saint Teresa: Religious Reform in a Sixteenth-Century City* (Ithaca, N.Y., 1989).

sacraments they conferred, and a codified uniform doctrine rendered into vernacular catechisms that articulated the modern standard of behavior and belief for Tridentine Catholics.[19]

Trent's was an ambitious program, and, despite its emphasis on clerical power, it depended on lay acceptance and promotion for success. To achieve it, reformers created new kinds of lay confraternities that supported the Tridentine vision of orthodox, parish-centered piety and a transnational church. In the past, the associations of pious lay people known as confraternities had been based on occupation or local politics. Tridentine confraternities turned the laity's attention to more universal causes: catechesis and devotion to the Virgin, who presided impartially over all of Catholic Christendom.

Women were especially drawn to both types of Tridentine confraternity. Devotion to Mary was a tradition of long standing among women, and the educational aims of the confraternities dedicated to teaching Christian doctrine were well suited to women as well. Mothers were their children's natural first teachers, and enlisting them in religious instruction was a reasonable way to harness female piety. As the sixteenth century progressed, Catholic women hungry for a religious outlet took up the causes of universalist devotion and Catholic orthodoxy and swelled the ranks of the new confraternities, often assuming leadership positions.[20] Some of them took their dedication to the next level. To carry the banner of Catholic reform higher and farther, they left marriage, motherhood, and ordinary lay confraternities behind and developed new female religious congregations. For a time, at least, the church fathers were so glad of the help they did not worry about the surge of women creating a column of their own in the Tridentine army.

19. See, for example, Delumeau, *Catholicism between Luther and Voltaire;* Philip T. Hoffman, *Church and Community in the Diocese of Lyon, 1500–1789* (New Haven, Conn., 1984); Sara T. Nalle, *God in La Mancha: Religious Reform and the People of Cuenca, 1500–1650* (Baltimore, 1992); and Kathryn Norberg, *Rich and Poor in Grenoble, 1600–1814* (Berkeley, Calif., 1985).

20. Christopher F. Black, *Italian Confraternities in the Sixteenth Century* (Cambridge, 1989), 35–38, 103–104; Marie-Hélène Froeschle-Chopard, "La dévotion du Rosaire à travers quelques livres de piété," *Histoire, Économie, et Société,* X (1991), 299–316; Hoffman, *Church and Community,* 114; Kathryn Norberg, "Women, the Family, and the Counter-Reformation: Women's Confraternities in the Seventeenth Century," *Proceedings of the Sixth Annual Meeting of the Western Society for French History,* VI (1978), 55–63.

The Ursulines were at the head of that column. In 1532, in the northern Italian town of Brescia, a middle-aged spinster named Angela Merici founded a religious congregation for women in an effort to maintain order and religious observance in her town. A member of a religious movement called the Oratory of Divine Love that coupled intense personal piety with charitable works, Merici responded to mounting social and religious disorder around her. Brescia was part of the territory in dispute between Louis XII of France and the Republic of Venice. Troop movements brought violence, large numbers of transient young men, and syphilis to the town. When Brescia rebelled against occupying French forces in 1512, reprisals included violent assaults on civilians, looting, rape, and violation of monasteries and convents. Peace returned with Venetian rule in 1517, but the association with the republic brought a different danger. Venice was a center of publishing, and Martin Luther's early tracts were being printed there and distributed in surrounding territory. The tentacles of the Protestant heresy found their way into Brescia.[21]

Brescia needed tending, body and soul. Angela Merici became known to church leaders for her dedication and energy as she joined with other members of the Brescian chapter of the Oratory of Divine Love to found a hospital for the victims of syphilis, orphanages, refuges for the rehabilitation of fallen women, and ministries to the imprisoned. In 1532, she recruited twelve unmarried women for an association named after Saint Ursula, a fourth-century missionary princess who went to her martyrdom in the company of her virgin companions. Together Angela and her associates set out not only to restore and sustain social order but also to create a bulwark of orthodox Catholic faith in the face of the Lutheran advance.[22]

Merici's organization borrowed aspects of both women's monasticism and the informal modes of female religious life that had flourished briefly in late medieval Europe—the beguines, beatas, and tertiaries—but it was innovative in not adopting communal living arrangements while embracing the chastity and formal religious observance of monasticism. Unlike beatas, beguines, and most tertiaries, sisters of the Company of Saint Ursula were not typically middle-aged spinsters and widows but might be as young

21. Teresa Ledóchowska, *Angela Merici and the Company of St. Ursula: According to the Historical Documents,* trans. Mary Teresa Neylan (Rome, 1967), 30–41; Peter Maurice Waters, *The Ursuline Achievement: A Philosophy of Education for Women: St. Angela Merici, the Ursulines, and Catholic Education* (North Carlton, Victoria, Aust., 1994), 21, 24–25.

22. Ledóchowska, *Angela Merici,* 34–51.

as twelve years of age. They took no vows, wore no habit, and did not make a lifelong commitment to a religious vocation, but they did follow a common rule and upheld distinctly modest standards of behavior and dress. Although Ursulines resided with their families, they called themselves a "company," received gifts and bequests to support their work, and placed themselves under the governance of a board drawn from both sexes of the laity. To the traditional religious duties of charity and observance, they added Christian education.[23]

The early history of the Company of Saint Ursula illustrates clearly how the intersection of religious revivalism, the absence of sufficient outlets for women to act on extraordinary levels of individual piety, and threats to the social and religious order combined to give birth to a new women's religious congregation. Extraordinary circumstances sometimes give rise to remarkable—and ephemeral—organizational responses under the leadership of charismatic figures. Survival beyond the first flush of founding enthusiasm depends on continuing leadership and a sustaining environment. By 1539, the Company of Saint Ursula had grown to 150 members, but, when Angela Merici died in 1540 and deprived it of its unifying vision and inspiration, it foundered.[24]

The Ursulines probably would not have persisted and spread if a leading figure of Catholic Tridentine reform, Archbishop Carlo Borromeo of Milan, had not recognized the potential of the company to advance the aims of the church fathers. In 1568, he invited twelve Brescian Ursulines to Milan and put them to work. He reasoned that these women, who pledged to attend Mass daily and make confession, would demonstrate and advance the sacramental piety that the Council of Trent wanted the laity to adopt. The women's commitment to teaching Christian doctrine would help assure the conformity in belief and devotional practice that was another of Trent's chief aims—a goal that gained new urgency with the spread of Protestantism. In 1584, six hundred Ursulines were teaching in sixteen schools in Milan, but there were no plans to expand beyond the city.[25]

23. Angela Merici, "Rule," 1536, trans. Teresa Ledóchowska, in Ledóchowska, *Angela Merici*, 276–288.

24. Waters, *Ursuline Achievement*, 23.

25. Borromeo has been accused of forcing cloister on the Ursulines. What he actually did was modify their rule, in 1582, so that they could live communally, if they chose to do so. Many of the early Ursulines who worked in orphanages and hospitals that required them to be in attendance or available at all hours welcomed a modifica-

In the 1590s, pious women in southern France faced much the same cli-mate of social unrest and religious ferment that had characterized Angela Merici's Brescia decades earlier. France was embroiled in civil war between Protestant Huguenots and Catholic partisans during the last forty years of the sixteenth century. When women in Avignon sought approval to found a religious community to administer charity and promote Catholic doctrine, their archbishop, who was within Borromeo's orbit of influence, steered them toward the Ursuline rule. Led by the enterprising catechist, Françoise de Bermond, the group embraced the suggestion and gained recognition as an Ursuline community in 1597. The Avignon initiative set off a wave of Ursuline foundations across the Midi: some twenty-nine were established in the first decade of the 1600s. The movement quickly spread northward into the heart of France. In 1612, a community was formally established in Paris. Dozens more were established throughout France in the 1620s.[26]

Although the Ursulines had their beginnings in Italy, they grew most rapidly and widely in France. The factors operating throughout Europe that created the match between individual aspiration and societal needs to make space for a new chapter in female religious life prevailed there. At the same time, the aftermath of France's wars of religion created an environment that was uniquely open to the educational apostolate of the Ursulines. The Edict of Nantes, issued by Henry IV in 1598, granted limited toleration to the kingdom's Huguenots, bringing the bloody religious wars to an end.[27] If Catholicism was going to turn back the Protestant heresy in France, it would have to be by means other than royal policy and the force of arms. Souls would have to be saved, one by one, through education. Heretics quite literally had to be converted through evangelization, and the young had to be indoctrinated in the true faith to inoculate them against the spiritual evil around them.

-----

tion that allowed them to live more conveniently. The archbishop did constrain the Ursulines' independence, however, when he imposed a new governing structure that supported the Tridentine organizational hierarchy. Borromeo took authority away from their lay governing body and made the bishops the superiors of Ursuline com-munities within their dioceses. The Ursulines lost the autonomy and flexibility that local lay control had given them, though they gained a powerful protector and spon-sor and a structure that facilitated their international growth. See Elizabeth Rapley, *The Dévotes: Women and Church in Seventeenth-Century France* (Montreal, 1990), 50.

26. Ibid., 50–51, 53, 58–59 (graph 1).

27. Mack P. Holt, *The French Wars of Religion, 1562–1629* (Cambridge, 1995), 162–165.

The devout women of France seized and were seized by the moment. Religious awareness and energy reached fever pitch at the turn of the seventeenth century, and a movement took shape that holds a more legitimate claim to the label "Counter-Reformation" than the actions taken by the Council of Trent decades before. Even as Catholic partisans were forced to lay down their arms, Jesuit priests moved from city to city, preaching, leading retreats, and hearing confessions, bringing men and women to new levels of personal piety and commitment. People wanted to act, and the first move for many, having been touched by the fire of devotion, was to join one of the Marian confraternities founded by the Jesuits as they made their way around post-Nantes France. Others, however, wanted to do more. Men could answer the call to serve God and his church by entering the priesthood. Women, in one town after another, answered it by establishing communities of Ursulines (see Figure 1).[28]

The early Ursulines of Italy performed a fairly wide repertoire of charitable activities that included nursing and ministering to the poor and imprisoned along with teaching Christian doctrine. The French Ursulines quickly became specialists in female education. Developing good Catholic mothers who would raise their children in the true faith was critical to the survival of the post-Nantes church. The Protestant heresy advanced by the power of the written word, and the Ursulines made literacy central to their crusade to mobilize women as defenders of the faith. Setting up camp in a corner of the parish church, or in their fathers' shops and homes, they taught the girls of their villages catechism, reading, and writing.[29]

The introduction of a new female religious congregation that promoted a skill for women that many men thought inappropriate to their sex would probably have been suppressed in another time and place. But the times were extraordinary in early-seventeenth-century France, and a surprisingly broad base encouraged the Ursulines. The Jesuits, who were sometimes in-

28. Louis Châtellier, *The Europe of the Devout: The Catholic Reformation and the Formation of a New Society*, trans. Jean Birrell (New York, 1989). At least one Ursuline community, Rennes, got its start when a group of women who had attended the course of preaching and retreats offered by a traveling Jesuit sought his advice on how to preserve and organize their dedication to advancing the faith. He pointed them toward the Ursuline rule. [Une Ursuline], *Monastère de Notre-Dame de Bon-Secours des Ursulines D'Hennébont* (Lorient, 1905), 13.

29. Linda Lierheimer, "Female Eloquence and Maternal Ministry: The Apostolate of Ursuline Nuns in Seventeenth-Century France" (Ph.D. diss., Princeton University, 1994), 22, 25, 27, 250–253.

T.IV. p. 150.

Ancienne Ursuline Congregée
en Provence.

36.

Poilly Jun f.

Figure 1. Ancienne Ursuline congregée en Provence. *From Pierre Hélyot,* Histoire des ordres monastiques . . . , *IV (Paris, 1715). By permission General Research Division, The New York Public Library, Astor, Lenox and Tilden Foundations*

strumental in establishing new Ursuline communities and lent the French movement the outline of their educational program, consistently championed them. At the same time, bishops and wealthy laywomen numbered among their patrons. The queen was an advocate and sent her son, the dauphin, to a catechism class offered by the early Ursuline leader, Françoise de Bermond. In 1611, Louis XIII authorized the new congregation "under the name of the blessed Saint Ursula, for the purpose of instruction."[30]

This tide of support from the powerful was critical to the Ursulines' ability to face down substantial opposition from other quarters. A friar in Langres threatened a campaign against the Ursulines because it was "an abuse for women to teach in public," and a preacher in Grenoble took his disapproval a step further and denounced them from the pulpit.[31] The Ursulines survived, but the current of clerical disapproval continued to flow. As the ranks of the Ursulines grew and other new congregations were born and drew thousands of women of diverse means and backgrounds into active religious life, church fathers grew increasingly anxious about the force they had unleashed and attempted to limit and control the women's activities.

The most dramatic move was to cloister the Company of Saint Ursula. In 1612, the women living as Ursulines in Paris sought recognition as a canonical, enclosed religious order, a step that would gain them permanent recognition by church and state and enable their community to build the financial base they needed to secure the future of their apostolate.[32] The other Ursuline communities of France were not all as eager as the Parisian foundation to seek canonical status as an order. The 1566 papal constitution issued on the heels of the Council of Trent had decreed that all women's religious orders were to be cloistered. The measure was the Council's unimaginative way of settling the issue of how to control female religious life. Now the Ursulines faced a roadblock and the church a conundrum. Teaching Ursulines were by 1612 seen as essential to keeping France Catholic, but, if they became a canonical order, they had to be cloistered. The definition of cloister ordained not only that the nuns stay inside the walls of a recognizable convent compound; it dictated that no one from the outside was allowed within.

---

30. Rapley, *The Dévotes*, 53.

31. Marie-Augustine de Pommereu, *Les chroniques de l'ordre des Ursulines recueillies pour l'usage des religieuses du mesme ordre*, I (Paris, 1673), 81 (quotation), 84, quoted in translation in Rapley, *The Dévotes*, 53.

32. Rapley, *The Dévotes*, 56–57; Lierheimer, "Female Eloquence," 32–33.

The rule of cloister would forbid Ursulines contact with their students and effectively rendered impossible the teaching apostolate that was their raison d'être. Rome's solution to the problem posed by a teaching order of canonical nuns was ingenious. The papal bull of 1612 that established the first cloistered Ursuline community in Paris recognized, not the usual three solemn vows of medieval monasticism, but four. Ursulines vowed to practice poverty, chastity, obedience, and teaching. The bull remained diplomatically silent on how teaching and *clausura* would be reconciled.[33] Both parties benefited from the internal paradox of the bull. Church fathers gained official compliance with Tridentine policy as well as the physical and symbolic evidence of their control of the Ursuline movement represented by cloister. Ursulines achieved formal papal sanction for their departure from the strict contemplative tradition in favor of a new mixed rule. Sisters in the Order of Saint Ursula said holy office daily, as nuns had always done, but they also opened their convent daily to teach, as nuns had never done. Between 1612 and 1650, all but a few of France's Ursuline communities accepted cloister, many of them reluctantly. The change initiated a massive construction program that saw impressive Ursuline compounds raised in the centers of dozens of French cities and towns. Their physical prominence in the town landscape was paralleled by a tendency for Ursuline communities to grow more socially exclusive. Bourgeois fathers who might have opposed their daughters' joining the pioneering Ursulines in their rented

33. Philippe Annaert, *Les Collèges au Féminin: les Ursulines: enseignement et vie consa-crée aux XVIIe et XVIIIe siècles* (Brussels, 1992), 44. The papal resolution of the contra-diction between the rule of cloister and the Ursuline teaching apostolate set French female religious life on a path that differed significantly from that of the other major Catholic Atlantic colonizer, Spain. Spanish nuns remained cloistered in the strictest sense, which effectively prevented them from developing an educational apostolate. Elite young women could enter Spanish and Spanish colonial convents to be edu-cated, but they did so only by submitting for the term of their education to the same rule of cloister observed by the nuns, a condition that precluded both the day stu-dents and short-term boarding students that characterized French teaching orders like the Ursulines. The first community of teaching nuns introduced into a Spanish colony was established in Havana, Cuba, in 1803 by a group of New Orleans Ursulines who fled the mainland on the eve of the Louisiana Purchase. For a full discussion of differences between French and Spanish female religious life and some of their im-plications in the colonial setting, see Emily J. Clark, "A New World Community: The New Orleans Ursulines and Colonial Society, 1727–1803" (Ph.D. diss., Tulane Univer-sity, 1998), 252–281.

communal lodgings looked more favorably on the propriety represented by the cloister. Exchanging convent walls for the supervision of their fathers, the daughters of pious merchants and lawyers filled the new Ursuline compounds.[34]

Even as the Ursulines retreated from the streets of their communities to the cloister, another branch of female piety was developing a different apostolate. As the French Counter-Reformation shifted from ideals to action and the creation of a model Catholic society, its bourgeois constituency of pious activists known as *dévots* mounted campaigns of institutionalized charity against the moral evils that plagued their communities. The sick poor, the mentally unfit, unwed mothers, foundlings, orphans, and wandering masterless men all represented social problems they wanted to reform in order to make France the moral paragon God meant it to be.

The emergence of a market economy that brought prosperity and status to a small group of people in early modern Europe and poverty and discrimination to a vastly larger number of others gave rise to France's infamous seventeenth-century *renfermement*. France's dévots, drawn from the ranks of the privileged, addressed the problem of those they deemed social outliers by building, supporting, and administering a network of charitable and reformatory institutions. Huge multipurpose *hôpitaux généraux* housed a wide range of unfortunate men, women, and children whom the town fathers categorized as unfit in mind, body, or spirit. *Hôtels dieux* cared for the sick poor, and a myriad of smaller institutions aided or rehabilitated special populations like the syphilitic, the elderly poor, foundlings, and orphans. In thousands of such institutions all over France, the men, women, and children who did not live in circumstances of Catholic social perfection were to be cared for and transformed into productive, moral members of society.[35]

34. Rapley, *The Dévotes*, 59–60.

35. Emmanuel Chill, "Religion and Mendicity in Seventeenth-Century France," *International Review of Social History*, VII (1962), 400–425, remains a classic study of the role of the Company of the Holy Sacrament, a prominent association of dévots, in moral reform in Counter-Reformation France. There is a great deal of literature on the French *renfermement*, literally, "the confinement." Properly speaking, the "Grand Renfermement," or Great Confinement, was the internment of beggars and vagrants in the hôpital général of Paris in compliance with a royal edict issued in 1656. The label "renfermement" has been applied more loosely to a larger movement prosecuted mostly by dévots throughout France that originated as early as the 1630s. Michel Foucault, *Discipline and Punish: The Birth of the Prison*, trans. Alan Sheridan (New York, 1977), is probably the most famous work on the subject, but more historically de-

The hôpitaux généraux and hôtels dieux were not hospitals in the modern medical sense. Until the advent of clinical medicine in the late eighteenth century, they were institutions that sheltered a wide range of social services. Women had long staffed the medieval hostels for travelers and disabled paupers that were their forerunners. Pious women of humble origins who had neither the academic backgrounds nor the financial resources to gain acceptance to Ursuline convents found that their willingness to dirty their hands with the practical work of nursing gained them a niche of their own in religious life. Another match was made between a population of spinsters who wanted to lead lives of holy service and a patriarchal society that perceived a pressing need that could only be answered by enlisting the aid of women who were neither wives nor mothers.

The best known of the new groups to emerge from this development were the Filles de la Charité organized by Vincent de Paul and a peasant woman named Marguerite Naseau. Recognized in 1633, the Filles performed hands-on nursing care, cooked, cleaned the hospitals, and kept their own books. Neither Vincent nor the women drawn to his vision of ministering to the sick and socially marginal wanted recognition as a religious order. The Filles tended the poor where they found them, which was often on the road or in the city square. Even after the renfermement gathered into hospitals many of their charges, a cloistered order required to spend much of its day reciting holy office would not have been able to meet the practical demands of ministering to the diverse population of the hôpitaux généraux. Vincent was thus careful to define his Filles as a congregation, not an order, and, although they lived communally and maintained chastity, poverty, and obedience to their superiors, the Filles de la Charité were not nuns.[36]

In the last third of the seventeenth century, French civil and ecclesiastical authorities institutionalized the program of moral and social reform that the dévots had started. The number of hospitals grew. In the eighteenth

---

tailed studies of the institutions and the ideas and social circumstances that engendered them are Fairchilds, *Poverty and Charity in Aix-en-Provence;* Jones, *The Charitable Imperative;* and Jütte, *Poverty and Deviance,* 176–195; the latter provides a good brief overview. Colin Jones and Michael Sonenscher, "The Social Functions of the Hospital in Eighteenth-Century France: The Case of the Hôtel of Nîmes," *French Historical Studies,* XIII (1983), 172–214, gives an excellent description of the functions of hôpitaux généraux and hôtels dieux.

36. Rapley, *The Dévotes,* 83–88; Jones, *Charitable Imperative,* 38.

century, there were more than two thousand, and the boards and individual patrons who administered them relied almost entirely on the Filles de la Charité, or other hospitalier orders modeled on them, to operate the institutions.[37]

The proliferation of hospitals and their integration into civil administration formalized relations between the hospitals' governing boards and the nursing sisters whose services were now recognized as essential. From the 1670s, it became standard practice for the Filles de la Charité to negotiate formal service contracts with hospital administrative bodies. Hundreds of contracts survive and reveal the Filles as practical women who were used to earning their own way and knew their worth. In addition to the medical equipment and furnishings necessary to operate a hospital, they required housing, clothing, food, travel expenses, and provisions for the care of ill and elderly sisters who had reached the end of their working days. The contracts stipulated how many Filles were to staff the hospital and at what rate they would be paid. Many contained provisions for expanding the number of sisters if the patient rolls required it.[38]

The terms of the Filles' contracts delineate a realm of autonomy and authority for them and convey a sense of assurance and even assertiveness that was certainly at odds with the contemporary ideal of submissive womanhood. Yet the civil and ecclesiastical male leaders of one town after another, anxious to purge their streets of people who undermined their vision of order, signed the contracts and continued to seek the services of the Filles. The congregation's superior noted at one point that they received almost daily requests for additional service arrangements. By the end of the seventeenth century, the Filles had a waiting list for their aid. In the 1720s, they were flatly turning away requests.[39]

In 1700, religious women, deployed by the thousands, were doing the daily work of making good Catholics in France. Decades before, as the French reform movement took wing, a cleric commented caustically about the failure of his colleagues to lead: "Most priests stand aside with their arms crossed; God has had to raise up laymen—cutlers and mercers—to do the work of these idle priests." Clearly, women were raised up as well, perhaps in much greater numbers, and certainly to more lasting effect. The Company of the Holy Sacrament, which was the vehicle for most of these

37. Jones, *Charitable Imperative*, 163–171.
38. Ibid.
39. Ibid., 173.

crusading men, was dissolved in the early 1660s. The Ursulines and the Filles de la Charité, along with the other new women's religious orders and congregations, persisted and grew, developing two distinct apostolates.[40]

Ursulines and members of other educational orders and congregations took on the work of Catholic Christian formation. Identifying the centrality of mothers to the propagation of the faith, their mission was to ensure that young women assumed their adult responsibilities armed with the knowledge, habits, and skills needed to sustain a moral, Catholic society. The Ursulines developed an approach with an intellectual and devotional emphasis that was preparatory, not reformatory, in its intent. Filles de la Charité and similar congregations took on the work of ministering to the physical and spiritual needs of those whom society considered deficient—in age, ability, circumstance, will, or spirit. Their work was custodial and often remedial, rooted in the kinds of practical ministrations to body and soul they might have practiced as mothers and daughters in the humble households of artisans and farmers (Figures 2 and 3).

Each of these two branches of apostolic female religious life served functions that were important to sustaining the social order, yet they addressed distinct purposes, served different populations, and did not reach their apogee at the same time. Ursuline communities sprang up when ideological anxiety was acute. Their program to wage what was essentially a missionary effort in their own land was apposite in the early part of the seventeenth century, and this was their period of greatest growth. At the height of their expansion in the 1620s, as many as sixteen new communities were founded in a single year, and until midcentury new foundations were added every year. Their progress slowed dramatically in the 1640s, and the last three decades of the seventeenth century saw only three new communities established. The rate of profession for Ursulines paralleled this developmental course: as the seventeenth century advanced, fewer women entered Ursuline convents.[41] The Filles de la Charité appeared in organized form more than thirty years later than the Ursulines, at a stage when the French reform element had grown more interested in right behavior than in right thinking. The Filles enjoyed their growth spurt in the late seventeenth century. New communities of Filles de la Charité were founded well into the eighteenth century, as town officials continued to employ them to anchor their campaign to bring health, morality, and order to France.

40. Adrien Bourdoise, quoted in Rapley, *The Dévotes*, 75.
41. Rapley, *The Dévotes*, 59 (graph 1), 198–199 (graphs 2, 3).

T. IV. p. 165.

Loisy Jun. f.

38

Ursuline de la Congrégation de Paris.

Figure 2. Ursuline de la Congrégation de Paris. *From Pierre Hélyot,* Histoire des ordres monastiques . . . , *IV (Paris, 1715). By permission General Research Division, The New York Public Library, Astor, Lenox and Tilden Foundations*

Figure 3. Soeur de la charité. *From Pierre Hélyot,* Histoire des ordres
monastiques . . . , *VIII (Paris, 1719). By permission General Research Division,*
The New York Public Library, Astor, Lenox and Tilden Foundations

For the first three decades of the 1600s, France looked favorably upon the Ursulines and their apostolate. From the French state's perspective, the restoration of universal Catholicism to which these nuns were dedicated was a way to achieve not only peace but the absolutist ideal to which Louis XIII and Louis XIV aspired. But there were always objections to certain things about the nuns. Their communities grew quickly and became quite large and quite rich. They bought sizable sections of prime real estate in French towns and cities on which they built sprawling convent complexes, driving up prices for others. They alienated significant amounts of French wealth from the control of patriarchal families and the civil economy—nuns took dowries to the convent with them, and, once pooled with convent resources, that wealth could never again be used to advance family interests or the secular economy. And in the mid-seventeenth century they refused to cooperate with French authorities who wanted them to deemphasize teaching and undertake the same sort of reformatory work that was the specialty of the Filles de la Charité.[42]

The deterioration of support for the Ursulines accelerated significantly after 1689, when Louis XIV demanded that all religious orders pay something called their *dues amortissement*. The king had traditionally excused religious orders from paying this royal levy, but in the late seventeenth century Louis XIV was short of cash. Religious orders, particularly the swollen ranks of women religious, made a good target not only because they were wealthy but also because they were perceived as being less useful in the 1680s than they had been in the early part of the century. The nuns had done their work all too well. By the late seventeenth century, Catholicism had been restored in France. In 1685, Louis XIV revoked the Edict of Nantes that granted tolerance to Protestants: he no longer needed the Ursulines' help to keep France Catholic.[43]

Assessing the dues amortissement and pressing nuns to exchange their educational mission for reformatory work created a mildly adversarial relationship between convents and the French state. In the eighteenth century, relations became more hostile. In 1727, the crown set up something called the Commission des secours (Commission on Assistance). This benign title was misleading. The Commission des secours was an investigative body set up to assess the financial stability of religious houses. France was reeling

42. Elizabeth Rapley, *A Social History of the Cloister: Daily Life in the Teaching Monasteries of the Old Regime* (Montreal, 2001), 27–48, 78–94, 244–256.

43. Ibid.

from the economic disaster of the Mississippi Bubble in the 1720s, and John Law's failed scheme had a direct impact on nuns, who had been forced by the king to buy shares in the project. Now nuns, like many other investors, found themselves impoverished by the debacle. The crown wanted to make sure that destitute religious sisters did not become a burden on the French state. The Commission des secours was ordered to investigate the finances of religious institutions and to close them down if they seemed too poor to survive.[44]

When the Ursulines came to Louisiana in 1727, the order was embattled. The Filles de la Charité and religious women like them who ran reformatory institutions still served a function that was deemed vital by public authority in France. Enthusiasm had waned, on the other hand, for the Ursulines and their plan to save souls through female education. In 1727, the Ursulines' zeal for saving the world was undiminished, but official public attention had turned from salvation in heaven to reformation on earth. How Louisiana came to be the instrument of revival for the Ursulines' missionary dreams is a story of serendipitous failures and seized opportunities.

44. Ibid. For a description of John Law's scheme for financing the colonization of Louisiana, see the introduction to Part 1, below.

part one

TRANSPLANTATIONS THE FRENCH LEGACY

France established Louisiana as a colony in 1699 to protect its strategic interests, securing a crescent of territory reaching from Quebec down the Mississippi Valley to the Gulf of Mexico. Louisiana acted as a wedge between the English to the east and the Spanish to the west and kept France among the mainland players in the game of Atlantic world exploitation. Despite the boldness of its geographic claim, however, France was a reluctant colonizer whose geopolitical passions and financial priorities lay elsewhere. Louis XIV, who reigned from 1661 to 1715, sought glory on the European continent through the time-tested but expensive strategy of war. His mind and the bulk of his treasure were directed toward a succession of ambitious military campaigns launched to achieve French supremacy in Europe. He recognized that the possession of mainland American territory was indispensable to his project, but he never saw it as more than a troublesome adjunct. Desperate for money to finance his grandiose and often ill-advised military exploits, he sought quick returns from the colony of Louisiana without ever making the investment of funds, talent, and manpower required for success.[1]

1. W. J. Eccles, *France in America*, rev. ed. (East Lansing, Mich., 1990), discusses French motivation for colonizing Canada (1–39) and its strategic interest in planting a colony in Louisiana (107–108). The 1699 foundation was not France's first attempt to colonize the Lower Mississippi Valley. After nearly completing an exploratory voyage down the Mississippi River, René-Robert Cavelier, sieur de La Salle, asserted France's claim to all lands drained by the river in April 1682 and dubbed the territory "Louisiana" in honor of the French monarch. La Salle was murdered by mutinous members of his party in 1687, and in 1689 the remnants of the colony he attempted to plant on what is now the Texas Gulf Coast were suppressed by Spanish troops. Canadian natives Pierre Le Moyne, sieur d'Iberville, and his brother Jean-Baptiste Le Moyne, sieur de Bienville, headed the expedition that planted a successful settlement in 1699 on the Mississippi Gulf Coast near present-day Biloxi (Bennett H. Wall, ed., *Louisiana: A History* [Wheeling, Ill., 1997], 18–22). The best discussion of France's negligent

At the heart of Louisiana's failure was its population. During its first forty years, the colony never had enough people, and the people who were there were not the right sort. With twenty million inhabitants, France was the most populous country in Europe. Its economy was largely agrarian and relied on scale, not acumen. In Louisiana, there were too few inhabitants to produce prosperity in the French mode. In 1699, eighty-two men lived in the colonial capital of Biloxi, including thirteen pirates. The dearth of women in the colony did not bode well for population growth. In 1708, there were only seventy-seven men, women, and children, exclusive of military personnel and enslaved Indians, but none of them had received farmland to cultivate. When Louis XIV died in 1715, the Regency turned Louisiana over to the proprietorship of Antoine Crozat, a merchant whose inept regime only worsened conditions. At the end of his administration in 1717, there were four hundred French inhabitants, an improvement, but hardly a sufficient population for such a vast territory. A few hundred soldiers and colonists, poorly supplied by unreliable shipments of food and arms from France, barely managed to survive and sustain the appearance of occupying and defending Louisiana. Far from enriching France's coffers, the colony represented a debilitating and dispiriting burden.[2]

The Scottish financier John Law proposed a remedy in 1717. Taking a page from the English joint-stock companies that launched successful colonial enterprises on the American eastern seaboard, Law proposed that the colonization of Louisiana be similarly promoted. Law's Company of the West, expanded and renamed the Company of the Indies in 1720, won proprietary rights to Louisiana. Law plied investors with promises of huge profits. Filling younger sons' heads with dreams of New World seigneurship, he persuaded them to become concessionaires who paid a fee for large land grants. Some remained absentee landlords, but others crossed the Atlantic with their families and entourages of indentured servants. With propaganda pamphlets that would have made the fulsome English colonial promoter

Louisiana policy is Mathé Allain, *"Not Worth a Straw": French Colonial Policy and the Early Years of Louisiana* (Lafayette, La., 1988).

2. Pierre Goubert, *Louis XIV and Twenty Million Frenchmen*, trans. Anne Carter (New York, 1972), 288. Gwendolyn Midlo Hall, *Africans in Colonial Louisiana: The Development of Afro-Creole Culture in the Eighteenth Century* (Baton Rouge, La., 1992), 3–9; and Daniel H. Usner, Jr., *Indians, Settlers, and Slaves in a Frontier Exchange Economy: The Lower Mississippi Valley before 1783* (Chapel Hill, N.C., 1992), 25, 32–35, 46–53, both provide good summaries of population in French Louisiana with only small variations in their estimates.

Richard Hakluyt blush, he sold Louisiana as an escape from the poverty that plagued France after the wars of Louis XIV had exhausted its treasury and its spirit. Thousands of men, women, and children responded between 1717 and 1721, including 119 concessionaires and their families, more than 2,000 indentured servants, or *engagés,* and some 1,300 German peasant farmers.[3]

These voluntary settlers were joined by more than twelve hundred forced French émigrés. Events leading to their departure began with the Peace of Utrecht, which ended the War of Spanish Succession in 1713. Military de-mobilization swelled the ranks of those looking for work in France, and the country moved into a peacetime economy that made work scarcer than ever. Vagabondage, petty thievery, smuggling, prostitution, and indebted-ness grew to proportions that could not be easily accommodated by prisons and reformatories. John Law, who needed more immigrant labor to make Louisiana profitable, suggested that some of the deviant surplus be sent over. What was meant to be a manageable trickle of undesirables who could be reformed into industrious farmers turned into an unruly tide. Women joined men on the forced pilgrimage to Louisiana. A spectator reported on "thirty carts filled with young women of middling virtue" on their way to ports of embarkation for Louisiana. "While traversing Paris, the wenches sang like men without care, and called by name those whom they recog-nized as former seductors."[4]

Official France, for its part, seems to have grown giddy at the prospect of achieving moral order through deportation and issued a spate of decrees

3. Hall, *Africans in Colonial Louisiana;* Usner, *Indians, Settlers, and Slaves.* See also Mathé Allain, "French Emigration Policies: Louisiana, 1699–1715," and Carl A. Bras-seaux, "The Image of Louisiana and the Failure of Voluntary French Emigration, 1683–1731," in *Proceedings of the Fourth Meeting of the French Colonial Historical Society, April 6–8, 1978,* ed. Alf Andrew Heggoy and James J. Cooke (Washington, D.C., 1979), 39–56. On John Law's project, see Pierre Heinrich, *Louisiana under the Company of the Indies, 1717–1731,* trans. Henri Delville de Sinclair (New Orleans, 1940), 111–142, 151–166; and Glyndwr Williams, *The Expansion of Europe in the Eighteenth Century: Overseas Rivalry, Discovery, and Exploitation* (New York, 1967), 52–55.

4. Glenn R. Conrad, *"Émigration Forcée:* A French Attempt to Populate Louisiana, 1716–1720," in *Proceedings of the Fourth Meeting of the French Colonial Historical Society, April 6–8, 1978,* ed. Heggoy and Cooke, 58. See also Marcel Giraud, *A History of French Louisiana,* I, *The Reign of Louis XIV, 1698–1715,* trans. Joseph C. Lambert (Baton Rouge, La., 1974), 249–323; Brasseaux, "The Image of Louisiana," in *Proceedings of the Fourth Meeting of the French Colonial Historical Society, April 6–8, 1978,* ed. Heggoy and Cooke, 47–56; Jean Buvat, *Journal de la Régence,* 2 vols. (Paris, 1865), II, 4, quoted ibid., 51.

aimed at identifying and shipping out its undesirables. Meanwhile, the infusion of more than a thousand mostly urban deportees who were unlikely to take to the plow with enthusiasm was not destined to have a stabilizing effect in the colony. Louisiana already harbored a large number of soldiers, always considered a problem because of their youth, poor social background, and bad pay. Between 1719 and 1721, the Company of the Indies shipped 1,628 enslaved Africans to Louisiana from its concessions in west and west central Africa.[5] Altogether, more than 8,600 individuals arrived in Louisiana between 1717 and 1721. More than 6,000 of them were enslaved people, indentured servants, soldiers, and forced exiles, an unstable foundation for Law's dreams of wealth to be created from indigo and tobacco plantations.

By 1726, there were only 2,228 French settlers, excluding soldiers, in Louisiana. Death and abandonment had claimed the rest. John Law's scheme, dubbed the Mississippi Bubble, had collapsed in 1720. The French government reorganized the Company of the Indies as a public venture and placed it in the hands of a body of commissioners who reported to the Royal Ministry of the Marine, which oversaw colonial affairs. After delegating interim authority to one of the colony's ex-governors, Jean-Baptiste Le Moyne, sieur de Bienville, the company detailed two commissioners to Louisiana to take charge of its administration. They arrived in April 1723, but only Jacques Delachaise survived the bout of fever that struck most new arrivals during their first summer in Louisiana.[6]

Louisiana in the 1720s was underpopulated and miserably poor. The climate was hot and humid, inviting a long annual fever season that kept mortality high. The alluvial land was rich but wild, infested with stinging insects, snakes, and alligators. The Indians were astute politicians who weighed their options carefully and played the English and French against one another as the Europeans vied for control in the southeast quadrant of the continent. Small numbers of poorly trained French troops were ill equipped to manage the Indians militarily, and inadequate funding and jurisdictional disputes kept the Jesuits who were there from an effective deployment of the missionary diplomacy that had often proved helpful in

5. Hall, *Africans in Colonial Louisiana*, 60 (table 2).

6. Charles R. Maduell, Jr., comp. and trans., *The Census Tables for the French Colony of Louisiana from 1699 through 1732* (Baltimore, 1972), 50; Giraud, *A History of French Louisiana*, V, *The Company of the Indies, 1723-1731*, trans. Brian Pearce (Baton Rouge, La., 1991), 3–11.

French colonial Canada. In 1729, Natchez Indians staged a devastating attack on the settlement at Fort Rosalie, some one hundred miles north of New Orleans. A growing population of enslaved Africans contributed labor and skill that advanced the colony's flailing agricultural efforts but represented a threat to order and security, staging both individual and organized acts of resistance throughout the decade.[7]

In the succeeding years of French rule, Louisiana made little progress toward realizing dreams of colonial prosperity, but it did achieve a measure of stability. Indian hostilities remained a problem, but the threat to the more densely populated settlements in the Lower Mississippi Valley diminished. The colony's population rose from just more than one thousand settlers of European descent in 1740 to approximately four thousand in 1763, when Louisiana was formally ceded to Spain. Enslaved Africans, who trickled sporadically into Louisiana during the French period, formed the basis of a population of some five thousand bondpeople in 1763, most of them young creoles born to African parents in the colony, a population less inclined to acts of rebellion than the new Africans who dominated in the 1720s and 1730s. If there were few French Louisianians who could claim real wealth, there were nonetheless a significant number who now made a reasonable living from farms and plantations that provisioned the growing population with produce and livestock and squeezed minimal profits from the fur trade, tobacco, and indigo.[8]

7. For overviews of conditions in French colonial Louisiana, see Hall, *Africans in Colonial Louisiana*, 2–27, 120–155; Charles Edwards O'Neill, *Church and State in French Colonial Louisiana: Policy and Politics to 1732* (New Haven, Conn., 1966); and Usner, *Indians, Settlers, and Slaves*, 13–43, 77–104, 147–278.

8. More recent scholarship has both supported and contested the characterization of Louisiana as retarded in its development of a plantation society. Ira Berlin, *Many Thousands Gone: The First Two Centuries of Slavery in North America* (Cambridge, Mass., 1998), 77–92, compares the development of French colonial Louisiana to that of the Chesapeake and the Lowcountry and finds that, although a concentrated influx of slaves in the 1720s constituted the foundation of a slave society in the Lower Mississippi Valley, the colony's failure to develop a profitable staple crop, coupled with a hiatus in the slave trade during the middle decades of the eighteenth century, created a devolution from a slave society to a society with slaves. Thomas N. Ingersoll, *Mammon and Manon in Early New Orleans: The First Slave Society in the Deep South, 1718–1819* (Knoxville, Tenn., 1999), 35–60, argues that a successful planter class and accompanying slave society emerged as early as 1730 and persisted throughout the colonial period.

During these formative decades, as Louisianians of widely diverse origins—French, German, Indian, and African—sought to survive and order their lives in the colony's chaotic mix of poverty, danger, and disease, they forged a society that bore the marks of their own origins and talents even as they responded to common experiences in their new environment that engendered new cultural and social patterns. From this crucible, a community emerged whose distinctive qualities continued to resonate throughout the colonial period. Among the formal institutions of European church and state that helped mold this New World society, only one survived the colony's passage from French into Spanish and, ultimately, American hands: the Ursuline foundation at New Orleans. The next three chapters follow the nuns as they made their way to America and established a ministry that served as an enduring element in the society that took shape at the mouth of the Mississippi.

MAKING A MATCH THE URSULINE
MISSION TO NEW ORLEANS

*If you could, Gentlemen, induce four good gray sisters to come and
settle here and take care of the sick, it would be much better.*
—Jacques Delachaise to the Company of the Indies, 1723

A map of New Orleans drawn less than four years after the arrival of the
Ursulines belies the poverty and social instability that were its hallmarks
in the 1720s. It shows a town graced with large private residences, formal
gardens, and carefully designed public spaces. Set at the focal point of its
grid of streets, the young colonial capital boasted a sizable parish church
that faced onto a public parade ground bordered by the official buildings
of the proprietors. The impression is one of a modest but proper French
urban space, replete with the basic ceremonial and aesthetic components
essential to creating a setting of civility (see Figure 4).

"Our city is very beautiful, well constructed and regularly built," the
Ursuline novice Marie Madeleine Hachard reported to her father shortly
after her arrival in New Orleans in 1727. "The streets are very wide and
laid out in lines," and the well-built houses are "whitewashed, paneled, and
sunlit." When they disembarked from their pirogues upon reaching New
Orleans, the Ursuline missionaries were taken to their temporary quarters, which Marie claimed was "the most beautiful house in the city." The
building had two stories and a garret and gave the nuns "all the necessary apartments." Yet, for all its fine attributes, the Ursulines' house was
located on the edge of the city, its garden bounded on two sides by the thick
woods from which the new urban space had only recently been cleared.
The dwelling was intended to serve as the convent only until a permanent building could be constructed to house the nuns. The future convent site was at the opposite end of the city, at the corner of the square of
cleared land that marked the settlement. Both spaces were situated as far

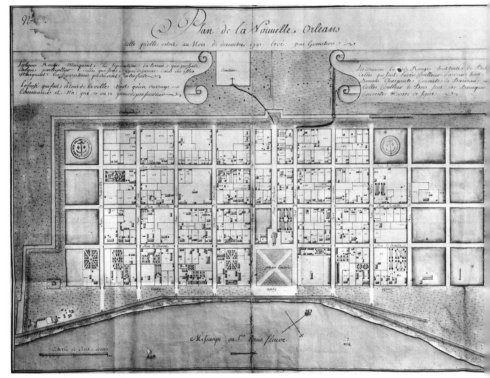

Figure 4. Plan de la Nouvelle Orléans telle qu'elle estoit au mois de dexembre 1731 levé par Gonichon. *By Gonichon. 1731. By permission Centre des archives d'outre-mer, Aix-en-Provence, France, FR CAOM 04DFC89B. The Ursuline property is at the extreme lower right of the plan. The key to the map notes: "House which they are constructing for the Ursulines. They are due to have the two squares marked R for their enclosure"*

from the town's physical centers of church and state as was possible (see Figure 5).[1]

The marginal siting of the nuns' two convents might have been unintentional, but it was a striking harbinger of the nature of the nuns' relationship with the official axes of power in the colony, who were at best lukewarm about their presence and at worst openly hostile toward them. Nor did the effusive description of New Orleans rendered by Marie Hachard comport with either the realities of the frontier capital or its tainted reputation in France. The mother superior of the little missionary band, Marie

1. [Marie Madeleine Hachard], *De Rouen à la Louisiane: Voyage d'une Ursuline en 1727* (Rouen, 1988), 72–74.

Tranchepain, and the chief colonial administrator of the colony, Commissioner Jacques Delachaise, were less sanguine in their assessments of both the city's promise and the prospects for a close and happy partnership between the nuns and the men who held the reins of civil and ecclesiastical authority. The tensions that characterized the relationship between religious women and male authorities in France in the 1720s leaped the Atlantic with ease. Yet, perhaps to everyone's surprise, the Ursuline establishment in New Orleans survived a rocky start, and the colonial capital began to take on the characteristics of a settled community.

In the early autumn of 1723, Commissioner Delachaise surveyed his realm of responsibility and despaired. Upon arriving in Louisiana the previous April, he promptly fell ill with the fever that afflicted all newcomers. Recovered, but still weak, he took stock of affairs in the colony from his vantage point in its capital, New Orleans, and began identifying the things he needed to turn the colony around. The condition of the public hospital was one of Delachaise's greatest worries, and he scrutinized its operations at the most basic level. At the height of the fever season, he advised his employers, there were as many as eighty of the colony's precious soldiers and inhabitants lying ill in the town's hospital, where things were not as they should be. "No one takes care of this place. We must rely on the surgeons and the male nurses." The surgeon, Delachaise continued, "pays scarcely any attention to it." "He has married a rich wife. He thinks only of his pleasures."[2]

The failure of the public hospital was not a small matter. In the 1720s, the Louisiana colony was still on the brink of failure, lacking on every count—population, economy, social stability—features that would reassure the financially pressed French government that it was worth sustaining. Its strategic importance alone secured its future. But Jacques Delachaise's own future fortunes as a senior bureaucrat rested on his ability to do more than maintain a miserable status quo. With a blend of aristocratic arrogance and bureaucratic stubbornness, he set out to turn Louisiana into a model outpost of French civility, one resting on a firm foundation of physical and mental health. A member of the bourgeoisie that had given birth to the *renfermement*, Delachaise understood the *hôpital* to be the lynchpin of a well-ordered urban center. He also knew that it served a second, critical function in the New World as well. The majority of its patients were the soldiers that Commissioner Delachaise depended on to enforce the com-

2. AC, C13A, VII, 19v, trans. Jane Frances Heaney. Heaney's unpublished translations of AC, C13A, correspondence relating to the Ursulines are housed in UCANO.

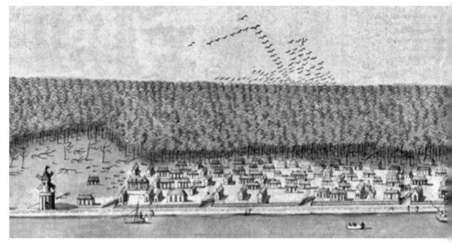

Figure 5. Veüe et perspective de la Nouvelle Orléans. *By Jean-Pierre Lassus. 1726. By permission Centre des archives d'outre-mer, Aix-en-Provence, France, FR CAOM 04DFC71A. The location of the future Ursuline convent is at the lower right corner of the sketch, at the edge of the settlement*

pany's trade monopoly against smuggling and black marketeering, to keep the civil peace, and to protect the colony's capital from Indian attack. His personal success turned on these men. If they spent most of their tour of duty incapacitated with fever or died in the hospital for lack of proper care, he would fail.

Delachaise believed he knew what would remedy his problem. "If you could, Gentlemen," he implored the directors of the company, "induce four good gray sisters to come and settle here and take care of the sick, it would be much better." Gray sisters—hospitalier nuns like the Filles de la Charité —would provide better care "than the male attendants, who steal the rations," Delachaise asserted. He added that he hoped that some of these gray sisters would be trained as pharmacists, because the colony's medicines "vanish as soon as they arrive." Delachaise believed that the surgeons in charge of the colony's medical care, who kept no dispensary accounts, were selling off the medicines for their own profit while the inmates of the hospital languished and died. "A good sister who will take charge of the medicines," he was sure, "will not deliver any except on receipts which will be explained."[3]

3. AC, C13A, VII, 20, X, 19v–20, translated in *MPA*, II, 312. Unless otherwise noted, translations are the author's. As the appointed commissioner of the proprietary Com-

Better health care was not the only reason that Delachaise and his employers sought the services of nursing sisters. The sisters and the institutions they operated in France catered to social problems as well as physical ills. From its earliest days, the official correspondence of Louisiana was filled with complaints about the moral and social deviance of the colonists, much of it centering on sexual relations. There was Indian concubinage at the first outposts at Mobile and Biloxi early in the eighteenth century. When French women began to arrive, official reports complained of prostitution, adultery, and polygamy. The arrival of twelve hundred forced emigrants under the Law regime exacerbated what officials perceived as a chronically disordered population. Like his bourgeois counterparts who governed the cities and towns of France and tried to impose the orderly industry and propriety they believed to be the keys to material prosperity, Commissioner Delachaise sought religious women and the institution of the hôpital to help him achieve his ends.[4]

Delachaise first wrote to the company asking for gray sisters in 1723. In 1726 the Company of the Indies reported that, in the three years since

pany of the Indies, Delachaise was the highest-ranking nonmilitary colonial officer in Louisiana. Together with a military commandant general, he bore ultimate responsibility for protecting the interests of crown and company in the colony. At the second tier of colonial administration, five councillors formed the Conseil Supérieur, or Superior Council, which discharged judicial and administrative functions.

4. AC, C13A, VIII, 418v–420; and see, for example, AC, C13A, III, 13–14, 48–49, IV, 187–191, VII, 21v, 47v–48.

he had made his request, they had been unable to persuade them, or any other nursing religious, to come to Louisiana.[5] At this point, the Jesuit superior for Louisiana, Ignace de Beaubois, stepped in and proposed a community of Ursulines as an alternative. At Trois Rivières in New France, Ursulines had agreed to add nursing duties to their traditional program of education, so there was precedent. There were several possible motives for Beaubois's intercession. The Jesuit and the Ursuline orders maintained close, friendly relations. Their Reformation origins were similar, and both practiced a spirituality in which self-examination, meditation, and retreats played a significant part, but it was their shared educational mission that made them natural allies. Both considered themselves better equipped than other orders to evangelize, particularly among the non-French. The most generous construal of Beaubois's promotion of the Ursulines is that he believed their educational approach was what the colony really needed.

More likely, however, Beaubois's purposes were strategic. He had traveled to France in the summer of 1726 to mend fences with the colonial proprietors and to settle the terms for the Jesuits' service in Louisiana. Beaubois had trespassed in numerous insidious ways on the apostolic territory of the Capuchin friars, who had pastoral charge of New Orleans. The Company of the Indies did not necessarily prefer the Capuchins to the Jesuits, but it did not like troublemakers, and Beaubois had made trouble. Using his order's good relations with the Ursulines to recruit a contingent to take charge of the New Orleans hospital, he would be able to make an impressive peace offering.[6]

5. AC, C13A, X, 75-75v. "Gray sisters" was used as a generic label for several congregations of nursing sisters, including the Filles de la Charité and the hospitalier sisters who operated the *hôtel dieu* of Montreal. In addition to these congregations of nursing sisters, there was one male order, the Brothers of Charity of Saint John of God. The Company of the Indies also approached this order for service in Louisiana (ibid). The male congregation was small, numbering only 355 members on the eve of the French Revolution, but it did supply brothers to one French colonial enterprise, the military hospital at Louisbourg, on the coast of Cape Breton, Nova Scotia. The Brothers of Charity served at Louisbourg between 1716 and 1758. See A. J. B. Johnston, *Life and Religion at Louisbourg, 1713-1758* (Montreal, 1996), 67-85.

6. Charles Edwards O'Neill, *Church and State in French Colonial Louisiana: Policy and Politics to 1732* (New Haven, Conn., 1966), 164-173. The Capuchins, a branch of the Franciscan order, had been given purview over New Orleans and the Gulf Coast settlements from 1704. The Jesuits, already established in the Illinois territory of the Upper Mississippi Valley, made various attempts from 1706 onward to insinuate

In the autumn of 1726, Beaubois brokered an arrangement between a small contingent of Ursuline nuns drawn from Rouen and several other towns in northwest France. The next spring, as he awaited the nuns' arrival, Beaubois seems to have grown increasingly nervous about the reception the little band of Ursulines would receive. Though he reported enthusiastically to the civil secretary of the Company of the Indies in Paris that the nuns' arrival was "[looked forward to] like that of the Messiah," he wrote more candidly to the religious supervisor of the company. Beaubois admitted that the Capuchin friar serving as the head ecclesiastical official in New Orleans, Raphaël de Luxembourg, thought it ridiculous to bring Ursuline nuns to the colonial capital.[7]

Beaubois's worries about the Ursulines' prospects for success were rooted in the friction between two colonial political factions that reverberated in disputes between the Jesuits and Capuchins over the division of missionary territory in the Mississippi Valley. It might have been that, as protégés of the Jesuit superior Beaubois, the Ursulines found themselves pulled into the fray. The Ursulines did, indeed, encounter difficulties in Louisiana, but their troubles did not begin and end with their association with the Jesuits. Rather, they grew from the ancient tug-of-war between religious women trying to win acceptance for their apostolate and authorities of church and state that reluctantly gave ground only when religious women offered them a solution to a problem for which there seemed no alternative.[8]

---

themselves as missionaries in the Capuchin domain. The Company of the Indies applied what it hoped would be a final solution to the dispute between the two orders with the agreement struck with Beaubois in 1726, which allotted the Capuchins the Lower Mississippi Valley and gave the Jesuits responsibility for the missions in the Upper Mississippi Valley from the Yazoo and Arkansas posts north (55, 70–77, 130, 162–173).

7. Reuben Gold Thwaites, ed., *The Jesuit Relations and Allied Documents: Travels and Explorations of the Jesuit Missionaries in New France, 1610–1791*, 73 vols. (Cleveland, Ohio, 1896–1901), LXVII, 273; and AC, C13A, X, 313.

8. O'Neill, *Church and State*, 189–212, provides the fullest account of the political squabbles between Beaubois, who associated with the faction supportive of the recently unseated governor of Louisiana, Jean-Baptiste Le Moyne, sieur de Bienville, and the new governing team of the Company of the Indies, led by Commissioner Jacques Delachaise and Commandant General Etienne de Périer. O'Neill's attribution of the Ursulines' early difficulties in Louisiana to their role in the partisan bickering remains the standard interpretation. Marcel Giraud, *A History of French Louisiana*, V,

Neither Jacques Delachaise nor Father Raphaël de Luxembourg wanted to bring Ursulines to New Orleans to educate women and girls. Like other French public officials in the 1720s, Delachaise wanted the practically oriented Filles de la Charité or similar sisters to help him turn his city into a model of bourgeois order through the agency of the *hôpital général.* His prescription for what would remedy the city's ills was not original. In Louisiana, the colonial clerics who complained that inhabitants barely discharged their annual obligation to attend Easter Mass and town fathers who decried drunkenness, gaming, fornication, and bastardy echoed their Old World counterparts in tone and substance. Although Louisiana had a notoriously bad reputation as a result of the deportation scheme that took place under John Law's administration, whether it was really substantially more disorderly than French towns is debatable. At one point in the eighteenth century, about forty thousand infants were abandoned each year in France, and in Paris the illegitimacy rate reached 20 percent.[9] Official tolerance vanished for anything smacking of dissipation, particularly among laborers, servants, soldiers, and sailors. The more fortunate beggars, drunkards, and others who failed to meet the test of sober productivity were rounded up and placed in *hôpitaux généraux;* the unlucky found themselves locked up in France's *dépôts de mendicité*—jails for the poor.

Delachaise simply followed his French counterparts in both his assessment of the problem and the means for its resolution. The sturdy, hardworking Filles de la Charité and similar nursing orders were well suited to the task of reformation, both in France and in Louisiana. They would not only operate his hospital and keep his soldiers alive, he reasoned, but look after orphans and abandoned children and run a small reformatory for the loose women and prostitutes who endangered the colony with venereal disease and threatened to bankrupt the public purse with the burden of unsupported bastards. Unfortunately, in the 1720s the Filles de la Charité were in such high demand that they were turning down potential clients in France. There was no way to induce them to cross the Atlantic to take on the project of Louisiana.[10]

The Company of the Indies, 1723–1731, trans. Brian Pearce (Baton Rouge, La., 1991), 87–97, also advances this interpretation.

9. Olwen H. Hufton, *The Poor of Eighteenth-Century France, 1750–1789* (New York, 1974), 318, 320.

10. Colin Jones, *The Charitable Imperative: Hospitals and Nursing in Ancien Regime and Revolutionary France* (New York, 1989), 173; AC, C13A, X, 75–75v.

Ursulines, on the other hand, were searching for a way to take their educational mission to the new colony. By the mid-1720s, the order and others like it were in a state of decline in comparison with their early-seventeenth-century heyday. Yet there remained a vital strain of the order's early evangelical enthusiasm, its original domestic object transformed into a zeal for colonial missionary work. Just as the early-seventeenth-century fervor of Catholic resurgence began to cool, the Jesuit Relations chronicling the dramatic missionary exploits of the Society of Jesus among the Indians of New France stirred a new generation of *dévots*. Indian conversion became a fresh, revitalizing interest among the pious and offered a new object for female zeal. The prospect of missionary work among the native population of New France exerted a ferocious appeal for the kind of women who, two generations earlier, would have found the original Ursuline enterprise compelling. But the New World offered these women an ambivalent reception. "The saga of women missionaries in seventeenth-century Canada," one historian observes, was "a story of female eagerness and official reticence."[11] Bishops and civil officials on both sides of the Atlantic discouraged their missionary aspirations. The women who persevered and came to New France, in turn, found themselves struggling to succeed in a missionary field they had to define for themselves.

The first Ursuline convent in New France was founded in Quebec in 1639 by a widow named Marie Guyart, known as Marie de l'Incarnation. Her project to make good Catholic mothers of Indian girls was never more than partially successful. She was sensitive to the value the public in her homeland placed on "the progress of the Gospel" among the Indians, but she either believed or came to believe that the work of instilling and perpetuating the faith among the French who would be mothers in the New World was equally important.[12]

In a letter to her grown son, she detailed the nuns' educational activities so that he could "reply to the rumours you say are put about that the Ursu-

11. Leslie Choquette, "'Ces Amazones du Grand Dieu': Women and Mission in Seventeenth-Century Canada," *French Historical Studies*, XVII (1992), 632.

12. Marie de l'Incarnation, *Word from New France: The Selected Letters of Marie de l'Incarnation*, ed. and trans. Joyce Marshall (Toronto, 1967), 337. For a general description of the educational program of the Ursuline mission to Quebec in the seventeenth century, see Vincent Grégoire, "L'éducation des filles au couvent des Ursulines de Québec à l'époque de Marie de l'Incarnation (1639–1672)," *Seventeenth-Century French Studies*, XVII (1995), 87–98.

lines are useless in this country and that the *Relations* do not speak of their accomplishing anything." As in France, in the late 1660s the work of Marie Guyart and her Ursuline sisters was eclipsed by the growing popularity of nursing sisters. Reports from New France made much of the work of the Chanoinesses Hospitalières de Saint-Augustin, who had charge of Quebec's hospital. Marie Guyart made a case for the significance of her order's work. "Great care is taken in this country with the instruction of the French girls, and I can assure you that if there were no Ursulines they would be in continual danger for their salvation," she wrote. The threat was as much carnal as it was spiritual, she noted tartly, because some parents were foolish enough to go out and leave their young girls at home with "several men to watch over them." Girls in such circumstances were "in evident danger, and experience shows they must be put in a place of safety." Preserving female virtue and providing young women with the spiritual armor to retain it was a crucial task for the nuns, who sometimes had only a year to teach their students "reading, writing, calculating, the prayers, Christian habits, and all a girl should know."[13]

Marie Guyart insisted that the Ursuline mission to New France was important. The nuns did what they could to convert Indian girls who would return to their villages to become mothers of Christian families in the wilderness, and they made certain that the French girls in Canada grew up to assume their essential duties as custodians of the Catholic faith. She blamed the public's failure to recognize the value of their labors on their cloistered state. "Our enclosure covers all," she noted. "It is quite otherwise with the Hospitalière Mothers; the hospital being open and the good done there seen by everyone." The watching world might be freer in its praise for the practical ministrations of the nursing sisters, but "ultimately they and we await recompense for our services from the One that penetrates into the most hidden places and sees as clearly in the shadows as in the light; that is sufficient for us."[14]

Such words were an inspiration to the French women who became Ursulines after the apogee of their order had passed. Marie Guyart's missives stubbornly proclaimed the continuing value of the order's work, even when it went unrecognized in the world. They conveyed the heroic nature of working to convert the nonbelievers in the New World but pointed out the equally meaningful task of preserving virtue and implanting Catholicism

13. Marie de l'Incarnation, *Word from New France*, ed. Marshall, 335, 336.
14. Ibid., 337.

firmly in the hearts and minds of French colonial girls. When the letters were published late in the seventeenth century, they gave new life and purpose to Marie Guyart's order and filled new generations of Ursulines with a desire to undertake the hybrid mission that she had pioneered. But the two small convents of Quebec had as many nuns as they needed. The zealous women who wanted to follow in Marie Guyart's footsteps had no place to go—until the call from Louisiana reached their ears.

As a young convert from Protestantism, Marie Tranchepain entered the Ursuline convent at Rouen in the last year of the seventeenth century and dreamed of being a missionary to the New World. It was a futile aspiration until, in middle age, "God made known to her that a Jesuit, whom she did not know and who did not know her, but who was then in France, was to be her guide and leader in a foreign land where He wished her to serve Him by establishing an Ursuline Convent." Marie Tranchepain's revelation bears a striking resemblance to the experience of the woman who inspired her, Marie Guyart. She, too, had been guided by a Jesuit, her spiritual director who told her that the vast mountainous landscape of her dream was Canada and that God meant for her to go there as a missionary.[15] When Ignace de Beaubois called on the Ursuline convent of Rouen to propose a Louisiana mission, Marie Tranchepain saw the hand of God and thanked him for hearing her prayer. That she and her sisters would have to add nursing to their educational program was a small price to pay for passage to the promised land.

"Would there be no means of advancing that happy day for which I have yearned for twenty-six years and which has not yet arrived?" wrote Marie Tranchepain from Hennebont as she waited in the autumn of 1726 to sail for Louisiana. The missionary spirit that infused Tranchepain drew companions to her from neighboring convents. Like her, they nursed an almost obsessive desire to be foreign missionaries. Madeleine Mahieu, from Le Havre, "was inspired by her heavenly spouse with the desire to consecrate herself to him anew through the mission to Louisiana, more than ten years before it was thought of to make an establishment there." Marguerite Salaon, of Ploëmel, had a "vocation for the missions," and, on hearing that

15. AC, C13A, X, 67, trans. Jane Frances Heaney; "Lettres circulaires," 207, UCANO. Linda Lierheimer, "Female Eloquence and Maternal Ministry: The Apostolate of Ursuline Nuns in Seventeenth-Century France" (Ph.D. diss., Princeton University, 1994), 47–50, discusses the importance of the Canadian mission to the identity and unity of the French Ursulines.

Marie Tranchepain was leading a group of nuns to Louisiana, she wrote to her "with fervor," asking that she be allowed to join them. Cécile Cavalier was so ardent in her desire to serve in a mission that she implored Saint Joseph with daily prayers and devotions, "contriving each day new ways to honor him" and promised to change her religious name from Sister Saint Marie des Anges to Sister Saint Joseph if her prayers were answered.[16]

These women joyfully left their convents in France to do the missionary work of education and conversion. The letters of Marie Guyart that guided them in their expectations and aspirations outlined a two-pronged challenge for Ursuline missionaries to the New World. First, they were to help spread Catholicism among the non-French by converting Indian girls and preparing them to propagate the faith after they returned to their own communities and became mothers. Equally important, they would ensure that frontier circumstances did not rob the French girls of Louisiana of what the nuns considered their birthright and the cornerstone of Catholic society: the retention of personal virtue and the acquisition of an orthodox Christian education.

The stories of Louisiana that filtered back to French Ursulines portrayed a frontier whose needs were perhaps even greater than those of Marie Guyart's New France. Travel accounts published in the late seventeenth century indicated that the work of Indian conversion south of Canada called for heroic missionary efforts. The recollect, Louis Hennepin, lamented of the Illinois Indians that "their Conversion is to be despair'd of, till Time and Commerce with the Europeans has remov'd their natural Fierceness and Ignorance, and thereby made 'em more apt to be sensible of the Charms of Christianity." Louisiana not only had intractable Indians but also a female population in dire need of the Ursulines' protection. The memory of convoys of convicts making their way to French ports to embark for Louisiana was still fresh and created the impression that the only people left in Louisiana were soldiers and reprobates. People on the streets of Paris made up jingles about the misery of Louisiana. The danger to the virtue of France's daughters in the colony was clear. Louisiana, the Ursulines must have reasoned, was crying out for their apostolate, and in September 1726 Marie Tranchepain and two other Rouenese Ursulines destined for New Orleans traveled to Paris to sign a contract with the Company of the Indies for service in Louisiana.[17]

16. AC, C13A, X, 67, trans. Heaney; "Lettres circulaires," 195, 203, 211, UCANO.
17. Carl A. Brasseaux, "The Image of Louisiana and the Failure of Voluntary French

The provisions and language of this contract reveal the architecture of the compromise between the limited practical objectives of company officials and the ideologically driven aspirations of the Ursulines. Patterned on the agreements that the Filles de la Charité drew up with public officials in France, the contract's twenty-eight articles stipulated that the company would transport to Louisiana and maintain six nuns at an annual salary of six hundred livres. Their energies were to be directed to the hospital. The contract allowed the nuns to undertake some educational work, but grudgingly. "They will take, if they judge proper, female pensioners at the rate which the Superioress will regulate," the contract directed, "but none of those who will be charged with the sick will be taken away from them or applied to the education of the pensioners." Only one nun, the contract dictated, would be assigned teaching responsibilities. The Company of the Indies recognized that, as vowed nuns, the Ursulines maintained a more demanding program of formal devotion than nursing sisters but noted that, although they were allowed "to govern themselves as to the interior of the house as to their rule and the Spirit of their Institute," it was to be effected so "that the service of the hospital will not suffer from it in the least."[18]

Marie Tranchepain, now acting as superior of the Louisiana-bound nuns, signed a contract that diverged quite dramatically from the Ursulines' usual program because she believed the nuns had been called to the colony. She must also have been aware that the difficulties that had besieged female religious life for some time and were soon to culminate in the royal Commission des secours boded ill for the growth of her order in France. Although the Company of the Indies was not disposed to loosen its purse strings to make sure the colony was a bulwark of Catholic motherhood, it would accept the Ursulines in lieu of nursing nuns and pay them to tend the sick and to protect their investment. Tranchepain, like the Company of the Indies, was forced by circumstance into an unlikely compromise tinged with mutual manipulation and, perhaps, outright deception. Even as Marie Tranchepain signed the contract, she and Beaubois had plans to bring more than six Ursulines to New Orleans. When the party of nuns sailed from Lorient in February 1727, they numbered twelve.

The mismatch between the Ursulines and the Company of the Indies was

---

Emigration, 1683–1731," in *Proceedings of the Fourth Meeting of the French Colonial Historical Society, April 6–8, 1978*, ed. Alf Andrew Heggoy and James J. Cooke (Washington, D.C., 1979), 47 (quotation), 51, 52.

18. AC, C13A, X, 88–99, trans. Heaney.

obvious, and it worried the bishop of Rouen, who had to give permission for Marie Tranchepain and her companions to leave their French convents and his diocese to take up new duties in Louisiana. "I cannot give this consent until I am assured that not only the King approves it, but that the King by his authority will render this establishment secure and permanent." Rouen's "unmanageable bishop," as Beaubois called him, must have been skeptical about the Ursulines' chances for success as they set off to do the unaccustomed work of nursing in Louisiana. If they failed in Louisiana, or grew infirm there, he did not want them to "become a care to their house of profession," straining the resources of France's struggling convents even further. No doubt reluctantly, with Beaubois ensconced at his residence pressuring him to relent, the bishop of Rouen signed the letters authorizing Marie Tranchepain and her companions to leave his diocese. The Ursulines were on their way to a missionary adventure that turned out to be as different from the Indian conversion campaign of Marie Guyart in Canada as it was from their schoolrooms in France.[19]

Two months after she and her eleven Ursuline companions arrived in New Orleans, Marie Tranchepain wrote to Abbé Gilles Bernard Raguet, the religious director of the Company of the Indies, with words that seem designed to reassure him that the Ursuline teaching apostolate was as welcome in the colony as their willingness to perform the accustomed duties of the Filles de la Charité. "All the inhabitants try their best to make us feel the joy which they experience to have us for the education of their children," she effused. Indeed, some inhabitants in and around New Orleans seem to have lost little time in taking advantage of what the nuns themselves were most anxious to offer. The first boarding students arrived in November 1727, about three months after the nuns moved into their temporary quarters in a rented house, and soon they were joined by girls, including Indians and Africans, who attended the free catechism classes offered during the day. A few months later, Marie Tranchepain wrote to Abbé Raguet of her relief at

19. AC, C13A, X, 28–29, trans. Heaney; Beaubois to Raguet, Sept. 18, 1726, AC, C13A, X, 319, trans. Heaney. In the same year that the Ursulines went to Louisiana, the bishop of Quebec defied the Ministry of the Marine in France and sent a single teaching sister of the Congregation of Notre Dame to Louisbourg to educate girls there. Civil authorities refused steadfastly to pay the sisters a salary for their educational services, though they readily supported the nursing ministry of the Brothers of Charity serving Louisbourg's hospital. Johnston, *Life and Religion at Louisbourg*, 67–108.

being settled enough to begin their educational work, "I confess to you that I have a sensible joy at seeing that we are not useless to the colony." In the spring, she reported that the nuns had "a large number of boarders and of day pupils with whose education the parents appear satisfied." She might have been voicing her vision, and not the inhabitants', however, when she averred that "they hope that it will produce in a few years great benefits in the colony where religion is little known and still less practiced." The youngest of the missionary band, the novice Marie Madeleine Hachard, wrote to her father that the nuns did indeed have a number of students. Her exuberant report, however, innocently confided, "Many people have treated our enterprise as folly."[20]

Tranchepain, nonetheless, remained fully committed to her order's educational mission and showed decided reluctance for her community to take on the nursing role that was their official entrée to Louisiana. "There is neither stable nor cattleshed that does not present more agreeable and commodious lodging," she complained after seeing the hospital for the first time, adding, "They say that there is very little sickness that would force one to this miserable shelter." From France, Raguet castigated Tranchepain for her lack of enthusiasm for the hospital. Reminding her that she was in Louisiana not only to educate girls but also to care for the sick, Raguet admonished, "I would have thought that you would run more rapidly towards this cross."[21]

Marie Tranchepain and the Ursulines, in fact, managed to avoid taking up that cross for nearly seven years. By holding company officials to the fine points of their contract and the rule of their religious enclosure, the nuns were able to pursue their educational work unencumbered by the hospital responsibilities the company had hired them to do. Unlike the Filles de la Charité and other nursing congregations, the Ursulines observed a modified form of cloister. According to their contract, the Company of the Indies was to provide them with a proper convent adjacent to the hospital so that they could operate it without breaching their rule. Plans for such a structure gathered dust while officials bickered over the cost and course of construction. The Ursulines took advantage of this bureaucratic inefficiency to advance their program and ignore the company's. While they conducted classes in their rented house and a hastily constructed student hostel at one

20. AC, C13A, X, 359, XI, 239v, 274, trans. Heaney; [Hachard], *De Rouen à la Louisiane*, 24.

21. AC, C13A, X, 359v, XI, 232, trans. Heaney.

end of New Orleans, patients languished in the hospital at the other end of town. "The Company has promised to have a convent built for us near the hospital," Tranchepain wrote to Raguet. "When it will have kept its word, we shall think about carrying out ours, for it is not fitting that we should walk, every day, from one end of the city to the other. Our duty does not oblige us to do that."[22]

The Ursulines' first duty, as they understood it in the context of their order's mission, was to establish the program of female education that they believed would transform the colony into a Christian society. In the jury-rigged Ursuline compound that was taking shape on the edge of the settlement, the nuns began to institute the rhythms of teaching and learning laid out in their rule, the *Règlemens des religieuses Ursulines de la Congrégation de Paris*. Through the *Règlemens*, we gain a sense of the daily routine of the twenty boarders of European descent, the seven enslaved boarders, and the "large number of day students and Negresses and Indian girls" who were students of the nuns in the spring of 1728.[23]

The days of boarding students were divided between academic lessons and religious devotion. They rose between half past five and half past six in the morning, depending on the weather. They were expected to be groomed and dressed at a quarter of seven, when they were to assemble in their classroom chapel or lesson room to say their prayers. At seven they proceeded to the convent chapel and heard Mass with the nuns. After Mass, they spent half an hour breakfasting and then filed into their classroom, seated themselves according to their age and attainment, and began their lessons. At a quarter past ten, they put their schoolwork aside to recite the litanies of the Virgin and then went to the main meal of the day, dinner, which was accompanied by inspirational readings. Boarding students enjoyed recreation between their mid-morning meal and noon, and at a quarter past twelve they returned to their classrooms for afternoon lessons, which lasted until shortly after two o'clock, when they broke for Vespers. Between three and five o'clock in the afternoon, they studied spelling and the catechism and learned their prayers. The students ate supper at five in the evening and enjoyed another recreation period until seven, when they filed into the convent chapel to say the final service of the day, including the Little Office of the Virgin. Afterward, they retired to their dormitory, examined their consciences, said their prayers, disrobed, and went to bed at about eight

22. AC, C13A, XI, 280, trans. Heaney.

23. *Règlemens des religieuses Ursulines de la Congrégation de Paris* (Paris, 1705).

o'clock.[24] Altogether, boarding students spent about six of their fourteen waking hours in the classroom studying a half-dozen classroom subjects: reading, writing, spelling, figuring with the aid of counting beads called *jetons*, needlework, and the catechism. The curriculum and division of the day reflect the responsibilities of pious Catholic women. They were to acquire an education in academic, domestic, and religious subjects and to sustain a regular regime of personal devotion.

If the days of the boarders were full, the days of the nuns were fuller. Educational duties probably commanded the attention of about half the little community in 1728, but other responsibilities kept the convent a place of continual activity that could range from the sedate keeping of accounts to rigorous forms of physical labor. While two to four of the nuns tended to the boarding students, another two managed the program for the extern students, a course of study that focused primarily on religious education and added the rudiments of reading and writing. Another sister took charge of the daily two-hour catechism sessions for enslaved Indian and African women and girls. Sickness was persistent among the denizens of the compound, and the nun who served as infirmarian was doubtless continually busy ministering to incapacitated sisters and students. She was probably also charged with looking after the three orphans placed with the nuns in 1728 by colonial officials. A treasurer managed accounts and procurement for the community, no easy task in the late 1720s when basic supplies in Louisiana were expensive and of poor quality, and cash to buy them was scarce. The mother superior, Marie Tranchepain, fell ill on the voyage to Louisiana and seems never to have regained her full strength; nonetheless, she kept up a fierce pace of negotiation with authorities in Louisiana and in France and assisted in the drudgery of correspondence by the young Marie Hachard, who served as chapter secretary. Renée Yviquel, descended from a family of prosperous French lawyers, showed her adaptability to the physical demands of her missionary work when she picked up an ax to chop firewood and stood at the steaming laundry kettle on washdays.[25]

Less than a year after their arrival, the Ursulines had created a buzzing center of female educational activity. Large numbers of young women,

24. *Règlemens*, 110–114.

25. "Lettres circulaires," and "Délibérations du Conseil," UCANO. The term "orphan" was applied not only to describe children whose parents were deceased but also those whose parent or parents had relinquished or forfeited their custody for reasons of financial exigency, illness, or criminal activity.

including enslaved Indian and African girls, regularly streamed into the convent, a respectable number of girls enrolled in their boarding and free day schools, and, during their first Holy Week in the colony, hundreds of women attended the course of sermons offered by a Jesuit priest at their compound. Despite official reluctance that soon turned into official consternation, the Ursulines refused to put the priorities of their earthly sponsors ahead of the work they believed God had called them to do. The New Orleans nuns remained steadfast in their determination to tend to the souls of Louisiana, even though by the time they arrived in New Orleans religious women were deemed best suited to work that was essentially domestic: nursing and sheltering. One historian has noted that the centrality of religious women to Counter-Reformation piety was always under attack in early modern France. The attack had clearly intensified as the reformation of ideas gave way to the reformation of manners over the course of the seventeenth century. The Ursulines, whose vocation lay in the apostolic work of catechesis that had been crucial in the years following the Edict of Nantes, had lost support in France in favor of religious women like the Filles de la Charité who turned their religious devotion to practical effect. In Louisiana, their reluctance to yoke their energies and commitment to the objectives of their employers created a fractious *mésalliance*. The Ursulines never enjoyed the unqualified support of authorities in the colony and had to fight more than once to remain there. In 1728, they nearly left for Saint Domingue in a dispute over their right to clerical self-governance, and in the 1740s colonial officials cut their budget, accused them of graft, and threatened to have them suppressed.[26]

The Ursulines persevered, nonetheless. Within a few short years of their arrival, they began to make progress in their desire to bring all who lived within the temporal boundaries of France's colony into the spiritual realm of Catholicism. The community of Christian womanhood that the nuns drew together in their little compound on the edge of town differed from what they had imagined as they made their Atlantic crossing. Their response to that challenge was to leave a visible imprint on the society that grew up beyond the convent walls.

26. [Hachard], *De Rouen à la Louisiane*, 78–80; Choquette, "'Ces Amazones," *French Historical Studies*, XVII (1992), 630; Jane Frances Heaney, *A Century of Pioneering: A History of the Ursuline Nuns in New Orleans (1727–1827)*, ed. Mary Ethel Booker Siefken (New Orleans, 1993), 69–91, 124–126 (written as Ph.D. diss., Saint Louis University, 1949).

chapter 2

THE ORDER WAS WELL KEPT CREATING

AND SUSTAINING COMMUNITY

On July 17, 1734, the inhabitants of New Orleans were treated to a festive spectacle. A procession of nuns, pious women, young girls, clergy, and inhabitants walked ceremoniously from the Ursulines' temporary quarters at one end of town to the new convent that had been built for the nuns at the opposite edge of the settlement (see Figure 6). The streets were a quagmire after three days of unremitting rain. Dozens of little girls, pent up all day waiting for the skies to clear, were restless. They broke into spirited song when the procession finally marched forth at five o'clock that evening. Military fifes and drums added to the noise and excitement. Yet "no one got out of order," the Ursuline chronicler tells us, "in spite of the mud and the singing of the children."[1]

In the muddy streets of the frontier town, rank and class still mattered to the nuns. "Messieurs Bienville, Governor, and Salmon, Intendant, honored us with their presence," the chronicler noted, "as did almost all the people of both the upper and the lower classes of the city." The Ursulines mirrored this attention to rank as they took up their places in the procession. The nine women constituting the little religious community "went out in order," and the mother superior and assistant superior took pride of place behind the canopy sheltering the reserved sacrament. At first glance, this processional display of social order gives an impression of traditional hierarchies, but a closer look reveals some surprises. Marching in the parade in places of honor were women who belonged to a lay confraternity, a devotional organization that saw plantation mistresses fall into step beside carpenters' wives and women of color. And Indian and African girls joined the chorus of singing students.[2]

The procession of 1734 tells us who the Ursulines were and what they

1. "Délibérations du Conseil," 253–255, UCANO.
2. Ibid., 253.

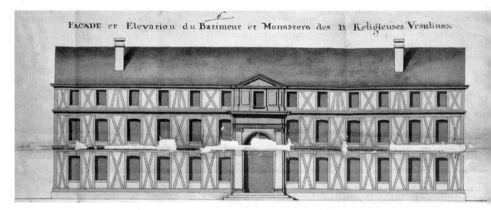

Figure 6. Façade et élévation du batiment et monastère des d. religieuses Ursulines; coupe profil du batiment et monnastère des dames Ursulines de cette ville à la Nlle Orléans le 14 janvier 1732. *By Ignace-François Broutin. 1732. By permission Centre des archives d'outre-mer, Aix-en-Provence, France, FR CAOM F3/290/6. Architect's drawing of the first Ursuline convent, where the procession of 1734 terminated*

were in New Orleans to do. Employing imagery from the fourth-century myth of the first female Christian missionary, Saint Ursula, it speaks to the nuns' determination to transplant their French version of her legacy to the New World. These eighteenth-century female missionaries remained true to their order's seventeenth-century origins: they were bent on extending the spirit of the French Counter-Reformation to Louisiana and transforming every woman there into an agent for the propagation of the faith. Yet their seventeenth-century universalizing religious imperative took them in an unanticipated direction in Louisiana. Diversity of social rank had marked the original Ursuline project in France. In the colony, race added a new dimension to the Catholic community they hoped to build. Women of every rank and color came to embrace and affirm the Catholic orthodoxy the nuns promulgated in their temporary convent and followed the nuns in public procession to their new cloister in 1734. At the end of the century, women of all social and racial backgrounds still found a place in the nuns' enclosure. This inclusive tradition was not easily preserved.

The Ursulines' first order of business in their project to create a community of colonial Catholic mothers was to establish themselves. Paralleling the development of the colony itself, the small band of nuns overcame threats that mortality and attrition posed to their stability. In the early years of their mission, they surmounted a frontier climate of moral lassitude and succeeded in bringing the women of the city within their orbit.

With each succeeding generation, however, the nuns had to find a way to keep the changing female community of New Orleans faithful to their original French project. Waves of African immigration, the change to Spanish dominion in 1763, the arrival of Anglo-Americans in the last decades of the eighteenth century, the rise of a successful plantation economy in the 1790s, and a burgeoning community of free women of color, each tested the adaptability and elasticity of their apostolate. Holding fast to their own French identity and rigid customs of convent rank and order, they kept the loyalty of a changing, diverse population of women by the contradictory strategy of making their convent a space that resolutely welcomed women of all races, classes, and nationalities through the end of the colonial period.

The Ursulines were able to preserve their universalist vision in the face of increasingly divisive forces turning on race, class, and national identity precisely because they clung to the terms and forms of a ministry forged in France in an earlier age. The Counter-Reformation imperative to restore France to Catholicism allowed early-seventeenth-century Ursulines to ignore social status as a requirement for admission to their schools. With the passage of that exigency, the ascent of the bourgeoisie in its membership and the sisters' attention to the formalities of rank allayed concerns about the subversive potential of universal female education and secured the future of the order and its mission. This European legacy provided the Louisiana nuns with the shield of tradition, allowing them to ignore the categories that were structuring relations outside the convent walls. To modern eyes, the Ursulines appear boldly progressive in their refusal to exclude women for reasons of race or class yet rigidly traditional in their adherence to fusty categories of gentility and social status. Their progress through the eighteenth century, like their march across New Orleans in 1734, used a revived religious imperative and long-established rules of rank and order to support a program of radical potential.

In early modern ecclesiastical processions, rank ascended from front to back. When the participants were all male, the hierarchies of office, social status, and age were traced in the arrangement of the marchers. The clergy stood at the rear, and just before them were the highest-ranking civil officials, preceded by other participants. In their New World procession, the nuns bowed to the accepted status of male clergy, placing them at their procession's rear, but the rule of gender hierarchy stopped there. In the great religious processions of Paris, the king took the position of honor behind the reserved sacrament. In New Orleans, the highest-ranking Ursulines stood beside the canopy while His Majesty's representatives looked on as honored spectators. Nor were soldiers, the human manifestation of military might and the king's glory, part of the main column. Instead, they were "drawn up on both sides of the street, marched in perfect order, single file, leaving between them and us a distance of about four feet."[3] By excluding the representatives of civil power from their procession, the Ursulines delineated a universe where the power of God was unambiguously superior to worldly authority. When they placed themselves and three groups of women and girls between the clergy and the male and female inhabitants who led the procession, they proclaimed their belief that women represented the link between the holy and the profane.

During the seventeenth century, the Ursulines crafted a spiritual tradition that built on the notion of women as the central agents of conversion and salvation.[4] In the early-seventeenth-century milieu from which the French variant of the order sprang, the clergy lacked a successful strategy for effecting the orthodox compliance that was the Council of Trent's ideal. Conformity could be imposed in theory, but in practice legislating piety was not enough to achieve conformity. Someone had to lead people to the baptismal font and Communion rail, where priests endowed with sacramental authority waited to receive them. With the careful separation of the sacred from the profane and the definition of the clergy as a class apart, the priest could not move easily between the altar and the hearth.

The seventeenth-century Ursulines employed mythology and imagery relating to their patron, Saint Ursula, and their foundress, Angela Merici, to create a literature and a historical tradition that supported their apostolate as teachers who brought people to God through the ministry of women. According to legend, Ursula was a fourth-century British princess who wanted

3. Ibid., 355. For descriptions of processional order and a discussion of the role of these ceremonies as vehicles for political and social expression in early modern Europe, see Barbara B. Diefendorf, *Beneath the Cross: Catholics and Huguenots in Sixteenth-Century Paris* (New York, 1991), 38–41 (esp. 39); and Brian Pullan, *Rich and Poor in Renaissance Venice: The Social Institutions of a Catholic State, to 1620* (Cambridge, Mass., 1971), 52, 59–60.

4. This discussion of the Ursuline apostolate and spirituality is drawn from Elizabeth Rapley, *The Dévotes: Women and Church in Seventeenth-Century France* (Montreal, 1990), 3–22, 48–60, 74–75, 142–154; and Linda Lierheimer, "Female Eloquence and Maternal Ministry: The Apostolate of Ursuline Nuns in Seventeenth-Century France" (Ph.D. diss., Princeton University, 1994).

to dedicate herself to God in a life of perpetual virginity. She agreed to marry, on condition that her betrothed allow her to make a missionary voyage of conversion in the company of eleven thousand virgins for three years before they wed. She and her companions were martyred by Huns at Cologne. More than a thousand years later, Angela Merici was believed to have been inspired by a vision of a ladder, bathed in supernatural light, upon which a company of young women clothed in shimmering white robes and crowned with diadems descended in the company of angels from heaven to earth. Hearing a voice telling her that God wanted her to found a company of virgins to do his work, she named her congregation for the martyr whose eleven thousand companions had been the first female missionaries.[5]

In the intertwined myths of Ursula and Angela Merici, the ladder scaled by women becomes an important symbol. It represents the link that women create between heaven and earth, the sacred and the profane. It is also an image that vividly embraces hierarchy. Yet, at the same time, Ursuline writers in the seventeenth century used it to describe an apostolic dynamic that allowed for movement up and down the rungs of the ladder. Ursulines were admonished to keep in mind "an image of Angels, climbing and descending." Intended primarily as a directive about spirituality, the admonition to move up and down the ladder had a practical side as well. The early Ursulines were notable because they made the education of the poor as important as the education of the wealthy. The convent schools of seventeenth-century France rang with the voices of girls drawn from every rung of the social ladder, and Ursulines taught them all, descending and ascending as needed to draw their students onto and along the path to salvation.[6]

The Ursuline procession in New Orleans evoked this philosophy and history by including in its retinue a group of elaborately costumed girls who represented the mingled legends of Ursula and Angela Merici. A young girl

5. Lierheimer, "Female Eloquence," 110–142; David Hugh Farmer, *The Oxford Dictionary of Saints* (New York, 1978), 386–387; and Teresa Ledóchowska, *Angela Merici and the Company of St. Ursula: According to the Historical Documents*, trans. Mary Teresa Neylan (Rome, 1969), 16, 107.

6. "Maxime" of Marie de Sainte Thérèse, Prevotière, in *Journal des illustres religieuses de l'ordre de Sainte Ursule, avec leur maximes et pratiques spirituelles, tiré des chroniques de l'ordre, et autres mémoires de leur vie, composé par une religieuse du même ordre, au Monastère de Bourg-en-Bresse, divisé en quatre parties* (Bourg-en-Bress, 1684), III, 320, cited in Lierheimer, "Female Eloquence," 98 n. 15 (see also 26–27); Rapley, *The Dévotes*, 48.

dressed as Ursula "in a robe of cloth of silver with a long train" walked just ahead of the convent group.[7] The women and girls with close associations to the convent who stood between the nuns and the inhabitants at the head of the parade—orphans, students, and confraternity members—were part of the Ursulines' particular design for creating an orderly Christian community, the stuff of which the colony's ladder to heaven would be built. The makeup of its rungs in New Orleans reflected the mélange of frontier society. Girls of Indian and African descent were among the Ursulines' students. The confraternity that stood next in line to the nuns included poor widows, destitute orphans, and women of color alongside wealthy plantation mistresses. In the Ursulines' scheme, the nuns applied a spiritual universalism to the objects of their mission that blurred or rearranged social and racial distinctions in favor of a hierarchy of pious belief and practice. Although the community within their enclosure had its own system of stratification, there was a single requirement for general admission: gender. The procession of 1734 was a public proclamation by the Ursulines of their intentions. They brought the promise of order to the raucous tumble of human energy and aspiration of the frontier, and they planned to achieve it through the agency of women.

The convent suffered from mortality and despair in its early years like the rest of the colony. Of the eighteen nuns who made their way to Louisiana between 1727 and 1736, four died and four more returned to France or left religious life. In 1731, there were only six in residence to sustain the community. The arrival of a total of nine French nuns in 1732, 1734, and 1742 turned the tide, and another eight women left French convents for New Orleans in the early 1750s, before the outbreak of the Seven Years' War. In 1749, a postulant from the Illinois territory arrived. She broke the ban on creole entrants that the Company of the Indies had imposed as a condition of the original contract in an effort to steer the young women of Louisiana toward marriage and a contribution to the colony's natural increase.[8] By 1757, the

7. The procession in New Orleans seems to have been closely modeled on the ceremonial used when the first Ursulines of Dijon moved into their convent in 1614, which included a girl dressed as Saint Ursula, carrying a heart and arrows to reference her religious ardor and martyrdom, and eleven girls representing the eleven thousand virgin missionaries. This procession is described in Marie-Augustine de Pommereu, *Les chroniques de l'ordre des Ursulines recueillies pour l'usage des religieuses du mesme ordre*, I (Paris, 1673), 160–161. Lierheimer, "Female Eloquence," 154–155, discusses the Dijon procession and its imagery in detail.

8. The term "creole" is used throughout to denote individuals born in the Americas

community had swelled to twenty women and was the largest it had ever been (see Appendix 1). Along with the other inhabitants of Louisiana, the Ursulines met the onset of Spanish rule in 1763 as battered but successful veterans of French neglect.[9]

It took more than the mere strength of numbers to keep the French vision of the Ursulines alive. During their first half-century in New Orleans, the Ursulines sustained it largely by the infusion of immigrant nuns who carried their tradition straight from the convents of France to the mission in Louisiana. All of the twenty-one nuns who arrived during the convent's first two decades came directly from France. Such transplants dominated the convent population until 1774, when the cessation of new French arrivals caused by the Seven Years' War allowed women from Louisiana and Canada to draw even, posing the possibility of a new, creole vision for the community.

During its first twenty-five years, the New Orleans community was not only decidedly Old World in its origins, it was aging, a factor that favored cultural conservatism and kept the outlook of the Ursulines during this period firmly fixed in French—rather than colonial—intellectual, religious, and social contexts. As they began their New Orleans ministry in 1727, the average age of the membership was thirty-three. The oldest member was forty-seven, the youngest twenty-three. Ten years later, in 1737, the convent community was decidedly middle-aged, with an average age of forty-two. In 1750, the average age was nearly forty-nine, and half of the members were fifty or older. Near the end of the French period, in 1762, the average age was fifty-four, and nearly half of the community was sixty or older. The age

---

of predominantly transatlantic ancestry. It is used in conjunction with the national and continental labels "French," "Spanish," and "African" to fix ancestry more precisely.

9. The best discussion of France's negligent Louisiana policy is Mathé Allain, *"Not Worth a Straw": French Colonial Policy and the Early Years of Louisiana* (Lafayette, La., 1988). For the interdependent nature of colonial social and economic circumstances, see Gwendolyn Midlo Hall, *Africans in Colonial Louisiana: The Development of Afro-Creole Culture in the Eighteenth Century* (Baton Rouge, La., 1992), 2–27, 120–155; and Daniel H. Usner, Jr., *Indians, Settlers, and Slaves in a Frontier Exchange Economy: The Lower Mississippi Valley before 1783* (Chapel Hill, N.C., 1992), 13–43, 77–104, 147–278. For a revision of Usner's thesis, which posits a greater dependence by settlers in the Lower Mississippi Valley upon French farmers in the Illinois country, see Cécile Vidal, "Les implantations françaises au pays des Illinois au XVIIIe siècle (1699–1765)" (Ph.D. diss., École des hautes études en sciences sociales, 1995).

of women when they came to the New Orleans convent is also noteworthy. Between 1727 and 1762, the average age of French women entering the colonial foundation, nearly all of whom were already fully professed, was thirty-six. Only three entrants for whom data is available were under thirty; only one was under twenty; two were fifty or older. One woman made the trip to Louisiana at the age of fifty-seven. The missionaries to Louisiana were not impressionable young women; they were mature nuns whose views and practices were grounded in their European experience.[10]

For most of the eighteenth century, the nature of the colonial society upon which the nuns exercised their French cultural loyalty wore two faces, one reflecting the aspirations of a small elite, the other expressing the larger population's navigation of the practical realities of the colonial experience. A small number of bureaucratic officials and a handful of large planters exercised political dominance and nurtured public displays of status, control, refinement, and order from the 1720s on. France had one of the most advanced class sensibilities of eighteenth-century Europe. In addition to the descendants of the old aristocracy, the *noblesse d'épée*, the proliferation of venal offices in the seventeenth century produced a large population of bureaucrats with pretensions to social superiority, the *noblesse de robe*. The officials of French Louisiana in the 1720s worked hard to replicate the performance of these class distinctions in the colony. Although not all petty officials could claim to be members of the nobility, most appended to their names whatever honorific designation they could.[11] Perhaps more than other inhabitants of colonial Louisiana, officials of the proprietary Company of the Indies and their families engaged in the game of social posturing and elegant living that prevailed in their homeland. Chief Commissioner Jacques Delachaise inflated his claims to aristocratic lineage

10. Marguerite Bernard de St. Martin, who arrived in 1732 from Caen, lived to be eighty-eight (see Appendix 1, below). See "Registre [des Ursulines de la Nouvelle Orleans]," and "Lettres circulaires," UCANO.

11. The *noblesse de robe*, or nobility of the robe, were members of the aristocracy by virtue of offices they or their families had purchased. They were deemed inferior to the *noblesse d'épée*, nobles whose titles derived from feudal seigneuries. An expansion of venality of office took place under Henry IV and Louis XIII in the late sixteenth and early seventeenth centuries. William Beik, *Absolutism and Society in Seventeenth-Century France: State Power and Provincial Aristocracy in Languedoc* (Cambridge, 1985), discusses the rise of the noblesse de robe in his study of the rise of absolutism and early modern economic and social change.

and disparaged his fellow colonial officials as socially inferior. Efforts to uphold French manners sometimes escalated into the realm of the absurd. A surgeon nearly came to blows with his housemate when his dinner was served with inappropriate linen, and in 1725 a group of military wives disrupted Sunday Mass when an usher directed them to seats in a location they thought insulted their status.[12]

The backdrop to this performance of elite sensibility was a community marked by slippages in the boundaries between classes and races fostered by the exigencies of frontier life. Popular culture flourished and elite codes of behavior were met with defiance and indifference. Inhabitants imbibed cheap smuggled brandy and gambled in illegal makeshift taverns that thumbed their noses at the company monopoly on overpriced spirits. The elite ideal of social order was further compromised by faltering attempts to establish a plantation economy that rested heavily on the contributions of Indians and enslaved Africans. Only in the last quarter of the eighteenth century did the region around New Orleans achieve the demographic and economic foundation necessary to the effective extension of elite social dominance.[13]

The Ursulines negotiated the contested social geography of colonial New

12. Marcel Giraud, *A History of French Louisiana*, V, *The Company of the Indies, 1723–1731*, trans. Brian Pearce (Baton Rouge, La., 1991), 5; RSC, *LHQ*, III (1920), 418; and Carl A. Brasseaux, "The Moral Climate of French Colonial Louisiana, 1699–1763," *Louisiana History*, XXVII (1986), 36.

13. Giraud, *History of French Louisiana*, V, *Company of the Indies*, trans. Pearce, 269; Usner, *Indians, Settlers, and Slaves*, 31; Brasseaux, "Moral Climate," *Louisiana History*, XXVII (1986), 27–41; Henry P. Dart, "Cabarets of New Orleans in the French Colonial Period," *LHQ*, XIX (1936), 577–583.

There is a range of interpretations regarding the balance between elite and nonelite influence in shaping colonial Louisiana society. See, for example, Giraud, *History of French Louisiana*, V, *Company of the Indies*, trans. Pearce, 272–285; Thomas N. Ingersoll, *Mammon and Manon in Early New Orleans: The First Slave Society in the Deep South, 1718–1819* (Knoxville, Tenn., 1999), 35–65; Hall, *Africans in Colonial Louisiana*, 237–274; James T. McGowan, "Creation of a Slave Society: Louisiana Plantations in the Eighteenth Century" (Ph.D. diss., University of Rochester, 1976); Usner, *Indians, Settlers, and Slaves*, 8–9, 106–107, 276–277. Peter H. Wood, *Black Majority: Negroes in Colonial South Carolina from 1670 through the Stono Rebellion* (New York, 1975), 229–230, offers an early and influential discussion of the practical considerations on the frontier that favored more egalitarian social relations than were found in more developed settlements.

Orleans by means of the dualism that had long marked their order. They upheld elite French social pretensions and the differentiation of the bourgeoisie in the colony by retaining within their own little community the trappings of rank they had first embraced in the seventeenth century. There were two classes of nuns in French Ursuline convents: choir nuns and converse nuns. In their earliest days, there was no differentiation among French Ursulines within their communities, but, after enclosure and formalization as a religious order, they adopted the medieval classification that divided executive and support roles. Choir nuns took solemn vows, taught, sang the divine office, and were able to vote or hold office in the community. It was they who carried out the *institut*—the educational work that constituted the Ursulines' primary mission. Converse nuns, sometimes known as lay sisters, took simple vows and wore the habit, but their duties were analogous to those of a highly placed servant or housekeeper, and they could not vote or hold office in the community. Choir nuns came from middling and well-to-do families; converse nuns were drawn from the working people. Although Ursulines in the early seventeenth century were often daughters of artisans and small merchants, by the early eighteenth century Ursuline choir nuns were drawn mostly from the families of the noblesse de robe.[14] Their fathers were likely to be lawyers who held minor government posts and were able to provide the dowries that were expected of Ursuline postulants (see Figures 3 and 7).[15]

The Ursuline contingent bound for New Orleans maintained the stratified structure: it included ten choir nuns and two converse sisters. The three founding Ursuline choir nuns whose backgrounds can be reconstructed were typical. Renée Yviquel's family was of the noblesse de robe, with a tra-

14. Rapley, *The Dévotes*, 48–49, 178–179; Elizabeth Rapley, *A Social History of the Cloister: Daily Life in the Teaching Monasteries of the Old Regime* (Montreal, 2001), 166–167, 182–197; Lierheimer, "Female Eloquence," 26.

15. Dowry contracts for women entering the Rouen Ursuline Convent, for example, identify one father as "conseiller du Roy" and "maitre des requets" with the right to present cases before the Parlement of Normandy and another as the "generalle conseillor du Roy en sa grande chambre du Parlement du Rouen." A lump-sum dowry of 500 to 3,000 livres was generally accompanied by a lifetime annuity of 100 to 150 livres or another payment of 1,000 to 1,500 livres to be used for the nun's accommodations. See dowry contract of Marie Marguerite Catherine de Pontcarré, Rouen, Jan. 1, 1725, dowry contract of Catherine Busseuetre, Rouen, Mar. 16, 1701, and dowry contract of Luce Marie Clotilde Bulteau, Rouen, Dec. 4, 1728, folio D418, ADSM.

Figure 7. Soeur converse Ursuline de la Congrégation de Paris. *From Pierre Hélyot,*
Histoire des ordres monastiques . . . , *IV (Paris, 1715). By permission General Research*
Division, The New York Public Library, Astor, Lenox and Tilden Foundations

dition of legal service, Marie Madeleine Hachard's father was procurator in charge of accounts in Rouen, and Cécile Cavalier's father was an advocate at court in Elboeuf. Cavalier's dowry contract, the only founder's contract that could be traced, provided for the payment of three thousand livres as a capital donation to the convent and the payment of fifteen hundred livres to provide her bed and board during her novitiate, sums that are comparable to dowries of her contemporaries in France. Cavalier's dowry, which exceeded the annual salary of Louisiana's second-highest-ranking public official in 1727, Councillor Bruslé, is indicative of considerable family wealth.[16]

Renée Yviquel, Marie Hachard, Cécile Cavalier, and seven other choir nuns crossed to Louisiana in the company of two converse sisters, Sister Anne de Saint François and Marie-Anne Dain, known as Sister Saint Marthe. Neither stayed long. Marie-Anne Dain returned to France three months after she arrived, and Sister Anne followed six months later.[17] In order to know what kinds of women became converse nuns and what their lives were like, we must rely on the accounts given of those who came after them.

The New Orleans convent was rarely without a converse nun named Sister Saint Martha, after the New Testament woman who tended to the kitchen while her sister, Mary, sat in conversation with Jesus. Four of the convent's twelve converse sisters in the eighteenth century bore the name that signified their role in the convent: service to sustain the work of their sisters in religion who had "the better part."[18] Their backgrounds were marked by humble origins and, frequently, by the tragedy of loss. Their obituaries praise them for their practical and manual skills, their diligence, their piety, and their submissiveness.

The ranks of the converse nuns were replenished by girls who attended

16. Louis Yviquel to Emily Clark, Feb. 25, 1997; "Plumif," Oct. 1, 1706, folio C2716, ADSM; and dowry contract for Cécile Cavalier, Elboeuf, June 23, 1722, folio D376, ADSM. The records of the Rouen Ursuline Convent, from which four of the first New Orleans nuns came, were confiscated and transferred to civil archives during the French Revolution and are only partially preserved. None of the dowry contracts for the New Orleans founders were among those surviving for women who professed at Rouen between 1722 and 1770. See note 15, above, for typical dowries for Rouenese Ursulines who were contemporaries of the New Orleans founders. Councillor Bruslé earned four thousand livres per year (Glenn R. Conrad, comp. and trans., *The First Families of Louisiana*, 2 vols. [Baton Rouge, La., 1970], II, 229).

17. "Registre [des Ursulines de la Nouvelle Orleans]," UCANO.

18. The New Testament passage relating this story is Luke 10:38–42.

the free classes given for orphans. They sometimes felt called to religious life through their experience at the convent. When they were, they became converse nuns. Thérèse Lardas was the daughter of a Mobile surgeon. At sixteen, after several years in the orphan class at the convent, she asked to enter, and the community voted in June 1774 to receive her as a converse sister. Her obituary remarks of her only that she was fervent. Marthe Delatre, who entered in 1757, came of "an honest family of the city who placed her in the orphans' class." Marthe's father, Antoine Delatre, began life in Louisiana as an indentured servant working as a carpenter on a plantation north of New Orleans. By the time his daughter joined the Ursulines, he was referred to as a "master joiner," but neither his trade, his skill, nor his respectability merited status for his daughter as a choir sister. Marthe was admitted because the nuns had grown to know "her tender piety and great sweetness" during her long tenure with the orphan class. She was remembered as being especially good at needlework, but she was also a skilled nurse who had "acquired a great knowledge of medicine and the state of the sick and knew how to apply the proper remedies." This "hardworking" nun, "a resource of the Superiors for an infinity of things," lived until she was eighty-one, working until three days before she died.[19]

Converse sisters were cast in supporting roles and never enjoyed a life of full fellowship with the choir nuns. In French Louisiana, where frontier exigencies often blurred distinctions between middling and lower sorts who struggled equally with the challenge of survival, the Ursulines did not relax their institutional hierarchy. There are only a few clues about how converse sisters felt about their inferior status, and they must be filtered through the texts of obituary notices written by choir sisters who might have been reporting what they hoped, rather than what they experienced. The Acadian refugee Rose Leblanc was portrayed as a cheerful servant, "a useful person, adroit, of a gay humor, fervent and exact in all her work, rendering prompt service equally to all." Sister Saint Etienne was "a model for all the converse sisters" because she was "humble, simple, and silent."[20]

Born of an Indian mother and a French father, the métis Marie Turpin knew that she would be a servant if she pursued a life in religion. The boatman who brought her to New Orleans from the Illinois Territory in 1749 reported to the nuns awaiting her arrival that fellow passengers tried to dis-

19. "Livre de l'entrée des filles de choeur," 4b, 10, UCANO; "Lettres circulaires," 237, 249, UCANO; Conrad, comp. and trans., *First Families*, I, 108.
20. "Lettres circulaires," 232, 242, UCANO.

courage her from entering the convent by telling her she would be nothing but a servant. "Oh, that is all that I seek," she is said to have responded, "to serve the wives of Jesus Christ." The Ursuline chronicler praises Marie Turpin's piety at length and credits her with edifying the choir sisters by "the regularity [of her religious observance] and her courage in the face of all difficulties."[21]

Marie Turpin's mixed-race background alone might have been enough to consign her to converse status. Aspects of her background that she shared with other converse sisters, however, probably equally determined her status at the convent. The fathers of these women made their living with their hands or through trade. Marie Turpin's father was a trader. The Acadian Rose Leblanc's father was a "habitant," a simple farmer. Thérèse Lardas's father was a surgeon at a time when his skill was considered mechanical, not professional. Converse sister Rosalie Cierra's father was a blacksmith.[22] The occupations of these men did not bring the kind of wealth that paved the way for choir status. None of the converse sisters brought cash dowries with them, as choir sisters did.[23]

The New Orleans Ursulines did not need converse sisters as domestic servants: enslaved Africans filled these occupations.[24] Their retention of the converse category indicates a social conservatism that dictated an individual's role in the community according to family wealth, occupation, and perhaps race. Life on the frontier might have invited fluidity in many social

21. Ibid., 225–226.

22. Ibid. Cécile Vidal, "Antoine Bienvenu, Illinois Planter and Mississippi Trader: The Structure of Exchange between Lower and Upper Louisiana," in Bradley G. Bond, ed., *French Colonial Louisiana and the Atlantic World* (Baton Rouge, La., 2005), 111–133, describes the Kaskaskia–New Orleans trade and the milieu of Louis Turpin. "Livre de l'entrée," 17, 19, and "Lettres circulaires," 232, UCANO, describe the background of Rose Leblanc. "Lettres circulaires," 234, UCANO, notes the profession of the father of Thérèse Lardas. "Prise d'habit," 23b, names Augustin Cierra as Rosalie Cierra's father. Augustin Cierra (Sierra) is identified as a master blacksmith in Earl C. Woods and Charles Nolan, eds., *Sacramental Records of the Roman Catholic Church of the Archdiocese of New Orleans*, 16 vols. to date (New Orleans, 1987–), II, 255 (hereafter cited as *Sacramental Records*).

23. The reception and profession entries for converse sisters Marthe Delatre, Rose Leblanc, Angela Langline, Rosalie Cierra, and Genevieve Chemite, for example, make no mention of dowries. See "Livre de l'entrée," 10, 11, 23, 29, 79, UCANO.

24. The Ursulines' bondpeople and the nuns' relationship with slavery are discussed fully in Chapter 5, below.

relationships, but those among the inner circle of the nuns preserved a more formal order. The New Orleans Ursulines sustained the standards that had developed in France regarding wealth and family background, even though such qualifications were ill suited to the kind of work they expected a colonial choir nun to do.

The obituary notice of Françoise Marguerite Bernard de Saint Martin describes the ideal choir nun. When she died in 1763, after thirty years in New Orleans, her mother superior penned a long letter extolling her virtues. It opened with a paean to her breeding. Mademoiselle Saint Martin "was a girl of high birth and of a great lineage" who exercised herself with "extraordinary politesse" and wrote and spoke with an eloquence that her biographer thought "rare for a person of our sex."[25] This model nun, who served four terms as superior and held every other office in the community, was "extremely zealous for all the rules, observances, and ceremonies of the choir. . . . She had a cultivated taste in music and a beautiful voice." Praise for social standing and attainments flowed unselfconsciously from the chronicler's pen. Yet, at the same time, there were words that explained Françoise's practical contributions to a frontier convent. She "had great skill in all kinds of work and kept constantly busy until the last moment." During her years at the convent, there were sometimes as few as seven nuns on hand to look after thirty orphans, catechize Indians and Africans, run a boarding school, operate a hospital, and sustain a pious association of eighty-five women and girls. It is a good thing that Françoise Saint Martin had multiple skills and no wonder that she was continually busy.[26]

Françoise Saint Martin's ability to satisfy traditional French social standards and her willingness to trade the ordinary routine of a life of gentility for the work of God exemplifies the paradox that was at the heart of the Ursulines' success. In the early years, the work they did could be physically as well as mentally demanding, and the external differences between the nuns and their servants could sometimes be indiscernible. The choir nun Renée Yviquel, who died in 1763, ground corn, did the washing, and chopped wood during the convent's first few years.[27] Even when the days of such physical heroics were past, the apostolate of the choir nuns meant that they spent their days working among and for people who ranked well below them in wealth, privilege, prospects, and manners. From their first months

25. "Lettres circulaires," 229–230, UCANO.
26. See Appendix 1, below.
27. "Lettres circulaires," 228, UCANO.

in New Orleans, these well-bred ladies kept company with women and girls who would never have been invited into the parlors of colonial officials.

Theirs was an apostolate that consciously embraced all elements of the colony's female population. "At present we have nine boarders. We will receive as many more after Epiphany, and we will also instruct a number of day students. . . . We also have a class to instruct the women and girls among the blacks and savages. They come every day from one o'clock in the afternoon until two-thirty," the novice Ursuline Marie Madeleine Hachard wrote to her father on New Year's Day in 1728. The nuns depended on boarding students for much of their income, but the sisters assigned to teach the day students, typically called externs, were advised by their rule that they should have great affection for their work because "it is the occupation that imitates most closely the Son of God, who wanted during his life primarily to instruct the poor and the ignorant." Although the mission was reduced to ten nuns by the spring of 1728, the sisters maintained a full program that reached out to all the women and girls in New Orleans. In April, twenty French students and seven enslaved girls were boarding at the convent as well as three women and several orphans. According to Marie Madeleine Hachard, a "great number of day students, female blacks and female savages" still came each day for two hours of religious instruction.[28]

Marie Hachard's reports indicate that the Ursulines' student community was broadly inclusive. But what about the women of New Orleans who associated themselves with the convent and its apostolate? Given the refined backgrounds of the nuns themselves, the elite women of the colony might naturally be drawn to them. On the other hand, if these women were attempting to establish and cultivate an exclusive enclave within the colony, the open-door policy of the Ursulines might have put them off.

If elite women did harbor trepidation about sharing space with the wives of tradesmen and servants, let alone enslaved women and girls, they suppressed it during Holy Week in 1728, when the Ursulines' Jesuit spiritual director conducted a retreat for the nuns at their temporary convent. Several laywomen joined them in the full regimen of prayer and meditation, and sometimes as many as two hundred townswomen crammed onto the convent grounds to hear the Jesuit's daily sermons. At this date, there were barely two hundred women and marriageable girls of European descent in

28. [Marie Madeleine Hachard], *De Rouen à la Louisiane: Voyage d'une Ursuline en 1727* (Rouen, 1988), 68, 79; *Règlemens des religieuses Ursulines de la Congrégation de Paris* (Paris, 1705), 158.

New Orleans.[29] In a matter of months, the Ursuline convent had become a powerful focus for female piety and community. That role was cemented when the winter of 1729 brought tragedy and fear to New Orleans in an episode that expanded the Ursulines' ministry and strengthened its ties to the women and children of the city.

On November 28, 1729, Natchez Indians executed a surprise attack on the military outpost and settlement at Fort Rosalie, about one hundred miles upriver from New Orleans in Natchez country. Most of the men, perhaps as many as two hundred, were killed, along with an unknown number of women and children. About thirty orphaned girls turned up in New Orleans, where the Ursulines took them in. In the weeks following the attack, the little city was gripped with terror. As survivors made their way into town, they raised fears that a full-fledged Indian revolt was making its way downriver. Panic broke out when a woman "came running into the city from the Bayou Saint John with streaming hair, crying that the Indians had made a descent on the Bayou and massacred all the settlers there, and were actually pursuing her." Soon she was joined by others and, "the noise increasing, the alarm soon spread to all quarters." The shots the woman heard had been made by hunters, but the city remained tense. The presence of traumatized survivors cast a pall of grief and foreboding over the capital long after the rebellion was quashed.[30]

The settlers of New Orleans were used to privation and disease by 1729, but, until the attack on Fort Rosalie, violence from Indian attack had been a more remote hazard. Now New Orleanians felt freshly vulnerable. When those widowed and orphaned by the attack resettled in the capital, townswomen who had begun to develop an association with the convent came face-to-face with the human consequences of the tragedy and must have become acutely conscious of the fragility of their own lives. At the same time, their small settlement now had to absorb a large group of motherless girls.

29. [Hachard], *De Rouen à la Louisiane,* 78. The 1731 census for New Orleans lists 209 women and marriageable girls in residence. See Charles R. Maduell, Jr., comp. and trans., *The Census Tables for the French Colony of Louisiana from 1699 through 1732* (Baltimore, 1972), 123–141.

30. Giraud, *A History of French Louisiana,* V, *The Company of the Indies,* trans. Pearce, 309, 398–399; [Jean François Benjamin Dumont de Montigny], *History of Louisiana; Translated from the Historical Memoirs of M. Dumont,* in B. F. French, ed. and trans., *Historical Memoirs of Louisiana, from the First Settlement of the Colony to the Departure of Governor O'Reilly in 1770 with Historical and Biographical Notes Forming the Fifth of the Series Historical Collections of Louisiana* (New York, 1853), 99.

A few orphan girls who lacked the guidance and financial resources to keep them from a life of prostitution or concubinage were challenge enough. The sudden arrival of such a large group of endangered and dangerous girls would have been alarming for devout women already struggling against the frontier disposition of New Orleans society.

In May 1730, a few months after the attack on Fort Rosalie, eight women turned up at the Ursuline convent and asked the nuns to help them organize a women's confraternity. The composition of the little delegation and the organization that grew from it is remarkable. The wives of a carpenter and a soldier called on the nuns, together with two wealthy plantation mistresses. If the well-to-do women of New Orleans had ever hesitated about associating with the convent and its diverse collection of students, the crucible of crisis melted their doubts away. Between 1730 and 1744, the pious association grew to include eighty-five women and girls who called themselves the Ladies' Congregation of the Children of Mary and pledged to honor the Virgin, "not by their prayers alone, but by their morals, and by all the conduct of their lives." The historical record yields a portrait of the confraternity that testifies to the Ursulines' success at capturing the allegiance of the city's women without sacrificing their inclusive standard.[31]

Members of the laywomen's confraternity founded in 1730 came from diverse backgrounds. A significant number of the confreresses were, certainly, quite wealthy. In 1732, when only 13 percent of Louisiana's plantation households claimed ownership of 20 or more servants, the slaveholdings of some confraternity families indicate unusual affluence. The wives, widows, daughters, and stepdaughters of the wealthy Carrières, who counted 123 servants among their holdings in 1731, were members. They were joined by Antoinette Fourier de Villemont Rivard, twice widowed by wealthy Louisiana landowners and the mistress of 25 enslaved servants in 1731, and her daughters and stepdaughter. Rounding out the contingent of wealthy plantation mistresses was Marie Payen Dubreuil, who lived with her husband and two sons on a productive site upriver from New Orleans worked by 106 unfree laborers in 1731. Six women who were wives or daughters of colonial officials joined the wealthy plantation mistresses to make up the elite constituency in the confraternity.[32]

31. "Premier Registre de la Congrégation des Dames Enfants de Marie," 3, 7, UCANO; Emily Clark, "'By All the Conduct of Their Lives': A Laywomen's Confraternity in New Orleans, 1730–1744," *William and Mary Quarterly*, 3d Ser., LIV (1997), 769.

32. "Census of Inhabitants along the Mississippi River, 1731," in Maduell, comp.

Numbering nineteen, these women and girls of wealth or high social status constituted the largest group within the confraternity membership, but not a majority. Six members of the association lived in modest plantation households with fewer than ten enslaved workers.[33] Eight confreresses were married or related to artisans, merchants, or professionals with one to five enslaved laborers. Among them were Genevieve Caron, married to the carpenter Pierre Thommelin, Marianne Gandry, who kept an inn with her husband, and Marie Françoise Hero, whose husband Louis Drouillon was a smallhold farmer.[34]

---

and trans., *Census Tables*, 114, 116, 122; *Sacramental Records*, I, 22, 87, 233; RSC, *LHQ*, IV (1921), 523, V (1922), 264, 425; Alice Daly Forsyth and Ghislaine Pleasonton, comp. and trans., *Louisiana Marriage Contracts: A Compilation of Abstracts from Records of the Superior Council of Louisiana during the French Regime, 1725-1758* (New Orleans, 1980), 23.

33. For details about the finances and activities of Mathurin Dreux, husband of Françoise Hugo, see Conrad, comp. and trans., *First Families*, II, 30; RSC, *LHQ*, II (1919), 335, 470–471, IV (1921), 338, V (1922), 260; and *Sacramental Records*, I, 131. On François Dumont de Montigny, husband of Marie Baron, see ibid., 12, 91; [Dumont de Montigny], *Historical Memoirs*, in French, ed. and trans., *Historical Memoirs of Louisiana*, 1–125; Giraud, *A History of French Louisiana*, V, *The Company of the Indies*, trans. Pearce, 212, 450; and Usner, *Indians, Settlers, and Slaves*, 36, and plates 4, 5, 6. On Pierre Fillart, husband of Marie Françoise Bonnaventure, see Conrad, comp. and trans., *First Families*, II, 57; Forsyth and Pleasonton, comp. and trans., *Marriage Contracts*, 37; and RSC, *LHQ*, IV (1921), 233. On Jacques Judis, husband of Marie Jeanty, see Conrad, comp. and trans., *First Families*, II, 54, 63, 132; Maduell, comp. and trans., *Census Tables*, 116, 121; *Sacramental Records*, I, 137; RSC, *LHQ*, V (1922), 249, 601. On Nicolas Adam, called Blondin, husband of Marie Marguerite Roy, see Maduell, comp. and trans., *Census Tables*, 116; RSC, *LHQ*, VIII (1925), 485, IX (1926), 301; Giraud, *A History of French Louisiana*, V, *The Company of the Indies*, trans. Pearce, 125. On Pierre Voisin, father of Demoiselle Voisin, see RSC, *LHQ*, IV (1921), 512, 523, VII (1924), 702; Judy Riffel, "The Voisin Family," *New Orleans Genesis*, XXII (1983), 458–460; and Conrad, comp. and trans., *First Families*, II, 52, 58, 70.

34. On Pierre Thommelin and Genevieve Caron, see *Sacramental Records*, I, 41; RSC, *LHQ*, III (1920), 417, VIII (1925), 140, IX (1926), 289; Conrad, comp. and trans., *First Families*, II, 37, 69. On Marianne Gandry and Claude Reynaud, called Avignon, see Conrad, comp. and trans., *First Families*, II, 51, 74; RSC, *LHQ*, V (1922), 400, 410, IX (1926), 301. On Louis Drouillon and Marie Françoise Hero, see Maduell, comp. and trans., *Census Tables*, 131; Conrad, comp. and trans., *First Families of Louisiana*, II, 71; Stephen and Patricia Houin, "Drouillon Family," *New Orleans Genesis*, XXVIII (1989), 82.

A third group of confreresses was not among the slaveowners of New Orleans. Marie Lepron Sautier was a carpenter's wife, and Elizabeth Homart Henry was the spouse of a goldsmith of limited means.[35] Others of similar circumstances included the wives of a traveling trader, a gunsmith, a nail maker, a widow struggling to make ends meet, and a woman whose family seems to have taken in an orphan to take advantage of the rations that came with him.[36] Even these women of humble circumstances were accorded the form of address "Madame" in the confraternity roster. The names of a fifth group of confreresses are listed without such prefaces. Anne Dimanche was a widow who boarded with a couple in a household without servants. Catherine Henri and Suzanne Marchand were orphans living at the Ursuline convent. Three women, listed simply as "Marie Thérèse," "Marthe," and "Magdelaine," were almost certainly women of color and perhaps enslaved.[37]

35. On Marie Lepron and Jacques Sautier, see *Sacramental Records*, I, 235; Conrad, comp. and trans., *First Families*, II, 70; RSC, *LHQ*, IV (1921), 357, VIII (1925), 683. On Elisabeth Homart and her first and second husbands, Nicholas Henry and François Fonder, see *Sacramental Records*, I, 106, 127; Conrad, comp. and trans., *First Families*, II, 134, 142; RSC, *LHQ*, IV (1921), 334–337, IX (1926), 739, 741.

36. Confreress Besson was married to *voyageur* Besson, whose profession and business troubles are suggested in Conrad, comp. and trans., *First Families*, II, 39; and RSC, *LHQ*, V (1922), 265. The small salary and indebtedness of gunsmith Nicholas Brantan are documented in Conrad, comp. and trans., *First Families*, I, 229; RSC, *LHQ*, VII (1924), 680. The humble living conditions and trade of nail maker Guillaume Fauché are recorded in the 1732 census (Maduell, comp. and trans., *Census Tables*, 90). The financial desperation of widow Marie Anne Millart, La Violette, is suggested by her attempt to recover a small but very old debt in 1735 (RSC, *LHQ*, VIII [1925], 122). She did not own her dwelling, according to the 1732 census (Conrad, comp. and trans., *First Families*, II, 71). According to the 1732 census, the La Prairie family housed an orphan. Since rations came with such children, taking them in could be an advantage to families whose funds limited their purchasing power. See Conrad, comp. and trans., *First Families*, II, 73; Giraud, *A History of French Louisiana*, V, *The Company of the Indies*, trans. Pearce, 272.

37. Conrad, comp. and trans., *First Families*, II, 69; "List of Orphans Living at the Ursuline Convent, 1731," ibid., 154. Sacramental records and other colonial documents regularly inscribed only the given name of the enslaved, a practice that was apparently reserved only for people of color in the colony (see, for example, SLC-B1 and SLC-B2). In the late 1720s, a number of enslaved women were boarding students at the convent, and women of color are also documented as boarding students at the Ursuline convent during the 1730s when the confraternity was active.

TABLE 1. *Social Status of Confraternity Members*

Category	Number	Proportion
Wealthy planters, bureaucratic elite	19	41%
Modest planters	6	13
Artisans, merchants, professionals	8	18
Nonslaveowners	7	15
Socially marginal residents	6	13
Total	46	100%
Elite members	19	41%
Nonelite members	27	59
Total	46	100%

Sources: Glenn R. Conrad, comp. and trans., *The First Families of Louisiana,* 2 vols. (Baton Rouge, La., 1970); RSC, *LHQ,* I–XXVI (1917–1943); [Jean François Benjamin Dumont de Montigny], *History of Louisiana; Translated from the Historical Memoirs of M. Dumont,* in B. F. French, ed. and trans., *Historical Memoirs of Louisiana, from the First Settlement of the Colony to the Departure of Governor O'Reilly in 1770 with Historical and Biographical Notes Forming the Fifth of the Series Historical Collections of Louisiana* (New York, 1853); Charles R. Maduell, Jr., comp. and trans., *The Census Tables for the French Colony of Louisiana from 1699 through 1732* (Baltimore, 1972); Alice Daly Forsyth and Ghislaine Pleasonton, comp. and trans., *Louisiana Marriage Contracts: A Compilation of Abstracts from Records of the Superior Council of Louisiana during the French Regime, 1725–1758* (New Orleans, 1980); Earl C. Woods and Charles Nolan, eds., *Sacramental Records of the Roman Catholic Church of the Archdiocese of New Orleans,* I (New Orleans, 1987). For a detailed discussion of confraternity members with specific citations of sources used to determine their social status, see Emily J. Clark, "A New World Community: The New Orleans Ursulines and Colonial Society, 1727–1803" (Ph.D. diss., Tulane University, 1998), 74–79.

The membership of the confraternity testifies to the nuns' success at bringing the full range of New Orleans womanhood under their wing. Characteristics including holdings in land and enslaved workers, occupation, homeownership, indebtedness, and status as a widow or orphan suggest the five groupings for identified members of the confraternity summarized in Table 1. A cadre of wealthy planters and members of a bureaucratic elite were the largest group, but 59 percent of the identified members were drawn from four other constituencies: modest slaveholding planters, artisans, merchants and professionals who held enslaved workers, nonslaveholding soldiers and artisans, and a socially marginal group comprising poor widows, orphans, and women of color.

Confraternity leadership, as well as membership, reflected broad social participation. Although two elite women, the widows Carrière and Rivard, held the two offices of first and second prefect more frequently than any other member, the membership elected Madame Thommelin, a carpenter's wife, to both of these posts. A gunner's wife, Servan Banville Fabré, also served as second prefect and, later, as treasurer. Marie Lepron Sautier, whose carpenter husband held no human property, was named councillor five times. The wealthy Marie Payen Dubreuil, on the other hand, never held office. Wealth might have favored some as the confraternity selected its leaders, but it was not the deciding factor.[38]

This diverse group represented the realization of the Ursulines' plan for the town's women. They had achieved the French ideal of universalism, capturing every element of the settlement's female community and yoking them to their plan to transform New Orleans into a place made fully Catholic and orderly through the agency of womanhood. The confraternity met weekly at the convent for a prayer service, and members were supposed to serve as exemplars of feminine morality and piety, refraining from swearing and intemperance and avoiding unseemly company. Members formalized their association and their ties to one another by electing officers and subscribing to rules that bound them to tend each other in sickness and death. These laywomen affirmed their links to the convent not only by using it for their meetings but also by contributing funds to fit out its chapel and by submitting themselves to the governance and spiritual guidance of a nun assigned to supervise and assist their activities.[39]

The confraternity not only represented a successful episode in the nuns' campaign to support and expand a broad and inclusive community of faith, but its members became agents for it when they adopted the Ursuline apostolate to evangelize enslaved Africans in Louisiana. "Confreresses," the organization's constitution stipulated, "should have a special zeal for . . . the instruction of their children and their slaves." An analysis of sacramental

38. "Premier Registre," 281–285, UCANO.

39. Ibid., 189, provides an account of contributions made by members of the confraternity to purchase an altar for the convent chapel where they met as well as an enthroned gilt statue of the Virgin that could be used in processions and at the chapel.

records available for the years during which the confraternity was active shows that these laywomen made good on their constitutional promise. In 1732 and 1733, for example, confreresses and their close relations were involved in 23 percent of baptisms of enslaved infants, though they represented only 11 percent of the slaveowning population in and around New Orleans. In 1744, they participated as owners or godparents in nearly one-third of infant baptisms and adult group baptisms. Confreresses and their families were more involved in sponsoring baptism of the enslaved than any other group in colonial New Orleans, and in numbers disproportionate to their representation in the slaveowning population as a whole.[40]

While the women of the confraternity who enlisted in the campaign of internal conversion pursued their mission in their households and in the slave quarters, within the convent the Ursulines continued in their effort to make all the women of Louisiana Catholic. Unfortunately, any student records they might have kept during their first seventy years in New Orleans have been lost. Only a few scattered references survive to provide the identities of their students, but these offer assurance that the convent remained a place that accepted any female, regardless of race or social status.

In 1729, an enslaved Osage woman was freed by the will of François Viard, who also reserved a sum to be used to support her instruction in the Catholic faith. The acts of the Louisiana Superior Council record that the woman was sent to the Ursulines, and the money was transferred to them to pay for her board and instruction. In 1735, a man named Saint Julien placed a mulatto woman named Marie Charlotte as a boarder at the convent, where she spent at least two years. Joseph Moreau, an illiterate locksmith who dictated his will in 1736, noted that he possessed a few pieces of furniture, linen, clothing, and crockery and owed only one debt of thirty-seven livres to the Ursuline convent for his daughter's board. A thirteen-year-old girl named Marie Jeanne Coupart was a boarding student of the Ursulines in 1740. She had been placed there by her guardian, master carpenter Pierre Thommelin, the spouse of one of the confreresses. Well-born Charlotte Demouy, the daughter of confreress Charlotte Duval Demouy, was a boarding student for nine years, probably in the 1750s.[41]

Although this is a small sample, its diversity is nonetheless striking. In

40. Ibid., 7; Clark, "'By All the Conduct of Their Lives,'" 790–792.
41. RSC, *LHQ*, IV (1921), 355, VII (1924), 339, VIII (1925), 478, IX (1926), 310. "Livre de l'entrée," 11, UCANO, identifies Charlotte Demouy as the daughter of Charlotte Duval Demouy.

the late 1720s, there was a drop in the number of boarding students at the convent, and one historian wonders whether some French families might have worried that the institution of slavery was compromised by the proximity of their daughters to enslaved classmates.[42] If there was such sentiment, it did not change the nuns' policies about whom they accepted as boarding students, since the mulatto woman was a student in the late 1730s. Nor did it keep Charlotte Duval Demouy, the wife of an officer, from enrolling her daughter Charlotte Demouy. Like the women's confraternity, the community that was developing through the Ursuline boarding school was heterogeneous.

Through the lay confraternity they sponsored and their classes for girls and unconverted women, the Ursulines in New Orleans during the French colonial regime provided mechanisms that knit together a motley fabric of female community. The spiritual universalism of their approach was rooted in the French Counter-Reformation campaign to reinstate Catholicism as a unifying feature of French cultural identity. In New Orleans, the nuns' big tent Catholicism created a space in which a socially and racially heterogeneous female population came together to enact a particular ideal of French Catholic womanhood. The Louisiana experiment was, however, quite different from the French project that inspired it. The shared identity it created was limited, not to the shared ethnicity that France's reconversion to Catholic orthodoxy helped to cement, but to a shared femininity that cut across disparate geographic origins. The colonial achievement probably depended, to some degree, on the fluidity in frontier social relations. The colonial elite's own desire for social hierarchy and an increasingly constraining official discourse about race in both colony and metropole would have presented significant barriers to the nuns' apparent ambition to commission all women in the colony, regardless of race or status, as agents of the faith. When Louisiana passed from French to Spanish hands in the 1760s and grew gradually toward economic prosperity with the maturation of plantation slavery, the durability of their original apostolate was tested.

42. Giraud, *A History of French Louisiana*, V, *The Company of the Indies*, trans. Pearce, 308.

INNER SPIRIT, OUTWARD SIGNS

FRENCH FEMININE PIETY AT WORK

All women should be prohibited from learning to write and even read.
This would preserve them from loose thoughts, confining them to useful
tasks about the house, instilling in them respect for the first sex.
—Restif de La Bretonne, 1777

Among the dozens of marriage contracts scattered throughout the proceedings of the Louisiana Superior Council are two that represent very different kinds of families, one prominent and prosperous, the other humble and
ordinary. They nonetheless share one striking feature: they testify to the
unusual literacy of New Orleans women. Jean LaBranche took a bride in
1737. A simple farmer with a small habitation upriver from New Orleans, he
stood before a notary with a single friend at his side and agreed to share his
modest property with his future wife, an orphaned minor named Suzanne
Marchand. LaBranche, the notary recorded, did not know how to sign his
name, but Suzanne's signature, in a sure, round hand, marks her consent.
Twenty-five years later, on a May day in 1762, the members of the Rillieux
planter family gathered together before another notary in New Orleans
to execute and witness a marriage agreement between a colonial official
named Antoine Thomassin and one of the Rillieux daughters, Margueritte.
The marriage portion and dowry amounted to a substantial five thousand
livres, and the colony's treasurer and a prominent merchant attended the
groom. The witnesses for Thomassin signed their names with confident
flourishes; Margueritte and her sister penned theirs in a more modest hand.
Their twenty-six-year-old brother, Vincent Rillieux, however, declared to
the notary that he could not write or sign. Two women, one rich, the other
poor, signed. Two men, one rich, the other poor, could not.[1]

The signature patterns of the two Louisiana documents are inversions

---

1. "Jean LaBranche mariage avec Suzanne Marchand," Nov. 6, 1737, "Thomassin
mariage avec Margueritte Rillieux," May 7, 1762, RSC.

of gender and class norms for eighteenth-century literacy in the Atlantic world. Sex-based difference in literacy acquisition was common, but it was unusual to find women, rather than men, displaying superior attainment.[2] A survey of signature literacy in colonial Louisiana reveals that the LaBranche-Marchand and Thomassin-Rillieux contracts hint at a larger phenomenon. The women of colonial New Orleans had a higher rate of literacy than was typical for the era elsewhere, and it was not uncommon for an unlettered man to stand before the altar with a bride who could sign her name at the bottom of the priest's entry in the parish marriage register at Saint Louis Church, the parish church for colonial New Orleans.[3]

Literacy was among the most singular markers of the distinctive female piety forged by Ursulines in seventeenth-century France. This piety was notable as well for its invocation of a feminine ideal that spurred women to organized service and endowed them with a potentially empowering religious identity. And it sustained a long-standing dedication to eucharistic devotion that made women the principal source of congregational support for the colonial clergy.

The term *piety* has implications that reach beyond belief to practice. Derived from the Latin *pietas*—"dutiful conduct"—piety connotes action, referring generally to behavior that demonstrates religious belief and reverence and that is designed to honor the object of devotion. The words *devotion* and *devotional practice* are often used interchangeably with *piety* and refer to the same kind of action inspired by belief and duty. Drawn from the Latin word for "breath," a phenomenon that lacks embodiment, "spirituality" represents a different aspect of religious life. Although it is often used to describe both belief and the action springing from it, the term is imprecise in defining the border between thought and behavior or the relationship between the two. Ursuline spirituality was the intellectual and emotional framework that supplied the nuns with an understanding of the

2. Nancy F. Cott, *The Bonds of Womanhood: "Woman's Sphere" in New England, 1780-1835* (New Haven, Conn., 1977), 103; R. A. Houston, *Literacy in Early Modern Europe: Culture and Education, 1500-1800* (London, 1988), 131-137; Allan Greer, "The Pattern of Literacy in Quebec, 1745-1899," *Histoire Sociale/Social History*, XI (1978), 295-335; E. Jennifer Monaghan, *Learning to Read and Write in Colonial America* (Amherst, Mass., 2005).

3. The parish church of Saint Louis achieved the status of cathedral in 1788 upon the elevation of its pastor to auxilliary bishop of the Diocese of Havana. See Roger Baudier, *The Catholic Church in Louisiana* (New Orleans, 1939), 204, 219.

particular nature of their duty to God. Their piety was the "dutiful conduct" they performed in response to the imperative embodied in their spirituality. The Ursulines understood that imperative to be one that not only
commanded and directed their own action but that demanded acceptance
of that action by others. When the New Orleans nuns shunned the hospital obligation they owed the Company of the Indies and pursued their educational work, their spirituality dictated that their actions be read as the
proper ordering of their piety: duty to God naturally overrode duty to men
of the company.

The innovative features of early modern Ursuline piety were not the
products of equally new traditions in female spirituality. In fact, Ursuline
spirituality built on traditions in female spirituality that reached back for
centuries. In the Middle Ages, women used the unique biological attributes
of their sex and their role as mothers to fashion a symbolic rationale for
feminine sanctity, power, and authority in religious terms. Against Aristotelian formulations that presented the female body as imperfect and weak,
women developed and elaborated an alternate reading. They created a spirituality in which their own bodies became powerful symbols that recapitu-
lated and reenacted the sacrifice of Christ, opening a new, often dynamic
avenue for enacting religious belief.[4]

Women sought and achieved a sexless symbolic enactment of Christ's
corporeal sacrifice partly by revealing the male savior himself as the ultimate nurturer. Medieval works of art startle the modern eye with depic-
tions of Christ feeding his flock as a mother would, from his breast. In a
fifteenth-century Italian painting, Jesus offers a eucharistic wafer he has
pulled from his breast to a Poor Clare nun kneeling at his feet, and in another he squeezes blood from the wound in his breast and aims the stream
toward a chalice held by a woman representing Charity. The Christ shown
feeding his flock from his breast does not so much bend gender as he tran-

4. The following discussion on medieval female spirituality is based primarily on
Caroline Walker Bynum, *Holy Feast and Holy Fast: The Religious Significance of Food to
Medieval Women* (Berkeley, Calif., 1987), esp. 24–25, 280–295. See also Bynum, *Jesus as
Mother: Studies in the Spirituality of the High Middle Ages* (Berkeley, Calif., 1982), 256–
258; Richard Kieckhefer, "Major Currents in Late Medieval Devotion," and Bynum,
"Religious Women in the Later Middle Ages," both in Jill Raitt, ed., *Christian Spiritu-
ality: High Middle Ages and Reformation* (New York, 1987), 96–100, 131–134; and Donald
Weinstein and Rudolph M. Bell, *Saints and Society: The Two Worlds of Western Christendom, 1000–1700* (Chicago, 1982).

scends it to show the sexless nature of bodily sacrifice. Holy women who maintained virginity, fasted, inflicted pain on themselves, and rejected the vanities of dress and toilette were not rejecting their sex; they were using the body, as Christ had done, as an instrument of sacrificial passion.[5]

At the same time, however, the symbols and acts of sanctity that developed from a feminine spirituality that embodied sacrifice resonated strikingly with feminine life experience. Because women were biologically endowed to be nurturers of human life, through the womb and the breast, as they crafted a devotional practice they were especially drawn to the Eucharist and its miraculous food, the body of Christ. Women became avid devotees of the feast of Corpus Christi, received Communion when they could, and fervently adored the host at its elevation in the Mass when they could not.[6] Medieval feminine spirituality, with its emphasis on the body and food, forged a potent, mystical link between women and the sacrament of the Eucharist that might have been particularly important in the early modern period, when women became crucial allies in the campaign by parish priests to emphasize sacramental piety.

During the early-seventeenth-century French Catholic revival, women were a key constituency among those who supported the clergy's aims to recenter devotion around the parish and the sacraments administered by priests in the parochial setting. Women's motivation to join the clergy's cause must have been largely a response to increased opportunities for action within the organized life of the church. Parish priests sponsored new Rosarian confraternities that appealed to women, and these, in turn, gave women greater scope for leadership and participation in the organized dispensation of charity, expanding their formal participation in church affairs.[7] The lineaments of medieval feminine spirituality suggest another

5. Bynum, *Holy Feast and Holy Fast,* 271–276 (plates 25, 26).

6. Ibid., esp. 24–25, 280–295; Bynum, *Jesus as Mother,* 256–258; Richard Kieckhefer, "Major Currents in Late Medieval Devotion," and Bynum, "Religious Women in the Later Middle Ages," both in Raitt, ed., *Christian Spirituality,* 96–100, 131–134.

7. Christopher F. Black, *Italian Confraternities in the Sixteenth Century* (Cambridge, 1989), 35–38, 103–104; Marie-Hélène Froeschle-Chopard, "La dévotion du Rosaire à travers quelques livres de piété," *Histoire, Économie, et Société,* X (1991), 299–316; Philip T. Hoffman, *Church and Community in the Diocese of Lyon, 1500–1789* (New Haven, Conn., 1984), 114, 124–125, 145; Kathryn Norberg, "Women, the Family, and the Counter-Reformation: Women's Confraternities in the Seventeenth Century," *Proceedings of the Sixth Annual Meeting of the Western Society for French History,* VI (1978), 55–63.

explanation for why women did not simply embrace the new confraternities of Reformation Catholicism and ignore the sacramental aspects that were so important to the clergy. For women, the sacrament had long been vital as holy nourishment and as a way to experience the physicality of Christ; for priests, it was a crucial mechanism by which parishioners could be yoked to the rhythms and rules of a church-based piety over which priests ruled by virtue of their exclusive power to administer the sacramental mysteries. Women's eucharistic devotion, embedded in an older, well-established spirituality that sprang from features unique to women's bodies, positioned them as the allies of Tridentine priests intent on creating loyalty to parochial sacramental worship. That alliance was not imposed upon women but was assumed by them for reasons of their own. Women supported eucharistic observance, not from a blind obedience to the dicta of Trent or in unquestioning submission to the authority of priests, but because it expressed and affirmed their unique embodiment of the sacred.

The Ursulines were in the vanguard of those who advanced women's alliance with the clergy from private acts of individual commitment to public propagation of eucharistic piety. Their rule, which stipulates in minute detail their daily routine of prayer and teaching, places the Eucharist at the center of the devotional life they led and taught their students to undertake. Of the thirteen chapters in the rule that speak to the instruction of their students, eight relate in some way to Communion. Chapters 4 and 5 of the rule are completely dedicated to preparing boarding students for their first Communion, and other passages stipulate that boarding students were required to attend Mass daily and were to receive Communion at least once a month and on major feast days of the church.[8]

The legacy of medieval female spirituality may help explain women's general support for the clerical program of sacramental piety and the Ursulines' particular focus on it in the devotional practice they taught their charges, but it does not explain the most singular and startling innovation in early modern French female piety: its emphasis on education and action under the aegis of new women's religious orders. Women not only led the way by pious example but also by precept. Moving from the private, if not passive, role they played as devout models of bodily submission and sacrifice in medieval piety, they now asserted prescriptive and didactic authority that reached beyond their bodies and their families to a wider public realm.

8. *Règlemens des religieuses Ursulines de la Congrégation de Paris* (Paris, 1705), esp. 44–68, 111, 133.

To justify such actions, which clashed with prevailing definitions of appropriate feminine behavior, they elaborated the medieval spirituality in ways that moved beyond the sacred bodily mimicry of individual women to a symbolic abstraction of apostolic womanhood. Women employed a new constellation of sacred symbols to construct a holy femininity that used women's sexual difference to claim modes of action previously defined as male.

The early modern female spirituality upon which the Ursulines built their order celebrated women's unique generative capacity and used it to claim a special space for women within the post-Tridentine church. Maternity was central to this new spiritual foundation: the Ursulines relied heavily upon the ultimate example of the Virgin Mary and her essential role in human salvation. "If it is said that Plato thanked God he was born male and not female, the holy Virgin is better able to glorify than his sex, since to hers is reserved a mystery which men have never performed," an early Ursuline wrote. To the medieval claim to spiritual power by personal imitation of bodily sacrifice, Ursulines added a new basis for authority by virtue of the sex they shared with the mother of God, who made Christ's sacrifice possible by giving birth.[9]

Woman was not only the indispensable conduit through which redemption reached the world; she was salvation's active agent. Male humanity, in the person of Joseph, played the passive role of onlooker. Mary was the vessel through which incarnation was accomplished, and her womb and breast brought forth and nurtured the human fruit that saved the world. But she did more. She acted, in an exertion of her own will, to bring the birth of the Savior to pass. Ursuline writing stressed the importance of Mary's agreement, at the point of the Annunciation, and contrasted it to Eve's passive role as the mere instrument of the devil. An Ursuline chronicler wrote that "Eve was the serpent's instrument of seduction, and Mary was the cause and the organ of our reconciliation with Jesus Christ; the one suggested the first sin (to Adam) and the other procured our redemption." Eve's transgression is presented as an act of spineless accession, Mary's redemption as dynamic. Her act of cooperation was transformed into a heroic

9. Linda Lierheimer, "Female Eloquence and Maternal Ministry: The Apostolate of Ursuline Nuns in Seventeenth-Century France" (Ph.D. diss., Princeton University, 1994), esp. 90–153, 217–234 (quotation on 226–227). The following review of Ursuline spirituality relies heavily upon Lierheimer. Unless otherwise noted, translations from Lierheimer and other sources cited in this chapter are the author's.

deed by the Ursuline writer who called Mary "notre libératrice"—our liberator.[10]

Mary's agreement to bring Jesus into the world was not her only sacred act. She nourished him and taught him. When the Ursulines wrote of these deeds, they made clear that nurturing and teaching were inextricably intertwined: "When he took from her virgin breast the milk destined by heaven for his nourishment, she told him to love and adore God, she told him that he was his God and his father, and these words entered little by little into his soul, by the passage of his senses." And, as Mary taught Jesus the basic facts of his relationship to God, all human mothers were likewise to teach their children. The relationship between mother and son, human teacher and divine pupil, served also as a model of Christian humility and a justification for placing women in positions superior to men within the special relational bounds of maternity. An early Ursuline acknowledged the radical nature of this new interpretation of Mary's heavenly authority: "It is wholly astonishing that one who is God should obey a woman, a humiliation without example; and that a woman should so dominate God is a wonder that one cannot comprehend."[11]

Ursuline writers thus made a strong case for women's privileged place and authority in spiritual matters and the propagation of the faith. To justify the existence of a cadre of virginal women who eliminated the corporeal aspects of maternity from their lives, Ursulines perfected a spiritual version of motherhood with the apostolic act of teaching at its core. In doing so, they also relied on Mary's example, citing several episodes in her life when she worked to bring the message of Christ's redemption to the world. Scriptural reference to her presence at the Pentecost was interpreted as evidence that it was she who instructed the disciples to preach the Gospels. In this context, she was frequently portrayed as the Queen of Apostles. "It is true," wrote one religious leader in seventeenth-century France, "that outwardly Saint Peter, being the image of Jesus Christ, had power over her; but inwardly he submitted to the most Blessed Virgin." The Visitation, when Mary went forth to announce her sacred pregnancy, also came to serve as a model of apostolic action. "It is from the mystery of the

10. Ibid., 217–234. See, especially, Jeanne des Anges, *Entretiens spirituels ou très-pieuses méditations sur les douleurs, grâces, grandeurs, et gloires de la très-sainte Vierge* (1665; rpt. Paris, 1868), I, 4, II, 300, quoted ibid., 221, 224.

11. Jeanne des Anges, *Entretiens spirituels*, I, 90, quoted in Lierheimer, "Female Eloquence," 422, 423.

Visitation that apostolic men and missionaries ought to draw the graces of their sublime vocation. From the moment that she conceived and formed Him in her womb, she, first of all, went out at once to announce Him, and thus did what the Apostles later did by her example."[12] Ursulines made the simple, yet revolutionary argument that apostolic life could not be denied to women because a woman beyond human reproach had originated it.

Although Mary served as the primary model for mother as teacher, it was the example of two other female saints, Ursula and Angela Merici, that enabled Ursulines to legitimate the apostolic teaching activities of unmarried virgins who carried out their work, not from the platform of the nuclear family, under the rule of a human husband, but as members of a company of women commissioned directly by God. Ursula, the mythic British princess martyred in the fourth century, set a crucial precedent. As mentioned earlier, she remained a virgin, persuading her new husband to convert and postpone consummation of their marriage until her return from a three-year missionary campaign of heathen conversion, paid for by her father and in the company of eleven thousand virgin companions.[13]

Ursula and her company of virgin missionaries exemplified the teaching vocation of womanhood, but they gave up the opportunity to be biological mothers in order to bring the rebirth of conversion to the heathen. Taking her orders directly from God, Ursula was not only a spiritual mother; she was also a commander, waging a mighty battle at the head of a legion of militant women who bore God's standard of truth. She taught and converted men, and her own husband dispensed her from normal wifely duties. Saint Ursula perfectly illustrated how a woman might fulfill the full maternal promise of her sex without giving birth and rearing children of her own by accepting God's charge to act as a spiritual mother to multitudes. Her father and husband demonstrated the proper male response to this heroic variant of motherhood. Men should not only step aside and allow a woman to answer God's call; they should recognize that she could surpass her brothers in both the scope and virtue of her service. "Behold an excellent teacher, who in one single lesson educated 11,000 students . . . one

12. Jean-Jacques Olier, *Vie intérieure de la très Sainte Vierge,* quoted in Lorraine Caza, *La vie voyagère, conversante avec le prochain, Marguerite Bourgeoys* (Montreal, 1982), 86, 90, quoted in Elizabeth Rapley, *The Dévotes: Women and Church in Seventeenth-Century France* (Montreal, 1990), 172–173. See also ibid., 146, 170–171, 174; Lierheimer, "Female Eloquence," 414–434.

13. Lierheimer, "Female Eloquence," 12.

must admit that St. Ursula's students honored her better than the Apostles did Jesus-Christ . . . since they stood firm, suffering bodily harm, while the Apostles cowered, sending their Master into the hands of his enemies."[14]

The images of Ursula, the holy warrior, and Mary, the mother of God, provided powerful mythic prototypes for the spiritual motherhood of the French Ursulines. Angela Merici, the sixteenth-century founder of the Ursuline order, bridged myth and reality, past and present, by serving as a recent example of the qualities and actions that the congregation now promoted. She had died in 1540, fewer than sixty years before the first Ursuline communities were established in France. Angela, an unmarried woman who organized a company of young virgins to catechize and dispense charity, claimed Ursula as inspiration and showed that the saint's heroic, virginal maternity was not an exceptional event ordained by God in unique historic circumstances; it was part of his continuing plan. God commissioned contemporary women, Angela's work proclaimed, not just the women born in the distant age of early Christian martyrs.[15]

Ursulines fashioned a potent new model of female spirituality upon the tripod of the Virgin Mary, Saint Ursula, and Angela Merici. Its most singular aspect was its unambiguous femininity. Christ, of course, remained the ultimate focal point of faith and adoration, but the path to salvation for women was now through imitation of holy females, each of whom had in some way more perfectly embodied his sacrifice and executed his will than any male could. The cult of the Virgin was not new, but the valorization of her apostolic attributes and the weaving together of her example with those of Ursula and Angela created a new chapter in female spirituality that brought with it a turn in pious practice toward public action.[16]

The call to action that sprang from Ursuline spirituality focused on the educational aspect of maternity and made teaching and learning into prominent attributes of female piety. According to the Ursulines, a devout

14. Ibid., 110–142, 234; Marie-Augustine de Pommereu, *Les chroniques de l'ordre des Ursulines recueillies pour l'usage des religieuses du mesme ordre*, I (Paris, 1673), 7–8.

15. Lierheimer, "Female Eloquence," 110–116; Peter Maurice Waters, *The Ursuline Achievement: A Philosophy of Education for Women, St. Angela Merici, the Ursulines, and Catholic Education* (Victoria, Australia, 1994), 19–29.

16. On Marian devotion, particularly in the medieval period, see Kieckhefer, "Major Currents in Late Medieval Devotion," in Raitt, ed., *Christian Spirituality*, 89–93; and Marina Warner, *Alone of All Her Sex: The Myth and the Cult of the Virgin Mary* (New York, 1976).

woman was one who prepared herself to propagate the faith by becoming schooled herself. She first was duty-bound to learn by rote the tenets of the faith, but, given the importance of print and literacy in the advance of Protestantism, the good Catholic woman must also learn to read and write so that she could meet the enemy with an arsenal of equal strength. In the Ursuline formulation of women's Christian duty, it was essential that mothers, whom God placed as natural missionaries to their families, be literate. Given women's divine vocation as teachers, they, not male clerics or missionaries, would be called by God to dedicate themselves to the education of these mother missionaries.[17] Two related tiers of female piety thus developed in post-Nantes France, one for laywomen that required them to demonstrate their devotion by learning and then teaching their families, and another for vowed religious women who stepped outside the household to create the institutions that took responsibility for mothering the mothers. Both asked women to show their love of God not merely through prayer and religious observance but through active, apostolic behavior.

This active female piety had numerous implications. It rationalized literacy for women, engendered a sprawling institutional apparatus for female education and charity, and gave thousands of women a professional alternative to marriage and motherhood. No country in Europe knew anything like the sweeping Ursuline campaign to educate women, which involved hundreds of convents and thousands of nuns in France at the end of the seventeenth century and made an Ursuline school a common feature of town life. And, although the principal rationale for women's education was religious, the literacy a girl acquired at the convent had multiple uses and gave her at least cognitive passage into the realms of law, commerce, and literature.[18]

The institutions that proliferated in the wake of women's rush into religious life altered both the material and social landscapes of early modern France. The active pious work of the new religious women ultimately demanded a complex and sophisticated organizational base, and enclosed convents were better suited to the preservation and deployment of the material resources necessary for the women's apostolate. Although the Ursulines became cloistered in the first decades of the seventeenth century, their enclosure did not so much separate them from the world as anchor their

17. Lierheimer, "Female Eloquence," 61–153, 236–288; Rapley, *The Dévotes*, 42–73; and Waters, *Ursuline Achievement*, 19–96.

18. For a graphic representation of the geographic distribution of Ursuline schools in seventeenth-century France, see Rapley, *The Dévotes*, 49 (map 2).

place in it. The highly urbanized landscape of early modern France was well suited to making the Ursuline project visible and linked it to the rising fortunes of the professional and merchant communities. Their convents occupied large, prominent spaces in French towns and, like other public buildings, testified with their powerful physical presence to the important work that took place within. Convents played a prominent part in local economies, as consumers of food and clothing, as builders and landlords, as lenders and investors. And the institutions of various congregations of religious women—Ursulines, Filles de la Charité, and a dozen others—developed into the primary source of labor and administration for much of what would be called today the social service sector. The result was a network of hospitals, schools, reformatories, orphanages, foundling homes, and shelters for the poor and the abused operated by women who managed accounts, directed work, and negotiated the terms of their services with male authorities who sought them. Female piety wore a substantial institutional face, its gaze turned outward to the world.[19]

Finally, the new piety changed the ideal nun and holy woman from the contemplative whose prayers and body were offered to God in private sacrifice to the vigorous apostle who also showed her devotion through service to others. The benefits of women's piety now translated into measurable results for all to see. Children learned the catechism and attended Mass. Girls learned to read. The sick were tended, the orphaned sheltered, and the undisciplined reformed. Women made life in this world more bearable, even as they continued working for humanity's salvation in the next. Religious women did not abandon the old piety, with its attention to bodily sacrifice and sacramental observance, but to it was added a new regime of action that spread their influence outward.

The distinctive new female piety forged in seventeenth-century France traveled to the colony of Louisiana by two principal means. Most obviously,

19. On the contributions of religious women to the provision of social services, their construction projects, and their financial activity, see Colin Jones, *The Charitable Imperative: Hospitals and Nursing in Ancien Regime and Revolutionary France* (London, 1989); and Olwen H. Hufton, *The Poor of Eighteenth-Century France, 1750–1789* (New York, 1974), 148. Rapley, *The Dévotes*, gives the best sense of the proliferation of women's religious orders and congregations. For a description of the large Ursuline convent of Rouen, constructed in the 1650s, see Pierre Chirol, *Le Couvent des Ursulines de la Rue des Capucins* (Rouen, 1926). For the construction plans and elevations for the Ursuline convents at Rouen and Elboeuf and materials documenting convent finances, see folios C2716, D345, D376, D418, D419, ADSM.

missionary nuns embodied it in their perspectives, customs, and instruction. But their example was both guided and augmented by a material legacy of Ursuline literature that the nuns and their students studied, read aloud, and invoked in the colony. The Louisiana Ursulines literally brought some of this legacy with them in their luggage. Nearly fifty of the books in one inventory of the convent library were published before 1727, and many if not all of these volumes were brought to the colony by its first generation of nuns.[20]

Two books in the New Orleans Ursuline library would have played a particularly important part in transmitting the French pious tradition to Louisiana, *Les chroniques de l'ordre des Ursulines* of Marie-Augustine de Pommereu, published in 1673, and the 1705 version of the Ursuline rule, *Règlemens des religieuses Ursulines de la Congrégation de Paris*. The *Chroniques* of Marie-Augustine de Pommereu represented, at the time, the primary history of the order. Marie-Augustine, a member of the Paris Ursuline community, based her chronicle on memoirs of the founding and early years of Ursuline convents and on the *lettres circulaires,* or circular letters, disseminated by Ursuline convents upon the death of a member of their community. The latter are life histories of individual nuns, which were intended to serve as exempla for living Ursulines. They often provide detailed biographical information about individual sisters, speaking of the circumstances of their call to religious life and recounting the nature of the work they did as nuns. In setting down the early history of the order, the *Chroniques* was perhaps more instrumental than any other Ursuline writing in articulating the ideals of spiritual motherhood, presenting the rationale for the order's educational enterprise, and prompting emulation.[21]

The second book, the *Règlemens*, which dictates how Ursulines were to spend every waking moment of their days, whether in classroom, cell, or chapel, tells us that books like the *Chroniques* were read aloud to the nuns as they ate or did needlework, ensuring continuity in their knowledge and

20. The New Orleans Ursuline Convent library collection was inventoried and sold to the Historic New Orleans Collection in 1998.

21. The 1998 inventory of the New Orleans convent library included the 1673 edition of Pommereu, *Les chroniques de l'ordre des Ursulines,* but not a full copy of the 1705 version of the Ursuline rule, *Règlemens des religieuses Ursulines de la Congrégation de Paris*. References to the rule in eighteenth-century records of the convent make clear, however, that the nuns had a copy in their possession at the time. For a detailed discussion of Pommereu's work, see Lierheimer, "Female Eloquence," esp. 161, 175–176, 187–197.

practice of the piety of their foremothers. The *Règlemens* itself gives the fullest picture of the daily shape and rhythm of female piety for both the nuns and the future wives and mothers who were their students. Of all the books that the nuns brought with them, it was likely the most treasured and frequently consulted, for it served as the template for both nun and student in the propagation of the distinctive new femininity imagined and made flesh by the Ursuline project.

The *Règlemens* aimed to produce not simply generic Tridentine Catholicism but also a specifically gendered piety. It incorporated the older tradition of eucharistic devotion among women but was most prominently indebted to what was new in Ursuline spirituality. The Virgin Mary, the greatest of female saints, now stood at the forefront as both model and inspiration. Living women who emulated the Virgin's example taught young girls that their femininity was inextricable from their piety. The timetabled regularity of the days prescribed by the *Règlemens* invested the rhythms of student life with special, gendered meanings meant to order their lives as women long after they left the schoolrooms of the Ursulines.

The *Règlemens* was divided into two volumes. Volume I details in twenty chapters how the nuns were to care for and instruct their students, what their charges were to be taught, and what the daily prayer regimen was to be. Marian adoration and the sacraments of penance, confirmation, and Communion played central roles in both the daily rhythm of the students' lives and in the general contour of the curriculum. Boarding students heard Mass daily with the nuns before breakfast, recited Marian litanies at midmorning, and recited the Little Office of the Virgin before they went to bed each night.[22] The Virgin punctuated the students' daily prayer life; the Mass anchored it. The *Règlemens* emphasized the importance of the Mass not simply by requiring daily attendance but by outlining the intense effort that the Ursulines were expected to mount in the preparation of their charges for participation in sacramental life.

Whole chapters of the rule are dedicated to the preparation of students for their first confession and Communion. The *Règlemens* called on the nuns not only to teach their students how to examine their consciences and recount their faults to a confessor but required a teacher to meet individually with each first-time penitent to conduct the neophyte through self-examination step-by-step. "The teacher must take care always that they are prepared, lest the Confessor have nothing to hear," the *Règlemens* admon-

22. *Règlemens*, 110–114.

ished. The priest had the power of absolution, but it was the nuns who ensured that the sacrament of penance took place and was effective. Similarly, the nuns carefully prepared students for their first Communion, reviewing for them its meaning, directing them to read and meditate on appropriate inspirational texts, confining them to quiet, reflective activities on the day they were destined to receive the sacrament, and conducting them to the chapel. Perhaps most striking, if no sermon was to be preached at the Mass on a day when students were to make their first Communion, their teacher was to "make beforehand some lecture, to serve as the subject for their meditation." The students exposed to these preaching, teaching nuns absorbed lessons in feminine assertion along with their catechism. Women achieved holiness, not by retreating from the challenges of an imperfect world, but by meeting them armed with knowledge.[23]

The missionary nuns, too, were closely instructed by the *Règlemens* in the particulars of religious observance and daily piety, and the *Chroniques* offered the inspiration of past example. Their enthusiasm and resolve were also sustained by an additional, more immediate source: the lives of the nuns who lived before them and beside them that were memorialized in the lettres circulaires.[24] Thirty obituary notices for New Orleans Ursulines were composed during the colonial period and provide vivid evidence of how the women sustained Ursuline spirituality in Louisiana. The New Orleans lettres circulaires confirm that the life of action inspired by the example of the Virgin Mary and prescribed by the *Règlemens* remained both the ideal and the reality for Ursulines in the New World. Yet they also hint that in America the range and intensity of the nuns' pious work exceeded French experience.

Most of the lettres circulaires contain four sections. The first speaks to the circumstances of a nun's entry into religion, the second discusses the occupations she filled during her lifetime, the third comments on her religious observance, and the fourth describes her death. Nearly all of the

23. Ibid., 49–54.
24. The "Lettres circulaires," UCANO, contain obituary notices for each nun who died at the convent from its foundation in 1727 through 1896. Copies of these letters were also sent to France for circulation among French convents, as evidenced by opening phrases such as, "Very Reverend Mother, with eyes streaming with tears and a heart full of sorrow, I have recourse to your charity to obtain the suffrage of our holy order on behalf of our very dear Sister Madeleine Mahieu, called St. Francis Xavier" (195).

obituaries contain a passage that describes the work the nun performed. There are only three notices that do not. One describes a sickly nun who was "crucified by many infirmities." Two others comment simply on the spiritual qualities of the deceased. Each of these three notices is remarkable not only for the omission of references to work but also for its extreme brevity, a single short paragraph taking up about a third of a page. Obituary letters could run to four or five pages in a folio volume and were rarely less than a full page in length. Clearly, the Louisiana nuns who were held up as exempla for future generations of Ursulines were not those who simply bore great physical suffering or exhibited extraordinary religious fervor. Such women would have satisfied the standard of feminine holiness observed in the Middle Ages, but early modern Ursuline spirituality demanded more. The nuns held up as models in colonial Louisiana mixed lives of prayerful observance with active participation in the work of the convent. And the work that drew the most enthusiastic praise was that which reached beyond the parameters of the Ursuline project in France. The education of French and French creole girls in Louisiana was good; work that took a sister into unusual or unknown directions in response to colonial exigencies was better.[25]

Although education was the Ursulines' primary objective and other evidence speaks to their determination to keep it at the forefront of their colonial mission, the nuns' teaching abilities and efforts do not take center stage in the lettres circulaires. Indeed, comments about teaching, particularly in the sedate boarding division, can be almost perfunctory. Marie Thérèse Ramachard was tersely praised in her 1755 obituary for her "application to the task of forming our first creoles and injecting them with the pious sentiments that make good Christian mothers." Enthusiasm was a bit more forthcoming for her sister, Marguerite Ramachard, who was "zealous for instructing the young, trying by all sorts of means to inspire them about religion, and she was indefatigable in this work." Of Marie Madeleine Hachard, who wrote vivid letters to her father about the voyage to Louisiana and the convent's first months there, it was said upon her demise in 1760 simply that, "when death came, she was employed with the boarders." The only time an adjective is used to describe a nun's teaching is in the obituary of Catherine Lavadiere, who died in 1779, which reports that she "did perfect instruction." In all, teaching is mentioned in only seven of the thirty obituaries for colonial-era choir nuns. Education might have been the de-

25. Ibid., 229, 230, 232. Compare these brief entries with others in the volume.

fining apostolate of the Ursulines, but being a good teacher was not what brought an effluence of admiring words from the colonial eulogist's pen.[26]

The nuns who joyfully accepted the unexpected, unaccustomed tasks that God put in the colonial Ursuline's path are the greatest heroines of the New Orleans lettres circulaires. Mother Superior Marie Tranchepain and her successors insisted publicly on the primacy of the sisters' educational work, but in their private postmortem assessments of religious heroics they valorized those nuns who undertook work beyond the traditional bounds of the Ursuline apostolate in order to sustain the viability of the mission. Because they were the only religious women in colonial New Orleans, there were ample opportunities for the Ursulines to shoulder unaccustomed burdens. Marie Hachard reported to her father: "We are going to follow, all at the same time, the functions of four different communities, that of the Ursulines, our first and principal order, that of the Hospitalières, that of the St. Josephs and that of the Refuge." In France, there was a formally observed division of labor among the women's religious organizations that provided social services. The Louisiana Ursulines had already agreed to assume the work of the *hospitalières* when they signed their contract with the Company of the Indies. They assented to the company's request to shelter a woman in a compromising domestic situation shortly after their arrival, a service usually rendered in France by the Order of Our Lady of Charity of the Refuge. When they agreed to take in an orphan late in 1727, they stood in for the Sisters of Saint Joseph, founded to care for orphans.[27]

No work received greater praise than caring for the orphans who tested the nuns' resources and patience in the middle years of the eighteenth century. In 1729, the sudden arrival of some thirty girls orphaned by the Indian

26. Ibid., 222, 225, 234, 236.

27. [Marie Madeleine Hachard], *De Rouen à la Louisiane: Voyage d'une Ursuline en 1727* (Rouen, 1988), 68–70. "Refuge" was the name given to institutions that housed delinquent or abandoned women and girls. Hachard is probably referring here to the Order of Our Lady of Charity of the Refuge, which was founded in France in 1641 ("Our Lady of Charity of the Good Shepherd," *Catholic Encyclopedia* [http://www.new advent.org/cathen/06647c.htm]). The progenitors of the Sisters of Saint Joseph (Filles de Saint-Joseph) were authorized by the bishop of Le Puy to care for orphans that had been sent to the town's *hôpital*. The Sisters of Saint Joseph later expanded the range of services they provided, but their early identity with the care of orphans made the name of their congregation synonymous with this apostolate (Carol K. Coburn and Martha Smith, *Spirited Lives: How Nuns Shaped Catholic Culture and American Life, 1836–1920* [Chapel Hill, N.C., 1999], 20–35).

attack on Fort Rosalie stretched the seven nuns in residence to the limits of their endurance. The orphans were reported to have terrible manners, and the official subsidy the nuns received for them was never enough to provide for them adequately without dipping into other convent resources. The sisters who stepped into the breach and worked with this troublesome brood were marked for special praise.[28]

Jeanne Melotte and Charlotte Hebert both arrived in 1732, bringing some relief to the seven nuns who were struggling to accommodate the strain of the orphanage. Both earned admiration in their obituaries for their work with these charges. Jeanne Melotte delighted in bringing order and affection to the unruly girls. "The ruder these children were, the more endearing she was," her superior eulogized. Instead of despairing when the number of her difficult charges grew, Jeanne "had no greater satisfaction than the increase in their number, seeing it as the benediction of the house." Charlotte Hebert cared for orphans at the end of her day, when she finished with her primary duties as hospitalière. "She had zeal and charity for these poor children, with whom she was constantly employed." Elizabeth de Belaire battled ill health for years before she died at the tender age of twenty-nine in 1752, yet she, too, had charge of the exasperating and demanding orphans at one point and "sacrificed everything for them during epidemics of smallpox and scarlet fever, when she had as many as twenty-five sick children on her hands at one time, for whom she cared night and day with great charity."[29]

Caring for orphans drew Ursulines beyond the duties expected of members of their order in France. Another activity that brought special attention in the obituary letters lay within the educational objectives of the Ursulines but nonetheless represented untrod territory for the order: evangelization of enslaved Africans. The women who came to Louisiana in 1727 were aspiring missionaries, but they expected the objects of their evangelization to be Indians, not Africans. A member of the founding cadre of New Orleans Ursulines, Cécile Cavalier, was eulogized at length for the enthusiasm with which she embraced the unexpected nature of her missionary field. Cécile's efforts with her charges aimed at more than the inculcation of superficial sacramental piety. "There were a number" of enslaved people, apparently adults, "for whom she procured by her instruction the good for-

28. [Hachard], *De Rouen à la Louisiane*, 69; AC C13A, XI, 274v, XIII, 265, AC B59, 575v–576; "Lettres circulaires," 215, UCANO.

29. "Lettres circulaires," 215, 219, 226, UCANO.

tune to receive the sacraments of baptism and of the Eucharist, which they approached with edification having been, by her care and upheld by the grace of God, rid of their libertine ways." Cécile "had a boundless zeal for these tasks, which, on several occasions, caused her superiors to forbid her this work in order to moderate her activities." Fearing for Cécile's health should she keep up her relentless pace as teaching mistress of the enslaved, the mother superior altered her duties. Cécile was devastated, but her superior reported, "I did not relent at her prayers and remonstrances, and I changed her to the boarders, where she acquitted herself with all the fervor that should attend a good Ursuline." Cécile's obituary gives due recognition to the obedience she rendered in performing the kind of teaching that was the norm for her sisters in French convents, but the eulogy shines with admiration for her heroic dedication to her enslaved pupils and for the evidence of the success of her efforts with them. Upon Cécile's death, "these poor black women added to their tears and sorrow the care to pray to God for her" and pressed upon the sister then in charge of instructing the enslaved "considerable sums, in view of their limited means, to say masses for the repose of her soul."[30]

The presence of enslaved Africans in Louisiana offered Ursulines another yardstick by which to measure their piety. The physical suffering and emotional distress the women experienced in pursuit of their mission represented varieties of the self-denial and mortification that were abiding legacies among the Ursulines of medieval female piety. Many lettres circulaires recount the stories of nuns who sacrificed their physical comfort and the safety of the familiar, but the notice for Renée Yviguel is the most vivid. Arriving in 1727 with the first contingent of Ursulines, she "continued indefatigable night and day for thirty-six years." Renée never had only one job; she always performed two or three occupations at once, and especially sought the ones that were "most humiliating and disgusting." In the early years of the convent, she "did what our most lowly slaves did. She ground corn and rice, chopped wood, and did the washing." For Renée Yviguel, a well-born girl from Normandy from a family that produced several Ursulines, such pious action would not only have been unimaginable in the fine stone cloisters of France, but it would have been indescribable. The analogy of a nun to a slave held vivid resonance in Louisiana and created a new marker of virtuosic piety.[31]

30. Ibid., 211–213.
31. Ibid., 228.

Piety for the Louisiana Ursulines certainly bore the marks of the active tradition that had arisen in the order's formative years during the seventeenth century. The good Ursuline acted as well as prayed. But the nun worthy of greatest praise was the sister who understood and responded to the broader implications of Ursuline piety. Spiritual motherhood was, ultimately, a missionary adventure. Like Ursula, the Louisiana nuns sailed to a strange place and encountered people and situations for which they were unprepared. Praise flowed most freely for those who showed physical courage and emotional generosity when they encountered such challenges as an unexpected crowd of unruly orphans and a classroom of enslaved Africans.

The Ursuline piety of works in New Orleans was neither safe, clean, comfortable, quiet, nor predictable. Beyond the obituary notices, other evidence shows the range of the nuns' service. In addition to the hospital and the orphanage, which were large-scale departures from their order's accustomed duties, the nuns assumed a variety of other charitable burdens in the course of the eighteenth century that also lay outside their canonical portfolio. They sheltered battered women on several occasions, gave homes and work to poor widows, dispensed alms to the victims of fire and disease, and on at least one occasion acted as arbiters when the mental health of an enslaved woman was in dispute.

French law allowed a woman to seek legal separation from her husband when she could prove he had intentionally inflicted bodily harm upon her. Numerous women sought the protection of the law in colonial Louisiana. On more than one occasion, battered women spent time at the convent after petitioning for separation because of spousal abuse. Only a few months after the Ursulines arrived, Louise Jousset Laloire filed a complaint against her husband, a surgeon in the employ of the Company of the Indies. She specifically requested that she be allowed to retire to the convent and then stayed with the nuns for more than a month in the early spring of 1728. The episode turned out badly for the nuns when a disagreement over which priest might visit the convent to hear Louise Laloire's confession blew up into a bitter controversy over the convent's relationship to the clergy. The nuns nearly left New Orleans over the incident.[32]

32. [Petition of Louise Jousset Laloire], Feb. 15, 1728, RSC; AC, C13A, XI, 275. Laloire's presence at the convent revived disagreements over whether Jesuits or Capuchins should supply the nuns with their clerical superior in the colony. Faced with the possible imposition of an undesirable superior, the Ursulines threatened to leave Louisiana for Saint Domingue. For a full account of the controversy, see Charles Ed-

This inauspicious start did not end the Ursulines' aid to the abused wives of the colony, but it made them hesitant about rendering this particular service again. Their reception of battered women was customarily at the behest of colonial officials. The Superior Council ordered the nuns to receive Françoise Ruelan in 1745, when she filed a complaint against her husband for beating her and stealing and wasting the goods of her minor children. A long entry in the chapter minutes for November 1761 explains that the nuns agreed to admit Madame Bunel as a boarder at the convent because she "had difficulties with her husband," and the convent anticipated receiving an order from officials directing them to receive her. "This was the reason we decided to admit her, despite our distaste at having laywomen in the house," they noted. Three years later, they made a similar decision, when the mother superior "assembled the councilors to propose to them in the name of Mr. Foucault, *ordonnateur,* that we receive a woman in our boarding school . . . seeing that in the name of the King, he could oblige us to do so, it was agreed."[33]

When the decision to take in abused wives was theirs to make, the Ursulines were more likely to adjust the rules of cloister: on two occasions they willingly sheltered women in need. In 1755, the mother superior called the chapter together to propose that they take in the widow of a man named Maurice and her young daughter until she could find employment elsewhere. In exchange for room and board for herself and her child, she agreed to help in the convent kitchen. The nuns decided in 1757 to allow a woman who was suffering a temporary illness and apparently had no one to look after her to spend eight days in the convent, though, since they were too crowded to offer her a private room, they noted in their chapter minutes that she would have to sleep in the student dormitory. A will executed in 1763 tells an even more touching story. A widow named Anne Galbrun

wards O'Neill, *Church and State in French Colonial Louisiana: Policy and Politics to 1732* (New Haven, Conn., 1966), 189–212.

33. RSC, *LHQ,* XIII (1930), 663; "Délibérations du Conseil," 47, 49, UCANO. The attitude of the New Orleans nuns toward such boarders parallels that of seventeenth-century French Ursulines, who generally resisted civil authorities' attempts to place at their convents as long-term or permanent boarders women under various forms of duress. The financial difficulties of many eighteenth-century French convents prompted a reversal in practice, and many Ursuline houses welcomed such boarders for the revenue they provided. See Elizabeth Rapley, *A Social History of the Cloister: Daily Life in the Teaching Monasteries of the Old Regime* (Montreal, 2001), 245–256.

called a notary to her bed in a room in the convent enclosure, where she worked as a gardener. "She declared and dictated, by her own mouth, that she is under every possible obligation to the said Ursuline nuns who have taken very good care of her for about fifteen years, during which time she lived with them, in health and in sickness, and for the good care that they still show her, which renders her sorry not to be in a position to recognize in a fitting way all their goodness."[34]

Over the course of the eighteenth century, the Louisiana nuns forged a new version of Ursuline piety when they added to their educational project a wide variety of services that tended to the social welfare of the colony's inhabitants. Caring for the sick, teaching the young, sheltering the orphaned, the abused, and the destitute, they and their convent worked to lay a stable foundation of healthy, educated people for the growing city and acted as a safety net when families failed through death, poverty, or violence to carry out the tasks society asked of them. Had theirs been a cloistered convent of contemplatives in the medieval mold, the Ursulines would perhaps have inspired the admiration of the colonists, but they would have offered no practical comfort to the men, women, and children grappling with the disease, death, and economic uncertainty that plagued New Orleans for much of the eighteenth century. Nor was the limited educational apostolate of the French Ursulines sufficient in the face of colonial realities. The *Règlemens* was silent on how Ursulines should act in a place bereft of other religious women. So the New Orleans nuns improvised, arming mothers with knowledge and dispensing the balm of human charity from a sturdy convent that proclaimed security and refuge in an unstable world.

This new variant of Ursuline piety added to the range of devout action without supplanting or eliminating preexisting elements that were engendered by the medieval spirituality of bodily sacrifice and the original teaching apostolate of the seventeenth century. The lettres circulaires celebrate the active nun, especially those who stepped beyond what was expected of French Ursulines, but they pay homage as well to those who maintained the older practices of female devotion. The obituary of Renée Yviguel, who ground corn and chopped wood, gives an impression of perpetual motion, of a nun who, above all else, worked. Yet other aspects of her religious devotion receive nearly equal space in her death notice, alerting us to the complex nature of the piety the nuns practiced in Louisiana. Renée "prac-

---

34. "Délibérations du Conseil," 43, 44, UCANO; "Testament de Anne Galbrun," Mar. 27, 1763, RSC.

ticed extreme mortifications, eating nothing but what our slaves ate or the leftovers of the nuns." Other forms of piety thrived in the convent alongside the devotion that showed itself in work. Action was central, but the nuns continued to honor the older tradition of bodily sacrifice amplified in Louisiana by the presence of the enslaved.[35]

After her arrival in 1732, Charlotte Hebert was for thirty years the nun in charge of the hospital in New Orleans. She is frequently credited in popular memory with being the first professional female pharmacist in America. She served many years as treasurer for the convent, an occupation that called for considerable accounting skills, and, when she finished with these duties at the end of the day, she turned her attention to the orphans. Charlotte worshipped with her labor, and her obituary praised her for it. It is thus somewhat jarring to learn from her lettre circulaire that she also worshipped through the mortification of her flesh. "She gave herself with zeal to all the austerities which a spirit of penance could invent." Charlotte wore a hairshirt and belts of horsehair next to her body, girdled her body with iron chains, weighed down her wrists with iron cuffs, and flailed her back every day. "She never took but one meal each day, and in that one meal she never ate that but what was most common and crude."[36]

Illness and physical affliction provided nuns with another way to offer bodily suffering as a form of worship. Marie Ramachard was ill for seven years, "the prey of the most cruel sickness, which carried her often to death's door." "She sanctified these times by her patience and sweetness." Elizabeth de Belaire's act of religious profession was delayed because of her poor health, but "she understood that this was to test her; her submission to God was total." A page of florid detail describes her death, at the age of twenty-nine. Coughing up blood, she recited psalms ceaselessly and expired "a model of extraordinary piety." Françoise Du Plessis "showed heroic patience during six or seven years of asthma which made her suffer violently." "Sometimes she coughed for a quarter of an hour without stopping. She suffered in silence." Jeanne de Cormoray was "crucified by many infirmities," which she bore heroically as an offering to God.[37]

35. "Lettres circulaires," 228, UCANO.

36. Jane Frances Heaney, *A Century of Pioneering: A History of the Ursuline Nuns in New Orleans (1727–1827)*, ed. Mary Ethel Booker Siefken (New Orleans, La., 1993), 115, 118, 122 (written as Ph.D. diss., Saint Louis University, 1949); "Lettres circulaires," 226, UCANO.

37. "Lettres circulaires," 220, 221–223, 232, 235, UCANO.

The bodily sacrifices borne by these women, especially the extreme regimes of fasting and mortification that Renée Yviguel and Charlotte Hebert practiced, are clear echoes of the female piety of medieval women. This older tradition still commanded deep admiration and respect among the eighteenth-century New Orleans nuns, though it was no longer the dominant component of feminine devotional practice. Altogether, only six of the thirty obituaries mention some form of bodily sacrifice as a feature of the deceased's piety. However, another devotional practice linked to the feminine preoccupation with the body, Communion, is mentioned in nearly all of the Louisiana obituaries and figures prominently in the devotional routine created for the laywomen's confraternity that was active in the 1730s and 1740s.

Charlotte Hebert "wisely managed all her free moments to pray before the blessed sacrament" and "had the good fortune to be the first to visit her dear Spouse in the form of the holy sacrament, which she received as often as she could," according to her obituary. The workhorse Renée Yviguel "showed much zeal in approaching the holy table as frequently as she could." A nun's eucharistic devotion was almost invariably woven into observations of her devotional routine, and chroniclers were always careful to describe her final reception of Communion at the hour of her death.[38]

The lettres circulaires chart the evolution of a new form of Ursuline piety in which elements called forth by the circumstances of the New World were grafted onto the settled constellation of devotional practices that the nuns brought with them. A parallel phenomenon reveals itself among the laywomen and girls of French descent who came within the ambit of the missionary nuns. In addition to their own avid sacramental devotion, the nuns taught laywomen to participate frequently and properly in this form of religious observance. The Règlemens that set out the regime of lessons and activities to be used in Ursuline schools paid extensive attention to preparing young girls for their first confession and Communion, and daily attendance at Mass was required of boarding students.[39] Written material produced in Louisiana demonstrates another way the Ursulines promoted eucharistic piety among the women and girls of the colony. The constitution and rules for the laywomen's confraternity, the Ladies' Congregation of the Children of Mary, sponsored by the nuns from 1730 to 1744 reveals the centrality of

38. Ibid., 195–256 (quotations on 226, 228).
39. Règlemens, 25, 49–55.

confession and Communion to the devotional routine that the nuns taught female colonists to follow and confirms the transfer of this aspect of French female piety to American laywomen.

The Eucharist is mentioned prominently in the organizational materials of the confraternity, which stipulate when confreresses were to receive the sacrament and listed occasions when the confraternity and its members should arrange for special eucharistic observances. The first two articles of the constitution of the confraternity set out the basic devotional routine for confreresses. The section opens by stating, "These practices consist of the approach to the sacraments of penance and the Eucharist on all the feasts of our Lord and the Blessed Virgin." When a fellow confreress was dangerously ill, the fourth article advised, "They will attend to procuring the reception of the last sacrament," and, when death occurred, they should arrange for a requiem Mass. The confraternity's sacristan was directed to arrange two special Masses each year, "one in honor of the Blessed Virgin, to attain her protection for all the congregationists and the other for all those who are deceased." Confraternity funds were to be used to compensate the priest who performed these Masses.[40]

Later in the century, the nuns continued to encourage sacramental observance in a variety of ways. Antoinette de Bellaire was ninety-one years old in 1792 when she wrote a series of castigating letters to Ursin Bouligny on the subject of his first Communion. The young man was well past the usual age for this religious rite of passage, and his social prominence made his poor example scandalous in the nun's judgment. In the late 1790s, the Ursulines offered their new chapel as a venue for the episcopal rite of confirmation. In 1796, Bishop Luis Peñalver y Cárdenas laid hands on thirteen young men and women in the convent chapel, and in 1800 more than fifty received confirmation there. Some of the confirmands on these occasions were students at the Ursuline school, where they undoubtedly received their preparation for the rite. Henriette Tremoulet, Maria Jones, Melicer Doufouchar DeGruy, and Celeste Gueno all appear in convent student records within months of their confirmation. As noted, young men were also confirmed there, and the venue seems to have been favored by free people of color as well. At the confirmation ceremony in 1800, Eloisa Hortanza, "free quadroon," Narciso Relon, "free mulatto," and Eulalia, "free

40. "Premier Registre de la Congrégation des Dames Enfants de Marie," 8–9, UCANO.

negress," joined a diverse throng of young people and their parents and god-parents in the small chapel within the convent enclosure.[41]

The Ursuline focus on eucharistic devotion did more than ensure that New Orleans Catholics were made vehicles for the expression of female spirituality. By emphasizing the importance of sacramental piety, the Ursu-lines also played a crucial role in ensuring that the Catholic religion was practiced in New Orleans in a way that supported the parochial clergy. Other aspects of female devotion that they observed—the piety of works and bodily sacrifice—could be conducted without benefit of clergy. The nuns' promotion of confession and Communion helped ensure that some New Orleanians went to church not only for the rites of baptism and mar-riage, which served vital social as well as religious functions, but for the more purely religious celebration of the Mass on Sundays and feast days. The nuns' inculcation of eucharistic observance helped build a congrega-tion for parish priests who otherwise faced an uphill battle to fill their pews. During the French period, the clergy complained frequently about poor church attendance and in the 1720s could rely only on officials and their wives for regular observance of the Mass. Decades later, in 1791, the bishop of Havana lamented that fewer than two hundred of the colony's inhabi-tants discharged even the minimum sacramental duties of confession and Communion in the Easter season. John Watson's report on the state of New Orleans religion in 1805 suggests who made up the faithful two hundred. "The gentlemen in general seem exempt from religious service—they give no attendance at mass."[42]

41. Antoinette de Bellaire (Sister Marie Magdelaine de Jésus) to Ursin Bouligny, Jan. 3, July 26, 27, 1792, Bouligny-Baldwin Papers, Historic New Orleans Collection; Hewitt L. Forsyth, comp. and trans., *Libro primero de confirmaciones de esta parroquia de Sn. Luis de la Nueva Orleans: Contener folios y de principio al folio 1, consigne hasta g dios no senor . . . ea servido confirmacions* (New Orleans, 1967), 47, 97–99; "General Ac-counts, October 1797–October 1812," 321, 332, 334, 335, UCANO.

42. John F. Watson, "Notia of Incidents at New Orleans in 1804 and 1805," *Ameri-can Pioneer,* II (1843), 234. On poor church attendance in French Louisiana, see Carl A. Brasseaux, "The Moral Climate of French Colonial Louisiana, 1699-1763," *Louisiana History,* XXVII (1986), 27–41; Henry P. Dart, "Cabarets of New Orleans in the French Colonial Period," *LHQ,* XIX (1936), 577–583; Marcel Giraud, *A History of French Louisi-ana,* V, *The Company of the Indies, 1721-1731,* trans. Brian Pearce (Baton Rouge, La., 1991), 66, 270, 288; and Emily Clark, "'By All the Conduct of Their Lives': A Lay-women's Confraternity in New Orleans, 1730-1744," *William and Mary Quarterly,* 3d

Whether or not the eucharistic devotion practiced and taught by the New Orleans Ursulines was directly descended from the kind of female medieval piety that centered on food and the body, women formed the core constituency of communicants in the city at the turn of the nineteenth century. We also have sketchy but convincing evidence that portrays the nuns' role in creating and sustaining devotional habits that supported the church-centered, sacramental religion over which male clergy presided. Yet, although women faithfully practiced eucharistic devotion, a particularly enthusiastic aspect of their worship took a different form.

The Virgin Mary served as the chief source of inspiration and guidance for the active piety of charity and service that marked the lives of nuns and laywomen alike in New Orleans. The Ursuline writers of the seventeenth century had advanced an elaborate new hagiography for the Virgin that emphasized her multiple roles as redeemer, teacher, apostle, and protector. Her example legitimated and animated the Ursuline educational mission. The *Règlemens* tells us that invocations of her powers of protection and intercession accompanied imitation of her virtues, directing that Ursuline schoolgirls offer prayers to her twice a day and call on her to help them prepare for their first Communion.[43] The lettres circulaires, chapter minutes, and records of the laywomen's confraternity indicate that the *Règlemens* achieved its design. Marian devotion took root in Louisiana and permeated the prayer lives and senses of the colony's women, vowed and lay alike. There was little doubt that the mother of God was their model for an active life of charity and service, yet in Louisiana her example was put to work in new ways. Under the aegis of the Ursuline mission, colonial women wrote a new chapter in lay Catholic female piety that paralleled the nuns' achievement in which European legacies survived but were transformed by their adaptive expression in America.

The eight laywomen who made their way to the temporary Ursuline convent in 1730 and asked the nuns to help them set up a confraternity honoring the Virgin prefaced their request with a tribute to the "Ursuline religious of this city who are known for the glory of God and for the health of souls and for honoring the very blessed Virgin in all this colony." Pages of text in the confraternity's record book illustrate how the confreresses carried out their purposes, which did not necessarily match perfectly with those

Ser., LIV (1997), 788. Joseph, bishop of Havana, to Theodoro Tirso Henriquez, Nov. 29, 1791, AANO, reports the dismal rate of Easter observance.

43. *Règlemens*, 62.

of the male clergy who authorized the women's work. Pope Clement XII issued a plenary indulgence to the confraternity in 1740, and its text precedes the constitution and rule in the organization's record book. Confreresses would receive an indulgence so long as they confessed and received Communion on the principal feast of the congregation and prayed "for the union of Christian princes, for the extirpation of heresies, and the exaltation of our holy mother Church." They might receive additional indulgences if they observed all four feast days of the confraternity by attending Mass and if they gave alms to the poor, reconciled with their enemies, attended burials, walked in processions displaying the consecrated host, and prayed for the souls of the dead with the Pater Noster.[44]

When the confreresses laid out their purposes themselves, they reflected a priority of interests that did not match the preoccupations of the papal indulgence. The women noted that they "professed to serve the Blessed Virgin, to honor her not only by their prayers, but also by their morals and by all the conduct of their lives." Such conduct would include ministering to the poor, attending funerals, and praying for the dead, but the women neglected to include praying "for the union of Christian princes, for the extirpation of heresies, and the exaltation of our holy mother Church." Nor did they make a point of talking of reconciliation with enemies and walking in sacramental processions. They did, however, vow to emulate the teaching ministry of their patron, the Virgin, promising to instruct their children and those they held enslaved. And they chose the feast of the Immaculate Conception of the Virgin as their principal festival and days celebrating the Purification of the Virgin, the Assumption of the Virgin, the Nativity of the Virgin, and the Holy Rosary as their four subsidiary feasts. When they gathered on these days to confess and receive Communion and win the indulgence promised by the pope, they honored above all the maternal saint who inspired them.[45]

The devotional routine and customs of the confraternity reflected the women's preoccupation with the Virgin. The first, brief article of the confraternity's constitution directs confreresses to receive the sacraments of penance and Communion on feast days, but the much longer second article sets out the details of daily devotion based on a steady rhythm of Marian

44. "Premier Registre," 3–5, UCANO. For more on the laywomen's confraternity, see Chapter 2, above; and Clark, "'By All the Conduct of Their Lives,'" *WMQ*, 3d Ser., LIV (1997), 769–794.

45. "Premier Registre," 6–7, UCANO.

adoration punctuated by more occasional attendance at Mass. Recitation of the rosary was the anchor of the daily private prayer routine. Adoration of the Virgin dominated this devotion, which consisted of a sequence of fifteen decades of the prayer known as the Ave Maria, or Hail Mary, followed at the end of each decade by the Lord's Prayer, or Our Father, and accompanied at each decade by a meditation on one of the mysteries of salvation recognized by the church. On Sundays and feast days, confreresses made their way to their assembly room at the convent, where they recited the rosary and prayed to Mary to intercede on behalf of deceased confreresses. When the confraternity council met, they ended their session with an anthem to the Virgin, and, when the prefect stepped down from office, she begged her patron saint's pardon for any offense she might have given.[46]

The special prayers used by the confreresses offer striking insight into the importance of Marian devotion for these women and show their imagined relationship among themselves, Mary, and God. On the principal feast day of the confraternity, the Immaculate Conception, the prefect offered an oration before the enshrined statue of the Virgin in the confraternity's assembly room:

> Very Blessed Virgin and most honored mother of God, Queen of heaven and Earth, daughter of the father, mother of the son, wife of the Holy Spirit and temple of the most august Trinity, refuge of sinners, and of all those who have hope in you: We prostrate ourselves at the feet of your majesty, with an unspeakable register of the faults which we have committed against your service and of which we ask your most humble pardon, with the desire to do better we promise you, in the presence of the most holy Trinity and the entire court of heaven, to hold you as our most special mother, Lady and Advocate. We supplicate you from the bottom of our hearts.[47]

Here, this eighteenth-century prayer portrays Mary with the same august attributes conferred on her by such seventeenth-century Ursuline writers as Jeanne des Anges, whose *Entretiens spirituels* cast the Virgin as the vessel of redemption without whom there can literally be no Trinity. Recognizing her enormous power and key position, the prefect asks not simply that she intercede on behalf of the confreresses to gain mercy for their sins but also that she specifically pardon transgressions that have offended her

46. Ibid., 8, 10–12.
47. Ibid., 12.

in particular. Although not a confession in the strict sacramental sense, this passage honors Mary with the same admission of guilt and offering of contrition that are the principal features of sacramental penance.

The prayer continues with a supplication that Mary help secure confreresses' salvation at death:

> I submit this congregation to your holy direction, rendering to your grandeur the homage, the honor, the obedience which you deserve in the quality of your little subjects and very humble daughters. We have total confidence in your merciful bounty and believe we will feel the effects of your holy maternal protection and to that end we render ourselves to your very dear Son, supplicating you most humbly to help us at the hour of our death to give us all your holy blessing.[48]

When a woman joined the confraternity, she stood before the assembled membership and recited a prayer prescribed by the constitution:

> Blessed Virgin, Mary mother of God and ever Virgin, I choose you today as Lady and mistress, patron and advocate, and propose that I will never let you go, nor will I say or do anything against you, nor will I permit anyone under me to do so. Nothing will be done against your honor. I supplicate you most affectionately to please receive me as your perpetual servant, assist me in all my actions, and do not abandon me at the hour of my death.[49]

The women who joined the New Orleans confraternity trusted in the example and advocacy of Mary in their own quest for salvation. Hers was the life they imitated, hers the compassion they sought most fervently when they contemplated the judgment that would come at the end of their days.

The Virgin's image was deployed everywhere to inspire her vowed and lay daughters. The confreresses asked that they be allowed to set up an altar dedicated to the Virgin in a shrine holding a statue of the saint. A page in the confraternity register carefully records gifts totaling more than four hundred livres for a gilt image of the Virgin and a throne and gauze scarf to be used when it was carried in procession. Catherine Lavadiere, who was mother superior at the convent from 1762 through 1767, was so devoted to the Virgin that she had statues of her placed over every doorway in the convent. The New Orleans nuns acquired yet another statue of Mary in 1785 to

48. Ibid.
49. Ibid.

which at least one miraculous intervention was attributed. Françoise Alzas, a professed Ursuline from the French convent of Pont Saint Esprit, battled the opposition of Spanish clerics and financial difficulties to travel with two other Ursulines to join the New Orleans community. Despairing of ever overcoming the barriers to her transfer to Louisiana, she came across a diminutive, old, abandoned wooden statue of the Virgin in her French convent's attic. She promised to carry the image to New Orleans if the saint should answer her prayers and remove the obstacles to her plan. Françoise Alzas was given permission to travel to Louisiana the next day.[50]

In the privacy of their personal daily devotions, in ceremonial gatherings, at dramatic turning points, the nuns and laywomen of New Orleans called on their "Lady and mistress, patron and advocate," to show them how to discharge these roles themselves and to find the route to salvation. In imitating her, they imitated Christ, yet Mary offered them a model that was more susceptible to absolute emulation than anything available to men, who shared Christ's sex. A priest could act as the conduit for God's grace in the miracle of transubstantiation, but only a woman could duplicate the miracle of birth that made God incarnate and was the act without which there could never be the miracle of the Mass. Only a woman could fully imitate the maternal ministry of the Virgin, bringing new souls into the world and teaching them the way to God. Human men could never enact the fundamental miracle of incarnation. Priests could emulate the miracle symbolically when they presided over the transformation of bread and wine into sacred flesh and blood, but a layman could approach the mystery of God made flesh only by receiving the sacrament of Communion. He had no clear and active role in evoking the miracle, and his relationship to it was encapsulated in the sacramental event, which could not be naturally integrated into the broader rhythms and purposes of his life. All women, on the other hand, could reproduce the physical and spiritual maternity of Mary and had a way to incorporate her repertoire of holy actions into the cadence of their daily lives.

The imitation of some of Mary's attributes not only pointed the way to personal salvation; it gave women the power to transform their earthly families, their community, and not least themselves through learning,

50. Ibid., 189, 234; "Journal depuis 1727 jusqu'en 1853," 106–107, UCANO. The wooden statue brought by Françoise Alzas is known in the convent today as "Sweetheart." It is displayed in a museum at the New Orleans convent, decorated with a jeweled crown and surrounded by the written petitions of the faithful.

teaching, and service. The content and form of the Marian devotion of the New Orleans nuns and confreresses did not represent a departure from contemporary French experience. And its potential to empower women had long been in place in France, supplying the early Ursulines with the rationale for their apostolate. But the resonance of Marian devotion in Louisiana was different. When colonial women asserted their faith in Mary's protection, it was from within an environment far more dangerous and unpredictable than French town and countryside. When they displayed her image and erected shrines to her, they signaled their connection to and trust in what was known in an alien place. When they recognized the attributes of her transcendent power in their prayers, they also recognized their own capacity to master the difficult and strange circumstances of colonial life. And when they imitated Mary, the informed teacher of the Visitation, by extending education to a diverse community of colonial women, literacy became a marker and a tool with special meaning.

An unusually high rate of female literacy is among the most striking results of the emulation of the Virgin's example in New Orleans. Paradoxically, it is in the documents created to record the socially recognized subjugation of woman to man that the main evidence for New Orleans women's literacy lies, revealing that wives were not always inferior to their husbands in all things. In French Louisiana, the bride and groom customarily signed or made their marks in the parish marriage register, whether they were free or enslaved.[51] Records exist for most of the French period, from the early 1730s until the mid-1760s, allowing for comparison between male and female literacy rates at the beginning of the Ursuline presence in New Orleans and at a point thirty years later, when a full generation of the city's native-born girls would have grown up in the presence of their school.[52]

51. The analysis of literacy that follows is based on signatures in the sacramental registers of Saint Louis Cathedral, New Orleans. Signing ability serves as the most common indicator for literacy when there are no quantifiable records that speak specifically to the capacity of men and women to read. Surveys of signature literacy are generally based on some official record source that provides the signatures or marks of the broadest possible cross-section of a community over a significant period of time. Marriage registers are especially useful for constructing comparisons between male and female literacy rates because there are equal numbers of men and women represented among the principal parties. On the usefulness of marriage registers for measuring literacy as well as a discussion of the difficulty of estimating reading ability, see Houston, *Literacy in Early Modern Europe*, 117–129.

52. Unfortunately, a change in the way entries were made in the marriage register

TABLE 2. *Literacy by Sex, 1731–1732*

Couples	Literate Women (%)	Illiterate Women (%)	Literate Men (%)	Illiterate Men (%)
40	13 (32.5)	27 (67.5)	19 (47.5)	21 (52.5)

Source: SLC-B1.

In the early years of the Ursuline apostolate, the majority of Louisianians were illiterate. Only 40 percent of individuals who married in 1731 and 1732 could sign their names. Most of them were French-born. Of the forty marriages performed at Saint Louis Church in 1731 and 1732, thirty-five were between natives of France. Three enslaved couples married during this two-year period, two free people of color exchanged vows with one another, and a Frenchman married an Indian woman. Thirteen of the brides, or about one-third, signed, compared with just less than half of the grooms. Male literacy exceeded female literacy by 15 percent. All of the enslaved who married verified their presence with a mark, but the free man of color who married in 1731 signed his name (see Table 2).

Thirty years later, the literacy profile in New Orleans was significantly different, and the increase in white female literacy was particularly dramatic. For 1760–1762, overall literacy for whites had risen to 71 percent, an increase of 31 percent over the figure for 1731–1732.[53] At 70 percent, white male literacy had risen an impressive 17 percent, but the most dramatic

------

in the Spanish period makes an analysis over the entire colonial period impossible. From the late 1760s at Saint Louis Church in New Orleans, priests entered and signed records for free and enslaved people of color and did not give the parties an opportunity to sign the record of their nuptials themselves. In the marriage registers for whites, some records were signed by the bride and groom, but there are no examples of entries bearing the marks of illiterate men and women. Perhaps during the Spanish period, the clergy gave literate white couples the option of signing their marriage record but did not extend this courtesy to illiterate whites or people of color. The changes in practices can be traced in the following sacramental registers: SLC-B4, SLC-B6, SLC-M1, SLC-M2, SLC-M3, SLC-M4, SLC-M5.

53. None of the twenty-two slave couples who were married between 1760 and 1762 signed, nor did either partner in the only marriage between free people of color. A comparison between literacy rates for 1731–1732 and 1760–1762 is thus made for free couples of European descent only.

TABLE 3. *Literacy of Whites by Sex, 1731–1732 and 1760–1762*

Years	Literate Women (%)	Illiterate Women (%)	Literate Men (%)	Illiterate Men (%)
1731–1732	13 (36)	23 (64)	19 (53)	17 (47)
1760–1762	38 (72)	15 (28)	37 (70)	16 (30)

Source: SLC-B4.

gains came among white women. Of the brides of European descent, 72 percent could sign their names, an increase in signature literacy for this group of 36 percent, bringing male and female literacy for free whites in New Orleans essentially to parity (see Table 3).

Although a direct connection is impossible to prove, the Ursuline school was likely responsible for the impressive literacy of New Orleans women in the early 1760s. Certainly, the increase in female literacy in Louisiana cannot be categorized as simply part of a larger French pattern. Female literacy lagged behind male literacy in France, a phenomenon evident in the literacy records of French women in Louisiana. Of the brides born in France who married in Louisiana between 1760 and 1762, only 42 percent were literate. Young women born in Louisiana, however, were much more likely to sign their names to their marriage records. Of the creole brides, 80 percent could sign their names. In other words, girls who were born and grew up in New Orleans were nearly twice as likely to be literate as French girls who came to Louisiana and married there (see Table 4).[54]

The absence of any educational institution in Louisiana for men during this period, by contrast, may explain why more than a few literate brides went to the altar of Saint Louis Church with illiterate husbands.[55] In 60 per-

54. Most studies of French literacy are based on surveys of marriage registers collected by a nineteenth-century school teacher, Louis Maggiolo. François Furet and Jacques Ozouf, *Reading and Writing: Literacy in France from Calvin to Jules Ferry* (Cambridge, 1982), is the most comprehensive of these. Houston, *Literacy in Early Modern Europe*, 135, provides the figures for female literacy in Lyon that illustrate the gap between male and female literacy.

55. Provision for the education of boys in New Orleans was sporadic throughout the colonial period. The Capuchin missionaries established a small school in New Orleans that was active between 1725 and 1731. It was usually staffed by a single schoolmaster and continuously struggled for sufficient funds. The maximum number of stu-

TABLE 4. *White Female Literacy, 1760–1762*

	Literate (%)	Illiterate (%)
French-born brides	5 (42)	7 (58)
Creole brides	33 (80)	8 (20)

Source: SLC-B4.

cent of marriages between 1760 and 1762, bride and groom were both literate; in 19 percent of marriages, both spouses were illiterate. In the remaining 21 percent of the couples, only one spouse was literate. In the eighteenth century, the expectation generally would have been that, if one spouse was illiterate, it would be the wife.[56] In New Orleans, however, this was not the case. Eleven couples went to the altar between 1760 and 1762 with unequal

---

dents recorded in attendance was nine. See Samuel Wilson, Jr., *The Capuchin School in New Orleans, 1725: The First School in Louisiana* (New Orleans, 1961), 20–27; Claude L. Vogel, *The Capuchins in French Louisiana (1722–1766)* (Washington, D.C., 1928), 69–83. There is no mention of a school for males in New Orleans again until 1771, when official Spanish plans called for one to be established. The books for the school's library were still stored in unopened boxes in 1780, however, indicating that plans for the school might never have been realized (Roger Philip McCutcheon, "Libraries in New Orleans, 1771–1833," *LHQ*, XX [1937], 152–158). Educational opportunity for boys in early Spanish Louisiana was generally poor (Caroline Maude Burson, *The Stewardship of Don Esteban Miró, 1782–1792: A Study of Louisiana Based Largely on the Documents in New Orleans* [New Orleans, 1940], 264–265). Late in the eighteenth century, the situation improved somewhat. In 1795, there were four schools for boys of European descent and one for free boys of color, including one Spanish-language school with about one hundred students and three French-language schools. See Joseph Maria de Rivas to Luis Peñalver y Cárdenas, bishop of Louisiana, Sept. 3, 1795, and the Reverend Antonio de Sedella to Peñalver y Cárdenas, Oct. 22, 1795, both in AANO (photostatic copies of original manuscripts).

56. On differences between male and female literacy rates in both Europe and America, see Houston, *Literacy in Early Modern Europe*, 134–136; Furet and Ozouf, *Reading and Writing*, 32–39; Kenneth A. Lockridge, *Literacy in Colonial New England: An Enquiry into the Social Context of Literacy in the Early Modern West* (New York, 1974), 38–42. Monaghan, *Learning to Read and Write*, is the most recent study of early Anglo-American literacy acquisition and provides a useful summary of signature literacy (esp. 383–385).

TABLE 5. *Literacy within White Marriages, 1760–1762*

Both spouses literate	32 (60%)
Both spouses illiterate	10 (19)
Literate husband/illiterate wife	5 (9.4)
Literate wife/illiterate husband	6 (11.3)

Source: SLC-B4.

literacy skills. In five instances, the husband was literate, and the wife was unable to sign; in the other six, the wife could sign, and the husband could only make a mark. Five of the literate wives who took illiterate husbands were born in Louisiana (see Table 5).

Literacy rates for inhabitants of African descent cannot be determined. The sacramental records do not record enough marriages of enslaved and free people of color to make a judgment. Evidence suggests, however, that some free girls of color were educated. At least two free girls of color attended the Ursuline boarding school, where reading and writing were part of the curriculum, one in the 1730s, and another in 1801. And, although the sacramental records in New Orleans cease to be a resource for determining signature literacy for free people of color during the Spanish regime, signed notarial records from this period confirm that some free women of color could sign their names. Luison Brunet, for example, whose granddaughter was a student at the Ursuline school around the turn of the nineteenth century, signed various bills of sale in the 1770s and 1780s. The confident signature of Marianne Dubreuil, who had once been the enslaved servant of Marie Payen Dubreuil, herself a member of the confraternity sponsored by the nuns, also appears in notarial records.[57] Such scanty evidence makes crediting the literacy of free women of color to the Ursulines impossible, but their school must have created a general expectation that basic literacy was the norm for the city's free women. The ability of Luison Brunet and Marianne Dubreuil to sign their names would not have surprised notaries in a city where women were just as likely as men to be literate.

The educational attainment of New Orleans women was, however, re-

57. For signatures of Luison Brunet, see Acts of Andrés Almonester y Roxas, January–May 1775, Feb. 14, 1775, 76, Acts of Juan Bautista Garic, Nov. 7, 1778, X, 501, Acts of Rafael Perdomo, July 1, Feb. 3, 1784, V, 75, 101, all in NANO. Marianne Dubreuil's signature appears on an act of sale, Acts of Fernando Rodriguez, Dec. 20, 1784, III, 916, NANO.

markable for its age. In late colonial British North America, for example, the male literacy rate was typically double the rate for women. In Europe, the numbers varied, but the gap between male and female rates was constant. Using signatory ability as a measure, men were consistently more likely to be literate than women. The parity between male and female literacy in New Orleans in the 1760s was an exceptional phenomenon.[58]

No letters or diaries tell us how the men of New Orleans felt about the city's high rate of female literacy. Notaries and clerics might have been habituated to the regularity with which women matched men in their signatory abilities, but we do not know whether they found this feminine proficiency praiseworthy or unseemly, or, indeed, whether they remarked on it at all. Nor do we know whether illiterate men experienced any discomfort when confronted by the superior skills of a woman. Did it embarrass the well-born Vincent Rillieux when he could not sign his name along with his sisters as his family gathered before a notary in 1760 to witness a marriage contract? Did the farmer Jean LaBranche and the soldier François Closeau resent when their Louisiana-born brides Suzanne Marchand and Marie Anne Daublin took quill in hand to sign their names in a practiced hand next to their husband's crudely formed crosses? What, in the end, did it mean to New Orleans society to have a female population that was unusually literate?

In a practical sense, husbands and fathers were not customarily the only members of the family who could read a contract before they signed it. When a young woman married, although her father decided the terms of her dowry, she did not have to rely on him to tell her what they were. If her husband should later fall into debt, he could not deceive her about the extent of her marriage portion or otherwise use her ignorance to his advantage. The world of the written word was not a mystery to New Orleans women, and so when they visited a notary to have a pleading drawn up to bring suit against a debtor or stood before a court recorder to give testimony

58. Cott, *The Bonds of Womanhood*, 103; Houston, *Literacy in Early Modern Europe*, 131–137. Monaghan, *Learning to Read and Write*, 286, 383–385, notes increased interest in promoting female literacy in the British mainland colonies after the middle of the eighteenth century, but, with the exception of female Connecticut deed signers, British colonial signature literacy fell below that of New Orleans women in 1760. Allan Greer's findings for mid-eighteenth-century urban women in French colonial Quebec, where Ursulines were also present, show higher literacy rates than for most British colonial female contemporaries, though they are not as high as those for New Orleans. See Greer, "Pattern of Literacy," *Histoire Sociale / Social History*, XI (1978), 299.

in their own defense, they could ensure that what they said was what was recorded. In the increasingly formalized public arena, where transactions were fixed by the act of writing, literate women had equal access to the power of unmediated comprehension. In New Orleans, women not only possessed certain legal rights, they had a powerful tool that helped them exercise them.

To be sure, there is ample evidence in the legal records of eighteenth-century New Orleans of attempts to take advantage of the inferior status assigned to women. But the same records frequently bear witness to women who brought to court formal complaints of mistreatment and assertion of their rights, testifying to a sense of confidence and power. Jean Baptiste LaCroix, a settler on the shores of Lake Pontchartrain just outside the city, found such qualities not at all to his taste. He complained to the Superior Council in 1748 that his wife, Jeanne Hervieux, was a spendthrift, changed her mind too much, neglected her housework, and spent too much time at her mother's house, from which she now refused to return. He asked the council to force his wife to relinquish the clothes she had taken with her and to pay for half the debts contracted during their marriage, and he begged the council's permission to "take passage to France in order to make a marriage that will hold better than here."[59] LaCroix's plea suggests that he expected to find more compliant, traditionally submissive women in France than in Louisiana. Widespread literacy among the colony's women might well have helped to create an assertive female population that dismayed men like Jean Baptiste LaCroix.[60]

59. Petition of Jean Baptiste LaCroix, Apr. 30, 1748, RSC. For examples of women's engaging in business transactions and court pleadings, see Acts and Court Proceedings of Pedro Pedesclaux, 1788–1803, Acts and Court Proceedings of Carlos Ximenes, 1790–1803, Acts and Court Proceedings of Francisco Broutin, 1790–1799, Acts and Court Proceedings of Narciso Broutin, 1799–1804, Acts of Andrés Almonester y Roxas, 1771–1782, Acts of Juan Bautista Garic, 1771–1779, Acts of Rafael Perdomo, 1782–1790, Acts of Leonardo Mazange, 1779–1783, Acts of Fernando Rodríguez, 1783–1787, all in NANO.

60. A number of scholars take a less sanguine view of the benefits of the education provided by French teaching sisters, suggesting that it was an obstacle to women's exposure to the more modern and rigorous intellectual content of the Enlightenment. See, for example, Jean Perrel, "Les écoles de filles dans la France d'Ancien Régime," in Donald N. Baker and Patrick J. Harrigan, eds., *The Making of Frenchmen: Current Directions in the History of Education in France, 1679-1979* (Waterloo, Ontario, 1980), 75–83; Martine Sonnet, *L'éducation des filles au temps des Lumières* (Paris, 1987); Linda

The curriculum laid out in the Ursuline *Règlemens* prescribed regular instruction in arithmetic as well as reading and writing. Students were to learn to recognize both Arabic and Roman numerals and to count to one thousand. Using beads, they were given simple addition and subtraction problems before advancing to complex calculations with pen and paper. They were next given word problems that taught them how to compute the cost of goods sold in a variety of measures and currencies. Although designed to equip young women with only sufficient numeracy to manage a household, these basic mathematical skills, when linked to literacy, would have enabled women to negotiate the realms of commerce and law with some degree of confidence, and there are indications that they did so. Notarial acts record women's direct participation in transactions well beyond the realm of petty marketing and housekeeping accounts. The civil law that governed colonial Louisiana allowed women to retain control of financial assets they held when they entered a marriage; literacy and numeracy supplied them with the skills necessary to manage those assets. A wide range of women, married and unmarried, appeared regularly before New Orleans notaries to execute pleadings, contracts, mortgages, and promissory notes, encounters with the realms of law and business that were not typically shared by women in British colonial America.[61]

In the eighteenth century, literacy and numeracy opened doors for women—particularly women of the laboring classes. Despite the academic limits of an educational tradition rooted in religious purposes, the women who attended Ursuline schools in both France and Louisiana acquired skills that gave them a degree of autonomy and power in their relations with men. The learning of New Orleans women had the capacity to shape gender relations in ways that were more favorable to women. Women might be thought intellectually inferior to men, but the realities of daily life in the colony vitiated that truism. Men could not count on feminine ignorance to give them the advantage in the myriad transactions that made use of pen and paper, nor could they rely on it as the basis for male claims to general superi-

---

Timmermans, *L'Accès des femmes à la culture (1598-1715): Un débat d'idées de Saint François de Sales à la Marquise de Lambert* (Paris, 1993). The major exception to this historiographical trend is Furet and Ozouf, *Reading and Writing*.

61. *Règlemens*, 84–86. These financial transactions are documented in the notarial records referenced in note 59, above. For the contrasting case of women in colonial Connecticut, see Cornelia Hughes Dayton, *Women before the Bar: Gender, Law, and Society in Connecticut, 1639–1789* (Chapel Hill, N.C., 1995), 79.

ority.[62] At least one eighteenth-century French commentator disapproved of women's sharing equal literacy skills with men because it undermined what he viewed as the natural inferiority of women. "All women should be prohibited from learning to write and even read," wrote Restif de La Bretonne in 1777. "This would preserve them from loose thoughts, confining them to useful tasks about the house, instilling in them respect for the first sex, which would be all the more carefully instructed in these things for the second sex having been neglected."[63] In New Orleans, the second sex was not neglected, and it was paradoxically by women enclosed, not by their households, but by a cloister that they were instructed in the skills La Bretonne would have denied them.

Literacy was only one of several ways in which the convent influenced the experience of the city's women, molding their sense of their place in the cosmic order and teaching them through prayer, precept, example, and sacred tradition to become women with the power to shape their families and communities. The piety fostered by the French Ursulines crossed the Atlantic to influence the behavior of colonial women and shape the developing institutions of church and community. Old patterns of medieval spirituality that emphasized eucharistic piety remained central to women's devotional lives and supported clerical aspirations for parochial loyalty, but it was the newer piety born in the seventeenth century that had the most profound impact on the colony and its inhabitants. A piety of action, organized and executed through corporate bodies of lay and vowed women, provided much of the institutional framework that supported colonial society. The centrality of female role models and imagery to devotional practice, together with the nuns' educational mission, influenced gender norms and expectations. Women claimed a superior form of holy emulation that was unique to their sex, and it, in turn, gave them an alternative to the Aristotelian assessment of female imperfection as they forged their identities

62. On the increasing advantage of the literate in such transactions, see Furet and Ozouf, *Reading and Writing*, esp. 302–320; and Lee Soltow and Edward Stevens, *The Rise of Literacy and the Common School in the United States: A Socioeconomic Analysis to 1870* (Chicago, 1981), 45–47.

63. N. Restif de La Bretonne, *Les gynographes ou idées de deux honnêtes femmes sur un projet de règlement proposé à tout l'Europe pour mettre les femmes à leur place et opérer le bonheur des deux sexes* (Paris, 1777), quoted in Furet and Ozouf, *Reading and Writing*, 340 n. 4.

and negotiated their relationships with men. Motherhood was valorized and made the rationale for female literacy, which endowed women with a practical power that mitigated the conventions of male dominance. In all of these ways, female piety, the active expression of religious belief, insinuated itself into the web of experience that was colonial New Orleans.

The French female piety promoted by the Ursulines, with its emphasis on education and corporately organized action, constructed both gender roles and society in the colony along particular lines. Free white women in colonial Louisiana, sometimes even women of color, were expected to be literate, thus guaranteeing a female population that could read the terms of a marriage contract and a bill of sale. The men of the colony claimed the privilege of their sex to govern, but in the market and in the courts they negotiated the practical limits of that privilege with women who might equal or surpass them in the lettered acuity necessary to succeed in the public realm. Beyond the market and the courts lay the commonweal, and here, too, feminine piety left its mark. Nuns and laywomen supplied the city with many of the social services deemed essential to maintaining a well-ordered society. They looked after the poor, the sick, and the homeless, and they sheltered women from violent husbands. Key institutions and acts of benevolence and education lay wholly in the hands of women, who played a central part in establishing and maintaining the infrastructure of social services that anchored a growing city.

part two

TRANSFORMATIONS OLD WORLD TO NEW

The Seven Years' War (1756–1763) brought an end to French control in Louisiana. By the terms of the secret Treaty of Fontainebleau, executed in November 1762, Louis XV transferred New Orleans and the Louisiana Territory west of the Mississippi to his Bourbon cousin, Charles III of Spain. The cession of Louisiana to Spain did not produce an abrupt political and cultural transition. The first Spanish governor, Antonio de Ulloa, did not take possession of the colony until 1767. He was forced from Louisiana late in 1768 by a rebellious cabal of French planters. The ringleaders of the revolt were deeply in debt and feared that the imposition of Spain's rigid economic policies would spell certain financial doom for their precarious enterprises. The French colonial Superior Council of Louisiana, which had not dissolved itself after the transfer and was at the center of the rebellion, presided over an outlaw government until the Spanish general, Alexander O'Reilly, arrived to quash it in the summer of 1769.[1]

O'Reilly quickly promulgated Spanish law and moved to install Iberian government at the local level by establishing in New Orleans a Cabildo, the traditional Spanish colonial town council. In naming to terms on the Cabildo a number of French creoles who had shown loyalty to Spain, O'Reilly presciently acknowledged the city's powerful ethnic roots. Spaniards never outnumbered the French and French creoles in Louisiana, and, although Spanish became the official language of church and state, the lingua franca and the cultural milieu of New Orleans and its environs remained French. Nevertheless, the Iberians' vigorous government and ambitions for the colony brought significant change to Louisiana, particularly in its demography. The immigration of French men and women to Louisiana stopped for several years at the end of the Seven Years' War and was negligible dur-

---

1. Daniel H. Usner, Jr., *Indians, Settlers, and Slaves in a Frontier Exchange Economy: The Lower Mississippi Valley before 1783* (Chapel Hill, N.C., 1992), 116–119, offers a concise overview of the rebellion and its suppression.

ing the rest of the century. Meanwhile, new groups made their way to the colony. Iberian officials and soldiers were among the first, of course, along with another group propelled to Louisiana by the changing boundaries drawn by war: Acadian refugees looking for a Francophone haven after their expulsion from an increasingly intolerant British Canada. They were joined by hundreds of Canary Islanders who began arriving in 1777, recruited by the Spanish government in a direct effort to increase Louisiana's population. The presence of Anglo-American and British merchants and their families grew as Spain modified and expanded its trade relations and the port of New Orleans gained importance with the settlement of the Trans-Appalachian United States.[2]

In the largest numbers of all, newly enslaved Africans poured into Louisiana. Between 1766 and 1788, the enslaved population of the New Orleans region increased by more than fifteen thousand, and most of the expansion came from the influx of new Africans. At the same time, even as the population of enslaved people mushroomed, Spanish laws that relaxed the procedures for manumission paved the way for dramatic growth in the city's number of free people of color, from ninety-seven in 1771 to more than fifteen hundred in 1805, when they made up 19 percent of the population of New Orleans. Together, the growth of all these different populations contributed to a substantial expansion in the size of the general population of Louisiana, from about ten thousand at the end of the French period to fifty thousand inhabitants at the end of the eighteenth century.[3]

Economic developments that moved the colony from its long frontier infancy toward staple crop plantation agriculture and commercial prominence matched this growth and diversification of Louisiana's population. Spanish policy favored the systematic enterprises of wealthy planters and herders and encouraged merchant activity in New Orleans. Planters expanded and consolidated their landholdings and invested in more slaves

2. Approximately one thousand Acadians immigrated to Louisiana between 1757 and 1770. See Carl A. Brasseaux, *The Founding of New Acadia: The Beginnings of Acadian Life in Louisiana, 1765–1803* (Baton Rouge, La., 1987), 73, 91; Gilbert C. Din, *The Canary Islanders of Louisiana* (Baton Rouge, La., 1988), xi, 51–52.

3. Gwendolyn Midlo Hall, *Africans in Colonial Louisiana: The Development of Afro-Creole Culture in the Eighteenth Century* (Baton Rouge, La., 1992), 278–287; Kimberly Hanger, *Bounded Lives, Bounded Places: Free Black Society in Colonial New Orleans, 1769–1803* (Durham, N.C., 1997), 22–23; Light Townsend Cummins, "The Final Years of Colonial Louisiana," in Bennett H. Wall, ed., *Louisiana: A History*, 3d ed. (Wheeling, Ill., 1997), 70.

to farm timber, tobacco, indigo, and, in the last decade of the eighteenth century, sugar. The fortunes of Louisiana tobacco rose in the 1780s at the expense of war-torn Revolutionary America, and refining techniques perfected in the mid-1790s allowed Louisiana sugarcane planters to profit when war and revolution disrupted the supply from Saint Domingue and other Caribbean sources.[4]

Louisiana's new prosperity came at a cost to the fabric of its community. Only the wealthy could capitalize fully on the opportunities to expand staple crop agriculture, and small producers found it increasingly difficult to maneuver in the regulated environment of Spanish Louisiana. Disparities in income among the colony's inhabitants widened. An elite that was not only wealthy but also controlling had definitely emerged by the last decade of the eighteenth century. This class division was paralleled by a deepening racial divide. Thousands of newly enslaved Africans worked the expanding plantations. Relations between planters and slaves hardened into the tense, repressive mode that characterized mature slave societies. Occupying an uneasy middle ground between rebellious new Africans and increasingly race-conscious whites stood a large population of free people of color, seeking their own place in a colony of crowded aspiration and narrowing opportunity.[5]

Spanish rule and passage into the last third of the eighteenth century mark distinct points of transition for Louisiana, but the Ursulines' transformation from French nuns to New World creoles was sometimes tied more to the internal rhythms of their convent community and its needs than it was to larger geopolitical and economic movements. A metamorphosis of the convent economy, for example, began with the nuns' arrival

4. John G. Clark, *New Orleans, 1718–1812: An Economic History* (Baton Rouge, La., 1970), 161–180, 183–249; Hall, *Africans in Colonial Louisiana*, 276–277; Usner, *Indians, Settlers, and Slaves*, 159, 188–190, 216–218, 278–285.

5. Hall, *Africans in Colonial Louisiana*, 276–277; Hanger, *Bounded Lives;* Usner, *Indians, Settlers, and Slaves*, 159, 188–190, 216–218, 278–285. For a discussion of the changing nature of European attitudes toward enslaved Africans linked to the development of colonial enterprises from societies with enslaved laborers to full-fledged slave societies, see Ira Berlin, "From Creole to African: Atlantic Creoles and the Origins of African-American Society in Mainland North America," *William and Mary Quarterly*, 3d Ser., LIII (1996), 251–288 (esp. 283–285). Adam Rothman, *Slave Country: American Expansion and the Origins of the Deep South* (Cambridge, Mass., 2005), provides a good analysis of the transformation of Louisiana's economy and the development of its full-fledged slave society in the late colonial and early national periods.

in Louisiana, but that economy followed an idiosyncratic path that did not always parallel the track of the colony's economic evolution. The nuns were plunged immediately into the ephemeral slave society of early French Louisiana and experienced its decline in the middle decades of the century, but they stood on the sidelines when it revived in the 1790s and did not join in the successful plantation economy that emerged in that decade.

In other ways, however, the convent community echoed transformations in the larger community beyond the convent walls. In the last quarter of the eighteenth century, nuns born in France were outnumbered for the first time. Novices born in Louisiana and educated by the nuns generally upheld the French legacy, but a steady stream of postulants from Havana tested the adaptability of the Ursuline community to a new strain of cultural diversity.

At the threshold of the new century, the Ursulines emerge from this composite portrait profoundly altered by their colonial experience yet at the same time recognizable descendants of their French progenitors.

chapter 4

DIFFERENCES OF NATION AND MENTALITY

*May God give you strength to get along with crazy people of different
types. — Father Pedro Velez of Pensacola in Spanish Florida to Father
Antonio de Sedella in New Orleans, 1786*

Pedro Velez, a priest serving in Spanish Florida, took up his pen in the
spring of 1786 to offer words of support to his beleaguered colleague in New
Orleans, Antonio de Sedella. Father Antonio found himself in the middle of
a power struggle at the Ursuline convent when three French nuns arrived,
without proper authorization, to join the community. "My most beloved
Father Antonio," he began, I "am ready to serve you in all things and wish-
ing that the holy nuns do not give you too much to do with the coming of
the three Frenchwomen." He continued, with what proved to be unfounded
optimism, "Your prudence will inhibit from the outset all occasion of discord between differences of nation and mentality."[1]

In fact, despite the interventions of Sedella and others much more highly
placed than he, "differences of nation and mentality" rent the Ursuline convent for much of the last two decades of the eighteenth century, as French
and Spanish factions among the nuns maneuvered for political dominance.
At stake were the tenor and composition of the feminine Catholic community the French nuns had nurtured since their arrival in the city. The
future of their American project seemed secure at midcentury, as French
creole women took Ursuline vows that bound them to the perpetuation of
the female apostolate through which they themselves were drawn to the
church. But changes in Louisiana's economy and social structure and the
introduction of Spanish creole nuns into the New Orleans monastery posed

---

1. Father Pedro Velez to Father Antonio de Sedella, Apr. 20, 1786, Notre Dame Archives, Catholic Church, Archdiocese of New Orleans (La.) Collection, University of
Notre Dame Archives, South Bend, Ind., IV-4-a A.L.S.

new challenges and elicited aggressively political responses from French and Spanish cliques within the convent walls.

French creole nuns represented a crucial link between the Ursuline mission and the larger community. Although young women born in the colony were originally forbidden to join the order as vowed religious, in time the prohibition was relaxed, and the purely French origins of choir nuns at the heart of the convent gave way to yet another form of diversity. Beginning in the 1750s, French creole girls of good families entered the convent as nuns, demonstrating the strong bonds between the convent and the city's socially prominent women. Marie Anne Rillieux, who entered in 1752, was the daughter of a prosperous plantation family. Charlotte Demouy's father was a retired officer and planter, and her mother, Charlotte Duval, was the daughter of a highly placed colonial bureaucrat. The Caue sisters, Antoinette and Anne, were daughters of the Guard of the Kings' Stores, François Caue, and of Françoise de Villemont, the daughter of one of Louisiana's early wealthy concessionaires.[2] Pierre François Marie Olivier de Vezin was proprietor of an iron foundry in Canada before he came to New Orleans in 1749 to serve as *grand voyeur,* surveyor and inspector in charge of Louisiana's bridges and roads. His daughter, Françoise Victoire Olivier de Vezin, became a postulant in 1773. Françoise Dufossat's father, Gui Dufossat, came to Louisiana as a military commander in 1751 and was honored with membership in the Order of Saint Louis under the French and a commission as captain of the Batallion of Louisiana under the Spanish. He married Françoise Claudine Dreux, whose father, Mathurin Dreux, was an early entrepreneur who had become wealthy by the middle of the eighteenth century. When Françoise Dufossat entered in 1773, her father had

2. "Livre de l'entrée," 11, 12, 14b, UCANO; Earl C. Woods and Charles Nolan, eds., *Sacramental Records of the Roman Catholic Church of the Archdiocese of New Orleans,* 16 vols. to date (New Orleans, 1987–), I, 95, II, 76 (hereafter cited as *Sacramental Records);* Glenn R. Conrad, comp. and trans., *The First Families of Louisiana,* 2 vols. (Baton Rouge, La., 1970), I, 223, 230, II, 36, 58; *LHQ,* IV (1921), 481–526; Alice Daly Forsyth and Ghislaine Pleasonton, comp. and trans., *Louisiana Marriage Contracts: A Compilation of Abstracts from Records of the Superior Council of Louisiana during the French Regime, 1725–1758* (New Orleans, 1980), 23, 81. Both of Charlotte Demouy's parents were deceased when she entered in 1765. For information about the family of Françoise de Villemont, see Conrad, *First Families,* I, 60, II, 5, 47, 128; *Sacramental Records,* I, 223; Marcel Giraud, *A History of French Louisiana,* V, *The Company of the Indies, 1723–1731,* trans. Brian Pearce (Baton Rouge, La., 1991), 177, 275, 418, 427.

recently been appointed a member of the city's colonial governing body, the Cabildo.[3]

These French creole nuns secured the place of the Ursuline convent as a center of female community in New Orleans as the eighteenth century advanced. By becoming Ursulines themselves, they assumed the ideals and missionary project of French foremothers on behalf of the developing creole society. In doing so, they made a commitment to a program of Christian education that was explicitly extended to enslaved and free women of color. The convent in which they were educated and in which they chose to live their lives in the service of God was characterized by the coming and going of a diverse tide of women and girls. The nuns' work was to mold them into an army of Catholic mothers who would instill and perpetuate the faith among their children with the same zealous energy the nuns displayed in the convent's teeming classrooms. As was true in France, there was an implicit paradox in the enlistment of elite young women in this venture. The presence of young women of high and middling social rank helped gain acceptance for the Ursulines in New Orleans just as it had for the French Ursulines of the seventeenth century. But the work to which Ursulines dedicated themselves in Louisiana, as in France, was subversive of many of the processes by which social hierarchies were maintained. In Ursuline schools in France, the privilege of education was not reserved for the few; the poor were not segregated from the middling and the wealthy. The classes in the Louisiana convent not only mixed rich and poor but European and African. When elite creole women entered the New Orleans convent, they distanced themselves from their families not only by the vows that severed their earthly ties but by the project they embraced.

When Louisiana's cession to Spain was recognized publicly in 1763 in the terms of peace that brought an end to the Seven Years' War, the change in sovereignty marked the first of several cultural confrontations that tested the Ursulines' ability to serve as a focal point and vehicle for female commu-

3. Stanley Clisby Arthur and George Campbell Huchet de Kernion, eds., *Old Families of Louisiana* (Baton Rouge, La., 1971), 260–261, 411–412; "Livre de l'entrée," 15b, UCANO; *Sacramental Records*, II, 104. For a discussion of the career of Mathurin Dreux, see Emily Clark, "'Not by Their Prayers Alone': A Laywomen's Confraternity in New Orleans, 1730–1744" (master's thesis, Tulane University, 1995), 28–29. Gui Dufossat did not allow Françoise to profess as a nun. She never married. See "Livre de l'entrée," 15b, UCANO; Arthur and Kernion, eds., *Old Families*, 261.

nity in New Orleans and to retain the tolerance of church and civil authorities. Changes in demography and government expanded the diversity of customs, classes, and colors that sought accommodation. The maturation of a plantation economy hardened lines of class and race. Spain's religious women were cloistered contemplatives who admitted only a small circle of elite girls to their monasteries for an equally cloistered education. Nothing in their experience prepared Iberian officials and settlers for the open convent of the Ursulines and their program of popular education. The French and French creole nuns found themselves at a crossroads. They could save their convent but lose the soul of their apostolate if they bowed to powerful trends favoring exclusion and division by closing their doors to women and girls of color and marginalizing students of modest means. Or they could continue to promote their aggressive inclusiveness and risk alienating the wealthy boarders who provided them with more than half of their income. The New Orleans Ursulines' response to these challenges was complicated by the admission to the convent of nine Spanish creole women between 1781 and 1785. Their understanding of the mode and purposes of religious life were at odds with the French Ursuline tradition, especially as it had evolved in Louisiana.

Becoming an Ursuline was a respectable choice for girls born into the upper social echelons in France and Louisiana, but it was not the socially desirable strategy monastic life was in Spain and the Spanish colonies. Iberian and Spanish colonial nuns all belonged to traditionally cloistered, contemplative orders. The elite young women who entered them did not compromise their social status by teaching or nursing. Such tasks were deemed unacceptable for genteel women because they would have brought them into continual physical proximity with their social inferiors. Spanish and Spanish colonial nuns prayed for the salvation of the souls of their families, sheltered from the eyes of their social inferiors by the convent walls. They upheld their family's social interests not only by limiting their activities to the unimpeachable practice of prayer and meditation but by ensuring through their vowed chastity their family's honor, which depended on the virginity of unmarried daughters, the sexual abstinence of widows, and the clear fidelity of wives to husbands. On occasion, an elite girl or two might be admitted to the convent to be tutored, but they, too, were expected to observe the strict routine of the cloister. Unlike the apostolic religious women who emerged in seventeenth-century France, elite Spanish and Spanish colonial nuns challenged neither the Tridentine definition of cloister nor the social and racial hierarchies that benefited their class.[4]

The Spanish colonial women who entered the New Orleans convent were ill equipped to understand, let alone share, the Ursuline approach to religious life. Here was a convent that only partially observed the rule of cloister: nuns remained within convent walls, but large numbers of girls came and went daily, transgressing the holy boundary that was supposed to separate the nun from the world. Moreover, elite choir nuns were expected to instruct not only their social equals but a veritable rabble of women and girls of every rank. To this unseemly academic enterprise was added an orphanage, entailing even more distasteful forms of intimacy with social inferiors. But perhaps most unsettling to the Habaneras who took the veil in Louisiana was the interracial nature of the New Orleans nuns' enterprise. Both the French and the Spanish exhibited race prejudice in the centuries before the antebellum elaboration of ideological racism, but the attitudes and practices of each nation took shape in different histori-

4. Jodi Bilinkoff, *The Avila of Saint Teresa: Religious Reform in a Sixteenth-Century City* (Ithaca, N.Y., 1989), provides a good overview of the social functions of early modern Spanish convents. The orders of early modern Spain that also had establishments in the New World were Augustinians, Cistercians, Conceptionists, Discalced Carmelites, Dominicans, Franciscans, and Hieronymites, all cloistered orders (Electa Arenal and Stacey Schlau, eds., *Untold Sisters: Hispanic Nuns in Their Own Works*, trans. Amanda Powell [Albuquerque, N.M., 1989], 338). On convents in the Spanish colonies, see Asunción Lavrin, "Ecclesiastical Reform of Nunneries in New Spain in the Eighteenth Century," *Americas*, XXII (1965), 182–203; Lavrin, "The Role of the Nunneries in the Economy of New Spain in the Eighteenth Century," *Hispanic American Historical Review*, LXIV (1966), 371–393; Lavrin, "Values and Meaning of Monastic Life for Nuns in Colonial Mexico," *Catholic Historical Review*, LVIII (1972), 367–387; Lavrin, "Women and Religion in Spanish America," in Rosemary Radford Ruether and Rosemary Skinner Keller, eds., *Women and Religion in America*, II, *The Colonial and Revolutionary Periods* (San Francisco, Calif., 1983), 42–78; Kathryn Burns, *Colonial Habits: Convents and the Spiritual Economy of Cuzco, Peru* (Durham, N.C., 1999); and Luis Martín, *Daughters of the Conquistadores: Women of the Viceroyalty of Peru* (Albuquerque, N.M., 1983). On honor and its relation to female virtue, see Julio Caro Baroja's influential essay, "Honor and Shame: A Historical Account of Several Conflicts," trans. Mrs. R. Johnson, in J. G. Péristiany, ed., *Honor and Shame: The Values of Mediterranean Society* (Chicago, 1966), 79–137. See Mary Laven, *Virgins of Venice: Enclosed Lives and Broken Vows in the Renaissance Convent* (London, 2002), on the elite convents of Venice.

cal contexts. French and Spanish religious and legal institutions developed distinct approaches to racial difference, the incompatibility of which had significant consequences in a convent shared by nuns representing both traditions.

The Spanish had an elaborately articulated concept of racial difference and an affinity for social hierarchies tied to Iberian superiority that would have made the untidy universal apostolate of the French Ursulines distasteful. Spanish convents were among the strictest conservators of Iberian notions of family honor and social stratification.[5] Both factors were tied in Spain to *limpieza de sangre*—purity of blood—a legacy of Muslim occupation and Christian reaction. After the Christian kingdoms completed their "reconquest" of the Iberian peninsula in the late fifteenth century, they—Castile in particular—developed national identities that rested on religious purity of ancient lineage. Only those families who could prove an unbroken ancestral chain of true Christians, untainted by mingling with either Muslim or Jewish strains, could attain Spanish honor and high social status. Ironically, Saint Teresa of Avila could not have joined her own order of reformed Carmelites after 1597. The trace of Jewish blood in her ancestry would have prevented her meeting the standard of limpieza de sangre that became in that year a requirement for entrance into the order. At the same time, Spanish exposure to Muslim slavery's discrimination between white and black slaves introduced the use of color phenology as an indicator of relative human value. By the eighteenth century, these two strains of Iberian experience merged in the Americas, and purity of blood and its social meanings attached not only to religion but to race as well.[6]

During the Spanish period in Louisiana, an elaborate repertoire of labels was introduced to classify people of color. *Pardo* indicated light skin, and *moreno*, dark skin; designations for lineage included *negro* for those of pure African descent, *mulato* for equal parts African and European, "cuarterón" for one-quarter African, *grifo* for children of dark- and light-skinned partners or mixtures of African and Indian. *Mestizo* indicated Indian and white parents, except in New Orleans, where it was sometimes applied to the off-

5. Bilinkoff, *The Avila of Saint Teresa.*

6. Ibid., 165; James H. Sweet, "The Iberian Roots of American Racist Thought," *William and Mary Quarterly,* 3d Ser., LIV (1997), 143–166. See also Verena Martinez-Alier, *Marriage, Class, and Colour in Nineteenth-Century Cuba: A Study of Racial Attitudes and Sexual Values in a Slave Society,* 2d ed. (Ann Arbor, Mich., 1989).

spring of Indians and persons of African descent.[7] With their complex cata-
log of racial phenotypes, the Spanish articulated and policed a clear boundary between an elite of European extraction and creoles of mixed blood.
They even extended their rigorous classification to the realm of faith: separate sacramental registers were kept in Spanish New Orleans for whites and
people of color.[8]

The French were certainly not indifferent to skin color. An official writing in 1715 in opposition to French-Indian marriage objected that, no matter
what might be said to the contrary, "experience shows every day that the
children that come from such marriages are of an extremely dark complex-
ion."[9] Yet sacramental records throughout the French period were kept in a
common register, the entries of slave baptisms and marriages intermingled
with those of free white settlers.[10] When they launched their mission, the
Ursulines seem not to have debated the racial integration of their school
or the women's confraternity they sponsored. Practical religious tolerance
persisted for some racial mixing, a feature that fits with France's own religious history.

Whereas Spain's early modern crisis of religious purity involved the presence of two distinct "intruding" populations that came to the Iberian peninsula through conquest and immigration, in France the threat to orthodoxy came from within. Towns and families might find themselves divided
against one another as Protestantism and Catholicism vied for the soul of
late-sixteenth-century France. The thrust of the French religious response
that took shape in the Counter-Reformation of the early seventeenth cen-

7. Kimberly S. Hanger, *Bounded Lives, Bounded Places: Free Black Society in Colonial
New Orleans, 1769-1803* (Durham, N.C., 1997), 15-16.

8. The practice began in 1777, when a new sacramental register recorded the baptisms of free and enslaved people of color (SLC-B8). A separate register for nonwhite
marriages was also kept from this date (SLC-M3). A separate funeral register holds a
few entries from 1777 (SLC-F3) but was only used regularly from 1790.

9. AC, C13A, 823, translated in *MPA*, II, 207. Guillaume Aubert, "'The Blood of
France': Race and Purity of Blood in the French Atlantic World," *WMQ*, 3d Ser., LXI
(2004), 439-478, traces the evolution in the seventeenth and eighteenth centuries of
the French concept of race from its origins, a rhetoric of bloodlines defined by social
and moral qualities, to one in which skin color became central.

10. There are nine surviving sacramental registers from the French period and the
transitional period between French and Spanish parochial administration; all reflect
this practice. See, for example, SLC-B1.

tury was not to purify through expulsion or segregation; it was to proselytize, convert, and restore unity.

The Ursulines, whose order was born in the crucible of the French Counter-Reformation, were heirs to this legacy of universal Catholic propagation. In the early years of their Louisiana career, they did not treat race as a barrier to a young woman's inclusion in their student community. In fact, the obituaries of the first generation of New Orleans Ursulines reflect the enthusiasm the nuns had for their work with women of color. Recall Cécile Cavalier's boundless zeal for teaching the enslaved in the 1730s and her unhappiness when her superior reassigned her to the predominantly European boarding class. Much later in the eighteenth century, as the slave society of Louisiana matured, the nuns remained steadfast in their determination to evangelize people of African descent. Françoise Olivier de Vezin, creole daughter of a wealthy planter family who entered the convent in 1773, taught catechism to the enslaved women of New Orleans for forty years. "She was a resource and a consolation for all these poor persons," her obituary noted, remaining undiscouraged in her apostolate, even in the face of the slave revolts that occurred near the end of her life.[11]

The campaign to universalize Catholicism that dominated seventeenth-century France and guided the Ursulines' New Orleans apostolate placed them generally at odds with the interests of colonial slave societies. There was no parallel episode in Spain's religious history, by contrast, to draw Spanish colonial nuns into practices that would counteract the progressive social and racial exclusion that characterized maturing colonial societies. The admission of Spanish colonial nuns to the Ursuline community made this disparity clear sooner than might otherwise have been the case. Spanish creole nuns accustomed to a cultural vocabulary of racial purity and exclusion might have found Françoise Olivier de Vezin's slave catechism class a distasteful but bearable fact of convent life. The enslaved met in a small building just inside the convent walls. That these same nuns might have found it more difficult to accept the presence of free girls of color among the privileged boarders who studied, ate, and slept in the main convent building is suggested by an episode recorded in the chapter minutes in 1797.

The nuns met in chapter on All Saints eve that year to discuss whether to admit mulattos as day boarders. They decided that, although they would continue their policy of admitting the legitimate daughters of quadroons and white fathers, "as they have been received up to now," they would ac-

11. "Lettres circulaires," 248–249, UCANO.

cept mulatto girls only if they were kept separate. The entry makes plain that the convent was accepting mixed-race students, but it also suggests that this development had become controversial. The discussion is about continuing a practice, not about an innovation. Indeed, although no student records before 1797 survive, another source confirms that a girl of color was enrolled at the boarding school in the late 1730s. Nothing suggests that the boarding division ceased accepting girls of African descent in the middle years of the eighteenth century only to admit them again in the 1790s. Something prompted a reconsideration of the terms of racial integration in the boarding school. External events offer one explanation. The outbreak of the Haitian Revolution in 1791 and the rapid development of a plantation economy in the Lower Mississippi Valley that took place in its wake combined to widen the social gulf between people of African descent and those of unmixed European ancestry in New Orleans. But the chapter minute entry does not indicate an attempt to impose the strict black-white divide that characterized the approved pattern of relations within a plantation society. Instead, it concerns itself with degrees of phenotype and legitimacy, both factors that echo long-standing Spanish and Spanish colonial traditions of limpieza de sangre, the honor conferred by legitimacy, and gradations in skin color that dictated precise social placement.[12] The decision of 1797 hints at compromise. Mulattos—darker-skinned and usually the offspring of illicit liaisons—would be admitted but kept separate from the lighter-skinned girls of color and students of European descent who shared a space in the boarding school. The spirit of inclusiveness born in the French Counter-Reformation and transported to Louisiana did not sail unassaulted and unchanged into the nineteenth century, but Spanish preference for exclusivity and rigid racial boundaries did not completely displace it.

There is no record of any verbal debate that might have taken place on the matter of mixed-race students or any other issue on which Spanish and French and French creole nuns might have disagreed as a result of their different legacies as religious women. Clearly, however, the nuns understood that numbers were the most powerful factor in deciding whose culture would dominate. Choir nuns voted on all major decisions affect-

---

12. "Délibérations du Conseil," 101, UCANO; Jack D. L. Holmes, "Do It! Don't Do It! Spanish Laws on Sex and Marriage," in Gilbert C. Din, ed., *The Spanish Presence in Louisiana, 1763-1803* (Lafayette, La., 1996), 162–182. See Chapter 2 for a description of the mulatto boarder of 1735.

ing policy and finances. Louisiana's unique version of the French aposto-late was more likely to prevail if the French element in the convent community outnumbered the Spanish. The election of French or French creole women as mother superior was also important, as this convent officer set the agenda for chapter meetings, determining which issues were considered.

The French sisters who had presided over the New Orleans convent for half a century took a variety of steps to preserve the French majority in the convent voting population when Spanish creole nuns began to enter in the 1780s. As the French and French creole nuns in New Orleans opened their doors to these young women, they imposed procedures designed to give an edge to French interests. The nuns reinstituted the long novitiate, which kept newly professed choir nuns from voting or running for office in the community for three years. They also required the Spanish creole postulants to board at the convent and learn French before clothing them with the religious habit that signified the start of their religious candidacy.[13]

Such delaying tactics were not sufficient, however. The French mother superior of the convent worked in the early 1780s to recruit three professed nuns from the community of Pont Saint Esprit in France to come to New Orleans. The mother superior studiously avoided seeking permission from the ranking ecclesiastic in New Orleans, Antonio de Sedella, and the nuns set sail for Louisiana before he could move to prevent their departure. He was faced with the unhappy prospect of causing further discord no matter what he did upon the French nuns' arrival. If he allowed the unauthorized recruits to stay, he would alienate the eight Spanish creole nuns then at the convent. If he insisted on their deportation, he lost all hope of future cooperation from the French faction, which included four French-born nuns and some proportion of the French creole population then numbering nine women. Sedella's colleague in Spanish Pensacola sympathized with his plight, which he thought was exacerbated by the gender of the antagonists. Pedro Velez prayed that God would grant his friend "strength to get along with crazy people of different types."[14]

13. Jane Frances Heaney, *A Century of Pioneering: A History of the Ursuline Nuns in New Orleans (1727-1827)*, ed. Mary Ethel Booker Siefken (New Orleans, 1993), 165–166, 194 (written as Ph.D. diss., Saint Louis University, 1949).

14. Velez to Sedella, Apr. 20, 1786, Notre Dame Archives, Catholic Church, Archdiocese of New Orleans (La.) Collection, University of Notre Dame Archives, IV-4-a A.L.S.

The elections of convent officers over the next seventeen years made it plain that the "different types" would not be easily reconciled. By 1785, there were twenty-one nuns at the New Orleans convent. Twelve were professed choir nuns who were full voting members of the community, a group comprising five Cuban women, four French women, and three French creole women. That year, shortly before the three French nuns arrived, a Cuban was elected superior for the first time, Antonia Maria Peres Ramos, who had entered as a postulant in 1778 (see Figure 8). She had the support of all five Cuban nuns, but she needed two more votes for a plurality. She likely found them in the French creoles Adelaide and Françoise Dusseau de La Croix, who had joined the order as teenagers and later showed solidarity with the Cuban nuns when the convent split at the colony's retrocession to France in 1803. In 1785, the La Croix sisters were twenty-two and twenty-three years old, closer in age to the thirty-four-year-old Ramos than to the French nuns qualified to serve as superior, who were all forty or older.[15]

The La Croix sisters represented the only French creole defection, and their allegiance was not enough to keep the Cubans in power. In 1791, Marguerite Du Liepure, a French woman, was elected superior. Others elected to her council were the French creole Françoise Olivier de Vezin and two of the nuns from Pont Saint Esprit, Françoise Alzas and Thérèse Farjon. Eligible to vote that year were five French nuns, five French creole nuns, and seven Cuban nuns. Even if the La Croix sisters had voted for a Cuban candidate, the French faction would have prevailed. Later that year, each faction gained a recruit. A Cuban woman, Maria Regle Lopez, and a French creole woman who had been a student at the Ursuline school, Emilie Jourdon, were accepted as novices. In 1792, the oldest French nun, Marguerite de Belaire, died at ninety-one, but a French creole girl, Rosalie Broutin, joined. The French maintained their majority (see Appendix 1).

The French slate swept the election of 1794, with eleven French and French creole nuns eligible to vote, compared to eight Cuban nuns. Two months after the election, Maria Jesus Sanchez arrived from Havana to enter the novitiate, but her addition was not enough to vanquish French domination. During the next election in 1797, eleven French or French creole nuns and nine Cuban nuns voted. The French prevailed again. In the elections of 1794 and 1797, the La Croix sisters must have voted with the

15. "Registre [des Ursulines de la Nouvelle Orleans]," UCANO. See also Appendix 1.

Figure 8. Antonia Maria Peres Ramos. Artist unknown. Early nineteenth century.
Courtesy, Archdiocese of Havana, Cuba

French faction. In 1800, they appear to have switched sides again. Antonia Ramos was elected superior on July 12 of that year.[16]

Through the blunt mechanism of partisanship in convent elections, the French and French creole nuns retained enough control in the closing years of the eighteenth century to see their views prevail. The French understanding of a permeable cloister dedicated to the universal propagation of Catholicism survived. The well-born nuns of the convent—French and Spanish—taught and otherwise ministered to all of the city's female population, even as this activity grew notably more incongruous with the interests of the class and race to which they belonged.[17]

Outside the convent, the Spanish governing body of New Orleans, the Cabildo, was more responsive to the interests of planters. Beginning in the 1770s, it enacted a series of measures that signaled diminishing formal tolerance for blurred and imprecise social and racial demarcations. There was a new array of provisions aimed at controlling the enslaved: brutal punishments, the creation of slave patrols to capture fugitives and forestall rebellion, and restrictions on assembly and movement. But there were also measures that seemed specifically aimed at counteracting the social impact of Spanish manumission laws, which produced a large body of free people of color in the last quarter of the eighteenth century. Free women of color were forbidden to wear expensive clothing that made use of gold or silver in 1777. Free and enslaved people of African descent were prohibited by a statute of 1781 to mask for festivals or dances and barred from dances held after dark. In 1784, free people of color were required to carry certificates of emancipation. The dances held at the public dance hall were officially segregated in 1792. As the plantation economy of Louisiana finally came to life at the end of the century, the elite of European descent beyond the convent walls publicly inscribed their superiority.[18]

16. "Registre [des Ursulines de la Nouvelle Orleans]," UCANO. See also Appendix 1.

17. Emily J. Clark, "A New World Community: The New Orleans Ursulines and Colonial Society, 1727–1803" (Ph.D. diss., Tulane University, 1998), 252–281, contrasts French and Spanish constructions of female religiosity and describes in detail the resulting conflict at the New Orleans convent.

18. Gilbert C. Din and John E. Harkins, *The New Orleans Cabildo: Colonial Louisiana's First City Government, 1769–1803* (Baton Rouge, La., 1996), 161, 164, 173. Thomas N. Ingersoll, *Mammon and Manon in Early New Orleans: The First Slave Society in the Deep South, 1718–1819* (Knoxville, Tenn., 1999), 184, attributes a hardening of slave treat-

Behind their walls, having adjusted their integration policies slightly with the decision of 1797, the Ursulines continued to admit girls of African descent to their elite boarding division. We know the identity of only one of the free girls of color who received her education in the Ursuline boarding school. Sophie Brunet, noted in the account book as "petite fille de Luison Brunet," was enrolled as a day boarder at the convent for six months in 1801. Her mother was a fairly prosperous woman and made regular use of notaries, who identified her as a free woman of color.[19] Sacramental records and notarial acts suggest a mixed-race background for three other students, Rosalie Baptiste, Louise Touton, and Victoire Rouby, but lacunae make positive identification impossible.[20]

---

ment in this period to Spanish imperial policies that fostered a successful plantation economy, including making certain that the trade in newly enslaved Africans returned to New Orleans after a hiatus of several decades during the French period.

19. "General Accounts, October 1797–October 1812," 317, 321, UCANO. Luison Brunet is identified in notarial acts sometimes as a mulatto, sometimes as a quadroon. See, all in NANO, Acts of Andrés Almonester y Roxas (January–May 1775), Feb. 14, 1775, 76 (Luisa Brunet, identified as a "mulatta libre," purchases a slave); Acts of Juan Bautista Garic, Nov. 7, 1778, X, 501 (Luisa Brunet, identified as a "mulatta libre," purchases a slave); Acts of Rafael Perdomo, July 1, 1784, V, 75 (Luison Brunet, identified as a "parda libre," sells property); ibid., Feb. 3, 1784, 101 (Luison Brunet, identified as a "cuarteróna libre," sells property). Luison Brunet was also identified as a mestiza, and at least one of her daughters employed this classification in her efforts to have the baptisms of the daughters of her legitimate marriage to a white man recorded in the white baptismal register. See Hanger, *Bounded Lives*, 93–94.

20. Free people of color were often baptized without surnames. Tracing family relationships is difficult. Even when surnames are known, pinning down racial ancestry is not always possible. Although separate sacramental registers were kept for whites and people of color, clerical vigilance in policing Spanish racial phenotypes varied widely, and many families of mixed race, like Luison Brunet's, passed back and forth as succeeding generations of free women of color married white men and claimed the racial privileges of their husbands for their children.

Rosalie Baptiste was a day boarder for a year, beginning in October 1798. In the sacramental records of late-eighteenth-century New Orleans, Baptiste is a surname that was used only by free people of color. A free girl of color named Rosalie was baptized in 1788 and would have been the right age to have been a student at the convent in 1798, and a free family of color carrying the Baptiste surname and living in the New Orleans area baptized a girl named Rosalie in 1806. See "General Accounts, October 1797–October 1812," 340, 341, 343, 348, 350, 388, UCANO; *Sacramental Records*, IV–XI; SLC-B12.

Students of privileged backgrounds did not abandon the Ursuline school, despite the presence of students like Sophie Brunet and the convent's refusal to join in the march toward racial exclusivity orchestrated by law and encoded in the segregated sacramental registers kept by Spanish Capuchins. In fact, records for overnight and day boarding students, which survive from October 1797 through 1803, show that the convent performed a function no other public institution did: it demonstrated that a community united by gender and faith could survive cultural and economic change that drove divisions elsewhere. In the 1790s, French creole girls shared their classrooms with the daughters of Spanish officials and Anglo-American merchants as well as free girls of color. Race and nationality were not the only differences reconciled within the convent walls. Diversity in income and occupation existed among the families of boarding students as well. The Ursuline student records paint a portrait of old loyalties sustained and new ties forged, creating a community within the enclosure that contrasted with developments taking place beyond the convent walls.[21]

Louise Touton, a boarding student for fifteen consecutive months in 1800 and 1801, might have been the granddaughter of Bartolomé Toutant Beauregard, whose mulatto daughter, Emelie, lived in 1805 with a free girl of color who would have been the right age to have been a student in the late 1790s. The girl's name is not listed in the census, but Emelie had a sister named Louise, for whom she might have named a daughter. See Acts of Francisco Broutin, Feb. 27, 1792, XV, 39, "Last Will and Testament of Bartolomé Toutant Beauregard," both in NANO; and Matthew Flannery, comp., *New Orleans in 1805: A Directory and a Census Together with Resolutions Authorizing Same Now Printed for the First Time from the Manuscript; Facsimile* (New Orleans, 1936), 46.

Victoire Rouby was a day boarding student for a year in 1798–1799 and might have been a member of a Mobile, Alabama, family of free people of color who moved back and forth across the Gulf Coast. They usually spelled their name Rabbi. A free woman of color named Marie Victoire Rabbi was baptized in New Orleans in 1815 and married in Mobile in 1833. See *Sacramental Records*, XI, 365; "Marriage Register," Cathedral of the Immaculate Conception, Mobile, Ala., Dec. 2, 1833 (microfilm at AANO).

21. "General Accounts, October 1797–October 1812," 287–362 (pages were used in reverse order, with the account for October 1797 on 362), UCANO. Student records appear in the form of notations in the receipts section of the general accounts book kept for the convent. Entries were made monthly, grouped by expense and income, with totals and the surplus or deficit noted at the bottom of the page and verified by the mother superior. Boarders are listed by name, with a notation of fees paid and the length of the term for which the fees applied. The student body of the boarding division of the Ursuline school, which included girls who ate all meals at the con-

The boarding school remained a traditional affiliation for families with deep roots in New Orleans. Student records name 245 individuals who attended between 1797 and 1803.[22] Of these, 70 appear in other colonial records that provide information about their family background, financial means, nationality, and race. Girls born to French or French creole parents made up the majority of this number. Their lineage reveals that bonds formed earlier in the century between the city's women and the convent remained firmly in place despite changes elsewhere, linking the school of the 1790s to the first flowering of the French female apostolate in New Orleans.

Twelve students in the late 1790s were descended from women who were members of the laywomen's confraternity founded in 1730. The Carrière clan, which had been prominent in the confraternity, contributed four descendants to the convent school student body.[23] Rose and Gertrude Du-

---

vent and stayed overnight as well as girls who ate only the noonday meal and slept at home, can thus be reconstructed for this period. The names of day students are not recorded. In 1800, there were more than one hundred students at the day school, but it still must have been a free service, since there are no notations of income received from this source for the period. The names of the girls who made up this portion of the Ursuline student body remain unknown. See Bishop of Louisiana to José Caballero, Oct. 13, 1800, AGI, SD, legajo 2645, fol. 419.

22. "General Accounts, October 1797–October 1812," 287–362, UCANO.

23. Susan Marguerite Sarpy de Lord and Emerance Despau were great-granddaughters of Marguerite Trepagnier Carrière. Susan Marguerite Sarpy is identified as the daughter of Marguerite Foucher (*Sacramental Records*, VII, 287). Marguerite Foucher is identified as the daughter of Marguerite Carrière (II, 128). Marguerite Carrière is identified as the daughter of confreress Marguerite Trepagnier Carrière (I, 42). Emerance Despau is identified as the daughter of Marie Sophie Carrière (IX, 111). Marie Sophie Carrière is identified as the daughter of Jean Carrière (II, 44). Jean François Carrière is identified as the son of confreress Marguerite Trepagnier Carrière (Sidney L. Villere, comp., "The French-Canadian Carrier's [sic] in Louisiana Province and Some of their Descendants," *New Orleans Genesis*, VIII [1969], 73). Josephine Laveau Trudeau was a great-granddaughter of Marie Arlut Carrière Tixerant. She is identified as the daughter of Charles Laveau Trudeau (*Sacramental Records*, IV, 303). Charles Laveau Trudeau is identified as the son of Marie Marguerite Carrière (III, 290). Marie Marguerite Carrière is identified as the daughter of confreress Marie Arlut (Villere, comp., "French-Canadian Carrier's [sic]," *New Orleans Genesis*, VIII [1969], 71). Desirée Montreuil was a great-granddaughter of Françoise Jalot Delasource Carrière. Marie Desirée de Montreuil is identified as the daughter of François de Montreuil (76). François de Montreuil is identified as the son of Marie Françoise

breuil were granddaughters of confreress Felicité Delachaise Dubreuil and great-granddaughters of confreress Marie Payen Dubreuil. Felicité Martina Eulalie Dubreuil was descended from three confreresses.[24] Antonia Celeste Dreux, Maria Celeste Macarty, Sophie Glapion, and Catherine Adam all were descended from confreresses, and Maria de La Merced Duffouchar Degruy was almost certainly the great-granddaughter of confreress Mathurine Guillemette Aufrere.[25]

Carrière (75). Marie Françoise Carrière is identified as the daughter of confreress Françoise Jalot (75).

24. Rose and Gertrude Dubreuil are identified as the daughters of Jacques Dubreuil (*Sacramental Records*, IV, 104, XI, 114). Jacques Dubreuil is identified as the son of Felicité Delachaise Dubreuil and Louis Dubreuil (I, 87). Louis Dubreuil is identified as the son of Marie Payen Dubreuil (I, 87). Felicité Martina Eulalie Dubreuil is identified as the daughter of Maria Eulalie Livaudais and Claude Joseph Dubreuil (IV, 104). Maria Eulalie Livaudais is identified as the daughter of Genevieve Babin Delasource Livaudais (III, 119). Genevieve Babin Delasource Livaudais is identified as the daughter of Françoise Jalot Carrière (Villere, comp., "French-Canadian Carrier's [sic]," *New Orleans Genesis*, VIII [1969], 75) and the wife of Jacques Livaudais (*Sacramental Records*, I, 97). Claude Joseph Dubreuil is identified as the son of Claude Joseph Dubreuil the elder (III, 297). Claude Joseph Dubreuil the elder is identified as the son of Marie Payen ("Dubreuil Family Lineage Chart," AANO).

25. Ursuline student Antonia Celeste Dreux is identified as the daughter of Pierre François Dreux (*Sacramental Records*, XI, 143). Pierre François Dreux is identified as the son of François Hugot Dreux (II, 99). Ursuline student Maria Celeste Macarty is identified as the daughter of Heleine Charlotte Fazende (IV, 89). Heleine Charlotte Fazende is identified as the daughter of Charlotte Dreux (II, 87). Charlotte Dreux is identified as the daughter of Françoise Hugot Dreux (II, 98). Catherine Sophie Glapion is identified as the daughter of Jean Christoph Glapion (Hewitt L. Forsyth, comp. and trans, *Libro primero de confirmaciones de esta parroquia de Sn. Luis de la Nueva Orleans: Contener folios y de principio al folio 1, consigne hasta g dios no senor . . . ea servido confirmacions* [New Orleans, 1967], 90, no. 3219). Jean Christophe Glapion is identified as the son of Jeanne Antoinette Rivard (*Sacramental Records*, II, 137). Jeanne Antoinette Rivard is identified as the daughter of confreress Jeanne Antoinette de Villemont Rivard (I, 223). Jeanne Antoinette de Villemont Rivard is identified as the daughter of confreress Antoinette Fourier de Villemont Rivard (I, 223). Catherine Adam is identified as the daughter of Andre Adam Blondin (IX, 2). Andre Adam Blondin is identified as the son of Marie Roy Adam Blondin (II, 1). Maria de La Merced Duffouchar Degruy is identified as the daughter of Antoine Degruy (V, 105). Antoine Degruy is identified as the son of Marie Thérèse Aufrere (V, 105). Marie Thérèse Aufrere was probably the daughter of Antoine Aufrere and Mathurine Guillemotte. If she was ap-

These twelve young women represented a French creole constituency in the boarding school that had ties of long duration to both the convent and the larger community. Their families had prospered since the early French period, and they continued to enjoy high social status in the late eighteenth century. Sophie Glapion's grandfather, Christoph Glapion, served as a member of the New Orleans Cabildo, for example, and Governor Esteban Miro stood as godfather to Celeste Macarty, his niece by marriage.[26]

The planter class was not the only group among the French creoles at the Ursuline school. Altogether there were thirty-four boarders whose families had been in the colony since the French period and another twelve whose mothers came of French creole stock. Although some of them were the products of illustrious family trees, others claimed more modest backgrounds. Eugenie Tricou, for example, was the granddaughter of Pierre Marchand, a wigmaker. Melanie Vitaud's grandfather was a baker, and master cutler Pierre Raby was the maternal grandfather of boarder Marguerite Delmas.[27] The presence of French creole girls from a range of social backgrounds attests to the nuns' ability to retain the loyalty of the descendants of the diverse population they had first come to serve. Not even the daughters and granddaughters of race-conscious planters defected.

The true test of the Ursulines' ability to negotiate the transformation of colonial society at the end of the century was not the retention of their traditional student base; it was their ability to attract newcomers. They succeeded by offering such students a place and an identity rooted, not in nationality, but in gender and piety. They also provided the families of

---

proximately fifty years of age at the baptism of Maria de La Merced Duffouchar in 1793, she would have been born during a period for which the New Orleans sacramental records are missing (1734–1743).

26. Din and Harkins, *New Orleans Cabildo*, 61; *Sacramental Records*, IV, 89.

27. The baptismal entry for Marie Anne Marchand, Eugenie Tricou's mother, names her as the daughter of Pierre Marchand, wigmaker, and Catherine Bernard (*Sacramental Records*, II, 194). Maria Marchand married Joseph Tricou in 1786 (IV, 302). Eugenie Felicité Tricou is identified as the daughter of Joseph Tricou and Maria Marchand (X, 425). Melanie Vitaud is identified as Anne Joly's daughter in her marriage record (VII, 314). Other sacramental records identify Anne Joly's father, Jacques Joly, as a master baker (II, 155). In the baptismal entry for Marie Magdalene Raby, mother of Marguerite Delmas, her father Pierre is identified as master cutler (II, 233). Jean Baptiste Delmas, native of Provincia, married Marie Magdalene Rabi in 1778 (III, 251), and Marguerite Delmas is identified as their daughter in the record of her own marriage of 1803 (VIII, 93).

TABLE 6. *Lineage of Boarding Students at the Ursuline Convent, 1797–1803*

Background	Number
Louisiana French creole, maternal and paternal	34
Anglo-American or British	11
Louisiana French creole, maternal; Iberian, paternal	6
French	7
Louisiana French creole, maternal; French, paternal	4
Saint Domingue	1
Free people of color	1
Unknown	3
Total	67

Sources: Student list drawn from "General Accounts, October 1797–October 1812," UCANO. Lineage of students based on Earl C. Woods and Charles Nolan, eds., *Sacramental Records of the Roman Catholic Church of the Archdiocese of New Orleans,* I–XI (New Orleans, 1987–1996); [St. Bernard, New Galvez, Baptisms of Slaves and Free Persons of Color, 1787–1857]; Hewitt L. Forsyth, comp. and trans., *Libro primero de confirmaciones de esta parroquia de Sn. Luis de la Nueva Orleans: Contener folios y de principio al folio 1, consigne hasta g dios no senor . . . ea servido confirmacions* (New Orleans, 1967); "Census of New Orleans," Nov. 6, 1791, Louisiana Division, New Orleans Public Library; Matthew Flannery, comp., *New Orleans in 1805: A Directory and a Census Together with Resolutions Authorizing Same Now Printed for the First Time from the Manuscript; Facsimile* (New Orleans, 1936); Acts and Court Proceedings of Pedro Pedesclaux, 1788–1803, Acts and Court Proceedings of Francisco Broutin, 1790–1799, Acts of Juan Bautista Garic, 1771–1779, all in NANO; Mrs. Fred O. James, "Premier 'Directory' de la Nouvelle-Orleans, 1807," *New Orleans Genesis,* III (1964), 112–119.

parvenus with entrée into an established community that might otherwise have been closed to them. Seven daughters of new French immigrants enrolled at the boarding school along with six daughters of Spanish fathers and French creole mothers, eleven girls of Anglo-American or British parentage, a refugee from Saint Domingue, and at least one girl of color (see Table 6).

Ursuline schools were part of the urban landscape of most towns in eighteenth-century France, so it would have seemed natural for the new French arrivals to enroll their daughters at the convent. The convent had a different appeal for Spanish fathers married to French creole women. The Spanish government strove to build loyalty and cooperation with the French creole community through both official and personal strategies. Appointments to the Cabildo were made from among French creole families, and Spanish officials, including Governor Esteban Miro, married French creole women to bind the new political order with ties of blood. When former *mayordomo de propios* Matias Alpuente, Captain Jose Vazquez Vaamonde, Galician Pedro Vizoso, and Captain Manuel Peres enrolled their daughters at the convent, they cemented those ties further and acknowledged the cultural legacy of their wives.[28] In the case of Thérèse Vizoso, family connections might have made more than the usual difference: her great aunt, Marthe Delatre, was a converse nun at the convent while she was a student there.[29]

Adjusting to New Orleans must have been particularly difficult for the Britons and Anglo-Americans who came to the city in increasing numbers after the American Revolution. The language, religion, and customs were all alien and exotic for them. An education at the Ursuline convent would have served the crucial role of acculturation for the eleven daughters of Anglo-American or British parents at the convent between 1797 and 1803. Rosalie Outran, Marie St. Colins, Charlotte Seth Hanchet, Nancy Rabesum, Rose Scara, Nancy Quil, Annet Jones, and a girl known only as Mlle. Helene were recorded in the account book with "anglese" penned next to their names. Henriete Cowperthwait and Marie Jones, whose entrepreneur fathers were

28. Governor Esteban Miro, for example, married Celeste Macarty, descended from a settler from the early French period, in 1779 (*Sacramental Records*, I, 174, IV, 213; Din and Harkins, *New Orleans Cabildo*, 9, 21–23). Matias Alpuente held the Cabildo post mayordomo de propios from 1788 to 1791 (Din and Harkins, *New Orleans Cabildo*, 72). He was married to Marguerite Duplessis, born in Louisiana in 1761 (*Sacramental Records*, II, 106). Jose Vazquez Vaamonde, captain of the Louisiana Regiment, and Brigitte Elena de Reggio are identified as the parents of Luisa Francisca Carlota Vazquez Vaamonde in the record of her 1789 baptism (IV, 306). Brigitte Elena de Reggio was the daughter of Elena de Flaurieu, daughter of a French colonial official (IV, 92). Celeste Antonia Peres was the daughter of captain Manuel Peres and Jeanne Catherine Dubois, according to her baptismal entry of 1784 (IV, 243).

29. "Lettres circulaires," 249, UCANO, confirms that Marthe Delatre was at the convent in 1798 and 1803, when Thérèse Vizoso was a student. Thérèse Vizoso's mother was Victoria Delatre, and her grandfather was Luis Delatre (*Sacramental Records*, V, 387). Luis Delatre and Marthe Delatre were the children of Antoine Joseph Delatre ("Livre de l'entrée," 10, UCANO; *Sacramental Records*, I, 72).

business partners, Angelica Hepp, and Marie O'Connor all leave more substantial traces in the record and confirm the probability that most, if not all, of these girls were the daughters of Anglo-American merchants.[30]

British and, later, American traders had been active in Louisiana since the French period, but their numbers and stature increased notably under Spanish rule, especially after 1797, when Spain effectively legalized American trading in the port of New Orleans. New York, Philadelphia, and Baltimore all contributed commercial immigrants to the city in the 1780s and 1790s.[31] According to most histories of the city, the Americans were never really assimilated into the society of the French and Spanish creoles, and travel accounts of the period bear out that assessment. "The French, Spanish, and Americans here, keep very separate society," noted the traveler John Watson in 1805. American women, he remarked, had an especially difficult time finding their way into creole social circles. "Ladies in this country never visit strangers *first*. All expect to be visited by the ladies newly arrived. Our ladies will not yield to this seemingly awkward position, and therefore they pass without native society."[32]

The Anglo-American girls boarding at the Ursuline convent sidestepped this social impasse. Three of them—Marie Jones, Angelica Hepp, and Marie O'Connor—were welcomed into the New Orleans community through fictive kinship. When Marie Jones was confirmed at the Ursuline convent in 1800, her godmother bore the French creole name Eulalie Daufine. At

30. "General Accounts, October 1797–October 1812," 294, 295, 300, 315, 327, 332, 343, UCANO. The fathers of Henriete Cowperthwait and Marie Jones were business partners in the 1780s: Acts of Fernando Rodriguez, March–July 1784, III, 929, NANO, records a contract between Jacob Cowperthwait and Robert Jones and a third party in 1784; Acts of Rafael Perdomo, January–July 27, 1786, VII, 192, NANO, records the dissolution of the partnership between Jacob Cowperthwait and Robert Jones in 1786.

31. Daniel H. Usner, *Indians, Settlers, and Slaves in a Frontier Exchange Economy: The Lower Mississippi Valley before 1783* (Chapel Hill, N.C., 1992), discusses English trading networks with Indians in the Lower Mississippi Valley during the French period. See also John G. Clark, *New Orleans, 1718-1812, an Economic History* (Baton Rouge, La., 1970), 161–166, 228, 232–250. Arthur P. Whitaker, "Reed and Forde Merchant Adventurers of Philadelphia: Their Trade with Spanish New Orleans," in Din, ed., *Spanish Presence*, 246–265, discusses two prominent Philadelphia merchants who were active in New Orleans between 1787 and 1803.

32. John F. Watson, "Notia of Incidents at New Orleans in 1804 and 1805," *American Pioneer*, II (1843), 228, 234.

Marie O'Connor's confirmation in 1801, a woman named Maria "Dufou-chard" served as her godmother. This woman was almost certainly her fel-low boarding student, Maria de La Merced Duffouchar Degruy. The French creole Leonide Verloin Degruy was godmother to Angelica Hepp when she was confirmed in 1801, during her term as a boarder. There is some evi-dence that these Anglo-American transplants embraced the French female apostolate that the Ursulines enjoined upon them. Although she was a stu-dent, Angelica Hepp, who might herself have been a convert, saw her sister abjure Protestantism and her eleven-year-old brother baptized according to the rites for adults. There is no evidence that student Henriete Cowper-thwait managed to convert her Pennsylvania Quaker father, Jacob, but she and other Anglo-American girls who were overnight boarders were none-theless included in a uniquely intimate aspect of French creole society.[33]

"Social and cultural life is as developed here as it is in Paris," the French envoy Pierre Laussat remarked of New Orleans in 1803, "elegance and good breeding prevail throughout. . . . There are numerous hairdressers and all sorts of masters—dancing, music, art, and fencing." Wealthy women in the final years of colonial Louisiana could compete in manners, attainments, and fashion with the ladies of Paris, but their "remarkable cleverness with natural elegance" was not the result of a sheltered education among their privileged peers. They read the plays of Beaumarchais and the fables of La Fontaine in the company of girls who did not share their prospects for lei-sured refinement and high society.[34]

The classrooms at the Ursuline school muted the differences in wealth and occupation that were hardening into class barriers in society at large. The convent housed the very rich, like the four daughters of Vincent Ril-lieux, whose estate inventory took up an entire volume of court proceed-ings, listing among his assets sixty-four slaves valued at more than forty

33. Forsyth, *Confirmaciones*, 138, no. 3527; *Sacramental Records*, VII, 167, VIII, 175. Forsyth *Confirmaciones*, 97, no. 2458, identifies "Maria Justina Jones" as daughter of Robert Jones and Ana O'Brien and her godmother as Eulalie Daufine. Henriete Cow-perthwait is identified as the daughter of Jacob Cowperthwait, Quaker of Pennsyl-vania, and Charlotte O'Brien, Catholic and native of Carolina, in the record of her baptism in New Orleans (*Sacramental Records*, V, 91).

34. Pierre Clément de Laussat, *Memoirs of My Life . . .*, trans. Sister Agnes-Josephine Pastwa, ed. Robert D. Bush (Baton Rouge, La., 1978), 20, 119 n. 31. The 1998 inventory of the library of the Ursuline Convent of New Orleans contains eighteenth-century editions of the works of Beaumarchais and La Fontaine.

thousand pesos. But it also took in middling- and working-class girls. Eight students were daughters of merchants and contractors whose slavehold- ings do not suggest unusual wealth.[35] Fathers of other students made their living in a variety of ways. Bernard Coquet, father of boarder Filipine Co- quet, was the coproprietor of the ballroom where the city's free people of color held their weekly dances in the late 1790s. Henriete and Aimée Tremoulet's father, Bernard, kept an inn near the wharves, where he had a free woman of color and a butcher as neighbors. Celeste and Madelaina Guenon's father, Pierre, was a baker who rented his building from his in- laws. Boarder Josephine Lambert's father, Pierre, was a gunsmith, and Jus- tine Fretté's was a glazier. When elite families like the Rillieux were not at their plantation homes in the countryside, they generally resided in town- houses in elegant sections of the city, eschewing the neighborhoods that gunsmiths, glaziers, and bakers shared with free people of color. Inside the convent compound, that social geography was suspended, if only for a time.[36]

35. "Estate of Vincent Rillieux," Acts of Carlos Ximenes, Mar. 22, 1800, NANO; Mrs. Rosario Centanni (Irna Elizabeth Adams), "The Legend of Perique," *New Orleans Genesis*, V (1966), 284, lists the children of Vincent Rillieux. Marie Melicerte Rillieux, born in 1783, Antoinette Rillieux, born in 1785, Basilia Rillieux, born in 1787, and Marie Eloisa Rillieux, born in 1790, were the right age to have been students at the convent in the late 1790s. Merchant Joseph Tricou owned seven slaves, Alexander Bodin four, Pierre Bousigue three, and Pierre Cenas two ("1795 Census of New Orleans," AGI, PC, legajo 211; Flannery, comp., *New Orleans in 1805*, 45). Alexander Bodin is identi- fied as the father of students Felonise and Josefine Baudin in their baptismal records (*Sacramental Records*, VII, 18). Eugenie Tricou is identified as the daughter of Joseph Tricou in her marriage record (X, 425). Louise Bousigue is identified as the daughter of Pierre Bousigue in her baptismal record (III, 35). Celeste Cenas is identified as the daughter of Pierre Cenas in her marriage record (VII, 56).

36. "1795 Census of New Orleans," AGI, PC, legajo 211, 64, 65, 73; Mrs. Fred O. James, "Premier 'Directory' de la Nouvelle-Orleans, 1807," *New Orleans Genesis*, III (1964), 112–119. Filipine Coquet is identified as the daughter of Bernard Coquet in her baptismal record (*Sacramental Records*, V, 86). On Bernard's connection with the dances organized by free people of color, see Hanger, *Bounded Lives*, 144; and Ronald R. Morazán, "'Quadroon' Balls in the Spanish Period," in Din, ed., *Spanish Presence*, 503. Bernard Tremoulet is identified as the father of Henriete and Aimée in their baptis- mal records (*Sacramental Records*, IV, 301, V, 371). Pierre Guenon is identified as the father of Celeste and Madelaina in their marriage records (X, 76). Josephine Lambert is identified as Pierre Lambert's daughter in her baptismal record (IV, 178). Justine

In 1803, a small fire broke out in New Orleans that sent its inhabitants, fearing a repeat of conflagrations that devastated the city in 1788 and 1794, running toward the riverfront. "Amidst screams and frightful confusion, the French as well as the Spanish and American languages mingled with one another on all sides," the French envoy Pierre Laussat remarked of the scene. At that moment, New Orleanians of disparate nationality, means, and race experienced a moment of common identity in the face of crisis.[37] Such episodes were rare in the lives of most inhabitants, but many young women of the city had an opportunity to have more than a fleeting encounter with the multicultural community that New Orleans could be. The Ursulines' compound bound together the French and the Spanish, the Quaker's daughter from Pennsylvania and the refugee from Saint Domingue, the governor's niece and the blacksmith's daughter, the rich planter's child and the daughter of a free quadroon.

The nuns did not employ a conscious strategy to achieve and preserve this environment of social and ethnic mingling. Just as their own high social standard and attention to rank in the early years of French rule had safeguarded their inclusive educational program, in the 1790s they continued to sustain a conservative, Old World system of social distinction that paradoxically created a site where newly drawn lines of social and ethnic distinction could be safely ignored. Under the aegis of practices steeped in the legitimacy of tradition, the Ursulines' preservation of their peculiar hierarchy outflanked contemporary forces pushing for a new orthodoxy of social relations.

The New Orleans nuns of the late colonial period ordered space and relationships inside their convent along rigidly conservative lines. The Ursuline pattern was set in France, where externs, the students who attended for only part of the day at little or no cost, did not mingle with fee-paying boarding students. The Ursulines' rule, the *Règlemens*, carefully delineated not only separate curricula for boarding students and externs but made it clear that boarders and externs must attend class in separate spaces. Even within the extern class there was attention to status, as the *Règlemens* di-

---

Fretté is identified as John Fretté's daughter in her marriage record (X, 190). The social geography of late colonial New Orleans can be reconstructed using the "Census of New Orleans," Nov. 6, 1791, Louisiana Division, New Orleans Public Library, and "1795 Census of New Orleans," AGI, PC, legajo 211.

37. Laussat, *Memoirs*, trans. Pastwa, ed. Bush, 85–86.

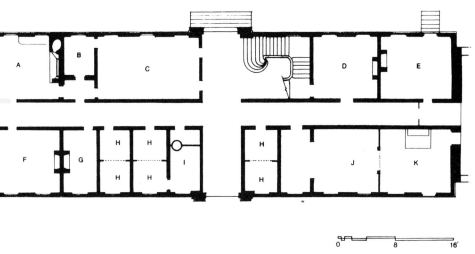

Figure 9. Ground Floor Plan of the First New Orleans Ursuline Convent. 1734. (A) kitchen; (B) office; (C) nuns' refectory; (D) recreation room; (E) room for the nun in charge of the hospital; (F) boarders' refectory; (G) superior's day room; (H) parlor; (I) room of the portress; (J) choir of the nuns; (K) chapel. Drawing by Rebecca Anderson after Ignace-François Broutin, in AC, C13A, XVII, 306

rected the nun in charge of externs to "be careful not to put girls of rank next to the most poor and ill groomed, in order not to disgust them."[38]

The layout of the convent and its grounds provided clearly demarcated, separate spaces for boarding students, externs, and orphans. Convents in the French cities of Rouen and Dieppe had separate, smaller classrooms for externs. In the first New Orleans convent, boarders and orphans had separate dormitories and classrooms, divided by a corridor, on the upper floor under the roof. Separate infirmaries made certain that distinctions were maintained even in illness (see Figures 9, 10, and 11). The second New Orleans convent, built on the same site as the first in 1745, put an entire story between the orphans, whose dormitory and dining room were on the ground floor, and the boarders, who occupied the third floor (see Figures 12 and 13).[39] Whether externs were taught inside the main convent build-

38. *Règlemens des religieuses Ursulines de la Congrégation de Paris* (Paris, 1705), 158–169 (esp. 168).

39. Plan of Ursuline Convent, Rouen, n.d., folio D419, and Plan of Ursuline Convent, Dieppe, n.d., folio D345, ADSM. Both convents were built in the seventeenth

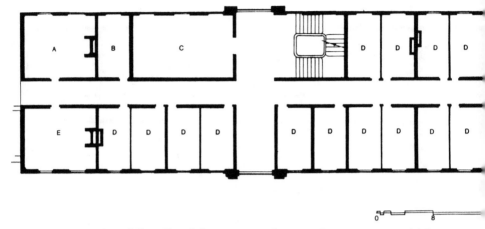

Figure 10. Second Floor Plan of the First New Orleans Ursuline Convent. 1734. (A) first infirmary; (B) room for the nun in charge of linen and infirmary; (C) chapter room; (D) nuns' cells; (E) second infirmary. Drawing by Rebecca Anderson after Ignace-François Broutin, in AC, C13A, XVII, 306

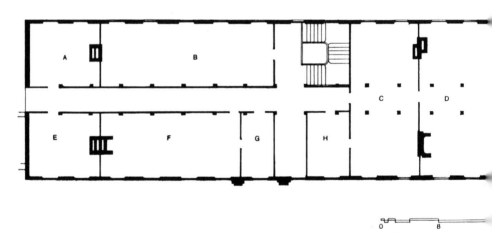

Figure 11. Third Floor Plan of the First New Orleans Ursuline Convent. 1734. (A) boarders' infirmary; (B) boarders' dormitory; (C) orphans' dormitory; (D) orphans' day room; (E) orphans' infirmary; (F) boarders' day room; (G) room for the mistress of boarders; (H) room for the mistress of orphans. Drawing by Rebecca Anderson after Ignace-François Broutin, in AC, C13A, XVII, 306

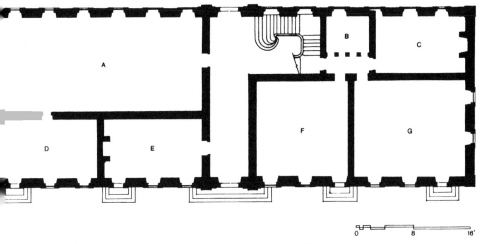

Figure 12. Ground Floor Plan of the Second New Orleans Ursuline Convent. 1745–1752. (A) orphans' dormitory; (B) office; (C) workroom; (D) orphans' classroom; (E) orphans' infirmary; (F) orphans' refectory; (G) nuns' refectory. Drawing by Rebecca Anderson after Ignace-François Broutin, in Ministere des Colonies, no. 10, Archives Nationales de France. Reproduced in Samuel Wilson, Jr., "An Architectural History of the Royal Hospital and the Ursuline Convent of New Orleans," LHQ, XXIX (1946), 605, plate 16

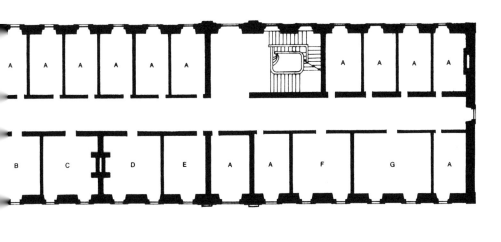

Figure 13. Second Floor Plan of the Second New Orleans Ursuline Convent. 1745–1752. (A) nuns' cells; (B) library; (C) nuns' infirmary; (D) infirmary chamber; (E) second infirmary chamber; (F) linen room; (G) wardrobe room. Drawing by Rebecca Anderson after Ignace-François Broutin, in Ministere des Colonies, no. 10, Archives Nationales de France. Reproduced in Samuel Wilson, Jr., "An Architectural History of the Royal Hospital and the Ursuline Convent of New Orleans," LHQ, XXIX (1946), 605, plate 16

ing in the early years is not clear, but in 1793 their classroom was housed in a separate structure just inside the convent walls. Here poor and enslaved girls came to learn their catechism. Even recreation was separate. Boarding students exercised in an outdoor area separated from the front court where the extern schoolhouse stood by the main convent building, chapel, and kitchen (see Figure 14).[40]

Despite all their careful spatial and curricular distinctions, the philosophy of the nuns nevertheless had radical potential. The 1705 *Règlemens* enjoined the very teachers who were supposed to keep poor, unkempt students from getting too close to their social betters to "carry this out with discretion, so that the poor will not think themselves scorned, and give to both sorts equal care and equal affection, not excepting any person."[41] The rhetoric of human equality was the property of only a handful of religious radicals until Revolutionary ideologues unleashed it late in the eighteenth century. It represents an admirable oddity in the pamphlets of seventeenth-century English Civil War sects and an inspiration in the evangelical voices of the First Great Awakening and the social experiments of Moravians in the Caribbean and British colonial America. Its fleeting appearance in an Ursuline manual suggests that these Protestants were not alone in their struggle to translate spiritual equality to the realm of earthly behavior and action. The nuns' experimentation in this regard is all the more striking because, unlike the Quakers, Moravians, Methodists, and Baptists of colonial America, they were not agents of an innovative, limited religious fellowship but an integral part of the largest established branch of Christianity in Europe and the Americas.[42]

---

century. The plans for the first convent in New Orleans, completed in 1734, are preserved in Centre des archives d'outre-mer, Aix-en-Provence, France, FR CAOM F3/290/6. The plans for the ground and second floors of the second convent are in FR CAOM F3/290/25, and reproduced in Samuel Wilson, Jr., "An Architectural History of the Royal Hospital and the Ursuline Convent of New Orleans," *LHQ*, XXIX (1946), plates 13–18.

40. See the certified copy of the plan of the convent grounds in "Cahier renfermant toutes les pièces relatives aux réclamations du fiscal pour le domaine royal du Roi D'Espagne: entre autres pièces curieuses se trouvent trois plans des terrains et bâtisses des casernes de l'hôpital et du couvent en ville," UCANO.

41. *Règlemens*, 167.

42. Of these groups, only the Quakers, who originated as an English Civil War sect, retained in the nineteenth century a significant practical commitment to racial equality. The Quakers formally prohibited members' ownership of enslaved people in

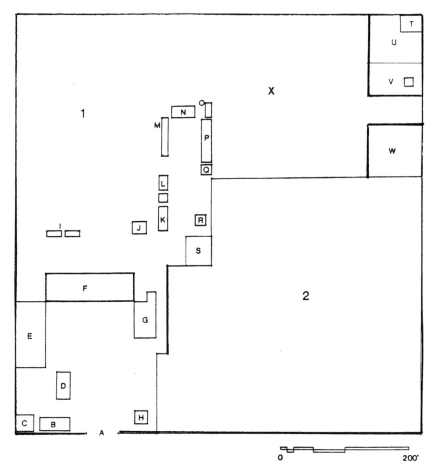

Figure 14. Site Plan of the Convent Grounds and Military Barracks. 1793. (A) cloister entrance; (B) externs' schoolhouse; (C) "ancient church"; (D) parlor; (E) church and choir; (F) convent, schoolroom, and lodging for boarders and orphans; (G) kitchen; (H) lodging for extern servant; (I) latrines; (J) store of timber for repairs; (K) provisions store; (L) henhouse; (M) ovens, hand mill, and kitchen for slaves; (N) lodging for convent slaves; (o) lodging for the housekeeper; (P) workshop for carpenters, shoemakers, and servants' hospital; (Q) washhouse; (R) storage? (S) nuns' burial ground; (T) house owned by nuns and rented to military officers; (U) and (V) military land given to Ursulines in exchange for property designated (W); (X) boarders' recreation area. Drawing by Rebecca Anderson after the plan drawn in 1793 by Gilberto Guillemard, copy preserved in "Cahier renfermant toutes les pièces relatives aux réclamations du fiscal pour le domaine royal du Roi D'Espagne: entre autres pièces curieuses se trouvent trois plans des terrains et bâtisses des casernes de l'hôpital et du couvent en ville," UCANO

The Ursulines in New Orleans faced a more complicated problem than their French sisters when they tried to give the changing, diverse female population of New Orleans "equal care and equal affection, not excepting any person." They solved it by adhering to an old set of rules that paid ostentatious attention to one set of boundaries but allowed them to blur others. They distinguished choir nuns from converse nuns, boarding students from extern students, servants from the served. They carefully allocated separate spaces within their enclosure in recognition of this stratified order. The convent succeeded in cultivating and preserving in a colonial setting a replica of the hierarchical European social order to which elites were attached, and which they despaired of achieving in the uncooperative environment of the Lower Mississippi Valley. Yet, even as they sustained this conservative social template, the nuns created a site that also subverted it when they invited all women to enter the larger physical space that was their compound and the spiritual space that was the church. Every woman, according to the Ursuline ideology worked out in the era of the Reformation, held God's commission to become a good Catholic mother and to propagate the faith. The Company of Saint Ursula's duty was to train them all for that mission, regardless of their status in earthly society.

In the closing decade of the eighteenth century, most of the women of New Orleans probably spent some time inhabiting the common ground sheltered by the convent walls, imbibing the gospel of Catholic motherhood. In 1795, 284 girls of European descent lived in New Orleans; 245 young women boarded at the convent between 1798 and 1803. Just fewer than four hundred girls of color, enslaved and free, resided in the city. Con-

---

the 1780s (*A Brief Statement of the Rise and Progress of the Testimony of the Religious Society of Friends, against Slavery and the Slave Trade* [Philadelphia, 1843], 47). The Moravian settlements in colonial Pennsylvania and North Carolina extended spiritual equality to enslaved and free blacks who sought and acquired admission to the Moravian fellowship. Unlike the Ursulines, they did not seem to impose spatial segregation in their communal living spaces; after 1822, however, white and black Moravians split into separate, racially segregated congregations (Jon F. Sensbach, *A Separate Canaan: The Making of an Afro-Moravian World in North Carolina, 1763-1840* [Chapel Hill, N.C., 1998], 121, 125–126, 211). On the waning Baptist and Methodist commitment to racial equality, see, especially, Sylvia R. Frey and Betty Wood, *Come Shouting to Zion: African American Protestantism in the American South and British Caribbean to 1830* (Chapel Hill, N.C., 1998), 176–181; and Christine Leigh Heyrman, *Southern Cross: The Beginnings of the Bible Belt* (New York, 1997), 66–69, 217–219.

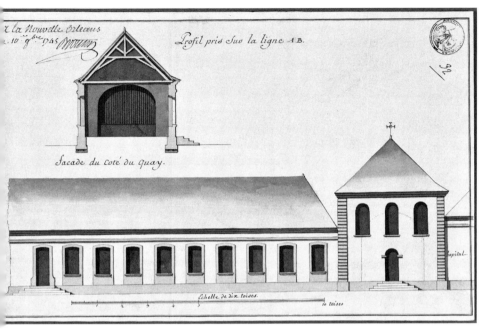

Figure 15. Profil et façade du côté du quay [du couvent des religieuses Ursulines].
By Ignace-François Broutin. 1745. By permission Centre des archives d'outre-mer, Aix-en-
Provence, France, FR CAOM F3/290/32. Architect's drawing showing the convent chapel,
where many Ursuline students and people of African descent were baptized in the late
eighteenth century

temporary accounts place the size of the extern class, which included enslaved girls who came for catechesis, at more than 100.[43] The composition of
the female population changed between those who first walked through the
convent gate in the late 1720s and those who sat in the nuns' classrooms at
the turn of the nineteenth century. As Indian slavery died out in Louisiana,
native women seem to have disappeared from the free catechism classes.
But the nuns retained their missionary bent, catechizing new Africans and
reaching out to Anglo-Americans. Their original mission—to sweep all the
women of the town into the ranks of Catholic motherhood—remained unchanged.

The monastery compound that demarked this heterogeneous feminine
enclave dominated a corner of the eighteenth-century city, spreading over

43. Bishop of Louisiana to José Caballero, Oct. 13, 1800, AGI, SD, legajo 2645, 419.

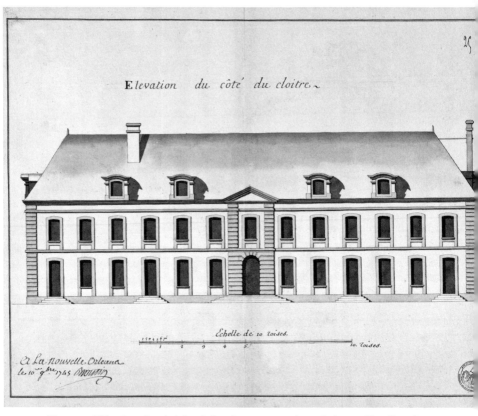

Figure 16. Elévation du côté du cloître [au couvent des religieuses Ursulines].
By Ignace-François Broutin. 1745. By permission Centre des archives d'outre-mer, Aix-en-Provence, France, FR CAOM F3/290/25. Architect's drawing of the second Ursuline convent, which the nuns inhabited until 1824

three square city blocks in a district that also had significant numbers of female propertyowners and heads of household. For the purposes of the census of 1795, New Orleans consisted of four quarters. The convent was located in the second quarter, where women owned approximately 16 percent of the occupied property and headed an equal proportion of households. In addition to the convent, women owned twenty-three of the properties in this district, eleven belonged to white women, ten to free women of color, and two to women of undetermined race. The convent complex covered about 20 percent of the ground area in the second quarter. Although calculating precisely the square footage owned or presided over by women in addition to this space is not possible, if the proportion of female-headed households was roughly equal to the proportion of land occupied we can estimate that female-headed households or institutions occupied more than a third of this neighborhood.[44]

The feminine presence in the second quarter was racially integrated outside the convent complex as well as inside it, and women of color shared to a significant degree in the power of propertyownership in the district. Although only 11 percent of the district's inhabitants were free people of color, free women of color represented nearly half the female propertyowners, and three of them rented to families headed by white men. Women, including large numbers of free women of color, owned substantial amounts of property in the third quarter as well, but only as private individuals. In the second quarter, beyond a riverfront row of cabarets and hotels, a diverse group of women inhabited and controlled an unusually large proportion of public and private space anchored by the convent. Perhaps some or many of the women who owned and rented housing in this neighborhood chose it because the Ursulines were there. In any event, one could not have walked the streets of the southeastern quadrant of the city without being aware of its women, black and white, presiding over so much of it.[45]

The church of New Orleans was even more distinctly feminine than the second district, for the women of New Orleans had responded to the Ursuline initiative by making it very much their own. In 1772, a Spanish cleric reported to his bishop that the women of the city were "more honest than in Spain, and live more in accordance with the precepts of the Church." More than thirty years later, John Watson's description of Holy Week celebrations in New Orleans portrays a scene dominated by motherhood and female piety. "Mothers bring their infants; some cry and occasion other disturbances; some are seen counting their beads with much attention and remain long on their knees." Watson's observations testify not only to the dominance of women in the life of the church but also to the notable participation of women of color. "Visit the churches when

44. Calculations derived from "1795 Census of New Orleans," AGI, PC, legajo 211.

45. Ibid. The census reveals that 23 percent of households in the third district were headed by women and that approximately 37 percent of the occupied properties in the third district were owned by women. Free women of color made up the majority of female propertyowners in this district, but free people of color also made up the majority of the population in the third quarter. Only in the second quarter is the representation of free women of color among female propertyowners high while their representation among the total population is low.

you will," he reported, "and the chief of the audience is formed of mulat-tresses and negresses." Watson's observations are substantiated by the sac-ramental records of colonial and early national New Orleans, which tes-tify to the leadership of women of African descent in the growth of a vital Afro-Catholic community that came to dominate the congregation numeri-cally.[46]

In 1734, the Ursuline procession had traversed the city with a column of women drawn from every rank and color in a public demonstration that claimed New Orleans for French Catholic motherhood. A community of women developed with the convent as a focal point, and, as the colony's capital grew and changed under the Spanish flag, the nuns continued to serve as its nexus. Holding fast to their unusual apostolate, the Ursulines created within their enclosure an enduring space for a sense of collective female identity among the city's diverse constituencies. The convent modu-lated the cacophony of competing cultures by providing young women with a common experience during the very time in the life cycle when indi-vidual identities form and there is a growing awareness of one's relation-ship to groups beyond the circle of family and household.[47] The activity that took place in the Ursuline enclosure lubricated the growth and transforma-tion that marked Louisiana's eighteenth-century passages—from France to Spain, from frontier settlement to maturing plantation society. It was be-yond the power, and indeed the intention, of the Ursuline apostolate to delay or oppose the development of a society increasingly locked into rigid structures of race, ethnicity, and class. But, when they were within the con-vent walls, women temporarily escaped that social paradigm for a com-munity that revealed alternate possibilities for the ordering of human re-lations.

46. Cirillo de Barcelona to Santiago Jose de Echevarría, Aug. 6, 1772, AGI, SD, legajo 2594; Watson, "Notia of Incidents at New Orleans," *American Pioneer*, II (1843), 230, 234. For a full discussion of the growth of Afro-Catholicism in colonial and early na-tional New Orleans and the role of women of African descent in this development, see Emily Clark and Virginia Meacham Gould, "The Feminine Face of Afro-Catholicism in New Orleans, 1727–1852," *WMQ*, 3d Ser., LIX (2002), 409–448.

47. Erik H. Erikson, *Childhood and Society*, 2d ed., rev. and enl. (New York, 1963), 261–263.

IT IS THE CUSTOM OF THE COUNTRY

THE URSULINE ENCOUNTER WITH SLAVERY

When missionaries left France for Louisiana, they took everything and everyone they thought they might need with them. The young Ursuline novice, Marie Madeleine Hachard, reported to her father that the Jesuits who crossed the Atlantic with the nuns on the *Gironde* in 1727 brought along a carpenter, a locksmith, and several other workmen to help them build and maintain their physical facilities. "As for us," she continued, "please do not be scandalized, it is the custom of the country: we are taking a Moor to wait on us."[1] Servants were not unusual in ancien régime French convents. Marie was concerned that her father might disapprove of the nuns' keeping an enslaved African. The precise nature of Monsieur Hachard's possible objection is ambiguous. Perhaps Marie thought that he harbored ethnic prejudice and would find it distasteful to think of his daughter in proximity to Africans. Or she might have known him to be troubled by the dissonance between the proud maxim, "There are no slaves in France," and the practical reality of colonial slavery with which his daughter would now become all too familiar. In any case, Marie's words to her father alert us to the young nun's own understanding that the Ursulines' encounter with slavery was something to be marked, one of the events that signaled the passage of the nuns from the comfortable realm of the familiar in France to the strangeness of their colonial adventure.

From the time the Ursulines embarked for Louisiana until the Civil War, they practiced the "custom of the country." They owned enslaved people, bought them, sold them, and used them to work their plantations. They

1. Marie Madeleine Hachard, who usually refers to enslaved persons of African descent as "nègres," explicitly uses "Morre" (Moor) in this passage: "Pour nous mon cher Père, n'en soyez pas scandalisé c'est la mode du païs, nous menons un Morre pour nous servir" (Hachard, *Relation du voyage des religieuses Ursulines de Rouen a la Nouvelle-Orléans en 1727*, ed. Paul Baudry [Rouen, 1865], 17).

never explicitly questioned the morality of the institution of slavery, and they relied significantly on the appropriated labor of their bondpeople to support their establishment. French women religious shaped, and were bound into and by, the slave society that eventually emerged in colonial Louisiana. The nuns' bondpeople were subject to the same system of regulation and exploitation as others enslaved in the colony, yet, at the same time, the women's religious values and policies resulted in a distinctive experience for their bondpeople, particularly with respect to family life. The nuns also had an impact on the enslaved who lived outside their convent, fostering the development of a robust Afro-Catholic community that affected the lives of bondpeople in New Orleans in social as well as spiritual ways.

Opinions about the degree to which religion could be a positive mitigating factor in colonial American slavery differ widely. Missionaries bent on saving the souls of nonbelievers are usually judged to have been spiritually well intentioned but ultimately complicit in advancing colonial aims that rested on racially justified systems of forced labor. For a missionary, the enslavement of a person and the prospect it brought for conversion to Christianity were preferable to earthly freedom and eternal damnation. Early modern European ideas about hierarchy also helped pave the way for missionaries' acceptance of slavery. Hierarchies among human beings, ordered according to social, cultural, and ancestral markers, were deemed natural. Missionaries differed from their secular contemporaries, when, indeed, they differed at all, not by promoting human equality on earth, but by holding all souls equally worth saving. If that position led them to be the instruments of colonial slave regimes that used the conversion rationale to legitimate themselves, it also led them, at times, into conflict with those same regimes. The consequences never seriously threatened the institution of slavery, but they could and did create spaces for alternative interpretations of social and racial order. And, within those alternative interpretations, some free and enslaved people of African descent found the freedom to maneuver within the rigid confines of the increasingly racist slave societies of the Americas.[2]

2. Frank Tannenbaum, *Slave and Citizen: The Negro in the Americas* (New York, 1947), first advanced the argument that religion and an associated body of law created a qualitatively different experience of slavery in Spanish colonies from that in English North America. Jane Landers, *Black Society in Spanish Florida* (Urbana, Ill., 1999), 114–135, revives and updates the Tannenbaum thesis for colonial Florida. For British colonial America, see Sylvia R. Frey, *Water from the Rock: Black Resistance in a Revolutionary*

The realm of religion is an admittedly limited one, but in early modern France it was uniquely central to national identity and royal authority. Rent by forty years of religious warfare between Catholics and Protestants, early-seventeenth-century France bought an uneasy peace with the Edict of Nantes in 1598. By granting limited toleration to Protestants, Nantes accepted a split cultural identity for France. Subsequently, when religious conformity became the cornerstone of Louis XIV's absolutist plan to build a strong French state, the king revoked the Edict of Nantes in 1685, officially conflating French identity with Catholicism. The only true subject of the king was a Catholic subject.[3]

This link between Catholicism and French identity had implications for France's colonial project. In the 1660s and 1670s, finance minister Jean-Baptiste Colbert promoted intermarriage between French men and Indian women in New France. The aim was to civilize and to make French subjects of the Indian women through conversion to Catholicism. The strategy failed to produce the large cadre of devout Catholic Indian wives that Colbert envisioned. Indeed, more commonly French men adopted the way of life of their Indian sexual partners. By the end of the seventeenth century, intermarriage between French men and Indian women had been abandoned as a means of incorporating the native inhabitants of New France into the French polity. From the turn of the eighteenth century, civil authorities routinely opposed such marriages officially. Far from advancing

---

Age (Princeton, N.J., 1991), 243–325; Frey and Betty Wood, *Come Shouting to Zion: African American Protestantism in the American South and British Caribbean to 1830* (Chapel Hill, N.C., 1998), 183–208.

Guillaume Aubert, "'Français, Nègres, et Sauvages': Constructing Race in Colonial Louisiana" (Ph.D. diss., Tulane University, 2002), generally resists seeing religion as a mitigating factor in French colonial race relations; he notes, however, the "uneasiness of a few missionaries regarding the emergence of racist ideas about Indians" in the French mainland North American colonies and chronicles Jesuit missionaries' continued support for mixed marriages between French men and Indian women as late as 1738 (see, esp., 8 [quotation], 237–238). See also Aubert's more recent "'The Blood of France': Race and Purity of Blood in the French Atlantic World," *William and Mary Quarterly*, 3d Ser., LXI (2004), 439–478. Sue Peabody, "'A Dangerous Zeal': Catholic Missions to Slaves in the French Antilles, 1635–1800," *French Historical Studies*, XXV (2002), 53–90, by contrast, suggests that the work of Jesuit missionaries was deemed by some contemporaries to be subversive of the racial order in the Caribbean, a factor that contributed to the order's suppression in the eighteenth century.

3. Mack P. Holt, *The French Wars of Religion, 1562–1629* (Cambridge, 1995), 173–188.

civilizing qualities, liaisons between French men and Indian women were blamed for the degeneration of French identity, with men embracing a native way of life that ignored the social norms and authority of the colonial regime.[4]

Although intermarriage fell from grace as a strategy for the extension of French empire and identity, conversion of the non-Christian inhabitants of France's colonies remained an explicit feature of French policy. Royal dicta were adamant that enslaved Africans were to become Catholics. Article 2 of the Code Noir of 1724, which governed slave treatment in Louisiana, mandated, "All slaves who will be in our province (of Louisiana), shall be instructed in the Catholic, Apostolic and Roman religion, and baptized; we order inhabitants who buy slaves newly arrived to instruct them and baptize them in a timely manner." The Code Noir tells us that the French crown wanted the enslaved baptized, but it does not tell us why.[5]

The Code Noir of Louis XIV, issued in the same year that the king revoked the Edict of Nantes and upon which the 1724 version was based, was part of the Sun King's program to enlarge and consolidate his kingdom at home as well as abroad. Catholicism played a central role in this program; indeed,

---

4. Jerah Johnson, "Colonial New Orleans: A Fragment of the Eighteenth-Century French Ethos," in Arnold R. Hirsch and Joseph Logsdon, eds., *Creole New Orleans: Race and Americanization* (Baton Rouge, La., 1992), 23; Aubert, "'Français, Nègres, et Sauvages,'" 74. According to Aubert, racial prejudice also played a significant part in the demise of officially sanctioned intermarriage between Indians and Frenchmen (see, esp., 4–5, 86–87, 90, 133). He posits a shift at the end of the seventeenth century from a cultural construction of difference grounded in Catholicism to a race-based categorization. This color-based social hierarchy grew from the failure of the intermarriage strategy in New France but was accelerated and crystallized with the emergence of the slave societies of the French Caribbean colonies and the Lower Mississippi Valley.

5. "Le Code Noir, ou Édit du Roi, servant de règlement pour le gouvernement et l'administration de la justice, police, discipline et le commerce des esclaves nègres, dans la province et colonie de la Louisianne; donné à Versailles au mois de Mars 1724," in *Le Code Noir ou recueil des règlemens rendus jusqu'à présent, concernant le gouvernement, l'administration de la justice, la police, la discipline et le commerce des nègres dans les colonies françoises: et les conseils et compagnies établis à ce sujet* (Paris, 1742), 321 (hereafter cited as *Code Noir*). Jerah Johnson links Colbert's promotion of Indian conversion and French-Indian intermarriage to the seventeenth-century campaign to enlarge the human realm of Louis XIV and suggests that similar motives shaped the Code Noir, but he severs the colonial policy from its religious context. See Johnson, "Colonial New Orleans," in Hirsch and Logsdon, eds., *Creole New Orleans*, 18–23.

loyalty to the crown was conflated with loyalty to the Catholic Church. In 1685, religion, not race, was the common denominator of French identity. Article 9 of Louis XIV's original Code Noir prescribed marriage between unmarried French men and enslaved African concubines who bore them children, making sure that all were duly baptized first. Everyone in the king's domain, whether a Huguenot in Paris, a Huron in Quebec, or an African in the Caribbean, was to be brought into the Catholic fold to secure the peace and prosperity of the kingdom.[6]

In time, tension grew between the drive for religious homogeneity in the French empire and the apparatus of racial distinction that was taking shape in the colonies to rationalize slavery. The crown revised the Code Noir in the 1720s to reflect the demands of maturing plantation societies in the French Caribbean. Although it retained the directive that enslaved Africans be baptized and buried according to the rites of the church, the version promulgated in 1724 in Louisiana forbade marriage between the French and Africans, sustaining in theory a unified spiritual community even as it signaled a new boundary in temporal relations.

French religious, however, were slow to let go of the implications of the old 1685 Code Noir for their work in the colonies. Although civil authorities clearly withdrew their official tolerance for interracial marriage in the colonies early in the eighteenth century, for example, French religious remained constant in giving more weight to uniform morality and the salvation of all souls than to racial distinction. Missionaries who favored sacramental marriage over concubinage continued to support such unions after the state began to oppose them. The curate of the French settlements on the Gulf Coast incurred the wrath of civil officials when he contravened their orders and performed marriages between French men and Indian women in the 1710s.[7]

6. Pierre Goubert, *Louis XIV and Twenty Million Frenchmen*, trans. Anne Carter (New York, 1972), 149–162; "Édit du Roi, touchant la police des isles de l'Amérique Françoise; du mois de Mars 1685; registré au Conseil souverain de S. Domingue, le 6 Mai 1687," *Code Noir*, 25–29.

7. AC, C13A, III, 17–18, 819–824. Peter A. Goddard, "Christianization and Civilization in Seventeenth-Century French Colonial Thought" (D. Phil. thesis, Oxford University, 1990), iii–vi, 5–14, argues provocatively that the Jesuits, in particular, saw Indian conversion as an extension of the general post-Tridentine campaign to impose religious conformity and moral order on the lower classes. Indians are conflated with the French peasantry and conceptualized as members of a single, lower social stratum rather than as a race apart.

Rooted in religious belief, the motivation to bring Indians and enslaved Africans into the church and moral society was less sensitive to the social and political forces that nudged slave law and policy toward more exclusionary practices. Devout Catholics believed that their own salvation depended on the extirpation of heresy in their midst. They fought the religious wars of the late sixteenth century to convert or kill the Huguenots, they joined religious confraternities and congregations by the thousands in the seventeenth century to promulgate the true faith and smother the dying embers of French Protestantism, and they embarked on missions to the Americas to evangelize the heathen, Indian and African alike.[8]

If one believed that one's own soul could be saved only if one had done everything possible to turn others from the path of heresy or nonbelief, missions to the Indians and the African slaves of the Americas made sense. Unlike the Calvinist doctrine of grace, Catholicism stipulated that the individual had to work for salvation through acts of devotion, charity, and proselytizing, whether at her hearth or on the frontier. In the closing years of the seventeenth century, Louis XIV's use of Catholicism as an instrument of national consolidation combined with the devout Catholic's search for salvation through the propagation of the faith to create a system of values and institutions in the New World that promoted an aggressively inclusive church.

In New Orleans, the Ursulines were the only religious establishment to answer, belatedly, the crown's call to extend the human borders of the realm by undertaking a large-scale and continuing program of catechesis among the enslaved. Although the Jesuits mounted significant slave evangelization in the French Caribbean, the terms of their agreement with the Company of the Indies prohibited them from preaching and catechizing in the capital city of Louisiana. The Capuchins, who were appointed to serve as the parochial clergy for New Orleans and thus had the right to organize

8. Natalie Zemon Davis, "The Rites of Violence," in Davis, *Society and Culture in Early Modern France: Eight Essays* (Stanford, Calif., 1965), 152–187; Barbara B. Diefendorf, *Beneath the Cross: Catholics and Huguenots in Sixteenth-Century Paris* (New York, 1991), 36–38, 49–63, 159–180; Philip T. Hoffman, *Church and Community in the Diocese of Lyon, 1500–1789* (New Haven, Conn., 1984); Kathryn Norberg, *Rich and Poor in Grenoble, 1600–1814* (Berkeley, Calif., 1985); Norberg, "Women, the Family, and the Counter-Reformation: Women's Confraternities in the Seventeenth Century," *Proceedings of the Sixth Annual Meeting of the Western Society for French History*, VI (1978), 55–63; Leslie Choquette, "'Ces Amazones du Grand Dieu': Women and Mission in Seventeenth-Century Canada," *French Historical Studies*, XVII (1992), 627–654.

a mass effort for slave conversion, lacked the manpower and perhaps sufficient will to take advantage of their clerical monopoly. To find either of these groups of French male clergy taking on catechesis of the enslaved in New Orleans would have been surprising. Jesuits were enthusiastic catechists, but they worked best at a distance from New World centers of civil and ecclesiastical authority. Indian missions in the upper Mississippi Valley and Great Lakes region and enslaved populations on remote Caribbean sugar plantations were more to their taste than an urban missionary field subject to the harsh glare and meddling hands of colonial officials. French Capuchins, unlike their Iberian counterparts, were not seasoned missionaries. The parochial clergy of New Orleans administered the sacrament of baptism to enslaved Africans, but the members of the order assigned to duty in New Orleans showed little desire to move beyond the baptismal font and altar rail in their conversion efforts.[9]

Ursulines, on the other hand, were exactly suited to the work of urban slave conversion. Their central purpose was catechesis, and town settings were their customary turf. In early modern France, the task of drawing people into church and preparing them for the sacraments rested with these nuns and the women they enlisted as their lay lieutenants. If the enslaved of New Orleans were to be converted to Catholicism in large numbers and in a meaningful way, the division of labor in the French church dictated that women would mount the effort. And, indeed, within a few months of their arrival, the nuns were at work among Africans and Indians. By the spring of 1728, a "large number" of African and Indian girls received religious instruction for two hours each day, and seven enslaved girls received special attention as boarding students at the convent. In 1730, the nuns extended

9. See Charles Edwards O'Neill, *Church and State in French Colonial Louisiana: Policy and Politics to 1732* (New Haven, Conn., 1966), 164–173; and Roger Baudier, *The Catholic Church in Louisiana* (New Orleans, 1939), 64–67, for the terms of the contracts between the Company of the Indies and the Jesuits and Capuchins. Caryn Cossé Bell, *Revolution, Romanticism, and the Afro-Creole Protest Tradition in Louisiana, 1718-1868* (Baton Rouge, La., 1997), 11–12, credits the Capuchins with incorporating "black New Orleanians into the life of the church" but bases this judgment on their baptismal activity alone. The chief Capuchin cleric in New Orleans, Raphael de Luxembourg, wrote at length in May 1726 of the school he was trying to establish for French children and, as an afterthought, asked for financial support so that he could add a little school for Indians. There is no mention of Africans (AC, C13A, X, 43–46v). A report by Raphael de Luxembourg on the state of the church in Louisiana in 1728 dwells on French immorality and ignores the issue of Indian and African conversion (AC, C13A, XI, 217–219).

their missionary reach to Africans when they provided sponsorship to the [...] [...]hich embraced the cause of slave catechesis.[10] [...]ms recorded between 1730 and 1803 in the sac[...] [...] rish church for colonial New Orleans testify [...]quency with which enslaved Africans and their children became Catholics in at least a formal sense.[11] These entries do not reveal, however, what function these sacraments and the religion they represented served for enslaved people living in the city. The Ursulines' practical and spiritual effects on bondpeople can best be seen for the enslaved kept by the nuns themselves because of the certainty of their exposure to the nuns' attitudes and actions and because the evidence about them is unusually abundant.

Sacramental records constitute the most revealing source of information about Ursuline bondpeople. The sacramental registers of New Orleans record the baptism and marriage of nearly 200 of the Ursulines' bondpeople between 1763 and 1803, providing details about family formation and community stability.[12] The convent council minutes record the sale, purchase, and emancipation of 106 individuals, often providing descriptive details of personality, skill, and family circumstances. In 1824, when they moved to a new site, the nuns recorded in a register the names, family relationships, ages, births, marriages, and deaths of their enslaved servants, including

10. [Marie Madeleine Hachard], *De Rouen à la Louisiane: Voyage d'une Ursuline en 1727* (Rouen, 1988), 79; "Premier Registre de la Congrégation des Dames Enfants de Marie," 7, UCANO.

11. For example, more than one thousand enslaved and free people of color were baptized over a period of five and a half years, between January 1, 1777, and June 14, 1783 (SLC-B8).

12. The Jesuits who served as the nuns' spiritual directors must have performed and recorded these sacraments for Ursuline bondpeople until the Society of Jesus was suppressed in 1763, because the first sacramental record for an Ursuline bondperson does not appear in the Saint Louis Cathedral registers until August 1763, just a few weeks after the order was officially expelled from Louisiana (SLC-B5, 22 bis, no. 4, Aug. 6, 1763). Although none of the Jesuit records have survived, the Ursuline bondpeople clearly were being baptized before 1763, since they served as godparents at the baptism of enslaved people belonging to others. See, for example, SLC-B2, 167, no. 3, Oct. 6, 1749 (Jeanneton, Ursuline bondwoman recorded as godmother to Marguerite, bondwoman of Monsieur Pontalba); SLC-B3, 40, Sept. 21, 1755 (Laurant, Ursuline slave recorded as godfather to Augustin, bondwoman of Madame la Valé); SLC-B3, 43, June 3, 1755 (Nicolas, Ursuline bondman recorded as godfather to Jean Baptiste, bondman of Monsieur La Croix).

many who had been with them since the eighteenth century. The civil law system that prevailed in colonial Louisiana relied heavily on royal notaries who recorded all formal contractual arrangements and served as clerks of court. Notarial records document acts of sale, emancipation, wills, successions, and court proceedings, contributing additional information about Ursuline bondpeople. These diverse documentary sources offer an unusually vivid portrait of the Ursuline slave community for the last forty years of the eighteenth century.[13]

Estimating the size of the Ursulines' enslaved population consistently over the entire colonial period is difficult. Infrequent censuses, several of them offering incomplete coverage, give figures for 1731, 1732, 1770, 1791, and 1795.[14] According to the censuses of 1731 and 1732, sixteen adults and three children lived on the Ursulines' plantation, and no one lived in town with the nuns as domestic servants. The census of 1770 reports that sixty-one enslaved people lived on the plantation. Censuses for the city of New Orleans indicate that in 1791 seventeen lived at the convent, and in 1795 there were twenty-four. Thus, we know how many bondpeople were living on the Ursuline plantation in some years and how many were living within the convent enclosure in others, but we are rarely given the size of the enslaved population at both places for the same year. Nonetheless, the censuses reveal that the Ursulines were substantial slaveholders. The number of bondpeople they claimed in 1731 put them among the top 30 percent of slaveowners among those with plantations on the Lower Mississippi River. In 1770, they were among the top 6 percent of slaveholders in this category (see Table 7). The public position of the Ursulines in colonial society, the size of their enslaved population, and the nuns' prominence as major slaveholders meant that the nuns' slave community was a conspicuous example to both the enslaved and slaveholder in the New Orleans area.[15]

13. "Délibérations du Conseil," 5–88, UCANO; "Livres ou sont les noms et les annés de la naissance des Nègres et Négresses qui sont venus au Couvent sur notre habitation le 2nd Octobre 1824," UCANO. More than one hundred volumes of records produced by eleven different New Orleans notaries survive from the colonial period. Nearly all of the notaries produced some references to Ursuline bondpeople.

14. There is also a 1777 census for the city of New Orleans, but the Ursulines are not listed in it.

15. Charles R. Maduell, Jr., comp. and trans., *The Census Tables for the French Colony of Louisiana from 1699 through 1732* (Baltimore, 1972), 113–122, 127; "Year 1770 Month of January: State of the Habitations of the Coast of the River below (the City) Beginning

TABLE 7. *Slaveownership on the Lower Mississippi, 1770*

Slaves	Plantations	Proportion
0	51	43%
1–9	31	26
10–29	20	17
30–49	10	8
50–99	5	4
100+	3	2

Source: "Year 1770 Month of January: State of the Habitations of the Coast of the River below (the City) Beginning at the Habitation of Madame Widow Lachaise up to the Environs of the Prairie aux Moucle Both of the (Right) Shore as Well as the Left Shore," in Albert J. Robichaux, Jr., ed., *Louisiana Census and Militia Lists, 1770–1789*, I, *German Coast, New Orleans, below New Orleans, and Lafourche* (Harvey, La., 1973), 92–114.

Family was clearly at the heart of this highly visible slave community. The most striking feature that emerges about the nuns' bondpeople is the predominance of nuclear families anchored by a mother and father living together under the official blessing of sacramental marriage. At least twenty-six such families formed, with nearly one hundred children distributed among them, whereas only five children were born to unmarried mothers (see Appendix 2). Although marriage between enslaved people was recognized and the slave family was somewhat protected under the French colonial regime, that support and protection by civil authorities was lost in the Spanish and American periods. The Ursulines, however, continued to promote marriage among their bondpeople, and, as the eighteenth century progressed, their example became increasingly unusual.[16]

Whether families began to form among their bondpeople during the

at the Habitation of Madame Widow Lachaise up to the Environs of the Prairie aux Moucle Both of the (Right) Shore as Well as the Left Shore," in Albert J. Robichaux, Jr., ed., *Louisiana Census and Militia Lists, 1770-1789*, I, *German Coast, New Orleans, below New Orleans, and Lafourche* (Harvey, La., 1973), 95; "Census of New Orleans," Nov. 6, 1791, 14, Louisiana Division, New Orleans Public Library; "1790 Census of New Orleans," AGI, PC, legajo 211, 68.

16. Gwendolyn Midlo Hall, *Africans in Colonial Louisiana: The Development of Afro-Creole Culture in the Eighteenth Century* (Baton Rouge, La., 1992), 168, 183.

Ursulines' first years in the colony is impossible to know. The Ursulines' contract with the Company of the Indies stipulated that they be allocated eight adult male enslaved Africans to work their plantation. Two of these first eight escaped into the woods only a few weeks after their assignment to the nuns. The first Ursuline bondwoman in the record is Gaïot, acquired in 1733, but not until 1756 is there evidence that their bondpeople were marrying and bearing children. That year, a group of six in three families stood accused of theft, and the nuns voted in chapter to sell them. Among them were two married couples and a creole boy in his teens. One of the couples was also creole, but the husband of the other was known by an African name, Equé, in addition to his given Christian name. This evidence suggests that the nuns were promoting sacramental marriage among the first-generation Africans as well as among creoles.[17]

One might easily imagine the nuns imposing marriage on their bondpeople without taking individual choice and affection into account, forcing unions among those living in their convent and on their plantation to effect both social control and the semblance of compliance with Catholic morality. No direct evidence exists for such behavior, but there are documented instances of the nuns' attempts to bring together enslaved people bound to one another by affection but separated by the geography of ownership.

In 1758, a woman petitioned to enter the convent as a permanent boarder and offered her bondwoman, Victoire, as part of her entrance dowry. Originally, the nuns were to receive Victoire and a cash sum, but they negotiated with a third party to forgo the cash in exchange for Victoire's husband, Joseph Leveillé. Much later in the century, they continued such interventions. In April 1795, they purchased a thirty-three-year-old woman named Victoria and her two-year-old son so that she could marry the father of her child, an Ursuline bondman named Ramón. The two were wed in a July ceremony, and the sacramental register carefully notes that the child, also named Ramón, was legitimated by the marriage. In March 1798, the convent council approved the purchase of a Guinean woman named Denise

17. [Hachard], *De Rouen à la Louisiane*, 29; "Délibérations du Conseil," 44, UCANO. Throughout, when referring to individual bondpeople I use the spelling of his or her name most frequently found in Ursuline records. If there is no reference to the individual in Ursuline records, I use the most frequent variant in other records, most typically sacramental registers. As a result, even in the Spanish period, some individuals are referred to by the French version of their name.

because "she might marry one of our slaves who had begged us to allow him to do so." The nuns paid Denise's mistress four hundred pesos in cash in May, and she and Ursuline bondman Charles were married that August.[18]

Sometimes the Ursulines could carry their promotion of slave marriage to unlikely extremes. Between 1798 and 1804, they engaged in a vigorous investigation to determine the validity of the marriage between two of their bondpeople. A woman named Teresa had originally been married to another of the Ursulines' enslaved servants, Mathurin. While on a trip up the Mississippi in 1776, Mathurin disappeared, and, although no body was ever found, he was presumed dead. The "widowed" Teresa married again. When her second husband, Domingo, died, she took a third, Estevan, also from among the nuns' bondmen. She bore him a child, and he, in turn, became stepfather to the five children she had borne to Mathurin and Domingo. In 1798, word reached the Ursulines and ecclesiastical officials in New Orleans that Mathurin had been sighted in Havana. Teresa and Estevan were separated, pending the outcome of an elaborate investigation that involved notarized depositions of enslaved people in Havana and the intervention of the archbishop himself. In 1804, six long years into the inconclusive inquiry, the superior of the New Orleans Ursulines wrote to the bishop asking that he end the case and pronounce Mathurin dead, "for the long separation is very harmful to the family of Teresa, her children, and her husband who has always considered her as his legitimate wife." She went on to say that the husband was "desperate and is continually asking me to let him marry another woman if he cannot have Teresa back." "I do not know what to do to tranquilize him." This episode reveals the Ursulines' continuing insistence on legitimating the sexual relationships of the enslaved through sacramental marriage and suggests that the enslaved themselves had either assimilated the nuns' values or chose to avoid the penalties for nonconformity.[19]

18. "Délibérations du Conseil," 45, 73, 81, UCANO; "Achat de Denise / Venus," act of sale notarized by Carlos Ximenes, May 16, 1798, UCANO; SLC-M3, 13, no. 77, July 14, 1795, 16, no. 42 bis.

19. The following are all in AANO. Translations are by Jane Frances Heaney, UCANO: Theresa St. Xavier Farjon to Bishop Luis Ignacio de Peñalver, Apr. 6, 1799; Josef de Basquez to Theresa St. Xavier Farjon, Apr. 19, 1799; Bishop Luis Ignacio de Peñalver to Theresa St. Xavier Farjon, Aug. 3, 1799; Francisco Jese de Bassave to Antonia Monica Ramos, June 9, 1801; Antonia Monica Ramos to Bishop Luis Ignacio de Peñalver, July 21, 1801; Pedro de Tamora to Bishop Luis Ignacio de Peñalver, July 27, 1801; Bishop Luis Ignacio de Peñalver to Pedro de Tamora, July 21, 1801; Notarized statement of Teresa, Sept. 13, 1802; Notarized statement of Angelica Regis, Sept. 15,

Deviation from the nuns' marital standard brought harsh justice, as their reaction to unmarried motherhood attests. In 1797, the convent chapter minutes record that a young woman named Touton was sold because of her "vices," as was another named Celeste in 1798 because of her "licentiousness." Eloise and Catherine, blood sisters, were sold in 1803 for "bad conduct." The vices, licentiousness, and bad conduct noted in the minutes left tangible proof in two cases. Celeste went to her new mistress with a month-old infant whose father was unknown, as did Catherine. The nuns literally banished from their community most women who bore children out of wedlock. They did allow Maria Juana, the creole daughter of Ursuline slaves Radegunda and Antonio, to stay after she bore Josef Maria Francisco out of wedlock in 1791, but she might have been shunned by potential creole marriage partners or prevented from marrying them by the nuns. In 1798, she married Domingo, a native of Guinea.[20]

The Ursulines' unwavering commitment to sacramental marriage among their bondpeople was not matched by the New Orleans slaveholding population as a whole. Marriage among the enslaved was not uncommon during the French period, but it almost disappeared at the end of the eighteenth century under Spanish rule. Baptismal records for three sample years during French domination, 1744, 1760, and 1765, show that between 12 and 19 percent of enslaved children were born to married parents. Of these years, only 1765 includes the baptisms of Ursuline bondpeople, illustrating that marriage among the enslaved did not take place only or even primarily between the enslaved servants of nuns or clergy. Such marriages may be partly attributable to compliance with the Code Noir directive that the enslaved be married by the church. Of the nine infants born to married parents in 1744, however, two belonged to Capuchin priests and three to families linked to the laywomen's confraternity sponsored by the nuns, while in the same year the bondpeople of a high official produced a child out of wedlock.[21] Religious observance, among both the laity and the clergy,

---

1802; Theresa St. Xavier Farjon to Patrick Walsh, June 11, 1804; Patrick Walsh to Theresa St. Xavier Farjon, June 12, 1804; Notarized statement of Angelica Regis, June 16, 1804.

20. "Délibérations du Conseil," 79, 88, UCANO; SLC-B12, 198, no. 1113, Jan. 3, 1791; SLC-M3, 16, no. 43 bis.

21. *Code Noir*, 325, article 7 (1724). Of the children born to married parents, two were slaves of Jean Claude Dubreuil (SLC-B2, 10, no. 4, May 12, 1744, 15, no. 4, June 4, 1744); one was owned by Monsieur Dreux (SLC-B2, 20, no. 4, Aug. 23, 1744). Capu-

TABLE 8. *Parental Marital Status of Slave Infants, 1744–1795*

Year	Slave Infants Baptized	Slave Infants Born to Married Parents (%)
1744	77	9 (12)
1760	141	27 (19)
1765	172	23 (13)
1775	136	10 (7)
1785	144	4 (3)
1795	215	2 (2)

Sources: SLC-B2, SLC-B4, SLC-B5, SLC-B7, SLC-B10, SLC-B13.

seems to have been a more powerful factor in encouraging marriage among the enslaved than the law. As the century wore on, religious motivation increasingly acted as the only thing that brought enslaved couples to the altar.

During the Spanish period, the proportion of enslaved children born to married parents dropped precipitously, to 7 percent in 1775, 3 percent in 1785, and 2 percent in 1795 (see Table 8). The change probably occurred for several reasons. Spanish law did not prescribe marriage for the enslaved as the Code Noir had, and clerics in the later eighteenth century charged such high fees for performing weddings that many people, free and enslaved, settled into common-law relationships to avoid the cost.[22] The "re-Africanization" of Louisiana's enslaved population might have contributed to the decrease in marriage, since Afro-creoles practicing Catholicism would be more likely to ask for the sacrament than "new Africans." Almost unique among the enslaved of New Orleans, the Ursulines' bondpeople regularly knelt before the altar to receive the nuptial blessing and ceremo-

---

chin slaves were baptized on Sept. 10, 1744, and Oct. 27, 1744 (SLC-B2, 22, no. 2, 25, no. 4). Claude, the slave of pay commissioner Salmon, was baptized on Aug. 23, 1744 (SLC-B2, 20, no. 5).

22. In 1800, the attorney general of New Orleans complained about the effect on the general public of the Capuchins' refusal to bury or marry anyone until their fees were fully paid. See Kimberly S. Hanger, *Bounded Lives, Bounded Places: Free Black Society in Colonial New Orleans, 1769–1803* (Durham, N.C., 1997), 90–92; Jack D. L. Holmes, "Do It! Don't Do It! Spanish Laws on Sex and Marriage," in Gilbert C. Din, ed., *The Spanish Presence in Louisiana, 1763–1803* (Lafayette, La., 1996), 168–169.

nial veiling at the hands of Catholic clergy. The four enslaved children born to married parents and baptized in 1785 were all Ursuline bondpeople, as were three of the four whose baptisms were recorded in 1795.[23]

The nuns no doubt insisted on sacramental marriage for their bondpeople for reasons of social control as well as religious morality. Settled families were likely to produce stable, reliable workers. At least one bondman's behavior deteriorated upon the loss of his family. The nuns sold their carpenter, Laurant, to a new master because he had taken to drink. The sale took place some years after Laurant's wife and child apparently died.[24] Neither such cold-eyed pragmatism nor financial interest, however, explains several instances when the nuns tried to help families stay together until children were grown. In 1777, they sold thirty-five bondpeople. All of them, except two bondmen in their late twenties, were sold as part of one of seven family groups. The act is notable because, unlike French law, Spanish slave statutes in force at the time did not require that children below the age of fourteen be sold only with their parents. Later in the century, the nuns preserved the cohesion of an enslaved family on the threshold of freedom. In 1789, when Louis and Cecelia approached the convent chapter asking to purchase their freedom and that of their four children, the nuns negotiated with them on the cost and payment terms so that the entire family was freed in a single act of manumission.[25]

23. Hall, *Africans in Colonial Louisiana*, 277–286; SLC-B10, 120, no. 526, Apr. 24, 1785, 136, no. 584, Aug. 6, 1785, 146, no. 623, Sept. 25, 1785, 152, no. 645, Oct. 30, 1785; SLC-B13, 184, no. 749, Mar. 8, 1795, 201, no. 803, May 10, 1795, 230, no. 911, Sept. 20, 1796.

24. "Délibérations du Conseil," 57, UCANO. Laurant had previously been esteemed enough in the community at large to serve as a godfather, but his wife, Jeanne, bore him only one child, in 1766, and the disappearance of both wife and child from the record suggests that they did not survive long afterward (SLC-B3, 40, Sept. 21, 1755; SLC-B5, 113, no. 3, Feb. 13, 1766).

25. Acts of Juan Bautista Garic, January–December 1777, VIII, Nov. 8, 1777, 402, NANO; "Délibérations du Conseil," 67, UCANO; Acts of Rafael Perdomo, June 13–December 1790, XVI, Mar. 24, 1790, 143 bis–144 bis, NANO. *Code Noir*, 348–349, articles 43 and 44 (1724), required that slave families be sold together and that no children under the age of fourteen be sold separately from their mothers. As Hans W. Baade, "The Law of Slavery in Spanish Louisiana, 1769–1803," in Edward F. Haas, ed., *Louisiana's Legal Heritage* (Pensacola, Fla., 1983), 54–58, explains, Spanish slave law in Louisiana was not articulated in a single code; it took shape through judicial decisions of the governor and municipal officials of the Cabildo. The preservation of slave families was neither an aim nor a result of Spanish colonial legislation. Hall, *Africans in*

The result of the Ursulines pro-marriage and family stance was a slave community marked by family groupings and networks during the last four decades of colonial rule. Nine families of Ursuline bondpeople were linked to one another through marriage (see Appendix 2, Families J, K, L, M, N, O, P, CB, and HB). The large family of Jacob C and Louise Eulalie forged ties through marriage with three other families, tying dozens of Ursuline bondpeople together (see Appendix 2, Family J). These families often sustained a multigenerational presence at the convent; thus, children born at the end of the eighteenth century might be surrounded by uncles, aunts, and grandparents. For example, the children of Alexis and Marguerite—Augustin, Santiago, and Adelaide—would have known their maternal grandmother, Teresa, and their paternal grandparents, Jacob C and Louise Eulalie, who remained on the Ursuline plantation that Jacob C managed for fifteen years after he was freed in 1796 on the condition that he continue to oversee operations at the farm (see Appendix 2, Family HB, IB). Augustin, Santiago, and Adelaide also would have grown up surrounded by their cousins Marie Therese, Louis Gonzague, Marie, and Henrique, the children of Louis Gonzague, Sr., and Marie Henriette. All of these children lived among a number of aunts and uncles (see Appendix 2, Families J, L, M, and LB).

Determining which bondpeople lived at the convent site in the city and which resided on the nuns' plantations is not possible.[26] Such information would help to establish the environment in which the slave community

---

Colonial Louisiana, 169–171, 304–305, provides several instances where slaves were inventoried and presumably sold in family groups during the French period but notes that during the Spanish period children younger than eight years of age were frequently sold apart from their mothers.

26. Before 1780, the Ursulines owned two plantations, both on the opposite bank of the river from the city. In 1777, they sold one of these, together with thirty-five bondpeople who worked on it. In 1780, they purchased a new plantation, which was the principal source of their dairy products and fresh fruits and vegetables. "Délibérations du Conseil," 57, UCANO, records the nuns' decision to sell their plantation to Mr. Dufossat and its thirty-five enslaved workers to Francisco Bouligny. Acts of Juan Bautista Garic, January–December 1777, VIII, Nov. 8, 1777, NANO, records the act of sale for the bondpeople. Acts of Juan Bautista Garic, June–December 1778, X, July 30, 1778, NANO, records the sale of the plantation by the Ursulines. "Délibérations du Conseil," 77, UCANO, records the convent chapter's decision in 1779 to purchase a piece of property on the same side of the river as the convent. Carlos Trudeau, Certification of Ownership and Survey, July 25, 1780, UCANO, describes and situates the new plantation.

took shape and would speak to the work of scholars who suggest that the agency of bondpeople was more influential than the precept, example, and demands of masters. We do know that in 1796 twenty-four Ursuline bondpeople lived within the convent compound in town, and perhaps another twenty lived on their plantation two miles upriver under the direction of Jacob C.[27] Thus, the community was split into a group that lived in proximity to the nuns and another group that had little or no contact with their mistresses. The full participation of Ursuline bondpeople in the rites of the Catholic Church suggests at least one connection, or tether, between the nuns and their bondpeople. But wedding customs and patterns of godparenting and naming suggest that the nuns' bondpeople used the rituals of Catholicism not only to satisfy their mistresses' demands for religious observance but also to strengthen the bonds of their own community.

Bondpeople who were not kin were often linked through godparenting. Between August 1763 and 1800, parents chose fellow Ursuline bondpeople to serve as godparents for forty-eight of the seventy-five infants born into the Ursuline slave community (see Table 9). In eight of these instances, all of them involving the children and grandchildren of Jacob C and Louise Eulalie, the godparents were aunts or uncles of the child. But in 83 percent of the cases, godparents were apparently unrelated to their godchildren. Married couples sometimes acted together as godparents, perhaps serving an especially important function around midcentury, before extended families had begun to form. In 1766, husband and wife Laurant and Jeanne, for example, were godparents to Marie Magdelene Rosalie, the daughter of Bartheleme and Angelique. Afro-creole slaves bearing children in the 1760s were likely the progeny of African mothers and probably would not have had many living siblings to rely on as potential guardians for their own children.[28] Nonblood ties forged through godparenting thus wove Ursuline bondpeople together in the second half of the eighteenth century, breaching the gaps in kinship created in the first generations of enslavement.

27. John W. Blassingame, *The Slave Community: Plantation Life in the Antebellum South* (New York, 1972), 41–42, 78–79; Herbert G. Gutman, *The Black Family in Slavery and Freedom, 1750–1925* (New York, 1976), 101–256. The 1795 census of New Orleans is recorded in AGI, PC, legajo 211, 68. The estimate of twenty enslaved workers at the plantation is a conservative estimate based on sacramental and notarial records.

28. SLC-B5, 150 bis, no. 2, Dec. 16, 1766. Hall, *Africans in Colonial Louisiana*, 169, 175, notes that the slave population grew before the 1760s through natural increase, but the woman-to-child ratio of 1.000 derived from the inventory of 1739 that she cites does not indicate large family groups.

TABLE 9. *Godparenting among Ursuline Slaves, 1763–1800*

Decade	Baptisms	Ursuline Slave Godparents/ Named for Godparents	External Godparents/ Named for Godparents
1760s	16	6/3	10/3
1770s	19	17/5	2/1
1780s	22	12/4	10/2
1790s	18	13/1	5/1
Total	75	48/13	27/7

Sources: SLC-B5, SLC-B6, SLC-B7, SLC-B8, SLC-B10, SLC-B12, SLC-B13, SLC-B15.

Naming was used to honor both fictive and nonfictive kin in equal proportions: thirteen infants were named for their nonkin Ursuline enslaved godparents, and eighteen were named for blood relations in the Ursuline slave community (see Table 10). Naming and godparenting maximized the number of individuals tied to the baptized infant: among the Ursuline bondpeople no relatives served as godparents and gave their names to a godchild at the same time. Rather, children were named after nonkin godparents, or after close kin who were not serving as godparents. For example, Cecelia's brothers Alexis and Santiago were godfathers to her sons Lucas and Josef María, respectively. Josef María was, in turn, named for his grandfather, Joseph Leveillé. Mothers and fathers gave their names to their sons and daughters. Marie des Anges, baptized in 1763, was named for her mother, Angelique, and Juan Josef was named for his father, Josef (see Appendix 2, Families G and R). Daughters might also be named for their fathers. Francisco gave his name to his daughter María Francesca, and Luis D named his daughter María Luisa (see Appendix 2, Families C and U). Henrique was apparently named for his mother, Marie Henriette (see Appendix 2, Family LB). Three boys were named for their grandfathers: Josef María and his brother Josef Martin were named for their paternal grandfather, Joseph Leveillé, and Santiago, the son of Alexis, for his grandfather Jacob C (see Appendix 2, Families HB and IB).[29] The intergenerational link-

29. SLC-B12, 51, no. 367, Feb. 8, 1788, 137, no. 869, Feb. 14, 1790; SLC-B10, 136, no. 584, Aug. 6, 1785; SLC-B5, 22 bis, no. 4, Aug. 6, 1763; SLC-B8, 232, no. 835, Sept. 23,

TABLE 10. *Ursuline Slaves Named after Kin, 1763–1850*

Grandmothers' names to granddaughters	1
Grandfathers' names to grandsons	3
Mothers' names to daughters	4
Mothers' names to sons	1
Fathers' names to daughters	3
Fathers' names to sons	6
Total	18

Sources: SLC-B5, SLC-B6, SLC-B7, SLC-B8, SLC-B10, SLC-B12, SLC-B13, SLC-B15.

ing of kin is especially evident in the two families whose descendants lived as Ursuline bondpeople over five generations, where the custom of naming children for their ancestors was carried into the late antebellum period. In one of these families, a son in each of four successive generations carried the name Louis Gonzague (see Appendix 2, Families LB, MB, and NB).

Ursuline bondpeople used godparenting not only to extend and strengthen the web of relationships among themselves but also as a vehicle for the exercise of leadership and the recognition of distinctive qualities, such as age, wisdom, or piety. Eleven men and women emerge from the records as unusually frequent godparents, serving at least twice at the baptisms of nonkin. Joseph Leveillé, for example, was the overseer of the Ursuline plantation in the 1760s and early 1770s. He was active as a godfather when he was in his late forties, standing at the baptismal font as sponsor four times between 1767 and 1770. Hélène and Nicole were both older women, perhaps in their fifties, when they were called on to be godmothers to four infants born in the late 1760s and early 1770s.[30] Angelique and Bartheleme were married to one another, and on two occasions they served together as godparents to the same individual. One of these ceremonies is notable. In 1772, Angelique and Bartheleme sponsored the baptism of the

---

1781, 313, no. 1095, Dec. 9, 1782; SLC-B15, 67, no. 236, Jan. 15, 1799; Acts of Juan Bautista Garic, January–December 1777, VIII, 402, NANO. Santiago was the Spanish variant of Jacob.

30. "Délibérations du Conseil," 57, UCANO, identifies Joseph Leveillé as the nuns' plantation overseer; his act of emancipation states his age as fifty-five (Acts of Juan Bautista Garic, January–December 1777, VIII, 485, Dec. 15, 1777, NANO). Hélène and Nicole were identified as "old" in the council minutes that recorded the nuns' decision to free them gratuitously in 1777 ("Délibérations du Conseil," 57, UCANO).

TABLE 11. *Frequent Godparents among Ursuline Slaves*

Name	Baptisms	Dates Active
Angelique	7	1771–1791
Bartheleme	4	1766–1781
Estevan	2	1788–1794
Hélène	2	1766–1770
Joseph Leveillé	4	1767–1770
Juan Bautista	6	1783–1799
María Luisa	6	1778–1785
María Teresa	2	1789–1795
Nicole	2	1766–1772
Radegunda	2	1770–1774
Vincent	6	1778–1795

Sources: SLC-B5, SLC-B6, SLC-B7, SLC-B8, SLC-B10, SLC-B12, SLC-B13, SLC-B15.

adult neophyte Vincent. Similarly, another married couple, Estevan and Teresa, stood as godparents to the new African Domingo when he was baptized in 1794 (see Table 11).[31]

Special importance and meaning might have been attached to godparenting new Africans. During the last third of the eighteenth century, the Ursuline slave community was made up almost entirely of creoles and Africans who came to Louisiana before 1744. Notarial acts, chapter minutes, and sacramental records indicate that between 1766 and 1803 fourteen new Africans joined the convent community.[32] When these adult

31. SLC-B7, 4, no. 4, Mar. 8, 1772; SLC-B13, 111, no. 426, Feb. 5, 1794.

32. Four Ursuline bondpeople are clearly identified in records as new Africans. Acts of Rafael Perdomo, June 13–December 1790, XVI, Apr. 10, 1790, 171, NANO, records the purchase by the Ursulines of two "negres bozales," or new Africans, who were probably Francisco, identified in his 1795 baptismal and marriage record as a member of the "Mande" nation, and Domingo, identified in his baptismal record of 1794 as a member of the "Maninga" nation (SLC-M3, 12 bis, no. 76, June 15, 1795; SLC-B13, 111, no. 426, Feb. 5, 1794). Roseta was identified as a member of the "Peyaya" nation when she married fellow new African Francisco (SLC-M3, 12 bis, no. 76, June 15, 1795). Adult slaves of the nuns baptized in the last third of the eighteenth century were also likely new Africans. There were ten: Marie (SLC-B6, 19 bis, no. 3, Apr. 10, 1768), Louis (SLC-B6, 68 bis, no. 5, Oct. 29, 1769), Vincent (SLC-B7, 4, no. 4, Mar. 8, 1772),

neophytes went to the baptismal font, they were often accompanied by bondpeople who were already prominent as frequent godparents. Angelique, in addition to joining her husband Bartheleme as a godparent to Vincent in 1772, sponsored the neophyte Ursula when she was baptized in 1790. Joseph Leveillé stood beside Marie when she received the rite for adults in 1768, and Juan Bautista, six times a godfather, took his place beside a new Christian who took his name in 1785. Vincent, who had been an adult neophyte himself in 1772, became one of the most active godparents and in 1785 gave his name and his promise to be a Christian guardian to a young man who was baptized together with his father.[33]

The characteristics of recurrent godparents and their prominence in the baptism of new Africans suggest that individuals played the role of elders in the Ursuline community. They gave the blessing of their protection to creole infants and oversaw the initiation of new group members into the cultural practices and network of relationships among the nuns' bondpeople. The pattern of frequent godparenting among the Ursuline bondpeople might have been an adaptation of African culture to New World circumstances. The Catholic tradition of godparenting provided bondpeople with the means to honor the experience, wisdom, and skill of their elders, and it gave older bondpeople a vehicle for authority that was supported by their mistresses and the powerful institutions of church and state that governed the colony. At the same time, the distribution of godparenting beyond the band of community elders broadened and strengthened the network of relationships among the wider circle of the nuns' bondpeople, helping to shape a sense of group identity and a communal history. Ursuline slaves made the most of godparenting, using it to serve two distinct but complementary functions that resonated with broad patterns of African culture and social organization.[34]

Antonio (SLC-B8, 158, no. 1, May 5, 1780), Felicité (SLC-B10, feuille volant between 122 and 123, May 14, 1785), Juan Bautista and his son, Vincent (SLC-B10, feuille volant between 164 and 165, Dec. 26, 1785), Sol (SLC-B10, feuille volant between 164 and 165, Dec. 26, 1785), Juan Bautista (SLC-B10, 118, no. 763, Oct. 15, 1789), Ursula (SLC-B10, 178, no. 1040, Sept. 10, 1790), Francesca (SLC-B10, 178, no. 1040, Sept. 10, 1790).

33. SLC-B6, 19 bis, no. 3, Apr. 10, 1768, feuille volant between 122 and 123; SLC-B10, feuille volant between 122 and 123, May 14, 1785, 178, no. 1040, Sept. 10, 1790; SLC-B7, 4, no. 4, Mar. 8, 1772.

34. For some examples of the social organization of African groups that figured in the Atlantic slave trade, see Michael A. Gomez, *Exchanging Our Country Marks: The Transformation of African Identities in the Colonial and Antebellum South* (Chapel Hill,

Ursuline bondpeople also used another life passage to bolster group cohesion and show solidarity with one another. Late in the eighteenth century, weddings were the site for demonstrations of mutual support among the nuns' bondpeople as they assumed responsibility for starting their own families and contributing to a widening web of kinship and community. The role of ushering couples over the threshold of marriage fell, not to parents or even to siblings, but to young men who were peers of the groom. Young male relatives and friends appear in eight of the nine marriages of Ursuline bondmen during the 1790s. Alexis, who married in 1791 at the age of twenty-eight, was the first of his cohort to wed, and he figures most prominently among the groomsmen. He witnessed the wedding of his brother Santiago four months after his own nuptials as well as that of fellow Ursuline bondman Ramón. With his brother Gabriel, Alexis also attended the weddings of his sisters, Marie and Marie Henriette, as well as the nuptials for Charles and Domingo, to whom they were not related. Juan Bautista witnessed five weddings of fellow Ursuline bondmen, and, when he married in 1795, his wedding was attended by Noel Carrière, captain of the militia of free men of color and the half-brother of an Ursuline bondperson. Vincent and Miguel each attended one wedding as a witness (see Table 12). Male friends of grooms of European descent frequently attended weddings and signed as witnesses in New Orleans. If Ursuline bondmen's practice was an emulation of this demonstration of male camaraderie, it was a replication of European male sociability denied to most of the enslaved population of New Orleans.[35]

_____

N.C., 1998), 95–100, which discusses the organization of religious societies in Sierra Leone, where older men and women might exercise particular authority; Gomez also notes the role of male and female elders in the Akan society of the Gold Coast (110–111). Hall, *Africans in Colonial Louisiana*, 52–53, notes the forms of leadership in the society of the Senegambians, who constituted a large proportion of the captive Africans brought to Louisiana. For a comparable use of godparenting among enslaved Moravians in North Carolina, see Jon F. Sensbach, *A Separate Canaan: The Making of an Afro-Moravian World in North Carolina, 1763-1840* (Chapel Hill, N.C., 1998), 137–143.

35. For examples of the European custom of male groomsmen, see the wedding of Francisco Alvarez, attended by Pedro Feo and Ignacio Briaga; that of Baltasar Dusciau, attended by Jose Devillie Degutin and Luis De Reggio; and that of Basilio Kreps, attended by Santiago Cadet Monlon, Juan Bautista Melleur, Luis Landreaux, and Felix Arnaud (Earl C. Woods and Charles Nolan, eds., *Sacramental Records of the Roman Catholic Church of the Archdiocese of New Orleans*, 16 vols. to date [New Orleans, 1987–], VI, 5, 109, 159).

TABLE 12. *Witnesses at Marriages of Ursuline Slaves, 1790–1798*

Date	Groom (Family)	Bride (Family)	Witnesses (Family)
November 22, 1791	Alexis (J)	Marguerite (L)	Pierre, free
April 16, 1792	Santiago (J)	María Martha, free	Alexis (J)
June 16, 1794	Vincent (Q)	Marie (J)	Juan Bautista, Alexis (J), Gabriel (J)
June 21, 1794	Louis Gonzague (M)	Marie Henriette (J)	Alexis (J), Gabriel (J)
February 14, 1795	Juan Bautista	Magdalena	Noel Carrière, free (K)
June 15, 1795	Francisco	Rosa	Juan Bautista, Miguel (FB)
July 14, 1795	Ramón (AB)	Victoria	Alexis (J), Juan Bautista
August 13, 1798	Charles (O)	Denis	Juan Bautista, Alexis (J), Gabriel (J)
August 16, 1798	Domingo	Maria Juana	Juan Bautista, Vincent (Q), Alexis (J), Gabriel (J)

Note: Family membership is indicated parenthetically. See Appendix 2.
Source: SLC-M3.

    The Catholic sacraments of marriage and baptism offered the Ursuline bondpeople ways to fashion a framework of supportive, intergenerational ties. The nuns' insistence on marriage and their protection of family groups, which survived long after law and custom withdrew support for these practices, promoted the continued stability of the community that began to form around family groups in the 1760s. New Africans arriving among the nuns' bondpeople came incrementally and were incubated in an environment that featured familiar forms of mentorship and peer support. The practical and, to some degree, emotional effect of the Ursulines' religious belief on the lives of their bondpeople is thus discernible. More difficult to ascertain is the extent to which Ursuline bondpeople embraced the spirituality that underpinned the nuns' promotion of family and the rituals and traditions from which the slave community drew structure and strength.

Some Ursuline bondpeople manifested genuine devotion. Before he died, Pierre instructed his daughter Ann to purchase her freedom from the nuns but to continue serving them so that she would "come to die here so that she would die like a good Christian." Joseph Leveillé, who was freed in 1777, sought a similar future for his six-year-old granddaughter, Julie. He asked the nuns in 1785 to manumit her without charge and keep her with them at their house "so that she will continue to be instructed in religion and good conduct."[36] Of the forty-one Ursuline bondwomen baptized between 1763 and 1803, twenty-nine (71 percent) were given the name Marie or Maria, presumably to honor and gain the protection of Catholicism's major female saint, the Virgin Mary (see Appendix 2).

The very prevalence of Ursuline bondpeople as godparents suggests that they exhibited sufficient understanding of Catholic doctrine and were observant enough in their own religious practice to be approved as sponsors at baptism. Canon law requires godparents to know the rudiments of Christian doctrine and to take an informed and "lasting interest in their spiritual child, and to take good care that he leads a truly Christian life." There is, of course, a difference between knowing and believing, and no proof exists that interior faith matched the external piety of African godparents. Ursuline godparents simply might have mastered a performance that secured them the use of a valuable cultural and social tool.[37]

36. "Délibérations du Conseil," 59, 64, UCANO; Acts of Rafael Perdomo, XVII, Jan. 10, 1786, 7–8, NANO.

37. Stanislaus Woywod, *A Practical Commentary on the Code of Canon Law*, rev. and enl., ed. Callistus Smith (New York, 1957), 393, 395 (quotation). For a discussion of such slave performances in the antebellum period, see Bertram Wyatt-Brown, "The Mask of Obedience: Male Slave Psychology in the Old South," *American Historical Review*, XCIII (1988), 1228–1252. Allan Greer, *Mohawk Saint: Catherine Tekakwitha and the Jesuits* (New York, 2005), 111–124, offers a fascinating analysis of the possible incentives for conversion among the Indians of New France. Jon F. Sensbach's *Rebecca's Revival: Creating Black Christianity in the Atlantic World* (Cambridge, Mass., 2005), sug-

The orthodox versions of Protestant and Catholic Christianity promulgated by the clergy fought popular belief in magic, mysticism, and pantheism in early modern Europe and its colonies.[38] The clergy managed to win some battles against alternative belief. They achieved orthodoxy in certain types of behavior—they persuaded more people to receive the sacraments of confession and Communion regularly and to seal their life partnerships with the sacrament of marriage, for example. The content of early modern European popular belief, however, often remained far from the clerical ideal.

The growth of slave godparenting suggests that, to the priests charged with judging the qualifications of godparents, Africans began to match Europeans in the outward expressions of religiosity that were the only practical measures the clergy had for assessing piety. In 1731, slaves or free people of color served as godparents in only 2 of the 162 baptisms that took place at Saint Louis Church, representing only 1 percent of the godparents in slave baptism. A generation later, the enslaved and free people of color had begun to participate more noticeably and were recorded as godparents in 21 percent of the slave baptisms registered at Saint Louis Church. As the century progressed, slaves and free people of color grew to dominate the sponsorship of slaves at baptism. In 1775, when the creole proportion of the New Orleans slave population was probably at its eighteenth-century peak, 89 percent of the godparents of slaves were of African descent. Even at the end of the century, when there were larger numbers of new Africans in the city who could not serve as godparents, the great majority of slave infants were sponsored by people of color (see Table 13).

The growth in godparenting among people of African descent was not a sudden phenomenon that can be tied to changes in regime. As Table 13 illustrates, it began during the French colonial era. Under the Spanish, it continued and peaked only to ebb a bit as the eighteenth century drew to

---

gests the importance of gender to successful conversion in his detailed study of a black female Moravian catechist and missionary.

38. Keith Thomas, *Religion and the Decline of Magic* (New York, 1971), esp. 636–639; Jean Delumeau, *Catholicism between Luther and Voltaire: A New View of the Counter-Reformation*, trans. Jeremy Moiser (London, 1977), esp. 169; William A. Christian, Jr., *Local Religion in Sixteenth-Century Spain* (Princeton, N.J., 1981); David D. Hall, *Worlds of Wonder, Days of Judgment: Popular Religious Belief in Early New England* (New York, 1989); Henry Kamen, *The Phoenix and the Flame: Catalonia and the Counter Reformation* (New Haven, Conn., 1993).

TABLE 13. *Participation of Godparents of African Descent in Slave Baptisms, 1731-1795*

Year	Slave Baptisms	Slave Baptisms with Godparents of African Descent (%)
1731	162	2 (1)
1750	75	16 (21)
1760	192	56 (29)
1765	197	135 (68)
1775	136	121 (89)
1785	144	122 (85)
1795	215	159 (74)

Note: The year 1731 was chosen because it is the first for which baptismal records are available. Records for 1740 are lost, so 1750 was used. The years 1760 and 1765 were chosen because they bracket the end of the Seven Years' War and show activity before effective Spanish rule began in 1770. Only infant baptisms were counted for the years 1775 and 1785 because the illegibility of adult group baptisms in those years makes it virtually impossible to determine the status of most godparents.
Sources: SLC-B1, SLC-B2, SLC-B4, SLC-B5, SLC-B7, SLC-B10, SLC-B13.

a close. The most plausible explanation for the rhythm and upward climb in slave godparenting lies in the community of the enslaved themselves. The growth tracks the generations of Louisiana Afro-creoles as they came of age and reproduced not only themselves but also their participation in the rite of baptism. Children born to mothers catechized and sponsored for baptism in the campaign of religious instruction carried out by the Ladies' Congregation of the Children of Mary in the 1730s became godparents in the 1750s, when the first significant growth spurt in slave godparenting appears. Whatever the role of the Ursulines and the Children of Mary might have been in the conversion of the first generation, the increasing frequency of slave godparenting, evident both in the Ursuline slave community and among the larger population, points to the enslaved's growing agency in their religious lives. It also suggests that enslaved and free people of color beyond the Ursuline community embraced the rituals and customs surrounding baptism and put them to the same purposes of network building and social support.[39]

For all practical purposes, the Ursulines led a successful effort to draw enslaved Africans into Catholicism. By extending their catechizing mission to people of color, they provided an institutional foundation for inclusivity in one of the key realms of colonial society and culture and laid an enduring foundation for a multiracial church that did not know congregational segregation until the era of Jim Crow in the late nineteenth century. Their promotion of baptism and sacramental marriage among their bondpeople protected the integrity of families and helped foster communal identity and strength.[40]

Notwithstanding these positive contributions to the quality of slave life, the nuns were full participants in establishing and maintaining the institution of slavery. They bought and owned human property from the start. They never hesitated about taking up the practice and never spoke against it, either in their private records or in public correspondence. Among the few eighteenth-century convent financial records that survive are six bills of sale in Spanish for individuals the nuns bought between 1778 and 1798. The sale and purchase of men, women, and children is recorded with mundane regularity in the council minutes of the community. These entries indicate that both financial concerns and issues of social control shaped the nuns' commercial transactions involving their human property.

39. For alternative interpretations, see James Thomas McGowan, "Creation of a Slave Society: Louisiana Plantations in the Eighteenth Century" (Ph.D. diss., University of Rochester, 1976), 268, 291 n. 17. Bell, *Revolution*, 65–66, accepts McGowan's explanation for the expanded participation of people of color in the church in the Spanish period. Thomas N. Ingersoll, *Mammon and Manon in Early New Orleans: The First Slave Society in the Deep South, 1718–1819* (Knoxville, Tenn., 1999), 113, asserts that the growth in slave godparenting was a manifestation of white aversion to involvement in slave baptism. He suggests that in 1759 "whites were clearly avoiding participation" in godparenting slaves. "Clearly, most whites had decided that it was socially acceptable to avoid this annoyance, and blacks were permitted to turn to their own community for godparents."

40. The segregation of the Catholic churches of New Orleans was not completed until the end of World War I. See Joseph Logsdon and Caryn Cossé Bell, "The Americanization of Black New Orleans, 1850–1900," in Hirsch and Logsdon, eds., *Creole New Orleans*, 259; James B. Bennett, *Religion and the Rise of Jim Crow in New Orleans* (Princeton, N.J., 2005), 136–199.

In 1734, they concluded a deal with a man named Larche for a plantation across the river from New Orleans to augment their holdings, trading him two bondmen, six hundred livres in cash, and two years' board and instruction in their school for the girl of his choice in lieu of the twenty-four-hundred-livre purchase price. The nuns negotiated a similarly complex deal in 1757, renting a plantation with "six adult male Negroes, two Negresses, four cows, two young bulls, two oxen, tamed, for 2,500 livres a year, the Negroes at twenty-five livres a month each." Although this is the only instance where the enslaved were categorized with animals, several other examples illustrate how clearly the Ursulines conceptualized their bondpeople as property and measures of their wealth. In 1758, they toyed with borrowing twenty-four hundred livres "to be invested in Negroes to increase the value of our plantations," and in 1762 they refused the request of the colonial commandant to transfer two of the bondpeople who worked one of their plantations to the staff of the provincial hospital, where the fruits of their bondpeople's labor would be lost to them. Only once did the notion of selling human beings seem to tweak the nuns' consciences. In 1759, they wanted to buy a family of seven for the large sum of ten thousand livres. The community agreed to the purchase "on condition of selling Pierre Borgne and his wife Mannon with one named Regis." They continued, as though apologizing to posterity, "We were not in condition to make this purchase without this help."[41]

Spanish legal practice made emancipation much easier than it had been under the French, and the nuns did manumit a number of their bondpeople, but rarely on terms that were disadvantageous to the Ursulines. In 1777, they freed "three of our old negresses," women who were undoubtedly past childbearing age and were probably no longer able to take a hand in heavy labor. The Ursulines freed Joseph Leveillé's six-year-old granddaughter, Julie, at no cost, but the chapter minutes note that this action was "only in her case, which will not serve as an example." Others obtained their freedom only at a price. Marie Reine's aunt, a free woman of color, gave the nuns two thousand livres in cash and a young bondwoman from Guinea in return for her niece's liberty. Lucienne achieved emancipation after paying only one hundred pesos, but free man of color Peter Claver had to pay the nuns six hundred pesos to gain the manumission of his goddaughter, Marie Angela, and Ann had to offer one thousand pesos for her freedom. The nuns also discovered the financial benefit of granting conditional manumission

41. "Délibérations du Conseil," 18, 44, 47, 49, UCANO.

to their enslaved overseers, requiring them to continue their duties as before in return for technical freedom, food, and lodging for themselves and their families, and usufruct of a piece of ground that exceeded the customary provision plot. Joseph Leveillé was freed on such terms in 1777, and Jacob C, in 1796.[42]

Their bondpeople's labor was a source of cash for the Ursulines. They rented out some of their skilled bondpeople, such as Vincent, who as a blacksmith earned monthly fees of 10 pesos. An unnamed cobbler contributed 7 pesos to the convent coffers in months when he made shoes for people outside the convent. Although the nuns seem not to have engaged in staple crop agriculture, they derived a steady income from the sale of surplus fruits and vegetables cultivated on their plantation. In 1799, produce brought in 679 pesos, which constituted 8 percent of the total cash income for that year.[43]

When bondpeople did not conform to the nuns' moral and behavioral standards, they did not hesitate to sell them away from the community. As mentioned earlier, six were sold in 1756 because they were "thieves and capable of spoiling the others," but numerous other sales of "bad Negroes" occurred throughout the French, Spanish, and American periods. In 1733, they exchanged a "very bad Negro" named Cuzart for one whose demeanor was more promising, and six years later they sold a young bondman named Jacob because he "was not likely to work well." The community approved the sale of "three couples of bad persons of our Negroes" in 1763 so that the nuns would be able to use the money to "own good ones in their place." Drinking, lasciviousness, and a nasty disposition were frequently cited by the nuns as reasons for selling bondpeople, particularly in the Spanish and American periods. They sold their carpenter in 1777 because he drank too much and their mason, Pedro, in 1796 because of his "bad behavior." And, as noted earlier, they often sold unwed mothers. The nuns' motives in these instances paralleled those of their fellow slaveholders. They sold "bad Negroes" lest they infect the rest of the slave community and to serve as a warning to those who remained. They aimed to build a workforce that was

42. Ibid., 57, 59, 62, 64, 74, 84; Acts of Juan Bautista Garic, January–December 1777, VIII, Dec. 15, 1777, 485, Acts of Carlos Ximenes, July–December 1796, XI, Mar. 18, 1796, 136–138 bis, both in NANO.

43. "General Accounts, October 1797–October 1812," UCANO, 336–347, 355–359. There is indirect evidence that the nuns tried their hands at sugar cultivation in the early nineteenth century.

not only morally upright and well behaved but also that was unfailingly productive.[44]

The Ursulines' educational mission and promotion of a sacramental life among the enslaved did have a positive impact on the lives of their bond-people and influenced the experience of the enslaved in the wider community as well. Nonetheless, this salutary effect seems largely to have been the unintended consequence of the nature of their order's mission and the enforcement of their religious mores. Yet the nuns appeared to be sensitive to the aspirations and feelings of their bondpeople and sometimes made an effort to respond directly to them. The thirty-five whom they rented to Madame and Monsieur Vallier in 1776 complained that they were poorly treated and asked the nuns to sell them to better owners. These people must have had some expectation of a sympathetic response when the group's representative made his way to the convent parlor to ask the mother superior to present the bondpeople's petition to the nuns in chapter. The mother superior did as he asked, and the nuns voted to accede to the request. A little more than a month later, they transferred the ownership of the thirty-five to Francisco Bouligny. Six years later, the nuns might have responded to a similar request. Cupidon and his wife, Catarina, were among the original group of thirty-five but had been sold again. In 1783, the nuns bought them back from a free woman of color named Teresa Cheval. In her old age, Catarina remained at the convent and showed her continued attachment to the Ursuline slave community when she served as godmother to an infant in 1799.[45]

Manumission records indicate that the nuns were generally inclined to facilitate freedom, even if they were not willing to give it away. They accepted modest prices and were flexible about payment. Recall Louis, who told the nuns that he could not pay market value to obtain freedom for himself, his wife, and four sons, from whom they accepted a lower sum in installments. The sisters also seem to have helped former slaves by lending them money or making purchases from them. Marie Thérèse, who was probably one of the elderly bondwomen freed in 1777, borrowed and repaid

44. "General Accounts, October 1797–October 1812," 18, 49, 57, 75, UCANO; "Délibérations du Conseil," 18, 32, 49, 57, 75, UCANO.

45. Acts of Juan Bautista Garic, January–December 1777, VIII, 433, Nov. 24, 1777, NANO; "Achat du Nègre Cupidon agé de 55 ans," July 28, 1783, UCANO; SLC-B15, 104, no. 342, Apr. 18, 1799.

two hundred pesos from the nuns in 1791, and Joseph Leveillé sold them two bondpeople in 1778, a year after he was conditionally emancipated.[46]

The nuns knew the enslaved wanted their freedom, understood their desire to earn money so that, once free themselves, they could liberate their family members, and recognized that not all slaveholders put the happiness of their bondpeople first. At some level, perhaps, they knew that the moral universe that dictated the enslaved should be full beneficiaries of the graces of Catholicism also ordained their liberty. Yet, at the same time, they might have longed for the kind of affirmation that Pierre gave when he instructed his daughter, Ann, to buy her freedom but remain with the nuns. They probably wanted to believe that the terms of slavery that they offered their bondpeople were received with a measure of gratitude.

The bondpeople of the colonial period indicated that even the benevolent ownership of the nuns was a poor substitute for freedom as they regularly sought to buy their liberty. During the Civil War, the Ursuline bondpeople told the nuns in the stark language of rejection that slavery on any terms was unacceptable. In the nineteenth-century record book of the convent's slave community, there is a series of terse notations.

> August 2, 1863, Theodore left us to claim his liberty from the federal military authorities in New Orleans and some days later his children Honoré and Adelaide left us also.

> August 1 or 2, 1863, André left us to claim his liberty from the military authorities of the city. Clementine his wife and their three children, Josephine, Justine, and André left us also. Thus too Leocardee, Clementine's sister.

> September 24, 1864, Maric Camille left us to take her liberty.

> November 1, 1864, Reine, daughter of Louis and Constance, left us for liberty.

> April 3, 1865, Julien, Marie Pauline his wife, and Eugenie their daughter left us to take their liberty. Hélène left us the same day."

46. Acts of Juan Bautista Garic, June–December 1778, X, 583, Dec. 22, 1778, Acts of Rafael Perdomo, January–June 12, 1790, XV, 143 bis–144 bis, Acts of Carlos Ximenes, January–December 1791, I, 147, Mar. 31, 1791, all in NANO.

As they left for freedom, members of some of the oldest of the convent slave families showed that the bonds of affection and loyalty that mattered to them were those that existed among themselves. Fifth-generation Ursuline bondpeople André, Theodore, Clementine, and Reine left the world of the convent behind without, it seems, a backward glance.[47]

Only two bondpeople are known to have remained with the nuns after the Civil War, Louis Gonzague and his wife, Constance. Louis's loyalty later revealed a bittersweet paradox. His will, made out in 1889 and carefully preserved in the Ursuline archives, left 12 dollars to the Ursulines for masses for his soul. Born in 1818, Louis had achieved the kind of true Catholic faith the nuns of the colonial era hoped to spread among the enslaved. Yet he left the bulk of his cash legacy, 150 dollars, not to the Ursulines, but to the African American Sisters of the Holy Family founded by a free woman of color, Henriette Delille. The money was, he said, to be used to pay for the education of his two daughters. Louis signed his will with a mark.[48]

The Ursulines never risked stretching the boundaries of slavery enough to give Louis Gonzague and his fellow bondpeople the education that might have been powerful enough to kill the institution. But, in a happy twist of fate, they planted seeds of piety among people of color that later bore sweet fruit: a religious order for women of color who served the enslaved and, later, freedmen. When Henriette Delille and the Sisters of the Holy Family took up the cause of Christian education in the 1830s, they acted in the tradition of the French apostolic women who were instrumental in introducing Afro-New Orleanians to Catholicism. When they founded an institution to educate the children of freedmen, they gave to Louis Gonzague's daughters what the Ursulines did not and pushed an educational ideal that was revolutionary in its potential to achieve the full measure of its promise.[49]

The Ursulines never intentionally acted to oppose or undermine the institution of slavery. Their Counter-Reformation apostolate, however, helped to create opportunities for the enslaved in New Orleans to build community and exercise leadership in a public institution. The nuns' pro-

47. "Livre ou sont les noms," 4, UCANO.

48. Louis Gonzague, Last Will and Testament, Oct. 24, 1889, UCANO.

49. On the development of religious leadership among free women of color and the prominence of Henriette Delille and her family, see Emily Clark and Virginia Meacham Gould, "The Feminine Face of Afro-Catholicism in New Orleans, 1727–1852," WMQ, 3d Ser., LIX (2002), 409–448.

Figure 17. Louis Gonzague III (1818–1894). Fourth-generation Ursuline bondman, circa 1890. Courtesy, UCANO

motion of marriage among their own bondpeople created a slave community marked by the enduring ties of family. The exodus of bondpeople during the Civil War was a family affair: Theodore, André, and Julien took their wives and children with them into freedom. The blood and fictive kin networks that knit the Ursuline bondpeople together served as an example not only to other slaveowners but also to other slaves, contesting assertions that families sacralized by the church were an unnecessary or unattainable ideal for the unfree. In the religious realm, at least, the experience of many of the enslaved was distinctive in New Orleans. French Catholicism and the religious women who promoted it among the enslaved in the formative colonial years made it so.

chapter 6

THE WAGES OF ZEAL CHANGE AND THE CONVENT ECONOMY

Nine women gathered in New Orleans on an October night in 1734 and decided together to negotiate the purchase of a plantation worth twenty-five hundred livres by offering the owner three hundred livres in cash, three hundred livres toward his debt with the colonial proprietors, two enslaved laborers worth one thousand livres, and two years of free tuition and board for the girl of his choice at their school.[1] Acquiring property in exchange for cash and enslaved laborers made these women typical of enterprising planters who invested their cash and slave capital to increase their wealth. Offering to close the gap in the terms of purchase with a voucher for fees at a girls' school was, on the other hand, an arrangement uniquely available to these women.

When they bought Jacques Larche's riverfront plantation in 1734, the New Orleans Ursulines displayed the specifically feminine nature of their central enterprise and their active participation in a financial realm perceived as distinctly masculine. The nuns continued throughout the eighteenth century to engage in a wide range of economic activities—agriculture, real estate development, buying and selling human property—in addition to maintaining their educational work. That they did so as a highly visible corporate body of unmarried women presents a contrast with eighteenth-century British colonial America. There women experienced increasing legal and ideological constraints on their independent agency in the decades approaching and following the American Revolution. British colonial and early national women negotiated this changing public climate with a variety of strategies that allowed them to shape economics and politics in the household and beyond. Women held property, participated in trade, organized resistance, and forged the political culture of the young American Republic in their drawing rooms. The consignment of women

1. "Délibérations du Conseil," 18, UCANO.

to the "private sphere" of domesticity and the rhetoric of "true woman-hood" lay ahead, in the nineteenth century. Still, eighteenth-century Anglo-American women did experience a recalibration of womanhood and its privileges. Where once property had provided some women with entrée into the realms of economics and politics, masculinity became the universal passkey for public participation. In the early Republic, women continued to exert influence over private finance and public affairs, but their status as wives was all but required for social and legal recognition of their activities, resulting in what one historian calls the "erasure of unmarried women from the public."[2]

In the convent, where no earthly spouse or father was present to make and execute a financial strategy, the Ursulines, like many widows and spinsters of British colonial America, proved willing and capable of doing so themselves. But for the nuns there was never the possibility of social and ideological rehabilitation through marriage or remarriage. These women would forever remain beyond the pale of a husband's benevolent rule. Nor could they simply be erased or ignored, as individual unmarried women might be. Neither invisible nor properly mediated by a husband, this community of women was not easily assimilated into the models of feminine agency that Anglo-American women had developed. Neither parlor politics nor republican motherhood was a viable alternative for celibate nuns who lived in a cloister.

The Ursulines owed their experience in corporate financial management to their French monastic origins, but the nature of the economic autonomy they achieved in Louisiana was different in crucial ways from what had gone before. Female religious customarily owned and managed property

2. "Republican motherhood" is the term coined by Linda K. Kerber to describe the distinctive form of female political agency forged by post-Revolutionary American women (Kerber, *Women of the Republic: Intellect and Ideology in Revolutionary America* [Chapel Hill, N.C., 1980], 11–12, 199–200, 227–231, 235, 276–288). Among the best studies that describe the eighteenth-century trend toward ideological and legal constraint of women's individual agency and women's responses to it are Linda L. Sturtz, *Within Her Power: Propertied Women in Colonial Virginia* (New York, 2002); Catherine Allgor, *Parlor Politics: In Which the Ladies of Washington Help Build a City and a Government* (Charlottesville, Va., 2000); Karin Wulf, *Not All Wives: Women of Colonial Philadelphia* (Ithaca, N.Y., 2000), 12, 17, 184–205 (quotation on 205); and Cornelia Hughes Dayton, *Women before the Bar: Gender, Law, and Society in Connecticut, 1639–1789* (Chapel Hill, N.C., 1995), 58–68.

in France, but the ultimate source of that property lay embedded in the matrix of patriarchy. The financial foundations of French convents rested on dowries provided by the nuns' fathers. The rules of their order forced the Louisiana missionaries to forfeit their dowries to their French convents upon departing for America. The absence of dowry capital coupled with an unreliable tuition revenue stream in the sparsely populated colony turned the colonial nuns into aggressive entrepreneurs during the early decades of the New Orleans convent. By the middle of the eighteenth century, they were the mistresses of two plantations and a part of the circle of major slave-holders. Although their plantations and bondpeople proved to be the foundation of their New World wealth, they were not the sustaining element of the convent economy. As the century drew to a close, the nuns' primary source of income was the money paid to them for services they provided. They received stipends from the Spanish crown for operating a hospital, sheltering orphans, and providing public education to girls in a day school. Fees paid by the better-off students became their largest source of financial support, growing substantially in the closing years of the colonial period when the maturation of the port of New Orleans brought wealth and population growth to the city. At a time when others in late colonial Louisiana pursued wealth through the lucrative cultivation of sugarcane by investing in larger labor forces and plantations, the Ursulines divested themselves of a substantial proportion of their bondpeople and land and depended on their school to support them. Cut off from the Old World patriarchal support represented by dowries at the beginning of the century, by the end of the era they had forged a financial strategy that distanced them from the emerging plantation economy and disturbed the gender hierarchy of the slave South.

The economies of the Ursuline communities of seventeenth-century France were enmeshed in the financial strategies of a patriarchal culture in which men acted to maximize family wealth and social prestige. In families of good social standing but limited means, a marriage made by the most promising of one's daughters, secured with the largest possible dowry, was strategically preferable to marrying off all one's daughters to husbands who offered no prospect of advancement. Convents required novices to enter with dowries, but the amount was considerably less than that required for a prestigious marriage. Joining a religious order represented a respectable, affordable alternative to families who wanted to preserve social standing without diluting their patrimony. Families were not in the habit of forcing daughters to take the veil, however. On the contrary, biographies of early modern French nuns suggest that most of the women who became nuns in the seventeenth and eighteenth centuries felt called to convent life, and many faced strong family objections to their vocations. Nonetheless, the trend toward concentrating and targeting family resources generally encouraged the choice of religious life among a larger population of young women than might otherwise have happened.[3]

Convents in seventeenth-century France thus served the interests of patriarchs who wanted to maximize their families' future prosperity and prestige. At the same time, nunneries were directly dependent upon decisions made by fathers about the distribution of family resources, for the dowries of entering novices provided an essential economic base for female religious communities. Patriarchy and convents were entwined in a symbiotic relationship that paradoxically helped ensure the survival of fictive families of women who presented a visible and viable alternative to traditional families headed by men. As the largest order of religious women in early modern France, the Ursulines were perhaps the greatest beneficiaries of the convergence of patriarchal strategy and feminine religious aspiration.

In the seventeenth and eighteenth centuries, the average dowry that ac-

3. Jean-Louis Flandrin, *Familes: Parenté, maison, sexualité dans l'ancienne société* (Paris, 1976), translated by Richard Southern as *Families in Former Times: Kinship, Household, and Sexuality* (Cambridge, 1979), is the seminal French work on early modern French family strategies. Julie Hardwick, *The Practice of Patriarchy: Gender and Politics of Household Authority in Early Modern France* (University Park, Pa., 1998), reveals that patriarchal strategies often operated in family networks beyond the nuclear family. A husband's interests could appear subservient to his wife's when in fact they were subservient to those of the men of his wife's family. Olwen Hufton, *The Prospect before Her: A History of Women in Western Europe*, I, *1500–1800* (New York, 1996), 67–69, provides a good summary overview.

The apostolic French orders did not share the social cachet of the cloistered contemplative orders that made Spanish and Italian convents popular destinations for elite young women. See the discussion in Chapter 4, above. On early modern French women's religious vocations, see, especially, Elizabeth Rapley, *A Social History of the Cloister: Daily Life in the Teaching Monasteries of the Old Regime* (Montreal, 2001), 148–163. The obituaries of the New Orleans Ursulines offer several examples of parental opposition to daughters' religious vocations. Marie Madeleine Hachard's parents tried to persuade her to abandon her plans to enter the Ursuline order and accept a "good match," presumably a marriage offer that would advance the family's social and financial position ("Lettres circulaires," 224, UCANO).

companied a woman entering an Ursuline convent was paid in cash.[4] This money was, in turn, invested in a financial instrument known as a *rente* (described more fully below). Reflecting the commercial bourgeois milieu from which most Ursulines came, their dowries were sometimes also made up partly of urban real estate, which brought rental fees. More rarely, rural agricultural land might make up part of an early modern nun's dowry. In a radical departure from medieval female monasticism, Ursulines also received revenue in the form of fees for services.[5]

The financial records of the Ursuline convent of Dieppe are some of the few that survived the French Revolution's dissolution of religious houses. The revenue report for 1716 is nearly contemporary with the foundation of the New Orleans mission and offers a useful example of how capital and earned income combined in a convent in the region of France that produced most of the Louisiana nuns. Rent from property, which was likely primarily urban real estate, constituted 42 percent of the Dieppe convent's income in 1716. Payments on rentes made up another 37 percent, and the fees of boarding students made up less than a quarter of convent income. Thus, the major proportion of convent revenue was passively earned through investments, which drew ultimately upon dowry capital (see Table 14).[6]

The data from the Dieppe and other contemporary convents suggest that convent investment strategies paralleled those of other charitable institutions of ancien régime France, which relied heavily on rentes, drawing between 57 and 100 percent of their income from this source.[7] Rentes represented a form of subterfuge against the church's prohibition against usury. With a loan, the principal sum was ultimately to be repaid, with interest. In the case of rentes, sometimes referred to colloquially as annuities, the capital was given with the understanding that the recipient would pay an annual percentage of the total in perpetuity, for as long as the donor lived, or in the unlikely event that the capital was fully repaid.[8]

4. See, for example, Dowry contract for Catherine Busseuetre, Mar. 26, 1701, folio D345, and Dowry contract for Cécile Cavalier, June 23, 1722, folio D376, ADSM.

5. Rapley, *A Social History of the Cloister*, 33–34, 40–45.

6. "Recettes et dépenses, 1707–1716 [Dieppe]," folio D345, ADSM.

7. Cissie C. Fairchilds, *Poverty and Charity in Aix-en-Provence* (Baltimore, 1976), is the classic study of such institutions. For the finances at convents in seventeenth- and eighteenth-century France, see Rapley, *A Social History of the Cloister*, 29–48.

8. This discussion of rentes is closely based on Fairchilds, *Poverty and Charity*, 58–60, 63–64.

TABLE 14. *Income at Ursuline Convent at Dieppe, 1716*

Source	Livres (%)
Rent from property	5,558 (42)
Payments from *rentes*	4,900 (37)
School fees	2,820 (21)
Total income	13,278 (100)

Source: "Recettes et dépenses, 1707–1716 [Dieppe]," D345, ADSM.

Although they bear the earmarks of a capitalist innovation, rentes were essentially a conservative investment strategy. In return for a limited sum, an investor received a small annual payment; the favored form brought returns at a rate of 4–5 percent. Risk was minimal, and the investment was close to home. Yet rentes were modern in the way they replaced face-to-face exchanges of products or specie with an intangible, symbolic representation of wealth. Rentes were also easy to manage: there was no need to supervise agricultural tenants or maintain property. Rentes were usually negotiated between institutions or individuals who knew one another, but the product of the transaction had no substance and was merely a value that might exist only in the form of notes or letters of credit. When communities of early modern religious women copied the investment strategy favored by the civic charities managed by male governing boards, they entered the realm of modern finance in which cash was favored over land in capital investment strategies.

Despite the financial sophistication suggested by their preference for the rente, at its foundation the convent economy was traditional and dependent. As already mentioned, the ultimate source of the French Ursulines' capital lay in the dowries given by families when their daughters entered the convent. Fees for services made an important contribution to convents like Dieppe's, but the New Orleans founders would have come from communities whose financial stability rested primarily on allocations made by fathers to their daughters. French Ursulines drew on a foundation of family wealth conferred upon them through the paternalistic instrument of the dowry to build their convents, furnish their classrooms, and set their tables. It was different in Louisiana.

On June 23, 1722, Cécile Cavalier stood in the great parlor of the Ursuline Convent of Elboeuf in northwest France and renounced all claims on her parents' estate in return for a dowry of fifteen hundred livres, to be deposited in due course with the community of nuns with whom she planned to live her life. The donation became irrevocable upon Cécile's solemn profession. Five years later, when she left Elboeuf as part of the Ursuline mission to Louisiana, her dowry stayed behind, as did the dowries of her nine companion choir nuns, all of whom had made similar contracts with their French convents.[9] The contracts that Ursulines executed when they entered the novitiate in France were between their families and a particular convent, not the order as a whole. Once given, their dowries could not be transferred or reclaimed. Louisiana's proprietors, the Company of the Indies, which had an interest in preserving the pool of marriageable women in the sparsely populated colony, included a prohibition against accepting creole nuns in their initial contract with the Ursulines. The first New Orleans missionaries did not have the Ursulines' traditional source of dowry capital at their disposal.

The prospects for substituting tuition revenues for returns on dowry capital were dim in Louisiana in the 1720s and 1730s. Louisiana was notoriously poor, and the European population was small. Whereas in France Uruslines subsidized their large free schools with returns on capital investments and tuition paid by boarding students, in New Orleans they could depend on neither to sustain their apostolate among the impoverished colonists and Indians they hoped to teach. The women who came to Louisiana thus crafted a new financial strategy, responding to the constraints and opportunities in their new environment. In the first instance, they expanded the range of services for which they received fees and aggressively sought better terms of payment. In addition, they made the most of the agricultural land that was allotted to them by the Company of the Indies and the bondpeople the company sold them on credit, taking advantage of every opportunity to increase their holdings in both. By combining the expansion of the established practice of charging fees for services with the innovation of slaveholding, the nuns transformed the convent economy.

The irrevocable terms of dowry contracts denied the New Orleans nuns their order's traditional source of financial security, leading Marie Tranchepain to execute a different kind of contract for her band of twelve missionaries in the autumn of 1726. Tranchepain signed an agreement with the Company of the Indies that stipulated an annual sum of thirty-six hundred livres be paid to the nuns for administering the colony's military hospital, which

9. Dowry contract for Cécile Cavalier, June 23, 1722, folio D376, ADSM.

the company hoped would secure the survival of the troops on whom the colony's success depended. Accepting responsibility for the military hospital represented the women's first foray into the unexplored territory that lay beyond teaching. The Ursulines were not nursing sisters, but their desire to find a way to establish a mission in the colony, coupled with their lack of dowry capital and uncertain prospects for tuition revenue, drove them to the task. The New Orleans convent, severed from its connections through dowries to fathers of blood, formed a new paternalistic relationship with the civic fatherhood of the state. Forged in compromise in an atmosphere of mutual wariness, the arrangement was to prove difficult throughout the colonial period, and the size and continuation of the stipend was the subject of frequent renegotiation.[10]

Although the Ursulines' contract with the Company of the Indies provided that an annual salary of six hundred livres be paid to six nuns to operate the military hospital, the same sum as paid to each Capuchin and Jesuit missionary in the colony, the apparent parity is deceptive. The annual payment to the Ursulines was capped at thirty-six hundred livres. The company contracted for six nuns, but twelve missionary Ursulines committed themselves to the project and made the voyage to Louisiana in 1727. They had to make do with a sum intended to support only six women.[11]

Indeed, the annual sum of thirty-six hundred livres fell far short of what it took to feed, house, and clothe the nuns in New Orleans. The small plantation they were allocated by the terms of their contract could be used to provision the nuns and their boarders but did not produce the cash they needed for other expenses, including paying for the enslaved workers the Company of the Indies sold them on credit. The annual rent on their temporary quarters, which they were expected to pay until their convent building was completed, was fifteen hundred livres. Reserving nearly half of their salary for housing left insufficient resources to cover the exorbitant prices of the commodities essential to everyday life. Goods shipped from France to New Orleans, which could be purchased only in the company storehouse, received a markup of 50 percent. When a pair of stockings of poor quality

10. The contract executed between the Ursulines and the Company of the Indies is at AC, C13A, X, 88–99 (certified copy at UCANO). For a discussion of the negotiations between the parties, see Emily J. Clark, "A New World Community: The New Orleans Ursulines and Colonial Society, 1727–1803" (Ph.D. diss., Tulane University, 1998), 15–17, 43–45, 49–50.

11. AC, C13A, X, 88–99.

that would sell for six sols in France brought six livres in Louisiana—an increase of 200 percent—the nuns would have found it difficult to replace the travel-battered clothes in which they arrived.[12]

The nuns thus understood from the beginning of their tenure in Louisiana that they would have to engineer their own financial survival and quickly moved to establish a basis for doing so. They turned first to what they valued most, teaching. Within weeks of their arrival in New Orleans, they invested in the construction of a building to house a classroom and dormitory for boarding students. Over the next several months, in the winter and spring of 1727–1728, the nuns enrolled some eighteen boarding students, bringing them at least an additional eighteen hundred livres and so increasing their annual income by 50 percent.[13]

Establishing their school was more critical to their morale than to their treasury, however. Tuition from eighteen students was not enough to support the nuns' enterprise. Another source of revenue soon presented itself. As the nuns tended their fledgling school in their first autumn in Louisiana, the Company of the Indies placed a female orphan with them, offering a small stipend in return. The sisters seem to have welcomed the opportunity to add to their income. By the spring of 1728, they had acquired three

12. [Marie Madeleine Hachard], *De Rouen à la Louisiane: Voyage d'une Ursuline en 1727* (Rouen, 1988), 62, notes the rent of the house; AC, C13A, XVIII, 111v, reports that the Ursulines owed Madame Kolly thirty-six hundred livres for three years of back rent in 1734. The Company of the Indies based the markup for its stores on the stores' distance from the capital. The markup was 50 percent at New Orleans, 100 percent at Illinois. See John G. Clark, *New Orleans, 1718-1812: An Economic History* (Baton Rouge, La., 1970), 35. [Hachard], *De Rouen à la Louisiane*, 25, provides 1728 market prices for eggs, milk, and bread. See also Marcel Giraud, *A History of French Louisiana*, V, *The Company of the Indies, 1721-1731*, trans. Brian Pearce (Baton Rouge, La., 1991), 263. The silver unit of ancien régime France was the écu, which was worth three livres tournois. A livre was worth twenty sols or sous, and a sou was worth twelve deniers. See John J. McCusker, *Money and Exchange in Europe and America, 1600-1775: A Handbook* (Chapel Hill, N.C., 1978), 88.

13. AC, C13A, X, 314v, XI, 161v; [Hachard], *De Rouen à la Louisiane*, 62. In 1732, a colonial official reported that the Ursulines charged three hundred livres per year for board. Although this rate was probably also charged in 1727, it is unlikely that all boarders remained for a full year. It was customary in the late eighteenth century for girls to board for a shorter period of three to six months, specifically to prepare for their first Communion. See "General Accounts, October 1797–October 1812," UCANO.

orphan girls and were actively seeking others "to provide them with a suitable education which puts them in a position to work to earn their living." Each orphan brought a food stipend of 150 livres from the company, increasing the convent income in 1728 by 450 livres. By expanding beyond their contractual responsibilities with the company, the nuns saw their income grow by 63 percent over their base stipend.[14]

This modest entrepreneurship took a disastrous turn in 1729, when the Indian attack on Fort Rosalie in Natchez territory produced some thirty orphaned girls who were summarily thrust upon the Ursulines with no financial provision for the additional costs of accommodating the new charges. It was one thing to stretch convent resources to find clothing, bedding, and crockery for three orphans. The influx of dozens of bereft and destitute girls was overwhelming. Pleas for an increase to their base subsidy directed late in 1731 to the crown's administrators in Louisiana fell on deaf ears. Timing was poor—the crown had taken over the colony earlier that year in large part because the Company of the Indies had been unable to make it financially successful. The ministry now in direct control of Louisiana sought to reduce standing expenditures and to that end capped the number of orphans for whom it would pay stipends. The crown did agree to pay the passage of two additional nuns to New Orleans to help the community, diminished through death and defection to six, shoulder its multiple demands. But the king's generosity stopped there. "His Majesty is willing for you to continue to have paid to the religious the board and room of thirty orphans . . . he forbids you to exceed the number of thirty. He orders you even to diminish it." With no additional payments from the crown and rising expenses associated with the orphans, debt was inevitable. When the sisters moved to their permanent convent in 1734, their bedding and furniture were so rotten and infested with vermin that they had to burn most of it and borrow money in order to give the orphans beds to sleep in.[15]

Meanwhile, another financial disaster loomed. Until their permanent convent was built, the sisters were excused from their hospital duties, but, with the move to their new home, they could no longer elude this unwelcome commitment. Their contract with the company, and subsequently with the crown, was to administer the hospital and oversee operations. Officials pressed the women in the 1730s to sign a new service agreement

14. [Hachard], *De Rouen à la Louisiane*, 79; AC, C13A, XI, 274v, XIII, 265.

15. AC, B59, 575v–576, trans. Jane Frances Heaney, AC, C13A, XIII, 120–123, 265v, XV, 74v–76v, AC, B57, 794v–795v, AC, C12A, XIX, 71–72v.

that included the provision of patient meals.[16] Aware that inflated prices and unpredictable availability almost guaranteed financial losses if they took on this responsibility, the nuns resisted renegotiating their contract until 1744, when a new chief commissioner, Sabastian Le Normant, coerced the women into signing a punitive new agreement.

Le Normant's dealings with the nuns were shaped by his own failure at his prior posting in Louisbourg, off the coast of Nova Scotia, where he had been unable to keep the hospital administered by the Brothers of Charity within its budget. The nuns were obvious candidates for sacrifice on the altar of Le Normant's pride. He accused them of profiteering by selling to outside buyers wine and spirits allocated by the crown for the sick and suggested that the nuns also redirected, for their own profit, the labor of seventeen enslaved Africans belonging to the king who were assigned to work in the hospital. If they did not agree to the new arrangement—which reduced the number of enslaved hospital assistants from seventeen to six, cut the food and heating budgets, and required the nuns to pay for replacement bedding, furniture, and equipment—Le Normant obliquely threatened to have the Ursuline establishment suppressed. When the women capitulated and signed the new contract, their financial position hardly reflected the successful skimming operation that Le Normant alleged. They were deeply in debt, and their financial position was made even more precarious by the failure of the crown to make good on its own parsimonious obligations to the nuns. The Ursulines were owed more than twenty thousand livres in salary, orphan subsidies, and hospital pay for the years 1743–1745.[17]

Seeking financial security by expanding their services had proven a disastrous strategy for the nuns of New Orleans. Although their contemporaries in France had also begun to take in small numbers of women boarders at the behest of the state, the colonial nuns surpassed their example in both the scale and variety of the responsibilities they added to their educational work, supplying the city with a full range of essential social services.[18] The

16. AC, C13A, XV, 75–76v, AC, C12A, XX, 221v, XXIX, 116.

17. A. J. B. Johnston, *Life and Religion at Louisbourg, 1713–1758* (Montreal, 1996), 75–78; AC, C11A, LXXXVI, 270–277, AC, C13A, XXVIII, 342–345. Le Normant's behavior was also consistent with the prevailing official attitude toward monasticism in France in the middle of the eighteenth century. Monasteries, particularly female religious houses, were subjected to intense financial scrutiny and presumed to be fiscally inept and of dubious social value. See Rapley, *A Social History of the Cloister*, 29–48, 78–95.

18. Rapley, *A Social History of the Cloister*, 244–256.

pattern of official stinginess and, in the case of Le Normant, transparent abuse, marks the failure of a financial strategy that would have shifted dependence from one set of patriarchs to another. That the nuns were doubly disadvantaged in their relations with male officialdom might have foreordained the disappointing outcome of their New World experiment. On the one hand, the crown and its representatives did not patronize the nuns, as they might have a female charity in France, but instead treated them as contractors for services subject to the cold rules of business. Civil authorities never softened either their contractual demands or their rhetoric when negotiating the terms of service with the nuns, making no allowances for their sex. Yet, at the same time, the nuns' sex made it easier for officials to target them when searching for ways to cut costs. Women, particularly religious women, were supposed to bear burdens willingly, make do with less, and refrain from complaint. They were not expected to fight back when attacked or abandon their responsibilities when they were underpaid. In crossing the Atlantic, the Louisiana Ursulines left behind more than their dowries. They lost the paternal protection and counsel that might have safeguarded them in their relations with civil authorities. Denied the traditional sources of male patronage and support, their long-term survival in Louisiana called for a new way forward.

The foundation for a distinctly New World survival strategy had been laid upon the nuns' arrival in Louisiana when they received a plantation from the Company of the Indies in 1727 as part of the terms of their contract. With a river frontage of eight arpents, their property was twice the size of allocations made to ordinary inhabitants. The plantation was intended "eventually to provide for their maintenance," though whether this meant that the company expected the nuns to provision themselves from the property or to engage in staple crop agriculture was not articulated. Whatever the intention, given the unreliability of supply shipments from France, the expense of food in the colony, and the general failure of staple crop agriculture in Louisiana in the first half of the eighteenth century, the nuns sensibly decided to use the plot to feed themselves, their boarders, and their enslaved servants. French nuns would have rented their lands for cash, with which they purchased food in urban markets. The value of land to the colonial nuns was tangible and edible.[19]

19. See AC, C13A, X, 75–77v, for the terms of the contract with the Company of the Indies. A census in 1770 reports that the Ursulines maintained a herd of forty-two cattle and a flock of twenty-five sheep on their main plantation (Albert J. Robi-

The laborers who worked the Ursuline's property, on the other hand, represented the potential for accruing cash assets. The nuns acquired, on credit, eight enslaved Africans upon their arrival in Louisiana. Two of them ran away almost immediately, but the nuns took advantage of an early opportunity to acquire more bondpeople. In 1733, the company offered the women four new African workers at seven hundred livres each. They minimized increasing their indebtedness to the company by trading "a very bad black named Cuzart." They returned all four of these bondpeople to the Company in 1734, probably to clear themselves of debt in preparation for the October 1734 transaction with Jacques Larche, described above. In exchange for part of the twenty-five-hundred-livre purchase price of his land, they negotiated to give Larche two brothers, Chaita and Touton, valued at one thousand livres and presumably owned outright by the nuns by this time.[20]

This first burst of investment activity was probably tied to the arrival of three nuns in 1732 who brought small annuities with them to the New Orleans convent. Marie Thérèse Ramachard and her sister, Marguerite Antoinette Ramachard, had a pension of 277 livres that was not bound to their French convent of profession. Marie Jeanne de Saint Marc signed over to the New Orleans Ursulines her deceased father's military pension of 150 livres.[21] These modest cash sums that were paid only during the lifetime of the beneficiaries were no substitute for the perpetual endowments created by dowries of 1,000–3,000 livres the nuns left with their French convents of origin, but, coupled with slave property, they allowed the New Orleans nuns to engineer the expansion of their material wealth.

The women invested what little capital came their way with a calculating eye. They seem to have used the pensions of the Ramachard sisters and Sister Saint Marc in 1737 to purchase, at significant expense, a bondwoman named Jeanneton from the estate of a deceased inhabitant. After 1731, no new Africans were brought to the colony until 1743. The price of bondpeople already in the colony must have risen, and there would have been an interest in promoting natural increase. When the nuns paid the high price

chaux, Jr., ed., *Louisiana Census and Militia Lists, 1770–1789*, I, *German Coast, New Orleans, below New Orleans, and Lafourche* [Harvey, La., 1973], 95). Convent accounts for the late eighteenth century record profits from the sale of produce only. See "General Accounts, October 1797–October 1812," UCANO.

20. "Délibérations du Conseil," 18.

21. Ibid., 25.

of one thousand livres for Jeanneton, they were undoubtedly investing strategically. Young males, on the other hand, might be more trouble than they were worth. A thirteen-year-old boy named Jacob was sold in 1739 because he "was not likely to work well." The fifteen hundred livres that he brought enabled the nuns to retire more of their debt to the Company of the Indies for the eight bondpeople advanced them in 1727.[22]

The occasional trading of the 1730s developed into a focused strategy in the 1740s, when the hospital crisis pushed the nuns into a vigorous campaign to increase their wealth through investment in the economy of slavery. For several decades, they participated feverishly in the slave market. They launched this entrepreneurial episode by borrowing thirty thousand livres to purchase twenty-four bondpeople in the 1740s. In 1756, their chapter minutes record that six individuals were sold to "purge the plantation of these bad persons" who were "thieves and capable of corrupting the others." The sale must have filled the nuns' moneybox with a sum that prompted them to contemplate a suitable investment, for in 1757 they arranged to rent a property furnished with eight enslaved workers, livestock, and ten acres of wax-producing myrtle. Wax was in high demand in the colony and would bring the nuns a cash income, and the chapter readily approved a four-year lease. The women continued to press ahead with similar moneymaking schemes. They arranged, in 1758, to acquire a capital sum of twenty-four thousand livres through a rente that would pay the lender the rather high annual rate of twenty-four hundred livres. The money, the chronicler noted, "is to be invested in blacks to increase the value of our plantations." When the contract fell through, they found another way to increase their slaveholdings the following year, when they sold a married couple and a young man, all probably in the prime of life, for the sum of eighty-five hundred livres. With the proceeds, they purchased a family of seven, comprising a married couple, four daughters, and a baby boy. The eldest daughter was fourteen, on the threshold of childbearing age. The nuns clearly anticipated a good return on this particular investment in the form of natural increase from four young bondwomen.[23]

Their relentless maneuvering to increase their holdings in land and human property placed the nuns among the major propertyholders of the New Orleans area. At the beginning of the Spanish era, they owned two

22. Ibid., 27, 32.
23. AC, C11A, LXXXVI, 275; "Délibérations du Conseil," 44, 47, UCANO. On myrtle as a staple crop in Louisiana, see Clark, *New Orleans*, 55.

large plantations, one on each side of the Mississippi River. With sixty-one enslaved workers, their establishment at Point Saint Antoine was one of the six largest of seventy-five slaveholdings enumerated along the lower banks of the Mississippi in the Spanish census of 1770. There was nothing marginal or tentative about the nuns' engagement with slavery as a financial strategy.[24]

The Ursulines left no clues to suggest how they felt about their decision to pursue material security through participation in the growing slave economy of the colony. Any negative judgments we might make based on their relentless pattern of trading are only partially mitigated by the knowledge that they did not engage in staple crop production during the colonial period. Instead, Ursuline bondpeople seem to have been occupied with supporting the large convent community and its various activities. A large number of the Ursuline bondpeople worked at the convent compound itself, where perhaps as many as eighty nuns, orphans, and boarding students lived at the end of the century. A detached institutional kitchen, henhouse, ovens, and hand mill suggest that a team of cooks was in residence. Workshops for carpenters and shoemakers and a laundry facility testify to the other sorts of work bondpeople living at the convent performed in addition to daily cleaning and maintenance (see Figure 14). Ursuline bondpeople living off the convent site tended livestock, ran a dairy, and raised produce for convent consumption and occasional sale. Until 1770, when the nuns relinquished the administration of the hospital, these workers also provided food for the patients at the hospital.[25] Whether because of the difficulties of plantation management, a distaste for the business of slavery, or simply a failure to forecast the lucrative future of staple crop agriculture in Louisiana, the nuns did not retain the plantation and slavery as part of a permanent, central financial strategy. In 1777, they divested themselves of nearly half of their bondpeople and one of their two plantations.[26] After 1780, their participation in the slave market diminished notably. Ninety percent of their sales and purchases of bondpeople took place before that date, and in the last two decades of colonial rule they were far more likely to sell and manumit enslaved workers than to buy new bondpeople, and more likely to

24. Robichaux, ed., *Louisiana Census and Militia Lists*, I, 92–114.

25. Convent accounts show revenues accrued from the sale of milk and produce only ("General Accounts, October 1797–October 1812," UCANO). See Chapter 5, note 26, above, for a description of the nuns' acquisition of the dairy in 1780.

26. See Chapter 5, note 26, above.

manumit than to sell. At precisely the time when other Louisiana planters took advantage of the resumption of slave shipments to Louisiana to build their slaveholdings and lay the groundwork for a profitable plantation system, the Ursulines virtually retired from the marketplace.[27]

They did not leave empty-handed. The nuns made fifty-seven thousand livres from the sale of enslaved workers and a plantation in 1777, by far the largest of their financial transactions in the colonial period. In an era when a dowry averaged between one thousand and three thousand livres, this sum represented the equivalent of nearly twenty generous dowries. Although it did not compare to the patrimonies of French convents that had been accruing dowries for six generations, the capital sum was respectable for the small missionary community of fifteen nuns.[28] Their hard-won financial security came at a cost, however. Most obviously, they achieved economic success only by denying men and women their freedom, pitting their lives against the convent's future. But their business transactions also reinforced an earlier change in the sisters' gender identity. Treated with cold calculation in their negotiations with French colonial officials, the nuns abandoned even the semblance of dependent passivity. When they took on the aggressive trading practices of colonial planters, they assumed a distinctive feature of the male identity evolving in the plantation societies of America. Although they did not pursue a future as full-blown planters, they were, for a time, masters in women's clothing.

The 1777 exercise in capital formation through slave trading might have challenged masculine prerogatives in a less subtle way as well. Two years before the transaction, the bishop of Havana intervened in the membership decisions of the convent, obstructing the entrance of some women while requiring the admission of others. Customarily, the professed sisters of a community exercised their own judgment regarding the suitability of candidates for admission to religious life. The bishop's formal permission was required but was generally a technicality that simply ratified the sisters' de-

27. Clark, "A New World Community," 187 (table 14) n. 55. On the shift in the economy of colonial Louisiana, see Gwendolyn Midlo Hall, *Africans in Colonial Louisiana: The Development of Afro-Creole Culture in the Eighteenth Century* (Baton Rouge, La., 1992), 276–281, 286, 308–310; and Daniel H. Usner, Jr., *Indians, Settlers, and Slaves in a Frontier Exchange Economy: The Lower Mississippi Valley before 1783* (Chapel Hill, N.C., 1992), 118–119, 148, 177–278, 281–282.

28. "Délibérations du Conseil," 57, UCANO; Acts of Juan Bautista Garic, January–December 1777, VIII, Nov. 8, 1777, June–December 1778, X, July 30, 1778, NANO; Clark, "A New World Community," 325–326.

cision. In 1775, the bishop of Havana made an issue of the absence of dowry capital at the New Orleans convent. Two years later, the Ursulines negotiated a sale that produced the equivalent of twenty dowries, signaling that they needed neither the dowries of the bishop's recruits nor his financial supervision.

Although the founding nuns forfeited their dowries to their French convents of origin, there was theoretically the potential for the New Orleans community to accrue such funds once creole women began to enter the convent. The colonial government delayed this possibility by imposing a ban on creole entrants in an attempt to encourage marriage and natural increase in the colony's French population. The ban was apparently lifted in the late 1740s, but the first five creole women who entered the convent after 1749 did not bring dowries with them. Marie Turpin, a métis woman, entered as a converse sister, a status that did not require a dowry. Marie Anne Rillieux, born into a prosperous planter family, entered in 1752, but poor health forced her to withdraw two years later before she made her profession and finalized her dowry contract with the convent. Charlotte Demouy was the first creole choir nun to persevere through postulancy and the novitiate to profess in the New Orleans convent in 1768, and as a wealthy boarding student she surely had the means to bring a dowry with her. The unorthodox nature of her entry may explain its absence. Charlotte left boarding school with regret, as the "world had become a boring place for her." Her parents had died, and she was lodged with her older brothers. She asked their permission to return to the convent to become a nun. They "wanted absolutely to stop it and put all possible obstacles in her path." Charlotte was determined. "Seeing that she was unable to obtain their consent, she asked if she could go to visit the nuns. When she arrived at the convent, she pleaded with them to open the door of the monastery to her, for she never wished to leave." Charlotte brought nothing to the convent but her headstrong ardor for religious life. It was enough for the New Orleans nuns, who did not know whether they would ever again receive sisters from France now that Louisiana was under Spanish rule. Two more creoles took their final vows at the New Orleans convent in the early 1770s, biological sisters Antoinette and Anne Caue. Neither brought dowries.[29]

The nuns' acceptance of these dowerless novices baffled Bishop José de Echevarría, who presided over the church in New Orleans from his episco-

29. "Livre de l'entrée des filles de choeur," 11, 13–14v, UCANO; "Lettres circulaires," 255–256, UCANO.

pal palace in Havana. The nuns lived in what he considered impoverished circumstances, with insufficient finances to support the community of sixteen nuns living at the convent in the 1770s. In 1775, he sent a set of terse interrogatories to Mother Superior Marie Madeleine Le Verme, threatening to refuse permission for the entry of three French creole aspirants unless he received reassuring answers to his questions. The first two went to the heart of the matter:

1. What is the amount which the Community requires for the dowry of the Religious?
2. How much finally, has the candidate?

When the bishop looked at the convent, he saw a community of women, and, in his experience, such communities were always supported by dowry capital, the only form of financial security appropriate and acceptable for such an establishment. The New Orleans convent possessed no significant capital of any kind when Echevarría posed his questions: the windfall from the 1777 sale of a plantation and bondpeople still lay in the future. In 1775, the sisters supported themselves with small crown subsidies for their catechism classes and orphanage, augmented with boarding school fees. Echevarría's remedy for this unconventional New Orleans convent economy was an infusion of dowry-bearing novices recruited from his congregation in Havana. This arrangement solved several problems for the bishop. He found a suitable place for young women who could not find space in Cuban monasteries that were oversubscribed, he brought dowry capital to the New Orleans establishment, and he introduced a cadre of creole Spanish women into the only monastic institution in Louisiana's capital. After sending three young women to New Orleans in 1778, Echevarría assured the mother superior that, should she wish more dowered novices from Havana, "I shall have no difficulty procuring them for you."[30]

30. "Livre de l'entrée des filles de choeur," 11, 13–14v, UCANO; José de Echevarría, bishop of Cuba, to Marie Madeleine Le Verme, mother superior, May 6, 1775, Oct. 13, 1778, trans. Heaney, UCANO. On convents in the Spanish colonies in the Americas, see Asunción Lavrin, "Ecclesiastical Reform of Nunneries in New Spain in the Eighteenth Century," *Americas,* XXII (1965), 182–203; Lavrin, "The Role of the Nunneries in the Economy of New Spain in the Eighteenth Century," *Hispanic American Historical Review,* XLVI (1966), 371–393; Lavrin, "Values and Meaning of Monastic Life for Nuns in Colonial Mexico," *Catholic Historical Review,* LVIII (1972), 367–387; and Luis Martín, *Daughters of the Conquistadores: Women of the Viceroyalty of Peru* (Albuquerque,

The bishop might not have known that the nuns had already secured a capital endowment through the sale of 1777, but it is unlikely that he would have been deterred from his plans in any case. Dowry funds remained the most appropriate financial base for a convent, making explicit the financial dependence of nuns upon their biological and church fathers. The Habanera recruits and their dowries carried a message about the distribution of authority between bishop and nuns, men and women that the bishop had every intention of delivering. Altogether, ten young women from Havana arrived in New Orleans to enter the convent as choir nuns between 1778 and 1794. They brought handsome dowries. The smallest recorded dowry brought by a Cuban sister was 1,500 pesos, and several were considerably larger; three given in the 1780s amounted to 9,000 pesos. A total of 10,500 pesos of 15,000 pesos of recorded dowry payments made between 1780 and 1794 came from Cuban nuns.[31]

Agency might have been denied the nuns in the acquisition of this dowry capital, but, once it was in their possession, they made their own decisions about its investment. Beginning in the 1780s, the nuns used it to buy urban real estate, a strategy that echoed the financial strategies of early modern French convents. They traded 9,000 pesos in dowries due from three novices to the Spanish Capuchin superior for New Orleans, Cirillo de Barcelona, for a lot in the vicinity of the parish church with a house that brought in 480 pesos per year in rent. When the house burned down along with most of the city in the great fire of 1788, the nuns invested 4,000 livres to replace it with two houses. The economic quickening that took place in the 1790s as the port of New Orleans grew in prominence and wealth might have influenced the nuns' aggressive acquisition of rental property at mid-decade. In 1795 they bought a large lot and house on Saint Ann Street, not far from their convent, and the following year they paid 1,630 pesos in cash "from the dowry of one religious and part of another" to build a house on a piece of land adjacent to their enclosure that they had acquired from the Spanish crown in an exchange of property. "The whole community agreed to the proposal, for the good and progress of the monastery," the chapter

N.M., 1983), esp. 186–188 (on dowries); Kathryn Burns, *Colonial Habits: Convents and the Spiritual Economy of Cuzco, Peru* (Durham, N.C., 1999).

31. "Livre de l'entrée," 20–21b, 29b, UCANO; Délibérations du Conseil," 83, UCANO; Acts of Leonard[o] Mazange, July–December 1781, IV, 962, Act of Carlos Ximenes, July–December 1792, III, 363–364v, July–December 1796, XI, 388, all in NANO.

minutes reported. Three years later, they bought a piece of land adjacent to their Saint Ann Street property in order to enlarge it and improve its security, thereby justifying a higher rent.[32]

The infusion of Cuban dowries was doubtless welcome at the New Orleans convent, but it amounted to an illusory reprise of old practices in which dowries formed the principal capital base from which investments were made. In fact, the fifteen thousand pesos paid to the convent in the 1780s and 1790s amounted to less than a third of the sum that the nuns had made from the sale of 1777. The rent payments derived from the property bought with dowries constituted only slightly more than a tenth of convent income at the end of the eighteenth century.

Two notable charitable donations that came to the nuns late in the century supplemented the modest funds from the rental property. During his tenure as governor, 1777 to 1785, Bernardo de Gálvez created a fund to support the education of a dozen orphans by giving to the nuns the income from sixteen small houses he had built on his New Orleans property. In 1798, the revenue from this source produced nearly eight hundred pesos a year.[33] The sisters gained another property in 1797, when a priest, Augustin Lemare, donated a house whose income was to be dedicated to scholarships for orphans in the boarding school. At the turn of the nineteenth century, revenue from these endowments brought in about 12 percent of the convent's income.[34]

The income derived from the nuns' flurry of investment in urban real estate, together with that produced by the charitable donations of Gálvez and Lamare, echoed familiar features of early modern French convents. Yet neither of these revenue streams restored the traditional calculus of the European convent economy. The Dieppe convent of 1716 received 79 percent of its income from its investments and proceeds from charitable con-

32. "Livre de l'entrée," 20–21b, 29b, UCANO; "Délibérations du Conseil," 83, 85, 95–96, 104, UCANO; Acts of Leonard[o] Mazange, July–December 1781, IV, 962, Acts of Carlos Ximenes, July–December 1792, III, 363–364v, July–December 1796, XI, 388, all in NANO. For discussions of the changing economy in the Lower Mississippi Valley at the end of the eighteenth century, see Clark, *New Orleans*, 161–180, 183–249; Hall, *Africans in Colonial Louisiana*, 276–277; and Usner, *Indians, Settlers, and Slaves*, 159, 188–190, 216–218, 278–285.

33. AGI, SD, legajo 2672, 53–55, Aug. 31, 1808, describes Galvez's donation. There are no contemporary documents recording the gift, but the revenue is regularly recorded in "General Accounts, October 1797–October 1812," UCANO.

34. "Délibérations du Conseil," 102, UCANO.

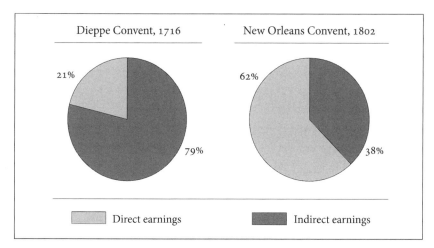

Figure 18. Proportionate Sources of Revenue, Dieppe and New Orleans. Sources: *"Recettes et dépences, 1707–1716 [Dieppe]," ADSM; "General Accounts, October 1797–October 1812," UCANO. Drawn by Emily Clark*

tributions; the Ursuline convent of 1802 received only 38 percent of its income from such sources (see Figure 18).

The nuns' willingness to accept novices without dowries, which had so disturbed the bishop of Havana in 1775, might well have derived from their understanding of a fundamental shift under way in their convent's economy that made the number of working nuns, not the amount of working capital, the crucial figure for the women trying to secure the mission's future. A review of convent finances at the end of the colonial period reveals that this particular community of women was supported in the main, not by charitable endowments or by returns on dowry capital, or indeed, by returns on the capital they had created themselves, but on payments received in return for their own labor. An analysis of two sample years bracketing the turn of the nineteenth century shows a female religious community that was literally earning its keep.

In 1798 and 1802, the nuns received nearly two-thirds of their revenue from fees for services rendered, mostly in the form of tuition paid by students in their boarding and day schools. School tuition made up an average of 36 percent of their income in these two years, with fees for orphans and salaries paid the nuns for other work, primarily their free catechism classes, contributing additional sums. Income from investments was significantly less. The sisters realized between 12 and 14 percent of their revenue from rents paid on property acquired with dowry capital, and slightly less from

TABLE 15. *Current Account Income at New Orleans Ursuline Convent,*
1798 and 1802

Source	1798 (pesos)	1802 (pesos)
Indirect Income		
Rent	979 (14%)	1,083 (12%)
Endowments for orphans	780 (11)	1,018 (12)
Miscellaneous	82 (1)	248 (3)
Plantation produce and slave rental	747 (10)	1,009 (11)
Total	2,588 (36%)	3,358 (38%)
Direct Income		
School fees	2,787 (38%)	3,001 (34%)
Orphan fees	600 (8)	750 (9)
Nuns' salaries	1,296 (18)	1,620 (19)
Total	4,683 (64%)	5,371 (62%)
Grand total	7,271 (100%)	8,729 (100%)

Note: Miscellaneous income includes a pension paid to one of the nuns as part of her dowry and small amounts earned by the needlework of orphans at the convent. *Source:* "General Accounts, October 1797–October 1812," UCANO.

charitable endowments given to support orphans at the convent. Planta-tion produce and slave rental accounted for another 10–11 percent. All told, passively earned income constituted just more than a third of convent reve-nues (see Table 15).

The turn-of-the-century convent economy is at its most striking when compared directly with that of the French convent of Dieppe considered earlier. Nearly 80 percent of the French convent's revenue was indirect in-come, whereas just more than 21 percent was directly earned. The New Orleans convent presents almost a complete reversal of that distribution, drawing more than 60 percent of its earnings from the work of the sisters (see Figure 18). Teaching—working in return for payment—this was the engine of the convent economy at the end of the century, and it relied on the nuns' ability to succeed, not in the slave market, but in the expanding marketplace of a budding consumer culture. In paying tuition to send one's daughter to the nuns' school, parents made a choice about the allocation of their financial resources among a diverse array of goods and services available to them in the growing port city.

The growth of the market itself played a crucial part in the nuns' ability to make tuition a viable base for convent revenue. In the last quarter of the eighteenth century, the city's free population grew quickly. The decade between 1777 and 1788 brought an increase of 55 percent, from about two thousand in 1777 to just more than three thousand in 1788. Between 1788 and 1791, a growth spurt of 60 percent brought the free population to more than five thousand. The relaxation of trade restrictions by the Spanish at this time brought a population of American merchants, and other immigrants were drawn to the city to cater to and profit from the commercial activity as shopkeepers, hoteliers, restaurateurs, and building contractors. Convent student records reveal that the Ursulines won a niche in the discretionary spending habits of these newcomers, and that achievement meant that the educational mission that had always supplied them their reason for being in New Orleans now indisputably also supplied them with the means to remain there on their own terms.[35]

The nuns struggled over the eighteenth century against male authorities and financial exigency to keep what they thought most important, their teaching apostolate, at the forefront. In France, the financial base provided by dowry capital meant that Ursulines could sustain their schools whether tuition revenue was plentiful or not. Their educational focus was never compromised, threatened, or suppressed. Such was not the case for the dowerless Louisiana nuns, who began their mission with a compromise that turned them into hospitalières and who went on to spend their first fifty years in the colony dividing their energies among multiple social services and trading restlessly in land and human property to keep their educational apostolate alive. Such efforts were not enough to secure either financial security or autonomy, and in 1775 they came under the scrutiny of a Spanish colonial bishop who deemed dowerless teaching nuns unacceptable. The bishop's plan to bring a cohort of properly endowed Spanish creole sisters to the New Orleans convent compromised the nuns' autonomy

---

35. Population figures are drawn from "Padrón general de todos los individuos de la provincia de Luisians," AGI, PC, 2351; "Resumen general del padrón hecho en la provincia de la Lusiana, distrito de la Movila y plaza de Panzacola," AGI, PC, 1425; and "Census of New Orleans," Nov. 6, 1791, Louisiana Division, New Orleans Public Library. On the students enrolled at the Ursuline convent in the 1790s, see Chapter 4, above.

but also threatened their mission. There was no precedent for teaching nuns in Spain and its colonies; the Ursulines might well have anticipated an attempt by the bishop and his recruits to turn their New Orleans convent into a cloister of contemplatives. Before the arrival of the Spanish creole women, the sisters attempted to fend off the bishop's intervention by negotiating a massive sale of land and bondpeople, an aggressive move that dwarfed all their previous financial transactions. The sale successfully capitalized the convent but failed to prevent the arrival of the Spanish creole postulants.

Fears about the Spanish threat to the teaching apostolate proved to be well founded. In 1793, the vicar-general of Louisiana, in response to correspondence from one of the Spanish creole nuns, launched a campaign to impose upon the Ursulines the traditional form of cloister they had long before abandoned. He demanded that students not be allowed to come and go from the convent compound without special authorization, which would have made it extremely difficult for the Ursulines to maintain their boarding school and impossible for them to continue their free day school and catechism classes for the enslaved. The French-born mother superior gave no quarter as she fought back. At one point, when the vicar-general asked to see, once again, the copy of the Ursuline *Règlemens* the nuns kept at their convent, the mother superior notified him that she and her sisters had decided that, "since you had had the book with you for nine months, this time it should be given to you in the parlor." The book would not be handed over to a courier and brought to the cleric so that he could pore over it in the comfort and privacy of his study. If the vicar-general wanted to review the finer points of cloister as defined by the Ursuline rule, he would have to come to the convent himself and examine it in the visitor's reception room while a nun looked on. The extraction of submission was not to be solely a male privilege in this confrontation.[36]

The *Règlemens* were not the mother superior's only source of confidence in waging this battle. She fought from a position of financial strength that was the product of the very activity the vicar-general sought to suppress. At the end of the eighteenth century, the New Orleans Ursulines were more fully independent of fathers of church, state, and blood than they had ever been. It was a status achieved, in the end, not by imitating the financial strategies of male planters, but by stubbornly persevering in their female

36. For a detailed discussion of the 1793 conflict, see Clark, "A New World Community," 252–277.

educational apostolate, holding on until New Orleans provided them with a convent full of paying students who vindicated their tenacity.

Louisiana's unmarried women of property had not disappeared by degrees from the public as Anglo-American women had over the course of the eighteenth century.[37] If anything, the colony's largest concentration of spinsters, though invisible behind convent walls, was more manifestly present, more obviously financially autonomous, and less inclined to the pretense of submission to male authority than it had been at the beginning of the century. As Louisiana stood on the threshold of the nineteenth century, the assertive femininity of the New Orleans Ursulines stood in marked contrast to the performance of womanhood that had taken shape in the young Republic of which it would soon become a part.

37. On this trend, see, especially, Sturtz, *Within Her Power*, 7, 11, 16, 17, 181; and Wulf, *Not All Wives*, 17, 23, 184–205.

part three

In the first two decades of the nineteenth century, the relative equi-
librium and stability that late colonial New Orleans had achieved was broken by a series of shocks and shifts in its economy and demography. Sugarcane cultivation became suddenly profitable, and sugar plantations manned
by large slave labor forces proliferated, pushing lower Louisiana firmly into
the ranks of slave societies. The colony was secretly retroceded to France in
1800, raising both hopes and fears among the inhabitants of New Orleans.
The largely French-speaking population had never been fully reconciled to
Spanish rule, yet the French republic that emerged from a bloody revolution was an unpredictable ruler. Even more unpredictable, and culturally
uncongenial, was the United States, which acquired Louisiana through purchase in 1803.

An economic and demographic movement brought large numbers of
Americans into the Lower Mississippi Valley in the years immediately pre-
ceding the Louisiana Purchase of 1803. Trans-Appalachian immigration accelerated in the years following the American Revolution, bringing farmers
into a hinterland rich in agricultural promise but constrained by an international boundary. The natural shipping corridor for the immigrant farmers'
produce lay to the west with the Mississippi, and, once Spain relaxed its
regulation on foreign trade on the river and at the port of New Orleans,
the trickle of American commerce grew quickly. The American commercial
agents and merchants who settled in New Orleans in the 1790s were a small
permanent presence representing a much larger population of farmers and
seasonal shippers whose prosperity hinged on access to the port. Satisfying their interests was increasingly critical to maintaining domestic political cohesion. The union of the young Republic hung in the balance. In 1795,
Pinckney's Treaty secured for these Americans full navigation of the Mississippi and the right to deposit goods tax-free at New Orleans for transfer to oceangoing vessels. But, like any diplomatic achievement, Pinckney's

Treaty was only as secure as continued good relations. The retrocession of Louisiana to France underlined the uncertainty of America's relationship to the Mississippi. In 1800, the future of Jefferson's republic was inextricably linked to a river and a city that lay in the hands of a foreign power whose own interests would not always converge with America's.[1]

There were two alternatives to what Americans viewed as the "Mississippi Crisis": a military invasion to seize control of the Lower Mississippi and its port or diplomacy. Jefferson chose the latter. When he dispatched James Monroe and Robert Livingston in 1803 to treat with Napoleon for the port and full navigation rights, they were unprepared for his counteroffer: all of the Louisiana Territory, from Canada to the Gulf of Mexico. With no time to seek permission, the envoys negotiated the purchase for fifteen million dollars and the settlement of outstanding claims against France. The execution of the purchase in May 1803 more than doubled the geographical extent of the young Republic. But, as the intrepid farmers and entrepreneurs who had made the acquaintance of New Orleans in the 1790s already knew, when the United States turned its gaze toward the new territory and its urban capital it would not see a reflection of itself. Instead, Americans confronted a mature colonial society with its own distinct identity.[2]

As a budding plantation society, Louisiana shared with several of its new American sisters the defining contours of staple crop agriculture and slavery, and its port hummed with the rhythms and rituals of commerce and shipping that marked New York, Philadelphia, Boston, and Charleston. Yet bound into even these common features were divergent cultural legacies that obstructed an easy amalgamation of Louisiana and the early Republic. America was emerging from the post-Revolutionary era with a fragile identity that balanced a bravely experimental republican government with a constellation of normative values rooted in its British colonial past.

Amid the dislocating change brought by revolution, independence, and an emergent commercial economy, religion was among the most important sources of orientation to early-nineteenth-century Americans. Protestant Christianity, though transformed by a proliferation of sects and denomi-

---

1. Peter J. Kastor, *The Nation's Crucible: The Louisiana Purchase and the Creation of America* (New Haven, Conn., 2004), 36–41, discusses the domestic politics that drove the acquisition of Louisiana. On the acquisition of Louisiana and its relationship to ideas about preserving America as an agrarian republic, see Drew R. McCoy, *The Elusive Republic: Political Economy in Jeffersonian America* (Chapel Hill, N.C., 1980).

2. Kastor, *Nation's Crucible*, 38–41.

nations in the early nineteenth century, retained sufficient continuities to serve as an anchor to an identity otherwise in flux. It was also the axis around which post-Revolutionary femininity was organized, undergirding an American republican ideology that valorized female moral virtue in a domestic context.

There was no comfortable place for the Ursulines in this changed world. The long-delayed flowering of a plantation economy was accompanied by the composition of hierarchies of race and gender that cast the slaveowning nuns as unnatural and dangerous. Neophyte republican creoles in New Orleans flexed their political will in ways that turned the nuns into opponents. Whereas nuns achieved a working relationship with republicanism in post-Revolutionary France by drawing on cultural tradition and proving themselves useful to social stability, the Protestant foundation of American political culture foreclosed such a path for the New Orleans Ursulines. The two decades that followed the Louisiana Purchase were filled with confrontation for the nuns.

The recovered story of the New Orleans Ursulines frames a broader understanding of the origins and persistence of American anti-Catholicism. Catholicism in general and religious women in particular complicated and disrupted the process by which America forged its national identity in the opening years of the nineteenth century. Catholic femininity, which embraced a class of unmarried women acting independently to advance the public good, was fundamentally incompatible with American Protestant womanhood as it developed in the early Republic. Antipathy toward Catholicism had deep roots among Anglo-Americans, reaching back to the Elizabethan hostilities with Spain and Ireland, cresting with the deposition of the Catholic James II in the Glorious Revolution of 1688, resurfacing with the Stuart Rebellion of 1745 and the passage of the Quebec Act in 1774. The Ursulines of New Orleans, and the rising tide of immigrant nuns who joined them in early-nineteenth-century America, renewed this historically embedded animosity and added a new dimension to it. The anti-Catholicism that culminated in the Nativist and Know-Nothing political movements owed no small part of its virulence to this earlier confrontation.

chapter 7

THE REPUBLIC ENCOUNTERS THE NUN

Benjamin Henry Latrobe was convinced that Catholicism was but a shadow of its former self when he visited New Orleans in the late 1810s. "The Catholic religion formerly was the only one permitted, and was carried on with all the pomp and ceremony of a Spanish establishment," he wrote in 1819. "The host was carried to the sick in great parade, and all those whom it encountered knelt devoutly till it had passed. All that is now over." But was it? By chance Latrobe encountered two public funeral processions that year, and both seemed quite replete with pomp and ceremony. Of one he wrote: "First marched a man in a military uniform with a drawn sword. Then came three boys in surplusses [sic], with pointed caps, two carrying staves with candelabras in the form of urns on the top, and the third in the center a large silver Cross. At some distance behind came Father Anthony and another priest." Four well-dressed men bore the coffin. Six white ribbons were attached to its sides, the ends carried by young girls "very well dressed in white, with long veils." Many in the large crowd that formed the rest of the procession carried lighted candles. From his perch atop a step, Latrobe counted sixty-nine such torches.[1]

That such a magnificent spectacle should not register in Latrobe's consciousness as a sign of Catholicism's thriving public presence may perhaps be attributed to the status of the mourners who constituted the showy, pious throng. They were "colored people, for the coffin was carried by men of that race, and none but negroes and quateroons followed it." When Latrobe later ventured to the cathedral for Holy Week services, he found it, too, a stage for black piety. "The congregation consisted of at least 4/5th women, of which number one half at least were colored," he observed. He went on to remark the intensity of their worship. "For many years I have

---

1. Benjamin Henry Boneval Latrobe, *Impressions respecting New Orleans: Diary and Sketches, 1818-1820*, ed. Samuel Wilson, Jr. (New York, 1951), 59, 61.

not seen candles offered at the Altars, but at each of the side Altars there were half a dozen candles stuck upon the steps by old colored women, who seemed exceedingly devout."[2]

Latrobe, like most of his white male fellow countrymen, measured religious strength or weakness in units of black and white, male and female. The colonial legacy of New Orleans's Catholic Church was deeply indebted to both women and people of African descent, and these constituencies dominated its ranks and gave it its public face when Latrobe visited the city in the 1810s. The church that Latrobe saw in New Orleans did not fit comfortably in a slave republic, where rigid racial and gender hierarchies were marshaled to uphold a white patriarchal regime. With their colonial ministry to enslaved and free people of color, Ursulines had helped to create this troublesome black church, and their financial independence confounded early American gender norms. In the years following the Louisiana Purchase, the nuns continued to act in ways that affronted expectations in a political culture that empowered white men through the exclusion of people of color and women. The Ursulines' confounding presence interrupted the smooth transformation of New Orleans into a model of southern republicanism and encountered predictable hostility.[3]

New Orleans grew to become one of the great urban centers of the American Republic in the twenty years that followed the Louisiana Purchase. In the 1820s, the marks of growth and commercial success were unmistakable. "When I visit the city, after the absence of a season, I discover an obvious change. New buildings have sprung up, and new improvements are going on," testified a northern sojourner at the beginning of the decade. A pair of northern clergymen stood on the riverbank and surveyed a river crammed with some fifty steamboats and fifteen hundred flat boats. "More cotton is shipped from this port than from any other in America, or perhaps in the world. I could never have formed a conception of the amount in any other way, than by seeing the immense piles of it that fill the streets," marveled one of the clerics. Sugar, too, stood heaped upon the wharves, along with grain and meat products from the Trans-Appalachian country upriver, lead-

2. Ibid., 60–62.

3. See Chapters 5 and 6, above, and Emily Clark and Virginia Meacham Gould, "The Feminine Face of Afro-Catholicism in New Orleans, 1727–1852," *William and Mary Quarterly*, 3d Ser., LIX (2002), 409–448.

ing the transfixed observer to proclaim the city of New Orleans "the great commercial capital of the Mississippi valley."[4]

The city's passage from its checkered colonial past to its emergence as the queen of the Mississippi begins with the epicenter of the Louisiana Purchase. For the Ursulines, as for many others, the events of 1803 triggered a dramatic response. When Louisiana's retrocession to France was finally made public in the spring of that year, the nuns feared the Napoleonic republic would seize their property and suppress their community. Sixteen of the sisters sought the protection of the Spanish crown and fled to Havana at the end of May. Eleven nuns remained in Louisiana to do the work of twenty-seven. They were stretched so thin that they had to train the orphans at the convent to sing Divine Office to maintain the daily observance required by their rule.[5] The remnants of the community carried on, and their enterprise, like so much else in the city, grew and prospered in the years following the Louisiana Purchase. That narrative of material success, however, obscures a more interesting story about the relationship between the nuns and the social and cultural accommodations New Orleanians made in order to take up their new identities as Americans in a slave society. That story is perhaps best approached in retrospect, beginning at a regular meeting of the New Orleans city council in October 1824.

The councilmen's first items of business reflected a prosperous community sprinting toward urban modernization. The men discussed mollifying a police captain, paying for the new public waterworks, and enhancing the port's facilities. Such matters of public order and improvement constituted the council's steady diet in the boom years of this decade. Tempering the exuberant tone of the council's typical agenda, however, was a perennial item that revealed the dark side of the city's explosive growth. At the end of

4. For descriptions of the commercial boom in early-nineteenth-century New Orleans, see [Pierre-Louis Berquin-Duvallon], *Travels in Louisiana and the Floridas, in the Year, 1802, Giving a Correct Picture of Those Countries,* trans. John Davis (New York, 1806), 145; and Timothy Flint, *Recollections of the Last Ten Years in the Valley of the Mississippi,* ed. George R. Brooks (Carbondale, Ill., 1968), 301–308 (quotations on 301, 308).

5. Monica Ramos, the first Spanish creole to enter the New Orleans convent, led eight other Spanish creole sisters, three French nuns, three Louisiana-born Ursulines, and one nun born in Scotland to Cuba, where she founded and became the mother superior of the Ursuline convent of Havana. See "Relation de ce qui se passa dans notre Communauté à l'Époque de la Rétrocession," "Délibérations du Conseil," 85–86, and "Private Archives IV, Part I," convent roster, both in UCANO.

each meeting, the city fathers considered applications from impoverished individuals for public relief. On this October day, the denouement to the council's agenda of civic expansion was to grant a supplicant woman five dollars in city funds.[6]

Wedged between the contrasting sets of civic responsibilities taken up by the council at that meeting is an item that reveals the connection between the two. Councilman Nicolas Girod proposed that the orphan girls kept at the Ursuline convent at city expense be transferred to the asylum recently endowed by a Protestant philanthropist. In a city where unmarried Catholic women had sheltered orphans for nearly a century, city fathers were reinterpreting women's public and private roles in ways that dictated an abrupt adjustment to the community's charitable infrastructure and a rejection of the construction of femininity on which it rested. In subsequent days, members of the city council visited the two institutions, reported on them, and ultimately authorized the transfer of the orphans.[7]

A simple reading of this incident buttresses popular historical traditions that explain city politics and society in this era as a power struggle between creole Francophone Catholics and Anglophone Protestant newcomers. Several generations of Louisiana historians have rung the changes on the theme of the "Americanization" of New Orleans. Fixing on signs of hostility between Francophones and Anglophones in antebellum New Orleans, they assert the city's preoccupation with the question, "Who was to rule in this community now jointly occupied by indigenous Latin inhabitants and hoards of parvenu Anglo-American migrants from a world of vastly different mores and traditions?"[8]

The removal of the city orphans from the Ursulines defies a pat analysis pinned to Francophone-Anglophone conflict—whether cultural, political, or economic. The city council of 1824 was dominated by Francophones, and the board of the new orphan asylum included Catholic as well as Protes-

6. "New Orleans Conseil de Ville Official Proceedings," Oct. 9, 1824, 356–358, City Archives, Louisiana Division, New Orleans Public Library (hereafter cited as "Conseil de Ville Proceedings").

7. Ibid., Oct. 9, 16, 1824, 359–365.

8. Joseph G. Tregle, Jr., "Creoles and Americans," in Arnold R. Hirsch and Joseph Logsdon, eds., *Creole New Orleans: Race and Americanization* (Baton Rouge, La., 1992), 132–137, provides an excellent summary of historical and popular writing that has perpetuated this view of Francophone creole–Anglo-American relations in early national New Orleans (quotation on 132).

tant members.[9] The forces provoking the change in policy were certainly partly cultural, but the cleavages did not run neatly along linguistic lines, nor were they rooted in immutable ethnic allegiances. Instead they were tied to the project of creating a white male citizenry in the city that was recognizably American despite its language and religion. The young Republic's extension of citizenship to white men required the exclusion of nonwhites and women, especially in the slave South, where whiteness became the property on which men without land or bondpeople founded their claim to citizenship. The creole planters and merchants of New Orleans, though propertied, were not good candidates as standard-bearers of this American citizenship grounded in exclusion. They shared their city with wealthy and prestigious free people of color, some of them slaveholders. A free black militia helped keep the peace and defend the city. The church was literally, if not figuratively, denied them as a stage for the performance of white masculine dominance, filled as it was with black women. And, for the education of their daughters and the provision of practically every social service, they depended upon a convent of nuns who submitted to male authority only in its heavenly manifestations. To become citizens, the city's creole men had to learn how to mitigate the features of New Orleans society and culture that called their republican manhood into question. The orphan controversy at the Ursuline convent was one of many gestures the creole men of New Orleans made to signal their fitness for American citizenship.[10]

The official transformation of Louisiana's inhabitants from colonial subjects to republican citizens did not immediately follow the territory's pur-

---

9. Those elected to serve on the asylum board in 1824 included Mrs. Depeyster and Mrs. Duplessis; the latter served as codirectress with Phoebe Hunter ("Proceedings of the Female Orphan Society of New Orleans; Vol. 2nd; from January 16, 1823 to May 3, 1832," Jan. 16, 1824, Poydras Home Records, Manuscripts Collection 69, HTML). The New Orleans City Council members present at the meeting of October 16, 1824, were Messrs. Christy, Meance, Naba, Davazac, Lanna, Génois, Wiltz, Gainnié, Blanc, Girod, and Cox. The minutes of the City Council were kept in French. See "Conseil de Ville Proceedings," Oct. 16, 1824, 359.

10. The discussion is indebted to Peter J. Kastor's conception of the incorporation of Louisiana and the centrality of race to the process (Kastor, *The Nation's Crucible: The Louisiana Purchase and the Creation of America* [New Haven, Conn., 2004], esp. 76–108, 135, 149). On whiteness as property, see Cheryl I. Harris, "Whiteness as Property," *Harvard Law Review*, CVI (1993), 1707–1791.

chase in 1803. Statehood was deferred until 1812, and territorial inhabitants champed at the bit for the privilege and power of home rule during the intervening years. Wary federal officials, meanwhile, lacked confidence in the inhabitants' loyalty and readiness for assuming the responsibilities of self-government.[11] Formally deprived of the privileges of political citizenship, New Orleanians found a setting, nonetheless, in which to exercise the right of self-government. The city's first attempts at home rule came, not in the statehouse, but in church.

Saint Louis Cathedral on March 14, 1805, was the stage for a Revolutionary-style drama over who should be the chief cleric in the city. The controversy raged for months, and, as the epistolary exchange seeking resolution dragged on, New Orleanians registered their impatience. "All the Catholics of this parish arose as one and in a body, asserting that as things had come to such a pass they would make use of the privilege that the freedom of the American government permits them and would appoint a pastor of their own choice." More likely, it was the city council and the parish trustees, a group of laymen who claimed to hold legitimate authority to appoint the pastor of their parish, who "arose as one and in a body" to take the decision away from distant prelates. In colonial New Orleans, the trustees and the city councillors of the Cabildo made their decisions without consulting the people they governed. Now, to demonstrate that they understood the mechanics of popular sovereignty, the city councilmen, freshly installed under a new city charter that made their offices elective, had the bell rung to call the faithful to church to vote for a new pastor. A crowd of four thousand reputedly showed up, and ballots were distributed. "A large number were holding their votes in writing in order to put them in the locked box prepared to receive them." The crowd, however, was not inclined to wait for the results of a formal secret ballot. They raucously proclaimed as their pastor the Capuchin priest Antonio Sedella and surged from the church toward the friar's residence. They conducted him forcibly thence

11. The correspondence of Louisiana's first territorial governor, William C. C. Claiborne, is among the best primary sources for the Anglo-American perspective on Louisianians in the two decades following the Purchase (*Official Letter Books of W. C. C. Claiborne, 1801–1816*, ed. Dunbar Rowland, 6 vols. [Jackson, Miss., 1917]). For an excellent study of the role of Louisiana in the young Republic's international diplomacy that offers some attention to the political culture of Louisianians, see Peter J. Kastor, "'Motives of Peculiar Urgency': Local Diplomacy in Louisiana, 1803–1821," *WMQ*, 3d Ser., LVIII (2001), 819–848 (esp. 822–823). For an expanded study of Louisiana's "incorporation" into the United States, see Kastor, *Nation's Crucible*.

to the sanctuary of the church, where, "after a courteous and polite discussion," he agreed to serve.[12]

Sedella's election did not go uncontested. The entire tumult, in fact, was prompted by a disagreement between Sedella and Father Patrick Walsh, a cleric of Irish ancestry who claimed the post and ecclesiastical authority in the city by virtue of his previous position as vicar-general under the Spanish. In the confusing aftermath of Louisiana's passage from Spanish to French and ultimately American hands between 1801 and 1803, the chain of ecclesiastical authority was unclear. The event that escalated into what is commonly known as the Schism of 1805 could be seen simply as the inevitable messiness inherent in the transition of church administration from one regime to another. Yet it was also a crucial setting for the assertion of popular will mediated by elected officials in a community denied the exercise of self-rule in the national political arena. Exploiting the temporary ambiguity in ecclesiastical organization that followed the Louisiana Purchase, Catholic New Orleanians announced their readiness for American citizenship.[13]

The *coup d'église* of 1805 echoed American Revolutionary antecedents in more than its claim to self-rule. Like much of the resistance of the Revolutionary age, it harnessed the power of mass popular protest to the interests of a local elite. The mob of four thousand that pressed Father Sedella into service was convened by the city council and the parish trustees. Under the French and Spanish regimes, the five trustees had fiduciary responsibility for the parish and were charged with maintaining the material fabric of the church. They were traditionally members of the social and economic elite of the colony, elected by eligible—white, male—parishioners. In both their composition and their function, there are thus obvious parallels with the institution of the vestry in the Anglican Church. Unlike colonial Anglican vestries, however, the trustees of Louisiana had always operated quietly

12. Casa Calvo to José Caballero, Mar. 30, 1805, in Stanley Faye, ed., "The Schism of 1805 in New Orleans," *LHQ*, XXII (1939), 107; John Kendall, *History of New Orleans* (Chicago, 1922), 67–71.

13. Charles Edwards O'Neill, "'A Quarter Marked by Sundry Peculiarities': New Orleans, Lay Trustees, and Père Antoine," *Catholic Historical Review*, LXXVI (1990), proposes a densely reasoned ecclesiastical interpretation of the Schism of 1805. He argues that creoles who supported Sedella were technically in the right regarding the validity of his claim over that of Walsh. O'Neill attributes a degree of political motivation to the trustees but roots it in colonial tradition and aversion to distant American authority, lay and civil.

under a colonial bishop and deferred to his authority in naming parish priests. After 1803, however, their understanding of their role changed. As one historian observes, the "trustees of New Orleans mistakenly thought that election of pastors was an accepted feature of Catholic practice in the United States of America." Subsequently, like the vestries of some colonial Anglican churches, the New Orleans trustees chafed at attempts by a distant central authority to impose its pastoral choices upon them.[14]

By means of the Schism of 1805, the city council and parish trustees of early national New Orleans explicitly embraced the political culture of the young Republic and attempted to demonstrate Catholicism's compatibility with it. They rejected precisely the kind of centralist, absolutist government to which the former colony had been subject. Far from positioning themselves in opposition to the Anglo-American constituency in the city, the creole trustees aligned themselves ideologically with the new regime and employed an ingenious strategy to achieve fuller inclusion in the city's and the nation's political life. By staging a dramatic performance of popular electoral politics, they consciously mimicked the processes by which the new Republic had been created. Finally, they made a show of their independence of papal and episcopal authority to reassure Americans who feared that religious allegiance to Rome could not be reconciled with civil loyalty to the Republic.

The Ursulines, meanwhile, put themselves in direct conflict with the council and trustees' assertion of their new republican identities. Upon Sedella's popular elevation to the pastorate, the nuns offered their premises to the priest whose claim they deemed more valid: Patrick Walsh. Walsh, in turn, proclaimed the Ursuline convent chapel the legitimate parish church and advised that sacraments performed elsewhere would be null and void. Bishop John Carroll of Baltimore, acting on authority from Rome, supported Walsh's position and confirmed the Ursuline chapel as the parish church and its chaplain as the pastor of the parish.[15]

The New Orleans nuns, like the city council and parish trustees, chose their course of action with acute consciousness of its larger ideological import. Their counterparts in revolutionary France had chosen to stand beside French clerics who refused to compromise their loyalty to the papacy

14. Ibid., 259. On the power of colonial Anglican vestries and their resistance to overseas authority, see, especially, Rhys Isaac, *The Transformation of Virginia, 1740–1790* (Chapel Hill, N.C., 1982; rpt. New York, 1988), 143–204.

15. Roger Baudier, *The Catholic Church in Louisiana* (New Orleans, 1939), 261–262.

by taking an oath in support of the republican church. Some paid with their lives for their stance: sixteen Ursulines loyal to nonjuring clergy went to the guillotine in 1794. As had their counterparts in revolutionary France, the New Orleans Ursulines supported episcopal and papal authority in defiance of local republican authority, a position that was no doubt reinforced by the election of a superior in 1812 who had herself been temporarily forced from religious life by the revolution.[16]

The Ursulines' episcopal alliance carried no fatal consequences for the New Orleans nuns, but it might well have been the cause of a demoralizing episode of public ridicule. As the drama of the Schism and its aftermath played out in 1805 and 1806, the city's only theater staged a comedy that the nuns complained was "calculated to bring their Order into disrepute, and to hold them up to the derision of the People." The women felt beleaguered enough to contemplate abandoning the city. In 1815, they wrote to the pope asking for permission to relocate to France if "spiritual assistance" and additional nuns were not forthcoming.[17]

Postrevolutionary women in both France and the United States sought new channels of influence when the secular republican regime adopted a mode of political action that specifically excluded women from its ideology of universal political rights. Early American women opened a new

16. Elizabeth Rapley, "'Pieuses Contre-Revolutionnaires': The Experience of the Ursulines of Northern France, 1789–1792," *French History*, II (1988), 453–473. Françoise Agathe Gensoul entered the Ursuline convent at Pont Saint Esprit in 1792 but was forced to renounce her vows and leave the convent shortly thereafter. She renewed her vows in New Orleans in 1811, less than a month after her arrival in Louisiana, accompanied by seven postulants. See "Private Archives IV, Part I," roster entry for Françoise Agathe Gensoul (Sister Saint Michel), UCANO; Jane Frances Heaney, *A Century of Pioneering: A History of the Ursuline Nuns in New Orleans (1727–1827)*, ed. Mary Ethel Booker Siefken (New Orleans, 1993), 230 (written as Ph.D. diss., Saint Louis University, 1949).

17. Sister Sainte Marie Olivier and Sister Saint Michel Gensoul to Pius VII, May 2, 1815, contemporary manuscript copy, UCANO. At the nuns' request, Governor Claiborne sought the mayor's help in suppressing the 1805–1806 play, a request that seems to have been completely ignored (William C. C. Claiborne to James Pitot, June 8, 1805, Claiborne to the mayor of New Orleans, June 24, 1806, in Claiborne, *Official Letter Books*, ed. Rowland, III, 84–85, 344–345 [quotation on 344]). Until the 1810s, there was a single theater in New Orleans, which offered its plays and entertainments in both French and English. See Liliane Crété, *Daily Life in Louisiana, 1815–1830*, trans. Patrick Gregory (Baton Rouge, La., 1981), 219–220.

route to public influence through an ideological keyhole in republicanism that enjoined women to participate in the production of a virtuous citizenry through education of the young. Though buoyed by religiosity, women's educational activity was justified and sanctioned by secular ideology and was explicitly yoked to motherhood. Postrevolutionary French women forged a different course. They recreated a vehicle for political influence and action by forming an alliance with the princes of the church, an alliance perceived by opponents to be against both republicanism and women's proper place within the family. The responses by French and American women to their exclusion from formal political participation are among the most marked of the differences between the two.[18]

French women turned to one of their traditional vehicles for public action: religion. The male ecclesiastical hierarchy, usually wary of growth in female religious life, embraced the female initiative and formed a powerful partnership with religious women in the first half of the nineteenth century. They were disposed to do so by their own relatively weak position at the turn of the century. In the 1790s, France had suppressed all institutions of the Catholic Church that were judged to be a threat to the new political and social order. Priests who swore to uphold the authority of the republic in church governance were allowed to remain in their parishes and administer the sacraments. Religious orders were suppressed, their property was confiscated, and their members were expelled from their convents, monasteries, and rectories. At the turn of the century, the republican government reassessed its policy on the church. Clergy and charitable and educational institutions operated by female religious orders were judged to be beneficial to the health and social order of the nation, and the French republic and the church negotiated an armistice in 1801 known as the Napoleonic Concordat. In its wake, France experienced a dramatic religious revival comparable in scope and energy to America's Second Great Awakening. French women, lay and vowed, seized the opportunity to fill the channels of action newly reopened to them.[19]

18. See Linda K. Kerber, *Women of the Republic: Intellect and Ideology in Revolutionary America* (Chapel Hill, N.C., 1980); Joan B. Landes, *Women and the Public Sphere in the Age of the French Revolution* (Ithaca, N.Y., 1988); Dena Goodman, "Public Sphere and Private Life: Toward a Synthesis of Current Historiographical Approaches to the Old Regime," *History and Theory*, XXXI (1992), 1–20.

19. The major work on the feminization of nineteenth-century French Catholicism is Claude Langlois, *Le Catholicisme au féminin: Les congrégations françaises à supérieure*

Through religious organizations and activities, and in partnership with the clergy, French women exercised political influence in ways that transcended or simply ignored the boundaries of secular politics. Their ideas and actions shaped educational and social policy and forced a relationship between religion and the state that lay outside the republican ideal. An educated citizenry, for example, was deemed to be a cornerstone of a successful republic. Ideally, the education provided in a republic should be grounded in the principles of secular Enlightenment thought. However, since women primarily taught in the populous French countryside and towns and since, more often than not, these women were vowed religious or were closely allied with the Catholic Church through lay associations, French children received an education with a distinctly religious cast.[20]

The august nineteenth-century French historian Jules Michelet decried women's alliance with the church as the most pernicious obstacle to the progress of the republican ideal. He placed the blame squarely on the shoulders of the church, which he claimed usurped the loyalty that good republican women should show to their husbands. Other nineteenth-century critics returned to old arguments about women's moral culpability to condemn the alliance. Women's partnership with the church grew from feminine irrationality and sexual weakness, which, in turn, left them susceptible to the spiritual, if not the literal, seduction of the shrewd clergy. Both schools of criticism accused priests of using women as pawns in their bid for political power in postrevolutionary France. Both women and priests were judged guilty of undermining the natural order that dictated women's submission to their husbands. Nineteenth-century French political culture and religion were thus dominated by an explicitly gendered conflict. The church became "feminized," both literally and figuratively, as it became the pre-

---

générale au XIXe siècle (Paris, 1984), revisited and extended somewhat in Langlois, "Féminisation du Catholicisme," in Jacques Le Goff and René Rémond, eds., *Histoire de la France religieuse*, 4 vols. (Paris, 1991), III, 292–307. In English, Hazel M. Mills, "Women and Catholicism in Provincial France, c. 1800–c. 1850: Franche-Comté in National Context" (D.Phil. thesis, University of Oxford, 1994), provides a comprehensive synthesis of the French scholarship on the subject and a pathbreaking study of women's agency and activism in the realm of religion. In a similar vein, Ruth Harris traces the powerful alliance formed between women and the clergy in the creation of a hugely popular pilgrimage in *Lourdes: Body and Spirit in the Secular Age* (New York, 1999).

20. Mills, "Women and Catholicism," 172–173, 204–274.

serve of women and clergy who had been denied access to political power in France.[21]

Although circumstances in America were similar in their broad outline, the British colonial Protestant heritage and separation of church and state made a significant difference. Like their counterparts in France, American women found themselves excluded from the formal political realm in the post-Revolutionary era. They responded by creating a new space for "public" action by building on the young Republic's educational mandate. Because a virtuous republic was thought to depend on an educated citizenry, women were able to gain a new source of support for education of and by women. Enlightenment influences that recognized intellectual equality had begun to have an impact among elite Anglo-American women in the eighteenth century. The Revolution endowed women's claim to educational access with political meaning that had the potential to justify other forms of public service, and American women subsequently expanded their activities to the realm of organized benevolence.[22]

In the nature of their organized public activities—education and charity—nineteenth-century French and American women paralleled one another. A fundamental difference lay, however, in the authority by which each of the two groups acted outside the private realm of the home. French women drew on the authority of the church, in both its heavenly transcendent form and its temporal, ecclesiastical manifestation. They built on a long-standing Catholic tradition of female religious institutions and a deeply rooted cultural acceptance of unmarried religious women. Their strategy lay in exploiting the revival of an ancien régime institution that preserved avenues of female political action that were not subject to the freshly articulated political ideology conflating masculinity with the crucial status of citizenship. The Protestant women of America had no such traditional alternative to press into service. Instead, they worked within the gendered republican paradigm that offered women a role in the creation and custodianship of citizenship through the ideologically sanctioned roles of wife and mother. Unmarried religious women in France who operated educational and charitable institutions acted on the heavenly authority of their god, living in fi-

21. Jules Michelet, *Du prêtre, de la femme, de la famille* (Paris, 1845); Mills, "Women and Catholicism," 1.

22. Kerber, *Women of the Republic*, 199–200, 227–230; Lori D. Ginzberg, *Women and the Work of Benevolence: Morality, Politics, and Class in the Nineteenth-Century United States* (New Haven, Conn., 1990), 11–97.

nancially independent communities that were not subject to the rule of an earthly husband. Although American women who organized and ran similar institutions might have acted independently, many were always subject to and acting with the assent of their husbands.

The Catholic women of New Orleans were conditioned by their history to emulate postrevolutionary French women, continuing to employ religion as a route to influence in the larger society. The convent compound and the city's churches were already, in effect, political sites where women and people of color made themselves, their interests, and the power of their numbers visible. The territorial status of early national Louisiana disrupted that pattern and made the church for a time a political space for white men as well. By deferring statehood, federal authorities in effect feminized Louisiana's male inhabitants. Like politically excluded women who were not recognized as citizens of the French and American republics, New Orleans men embraced the Catholic Church and made it an alternate site for the performance of the rhetoric and ritual of the Republic in which they sought the full rights of citizenship. For the trustees and their followers, their alliance with the church did not preclude their later participation in civic republicanism. In the longer term, it became an additional rather than an alternative theater of male republican authority in the city. Indeed, trustees continued to exercise significant control over the New Orleans church until 1844, long after Louisiana's inhabitants had been granted the more traditional mechanisms of republican power.[23]

When Father Walsh defied the trustees and established an alternative ecclesiastical authority at the Ursuline convent, he created a schism that went beyond issues of ecclesiastical legitimacy. By acting with the city council's approval and representing the parishioners' will, the trustees brought the white male leadership of the city's Catholic Church in line with civil power, forestalling the political estrangement and literal feminization of the church lay leadership that took place in France. Walsh's action, however, forced ecclesiastical authorities to take a position that was perceived as explicitly adversarial to popular white male opinion. Bishop Carroll of Baltimore, Bishop Dubourg of Louisiana, and the pope himself all contested or overrode the trustees and thus contravened male inhabitants' authority.

If the New Orleans church had remained undivided, the Ursulines' long-standing working relationship with city officials might have continued with

23. O'Neill, "New Orleans, Lay Trustees," *Catholic Hist. Rev.*, LXXVI (1990), 276–277.

only minor adjustments to the new regime. Walsh's refusal to bend to the will of the city's men foreclosed that possibility. In the face of resistance to central ecclesiastical authority, he did what many revolutionary-era French clergy had done; he called on religious women to provide a refuge and a power base. The Ursulines followed in the footsteps of their French counterparts and placed themselves in direct opposition to a city elite newly baptized in the waters of democratic republicanism.

Rather paradoxically, this allied the nuns with the federal authorities, who supported Bishop Carroll's position. Overlooking the long-term ideological implications of the trustees' actions, federal officials focused on the more immediate threat of rebelliousness. Such a position was understandable in the wake of the Burr conspiracy that aimed to make a separate republic of Louisiana, but it worsened the nuns' standing with the local elite. By a circuitous route, the New Orleans nuns found themselves in much the same position as their French counterparts: alienated from the leadership of the male citizenry.[24]

Postrevolutionary France enjoyed a functional rapprochement between republicanism and the religious women who operated the educational and charitable institutions that supported the progress of the state. Early-nineteenth-century French culture doubly secured the place of nuns. An ingrained acceptance of the presence of unmarried religious women of two centuries' standing withstood the republican belief that marriage was the lynchpin of civic virtue. The functional utility to the state of religious women already committed to education and social service provided further protection for the nun in France.[25] Neither circumstance obtained in

24. Ibid., 251–256.

25. Colin Jones, *Charity and Bienfaisance: The Treatment of the Poor in the Montpellier Region, 1740–1815* (Cambridge, 1982), 201–234; Mills, "Women and Catholicism," 275–335. Mills describes the particular benefit to the state of religious congregations that took on the dirty work of ensuring social welfare: "In the peasant and urban working-class women who became *Soeurs de la Charité* and their like, the state found a workforce prepared to deal with the most undesirable elements of society—the insane, the venereal, the 'fille soumise,' the petty criminal" (334). The French republican détente with nuns ended in 1905, when the Third Republic passed a series of anticlerical laws. The terms of the 1801 Napoleonic Concordat were dissolved, church and state completely separated from one another, congregations dissolved, and Catholic schools closed. On the centrality of marriage to the construction of republican virtue in the early American Republic, see Jan Lewis, "The Republican Wife: Virtue and Seduc-

America, where the Protestant tradition that dominated had long since suppressed female vowed religious life as an alternative to marriage. Marriage and the virtuous wife came to be seen, in post-Revolutionary America, first as an anchor for the morality that was essential to securing the Republic and subsequently as a means of defining social and racial hierarchies that served the interests of a rising middle class. The inculcation of republican virtue and the creation of a moral society that served the interests of early national elites were inextricably linked to marriage. In the young Republic, marriage and the apparatus of female benevolence that it spawned created a demand for education and social services that specified marriage as a prerequisite for participation. In the young Republic, the nuns' unmarried state deprived them of the route that married women took to gain entry to a realm of public action. Neither ideology nor social necessity created a safe space in which the New Orleans Ursulines could follow their calling.

The Schism of 1805 created a serious rift between the Ursulines and the local elite, but it was insufficient in itself to permanently poison the relationship between the parties. Other factors amplified the perception that the nuns represented a threat to the local power structure. On the eve of its cession to the United States, the plantation economy of the Lower Mississippi Valley finally came into its own. The full apparatus of a slave society fell quickly and permanently into place, imposing its firmly drawn categories of race and gender with the patriarchal force intrinsic to the system. At the same time, the port of New Orleans blossomed as a commercial center, embracing as it did key features of early national American urban culture. Both plantation slavocracy and urban commercialism embraced a republican gender order that sanctioned female agency only when it originated from within the supervised social spaces of home and family. The Ursulines not only operated outside the surveillance of patriarchal families but also subverted the gendered distribution of authority when the nuns assumed crucial aspects of planter and merchant identities. On occasion, the women even achieved markers of success that surpassed those attained by the city's men.

During the colonial period, the Ursulines appear never to have joined other slaveholders in the generally futile quest for profits from staple crop

tion in the Early Republic," *WMQ*, 3d Ser., XLIV (1987), 689–721; and Clare A. Lyons, *Sex among the Rabble: An Intimate History of Gender and Power in the Age of Revolution, Philadelphia, 1730–1830* (Chapel Hill, N.C., 2006), 288, 309–310, 354–355, 391–395.

agriculture. Early in the nineteenth century, however, they appear briefly to have joined the rush to reap the profits of sugar cultivation. In August 1805, they spent more than $6,000 for a plantation on the west bank of the Mississippi. Five years later, when property prices had skyrocketed in New Orleans, they approved the purchase of a piece of property adjoining it for the more substantial sum of $15,500. Although no direct evidence indicates that the new property was acquired and used for cane cultivation, the frantic negotiation for land around New Orleans and its rapid transformation into sugar plantations during these years suggest that the nuns were so inclined.[26]

The timing of the first property purchase, four months after the tumultuous election of Father Sedella launched the Schism of 1805, suggests that the nuns' decision might have been influenced by more than simple avarice. The profitability of sugarcane had been established for some years before the nuns made their initial investment, but in 1805 New Orleans was politically unstable, and the nuns' position had suddenly become acutely precarious. The American government had, at least, guaranteed them the right to hold property. Wealth provided an attractive insurance policy against capricious local politics.[27]

Convent sources yield no details about the returns on this investment between 1805 and 1810, but in the end it was unsuccessful and threw the convent into temporary debt in 1810 and 1811.[28] The nuns had apparently tried and failed to make their fortunes as planters. If the trustees, city council, and their supporters reveled in Fortune's rejection of the women's attempt to claim the masculine identity of plantation master, they soon found themselves confounded by the nuns' success in another masculine pursuit, urban property development.

The nuns fell into this venture as they sought a way to retire the debt from their failed plantation experiment. They were unable to find a buyer

26. "Livre du cofre à trois clefs: 12 Juillet 1888–Octobre 1851," 19, 21, UCANO; James Pitot, *Observations on the Colony of Louisiana from 1796 to 1802*, trans. Henry C. Pitot (Baton Rouge, La., 1979), 73–79.

27. Thomas Jefferson to Sister Thérèse de St. Xavier Farjon, May 15, 1804, UCANO.

28. "Livre du cofre à trois clefs," 21v–22, UCANO. The nuns pasted over several pages of their capital accounts book, obscuring the full details of this debt and its aftermath. They noted that they had taken bad investment advice and were having to make considerable sacrifices to regain a firm financial footing. Their strategies for doing so included selling at least eleven of their bondpeople between 1809 and 1812.

for the unprofitable property until 1812. In the meantime, they decided to liquidate another real estate asset that proved to be equally valuable, the dairy farm they had purchased in 1780. Fortuitously, the farm lay directly in the path of rapid urban expansion. In the aftermath of the Louisiana Purchase, the area directly upriver from the original French settlement beat out its competitor downriver as the favored site for new commercial and residential development. As the city's economy and population boomed, the plantations that made up this district, known as the Faubourg Sainte Marie, were successively subdivided and sold to eager commercial and residential buyers. The nuns hired surveyors in the fall of 1810 and charged them with creating a plan for the subdivision of the plantation into lots. The firm of Potier and Lafon mapped out a residential neighborhood with streets that still bear the names of mother superior Sister Saint Marie, treasurer Sister Saint André, and assistant superior Sister Sainte Félicité.[29]

The women made thousands of dollars from the subdivision that became known as Faubourg Nuns. The Ursulines not only involved themselves in the business of land development, but they did so in a manner that was deemed particularly unseemly. Not content with the spirit of the pledges made by buyers in their notarized purchase contracts, the nuns hired an attorney to enforce financial commitments that had fallen in arrears. "We feel all the repugnance which naturally arises from the idea of being obliged to make use of violent means," the Ursulines wrote to their lawyer in reference to the collection of a delinquent mortgage debt. "We are all however of the opinion that he should be told that it is our intention to seize our property for the balance due our order." When their Anglophone lawyer, A. L. Duncan, balked, the women dismissed him.[30]

The harried lawyer reminded the women in a letter protesting his dismissal that "their Convent was no longer in the opinion of some men [viewed] as a sacred Asylum." He went on to observe that the nuns were "at war with a powerful corporation in almost everything which related to their town property and involved in some difficulty with almost every person who was indebted to them." Duncan was alluding not only to the sis-

29. See Chapter 5, above, for details on the purchase and operation of this plantation. Sales of parcels of this tract are recorded in "Livre du coffre à trois clefs," 25, UCANO. For a full account of the origins of Faubourg Nuns, see Kathryn C. Briede, "A History of the City of Lafayette," *LHQ*, XX (1937), 906–908.

30. Sister Sainte Angele Johnston to A. L. Duncan, [1822], Duncan to Johnston, June 15, 1822, UCANO.

ters' development of Faubourg Nuns but also to their battle with city and federal authorities over the land on which their convent compound was situated.[31]

The nuns resolved a dispute with federal officials over the allocation of land for an expanded barracks and hospital complex abutting the convent enclosure in 1821.[32] Their altercation with city officials who wished to open a public street through the middle of their compound enjoyed a less pleasant resolution. Condé Street was a heavily used cross street in the original city grid that stopped short of a complete transverse of the town at the walls of the convent at the settlement's southeastern corner. The development of residential and commercial property east of the original city limits in the early nineteenth century made the street's truncated path newly inconvenient, and inhabitants pressed city officials in the late 1810s to open the street through the convent grounds. In the spring of 1819, Mayor August Macarty gave the nuns a year's notice that the city would satisfy the public's request. The nuns protested the invasion of their privacy and the breach of their cloister, and, when negotiations over construction of fences at public expense fell through, the women let it be known that if the street were opened they would relocate their entire compound.[33]

It was not an idle threat. When negotiations with the United States over the expansion of the barracks stalled in the late 1810s, the nuns applied some of the profits from the sale of various properties to the purchase of a large parcel of land downriver from the city. Lying well beyond the city limits and in the opposite direction favored by the city's expansion, the site the nuns purchased in 1818 would provide a convent location beyond the

31. Duncan to Johnston, June 15, 1822, UCANO.

32. The nuns prevailed in a dispute with the Spanish crown over title to their property and used this ruling as a basis for their negotiation with the United States authorities over a parcel of land adjacent to the military hospital ("Cahier renfermant toutes les pièces relatives aux réclamations du fiscal pour le domaine royal du roi d'Espagne," UCANO). After several years' negotiation, the nuns resolved the dispute by buying the parcel in question. See William Wirt to James Monroe, Apr. 11, 1820, contemporary manuscript copy, "Pièce concernant l'hôpital," Sept. 24, 1822, Louis William Dubourg to Madame de Saint Joseph Laclotte, Sept. 17, 1823, J. J. McLanahan to Dubourg, Jan. 28, 1824, all in UCANO. Heaney, Century of Pioneering, ed. Siefken, 253–259, provides a succinct and lucid summary of the negotiation.

33. Sister Sainte Marie Olivier to Archbishop John Carroll, Oct. 16, 1815, contemporary manuscript copy, UCANO; Heaney, Century of Pioneering, ed. Siefken, 259–260.

reach of city officials.[34] When their dispute with the federal government over title to some of the land within part of their enclosure was finally resolved in their favor in 1822, the nuns were free to subdivide and sell an entire city square of valuable urban real estate. They used the proceeds to elude their unpleasant stalemate with city authorities over opening Condé Street. In the spring of 1823, the nuns signed a contract in excess of sixty-four thousand dollars for the construction of a new convent on their property downriver.[35]

The main convent building rose rapidly on the banks of the Mississippi some two miles below New Orleans. It was an immense building of expensive brick, three stories high with a double gallery supported by twenty-six white wooden pillars running along its front. This extravagantly large edifice was an imposing testament to the nuns' ultimate triumph in the perilous waters of finance. During the very years that brought heavy losses to planters in the wake of the panic of 1819, the nuns prospered and built a new home for their educational enterprise that dwarfed the plantation homes neighboring it on the riverbank (see Figure 19).[36]

The Ursulines had now challenged male authority on multiple occasions, defying gender conventions and wounding masculine pride. They had refused to submit to male leadership in the Schism of 1805. They had presumed to try their hands as planters in a full-blown slave society that was secured by an ideology of patriarchal control. They entered into the fray of real estate development and laid mercy aside as they rode the crest of the city's boom to wealth at a time when many of the men of the city found themselves facing ruin. They eluded attempts by the city fathers to constrict, quite literally, their space. And, finally, they built a headquarters for their enterprise that dwarfed the plantation abodes of the patriarchs whose identities they had audaciously subverted for nearly twenty years.

34. The site of the Ursulines' acquisition lay beyond the settled areas of the city, downriver from the fortifications erected before the Battle of New Orleans in 1815. See "Plan of the City and Suburbs of New Orleans: From an Actual Survey Made in 1815 by I. Tanesse," Rollinson, sc. New York: Charles Del Vecchio, New Orleans: P. Maspero, 1817, Library of Congress, Geography and Map Division, Washington, D.C.

35. Heaney, *Century of Pioneering*, ed. Siefken, 260. The nuns made three payments between 1818 and 1820 totaling $34,640 for the parcel, which they purchased through an agent. See "Livre du coffre à trois clefs" [contract between Claude Gurlie and Joseph Guillot and the Ursuline Sisters of New Orleans], Mar. 25, 1823, UCANO.

36. "Livre du coffre à trois clefs," Mar. 25, 1823, UCANO.

Figure 19. Third New Orleans Ursuline Convent. Built 1824. Courtesy, UCANO

Along with the Ursulines' assaults on New Orleanians' masculinity other significant forces threatened the city's planter and commercial elite in the first two decades of the nineteenth century. Ironically, the twin bases of the city's prosperity—the heady sugar boom and the rapid growth of the port —each brought problems that endangered the stability necessary to sustain that prosperity. Expansion of sugar cultivation triggered rapid growth in the slave population, raising both the specter and the reality of rebellion. The continual influx into the city of disorderly "Kaintucks" bringing their goods downriver to market, joined by hopeful but poor immigrant laborers and criminal opportunists, undermined hopes of establishing a secure environment for the creation of wealth. A massive immigration of Haitian refugees in 1809–1810 added to the city's burden. Yellow fever epidemics punctuated the first twenty years, sapping the city's workforce and snuffing its optimism. Racial tension and antagonism, a disruptive mass immigration, public disorder, and disease all chipped away at the confidence and effective authority of the men who saw themselves as the city fathers.

Louisiana's sugar production took off with a sudden jolt in the 1790s.

The Haitian Revolution that broke out in 1791 cut off the main source of supply of the staple from the French Caribbean, which gave Louisiana an opening in the market just as a local planter perfected a new refining technique. Practically overnight, cane became profitable for Louisiana planters. The Lower Mississippi Valley was still relatively thinly settled, so the availability of land did not pose a significant obstacle. Acquiring and controlling a sufficient labor force posed a greater challenge. The demand for slaves in late colonial Louisiana was almost insatiable. Impatient planters bought laborers from every possible source. Enslaved people from all regions of the young United States, north, upper south, and lowcountry, were sold into the Spanish colony along with creole Caribbean bondpeople. Of an estimated twenty-six thousand unfree laborers imported into the Lower Mississippi Valley between 1790 and 1810, newly enslaved Africans formed the largest constituency, making up as much as two-thirds of this tide of forced immigrants.[37]

The rapid growth and re-Africanization of Louisiana's slave population brought more than economic change and a shift away from the slave community's creole cultural balance. Rebellion became more than the constant but dim specter it had been through most of the eighteenth century. Fifty-seven enslaved blacks and three Euro-Louisianians were convicted in 1795 of conspiring to raise a slave revolt in Pointe Coupee, some one hundred miles north of New Orleans. According to court records, the conspirators hatched an elaborate scheme to draw the district's planters to one location by setting a decoy fire. Once gathered, the slaveholders would be killed by armed laborers who would rally the district's workforce to a general assault on the slave regime of the entire colony. The rebellion was aborted, and the heads of twenty-three convicted conspirators were cut off and nailed to posts along the Mississippi River between Pointe Coupee and New Orleans. The rapidly maturing slave society of Louisiana had reacted to rebellion with emphatic brutality. This feature of master-slave relations gen-

37. Ira Berlin, *Many Thousands Gone: The First Two Centuries of Slavery in North America* (Cambridge, Mass., 1998), 342–346; Gwendolyn Midlo Hall, *Africans in Colonial Louisiana: The Development of Afro-Creole Culture in the Eighteenth Century* (Baton Rouge, La., 1992), 275–315; Allan Kulikoff, "Uprooted Peoples: Black Migrants in the Age of the American Revolution, 1790–1820," in Berlin and Ronald Hoffman, eds., *Slavery and Freedom in the Age of the American Revolution* (Charlottesville, Va., 1983), 149; Adam Rothman, "The Expansion of Slavery in the Deep South, 1790–1820" (Ph.D. diss., Columbia University, 2000), 70–76.

erally increased as planters anxious to increase their fortunes applied the most obvious, if not the most effective, means of subduing a resistant labor force. Observers of Louisiana in the early 1800s commented with some frequency on the liberal use of the whip.[38]

Although corporal punishment might have been effective in extracting labor and compliance in some instances, it did not stamp out the impulse to resist and rebel that was the planter's greatest fear. Some five hundred enslaved workers rose up in the winter of 1811, reportedly under the leadership of an enslaved man who was a native of Saint Domingue. Setting out from a plantation a short distance upriver from New Orleans, the rebels killed two people, burned three houses, and sent the whites in their path running to the city for safety. Local militia and federal troops put down the revolt, and the gruesome sight of severed heads once again loomed along the riverbank outside the city. The bloody spectacle masked the planters' self-inflicted powerlessness and their profound fear. Enthralled by their greed, they were unwilling to reduce the threat of future rebellion by restricting the domestic slave trade. Terrified by the possibility of another rebellion, they demanded that Governor William C. C. Claiborne permanently establish a full regiment of federal troops in New Orleans.[39]

Fear of slave revolt was heightened by the revolution in Saint Domingue and its particular aftermath in New Orleans. Fought between 1791 and 1804, the ultimately victorious slave revolution resulted in the establishment of the republic of Haiti. The conflict propelled successive waves of black and white refugees abroad for three decades. Ten thousand Saint Domingans fled in 1793 and settled in Baltimore and other Atlantic seaboard towns. In 1803, most remaining whites, a large number of free people of color, and enslaved workers belonging to both groups fled in the wake of the decisive defeat of Napoleon's troops by Haitian revolutionaries. Some thirty thousand free and enslaved refugees made their way to the temporary haven of Cuba. When Cuba deported large numbers of this cohort in 1809, their primary destination was New Orleans. More than nine thousand of the refugees reached the city between May 1809 and the early spring of 1810, join-

38. Hall, *Africans in Colonial Louisiana*, 344; Latrobe, *Impressions respecting New Orleans*, ed. Wilson, 53; C. C. Robin, *Voyage to Louisiana, 1803–1805*, trans. and ed. Stuart O. Landry, Jr. (New Orleans, 1966), 238.

39. *Louisiana Gazette*, Jan. 11, 24, 1811; Thomas N. Ingersoll, *Mammon and Manon in Early New Orleans: The First Slave Society in the Deep South, 1718–1819* (Knoxville, Tenn., 1999), 292–293.

ing the thousand or so who had made their way to Louisiana previously. In 1806, the city's population stood at roughly seventeen thousand. The sudden arrival of more than nine thousand newcomers would have been a traumatic event in any circumstance. The makeup of the immigrant wave did nothing to mitigate the impact of the event.[40]

The majority of the refugees from Haiti were people of African descent. Among those who arrived in 1809–1810, some 3,102 were free people of color, and 3,226 were enslaved, constituting 70 percent of the immigrant group. Congress reopened the slave trade to accommodate the free Haitians who arrived with enslaved people, exempting them from the 1808 ban on the importation of foreign slaves. Introducing more than 3,000 enslaved people tainted by the spirit of revolution into the volatile young plantation society of southeast Louisiana was a risk, and the refugees' welcome in New Orleans was mixed. When a story circulated that the leader of the 1811 slave revolt was from Saint Domingue, New Orleanians' fears that the refugees carried the seed of revolution with them were confirmed, though the actual origins of the rebellion might well have lain elsewhere.[41]

Whites among the Haitian immigrants might have been welcomed as reinforcements for Francophone cultural dominance, but their economic position reduced the attractiveness of the newcomers. Stripped of their land and their wealth, many were masters with enslaved laborers in search of an occupation. They were destined either to compete directly with creole planters for the scraps of land not yet taken for sugar cultivation or to be merchants and professionals whose interests might diverge from those of the planter class.[42]

Rebellion was the most extreme of the threats to the city's stability, but more mundane and pervasive corrosives continuously undermined civil order. "The city abounds with tippling houses," reported a French observer in 1802. "The low orders of every colour, white, yellow, and black, mix in-

40. Paul F. Lachance, "The Foreign French," in Arnold R. Hirsch and Joseph Logsdon, eds., *Creole New Orleans: Race and Americanization* (Baton Rouge, La., 1992), 103–105.

41. Ibid., 107; Ingersoll, *Mammon and Manon*, 292. The attribution of Haitian leadership in the rebellion of 1811 might have been more a product of white expectation than a reality: the revolt erupted the day after newspapers in New Orleans published accounts of Henri Christophe's defeat of French troops at Port-au-Prince.

42. Lachance, "The Foreign French," in Hirsch and Logsdon, eds., *Creole New Orleans*, 121, 123–125.

discriminately at these receptacles, finding a market for their pilferings."
Taverns contributed doubly to disorder, emitting intoxicated, brawl-prone
customers onto the city's streets and creating desperate paupers of the unlucky who succumbed to the games of chance that enlivened even the most
basic drinking houses. "Here the raw cullies from the upper country come,
lose all, and either hang themselves, or get drunk, and perish in the streets,"
lamented one observer. Less sympathetic assessments of the effects of gam-
bling noted its contribution to the criminal impulse.[43]

The ranks of transients in the city swelled in the early decades of the
nineteenth century with "a constant influx of strangers, particularly from
the western country," who brought flour, grain, and preserved meats downriver on barges and flatboats. "In the wake of these honest farmers and
traders could always be seen a horde of bandits and gamblers," commented
a New Orleanian born in the 1820s and raised on stories of the boom times.
Honest traders woke in the night to find representatives of the bandit horde
attempting to make off with the commodities stowed on their flatboats.
The steady undercurrent of larceny spawned a miasma of insecurity that
was exacerbated by an outbreak of arson in the 1820s, culminating spectacularly in the destruction of the State House. Although the city councils
of the 1810s and 1820s stoically reorganized and upgraded the city's police
and fire departments, the portrait that emerges reveals the persistence of
disorder and petty crime throughout the period. The city fathers held authority but were unable to impose the order they sought.[44]

Epidemic disease further eroded civic confidence. Set in semitropical
wetlands, the city was plagued with malaria from its earliest days in the
1710s. It was debilitating in the colony's early years, but its destructive
power paled in comparison to the outbreaks of yellow fever that began to
make regular appearances at the end of the eighteenth century. The first
epidemic ravaged the city in 1796, and the scourge reappeared in 1799 and
in 1804. For the next thirteen years, the city suffered only one major outbreak, in 1811, but in 1817 the disease returned and inaugurated a dreadful
succession of outbreaks. Two thousand succumbed to yellow fever in 1819,

43. [Berquin-Duvallon], *Travels in Louisiana,* trans. Davis, 53–54; Henry C. Castellanos, *New Orleans as It Was: Episodes of Louisiana Life,* ed. George F. Reinecke (1895; rpt.
Baton Rouge, La., 1978), 16; Flint, *Recollections of the Last Ten Years,* ed. Brooks, 310.

44. Castellanos, *New Orleans as It Was,* ed. Reinecke, 16–20; [J. G. Flügel], "Pages
from a Journal of a Voyage down the Mississippi to New Orleans in 1817," ed. Felix
Flugel, *LHQ,* VII (1924), 428; "Conseil de Ville Proceedings," Dec. 14, 1811, 123.

and the epidemic of 1822 took as many as thirty lives per day, mounting to some fourteen hundred by the end of the season in November. "The hearse is seen passing the streets at all hours," remarked one observer of the epidemic of 1824, which dealt a crushing blow to the spirit of a city still suffering the effects of three epidemics in five years. Yet, "notwithstanding the annual, or at least the biennial visits of this pestilence; although its besom sweeps off multitudes of unacclimated poor, and compels the rich to fly; notwithstanding the terror, that is every where associated with the name of the city, it is rapidly advancing in population." Striking most fiercely at the impoverished immigrants who poured into New Orleans during these years, the epidemics overwhelmed the city's charitable institutions. Widowed women and orphaned children far from friends and family strained city resources, overwhelming a limited array of benevolent institutions that could not keep pace with the burgeoning demand.[45]

Throughout the eighteenth century, the Ursuline convent provided the only shelter for female orphans. There public subsidies for orphans had existed continuously since 1728, and at the end of the colonial period thirty orphans were publicly supported at the convent. Occasional benefactions enabled the nuns to enlarge their capacity slightly, but the women were resolute in controlling the numbers of orphans to avoid overwhelming their larger educational mission. At some point after the Louisiana Purchase, the city negotiated with the nuns a subsidy of sixty dollars per annum for each of twenty-four orphans.[46] The immigration and epidemics of the early 1800s swelled the ranks of children whose parents had either perished or had fallen into such utter destitution that they could no longer support their families. By the mid-1810s, an acute need existed for an enlarged institutional response. The remedy emerged, not from the roots of the French tradition long established in the city, but in the new form that was spreading throughout the young Republic, Protestant female benevolence.

Nearly 150 women subscribed eight dollars each in 1817 to launch the Female Charitable Society to support an orphan asylum. Led by Phoebe Hunter, a native Philadelphian and Quaker who had followed her government geologist husband to New Orleans, the group's "endeavor to create

45. John Duffy, ed., *The Rudolph Matas History of Medicine in Louisiana* (Baton Rouge, La., 1958), I, 206–207, 356–369; Flint, *Recollections of the Last Ten Years*, ed. Brooks, 302, 311.

46. AC, C13A, XI, 145, XVI, 88v–89; AGI, PC, 538B; "Mandat de Payement, Pension des orphelines," Feb. 28, 1814, UCANO.

an association to benefit the suffering poor" was inspired by a particular population. "The unhappy sufferers" whose plight spurred the women to action were, not the victims of yellow fever, but "generally fugitives from the islands of St. Domingo and Cuba." The refugees, observed the founders, came to Louisiana unprepared to make their way honestly in the world. The daughters of planters rendered destitute by the Haitian Revolution were "accustomed to no exertion but that of commanding" and were "incapable of either mental or corporeal activity." Uneducated in the ethos of industry and civic virtue, the founders lamented the fate of the young refugees, "yielding to the temptations of vice to procure a momentary suspension of their wretchedness."[47]

The founders were convinced that these unfortunate young women were beyond redemption and "determined that they should serve the cause of humanity more effectually, if they could be enabled by care and instruction to prevent future misery." The women resolved to "form a plan for the maintenance and education of unprotected children of their own sex; to instil into the young and unformed minds of those children principles of religion and morality." And, to ensure that none would be tempted to earn a living by unsavory means, they stipulated that the inmates of their institution be given "an early habit of industry, . . . to qualify them to support themselves hereafter independently and respectably."[48]

In the end, wayward Haitians were little more than inspiration for the enterprise. When the Female Orphan Asylum opened its doors in February 1817, it admitted three widows with young children, a childless widow, and a child of nine years, none of them identified as having any connections to Haiti. In the later 1810s and 1820s, inmates were likely to be German and Anglo-American girls. Yet the perception of the founders that the Haitian influx posed a particular moral peril for the city holds a key to understanding the role the asylum came to play in the controversy of 1824 that stripped the Ursulines of their orphanage. The daughters of the Haitian planters had lost the wealth and property that secured their status as free white women in a plantation society. Bereft of the moral and financial protection their fathers provided in the lost plantation empire of Saint Domingue, these young women might be expected to fall easily into a life of sin. The loss of

47. "Board Minute Book, January 1817–January 1823," Poydras Home Records, 1–4, 59, HTML.
48. Ibid., 59.

their virtue would rob them of a defining feature of white womanhood, as it was ideally construed in antebellum America, rendering them racially ambiguous. That their moral and financial destitution was the result of a racial order turned upside down made these potential Magdalenes doubly disturbing. Phoebe Hunter and her fellow founders could not undo the Haitian Revolution, and no refugee plantation daughters seem to have presented themselves at the doorstep of their institution for moral restoration, but they could see to it that other white girls who found themselves destitute in the raucous boomtown kept the virtue that defined white womanhood and anchored the social order of the early Republic.[49]

The Female Charitable Society's focus on the Haitian refugees was rooted not only in the very real shock felt by a city still struggling to absorb a huge influx of refugees but also in the difficulties inherent in southeast Louisiana's rapid evolution into a plantation society. With hardly a backward glance, elite white New Orleanians embraced the rigid racial hierarchy and patriarchal gender order that undergirded the established plantation societies of Anglo-America.[50] Yet stubborn remnants of a different social order persisted. At the time of the Purchase, the city was home to a large population of financially secure free people of color. Their presence made the tidy conflation of freedom, economic independence, and whiteness impossible, especially in a city with a mounting population of poor whites.[51] The Philadelphia women met these realities already armed with a

49. Ibid., 84, 97, 101; Victoria E. Bynum, *Unruly Women: The Politics of Social and Sexual Control in the Old South* (Chapel Hill, N.C., 1992), 7, 10, 35–58, 88–110; Catherine Clinton, *The Plantation Mistress: Woman's World in the Old South* (New York, 1982), 204; and Jean Fagan Yellin, *Women and Sisters: The Antislavery Feminists in American Culture* (New Haven, Conn., 1989), 25, 94–96. The Philadelphia women's preoccupation with the sexual morality of Haitian refugees would have been in keeping with what Clare Lyons sees as elite early national women's participation in upholding by example and prescribing through benevolent intervention new standards of sexuality designed to advance upper- and middle-class interests. See Lyons, *Sex among the Rabble*, 322–348.

50. Of particular note are legislative acts that attempted to control and ultimately obliterate Louisiana's sizable class of free blacks, beginning with An Act to Prevent the Emigration of Free Negroes and Mulattoes into the Territory of Orleans, Apr. 14, 1807, and An Act to Prescribe Certain Formalities respecting Free Persons of Color, Mar. 31, 1808, in L. Moreau Lislet, *A General Digest of the Acts of the Legislature of Louisiana: Passed from the Year 1804 to 1827 Inclusive . . .* (New Orleans, 1828), I, 498–499, 499–500.

51. In 1805, 1,566 free blacks composed nearly one-fifth of the city's population;

commitment to uphold by example and promote through benevolent intervention new standards of sexuality designed to advance upper- and middle-class interests. In New Orleans, those interests called for carefully guarding the intertwined social, racial, and gender hierarchies that upheld a slave society.

The Haitian refugees represented a spectacularly obvious threat to the social order members of the Female Charitable Society were bound as republican wives to uphold. So did a convent full of unmarried women who not only managed their own affairs but also publicly opposed the wishes and injured the pride of city fathers. The Female Charitable Society provided a particularly comforting counterbalance to these disturbances to republican order. With the exception of Phoebe Hunter's daughter, Mary Ann, all nine officers of the society were married women, acting safely from within the bounds of the family. Early in its development, the society accepted a large gift from a wealthy planter and named the orphanage the Poydras Orphan Asylum, thereby acknowledging its indebtedness to male patronage. The officers were solicitous of the city council and gave the mayor the right to place young women in the asylum. And perhaps most crucial, the women pledged that the children in their care would be "instructed in reading, writing, spelling, and arithmetic, and principles of morality and religion." In addition, they would be "treated with kindness and taught such work as is best calculated for their future advantage." The inmates would, in short, be educated to take their places as virtuous, industrious women under the patronage of those who embodied this ideal. The young women raised in the asylum would be imbued with the defining qualities of white womanhood so that as adults they could help secure the settled racial order to which many white New Orleanians aspired.[52]

The Female Charitable Society did much to move the city toward compliance with the ideals of white plantation society, and, although the founders and officers were Anglo-American women, the society's subscribers were drawn from the ranks of prominent Catholics and Protestants alike.

----

many were propertyowners, and some were slaveholders. See Kimberly S. Hanger, *Bounded Lives, Bounded Places: Free Black Society in Colonial New Orleans, 1769-1803* (Durham, N.C., 1997), 22, 55-87; Lyons, *Sex among the Rabble,* 322, 348, 354-355, 393-395.

52. Notice published in the *Louisiana Gazette* [1817], quoted in Lillian Fortier Zeringer, *The History of Poydras Home* (n.p., [1977]), 12.

Their project was not a weapon in a war between Anglophones and Franco-phones for cultural dominance, nor was it a simplistic strategy to advance the "Americanization" of the city. It grew from the project of elite Anglo-American republican wives in cities like Philadelphia to create a virtuous, properly ordered society, but its foundation was also attuned to the city's struggle to redefine itself in the mold of a slave society.[53]

Of the two female educational enterprises in the city, one advanced these causes; the other ignored them, and on occasion subverted them. The autumn of 1824 brought a reckoning. For two decades, the Ursulines had perpetrated various infractions against the pride and authority of the city fathers. Now, in the shadow of the summer's crushing yellow fever epidemic, the patience of these men had run out. At the October 9 meeting of the city council, councilman Nicolas Girod announced that "he had been informed that the orphan girls, whose board the Corporation pays to the religious, were not treated properly." Girod went on to ask "that the Council take measures to remove them, and to place them in the Charity Hospice founded by Mr. Poydras."[54]

A fact-finding committee was quickly appointed, and its charge hinted at the festering resentment against the nuns harbored by the councilmen. The committee was to "find out first how the religious treated the orphan girls confided to their care." The care given the girls was not, however, the matter of greatest interest to the councilmen. The committee was also charged to ascertain "whether the said religious had, in leaving the City, provided for the establishment of a school in town for the externes," a pointed indication that the council was piqued at the nuns' abandonment of their urban location for a convent site beyond the reach of their direct command. Finally, the committee was directed to ask the nuns "why up to the present they never notified the Mayor of the choice which they made of the children destined to replace the vacancies that could take place among those placed by the Corporation in their convent." Unlike the officers of the Poydras Orphan Asylum, the nuns did not consult city authorities on admissions to the convent orphanage. The visiting committee wasted no time and

53. "Board Minute Book, January 1817–January 1823," Poydras Home Records, 2–4, HTML; Stephanie McCurry, *Masters of Small Worlds: Yeoman Households, Gender Relations, and the Political Culture of the Antebellum South Carolina Low Country* (New York, 1995), esp. 208–238.

54. "Conseil de Ville Proceedings," Oct. 9, 1824, 357.

returned to the council with a report on October 12. There seems to have been a hasty recognition that the Poydras Asylum should be examined before any decision was made, so the report was deferred until the committee could complete a visit to its premises. On October 16, the committee made its report on both institutions to the council.[55]

At the Ursuline convent, the committee met the fourteen orphans then in residence. The opening sentences of their report noted that more than half were barefooted and quickly revealed the nature of the concerns that drove their intervention. "The Committee remarked that in the present season shoes were as necessary to health as was required by decency in a country where the want of shoes and stockings is in some respect one of the signs of slavery." Undaunted, the mother superior remarked that the girls had shoes and stockings but did not wish to wear them. When asked to do so, the girls ran to fetch them and donned the footwear in the presence of the committee. The committee changed tack. "What measures," they asked the mother superior, "had she taken to continue at their own expense, the school where they taught at the old convent, reading and writing to externes." The nun answered that, as they had donated the use of their property in the city to the bishop for his use, they thought themselves "dispensed from continuing this establishment, but that they would receive with pleasure in their new convent the young girls who presented themselves to learn to read and to write."[56]

The committee decided to gather information from former inmates of the Ursuline orphanage to supplement the findings from their visit. Here they found the damning evidence that had generally eluded them at the convent. "From the testimony of several individuals separately interviewed it follows that the nourishment of these children is composed, for breakfast, of corn, boiled with salt, for dinner, bread and brisket without soup, and, for supper, bread, sometimes with butter." In addition to having to subsist on such a mean diet, the girls "serve the meals of the boarders, in a word that they do at the convent almost all the work of servants." At the convent, the committee asserted, "there exists between the orphans and the boarders a difference in dress, nourishment, education and occupation, necessary without a doubt, but which must certainly degrade these young unfortunate girls."[57]

55. Ibid., Oct. 9, 12, 16, 1824, 357–358, 359, 360–362.
56. Ibid., Oct. 16, 1824, 360–361.
57. Ibid., 361.

The committee's equation of slave status and bare feet is their most explicit reference to the crucial matter of hierarchy at the convent. Though left largely unsaid, the committee must have believed that the "difference in dress, nourishment, education and occupation" that existed between boarders and orphans was greater than that which existed between orphans and the convent's enslaved servants. The Ursulines' failure to attend sufficiently to proper differentiation between white and black, master class and slave, was insupportable in early antebellum New Orleans. Their antiquated, class-based hierarchy had in the 1790s allowed free girls of color with means to attend as boarders while poor white girls were consigned to the extern class. The nuns' transgression of a hardening racial order was less egregious now, but it was still more than the city councilmen would tolerate.

The city fathers' report on the girls at the Poydras Asylum underlines their concern with establishing racial hierarchy, even if it meant ignoring the existence of class distinctions between whites. "In this institution, one sees equality reign which is the foremost of all benefits, and that of all which childhood appreciates the most." At the Poydras institution, there was nothing to parallel the performance of social rank that took place at the Ursuline convent, where the daily routine of housekeeping and meal service inscribed an indelible boundary between server and served of the same race. Rather, for the inmates of the Poydras Asylum there was "no domestic care, no household work from which they are exempt, but this work is alternately the task of all and each of them serves, and is in her turn served by her companions." Class hierarchies were a social luxury in slave societies, where racial solidarity became politically essential in the second quarter of the nineteenth century. The nuns' failure to adjust their practices to advance that imperative gave the city council the ammunition they needed to discipline the women for their long string of infractions against masculine social and political objectives. The city council voted unanimously to remove the orphans and place them at the Poydras Asylum. There, finally, the orphans were brought within the sacred circle of a community properly ordered and governed by the fathers and masters of New Orleans.[58]

The city fathers' victory over the nuns and the threat they posed to republican racial and gender norms was Pyrrhic and temporary. The officers of the Poydras Orphan Asylum were wives of living husbands. Since pro-

58. Ibid., 360–362.

priety forbade their personal operation of the institution, they employed widowed and unmarried superintendents and governesses to attend to this task. Qualified candidates were difficult to find and harder to keep. The first two years of the asylum's operation saw three governesses come and go, and the tenures of their successors were only slightly longer. In the late 1820s, the officers experimented with having a married couple manage the operations of the asylum, but, "having tested the experiment of having a gentleman at the head of the Poydras Asylum by a trial of four months," they became "convinced of the propriety and necessity of returning to their original plan by placing the proper authority in the hands of a respectable female." At a special meeting held in the autumn of 1829, the board of the asylum, which remained exclusively female, voted to extend an offer of employment to "two ladies highly recommended to them." These ladies were, as it happened, "members of the benevolent community, known by the name of the Sisters of Charity." For the next seven years, nuns belonging to the Catholic order founded by Elizabeth Seton in Emmitsburg, Maryland, operated the Poydras Orphan Asylum.[59]

The Ursulines, meanwhile, flourished at their new convent and suffered no financial hardship with the loss of the city-sponsored orphans. In 1839, they began to take in orphans again, this time at their own expense. With what was doubtless unintended irony, they decided to admit twenty-five girls—one more than had been supported by the city.[60] The nuns accommodated themselves somewhat to the changed racial culture of New Orleans. When they moved to their new convent, they appear to have abandoned the education of free girls of color.

The Ursulines' apparent capitulation to racial segregation belies one of their lasting legacies. The free women of color who founded the Sisters of the Holy Family in the 1830s melded the Ursuline tradition that had shaped the religiosity of their foremothers with the new traditions of female religious activism that emerged in postrevolutionary France to wage their own assault on the confining race and gender hierarchies of the antebellum era. The chaste black nuns who served and owned enslaved African Americans

59. "Board Minute Book, January 1817–January 1823," Poydras Home Records, 27–28, 72, 87, HTML; "The Proceedings of the Female Orphan Society of New Orleans, Vol. 2nd. from January 16, 1823 to May 3, 1832," Sept. 2, 1824, May 8, Sept. 5, Oct. 1, 1829, Poydras Home Records, HTML.

60. "Délibérations du Conseil," July 12, 1839, UCANO.

and founded an orphanage of their own continued to frustrate the perfection of society envisioned by white men. Unmarried, black, female slaveholders could be reconciled even less easily than white Ursulines with the ideal of white domesticity that swept America, north and south, in the decades before the Civil War.[61]

61. Emily Clark and Virginia Meacham Gould, "The Feminine Face of Afro-Catholicism in New Orleans, 1727–1852," *WMQ*, 3d Ser., LIX (2002), 440–448.

epilogue

A WOMAN OF MASCULINE APPEARANCE AND

CHARACTER ANTEBELLUM ANTI-CATHOLICISM

Charlestown, Massachusetts, on an August night in 1834 was the setting for one of the most spectacular acts of mass violence against a group of women in American history. Before an audience of as many as two thousand spectators, a mob of sixty men attacked and burned down the town's Ursuline convent and school. The episode traditionally serves as the opening scene in the historical narrative of antebellum anti-Catholicism, setting the stage for a class-based, economic explanation for the eruption of the Nativist and Know-Nothing movements that jostled with abolitionism to raise the temperature of America's political culture in the decades before the Civil War. A report emerging from the trial of the rioters suggests, however, that class was not the only inflammatory agent at work that night: "Of the Lady Superior, to whose stern and unyielding course during the excitement and difficulties which preceded the riot, the disaster has been often attributed, there have been strange and contradictory rumors, both before and since the time of the trials. She was a woman of masculine appearance and character, high-tempered, resolute, defiant, with stubborn, imperious will."[1]

When one of the rioters shouted to a student standing at a convent window that trouble was about to break out and he would be happy to protect her, the mother superior "appeared at another window and told them she did not require to be protected." It was an offense against American man-

---

1. Daniel A. Cohen, "The Respectability of Rebecca Reed: Genteel Womanhood and Sectarian Conflict in Antebellum America," *Journal of the Early Republic*, XVI (1996), 419–461; ["The Charlestown Convent; Its Destruction by a Mob . . . Also the Trials of the Rioters, the Testimony, and the Speeches of the Counsel . . . Compiled from Authentic Sources"], *Trial Documents of the Convent Riot* (Boston, 1870), 80, quoted in Jenny Franchot, *Roads to Rome: The Antebellum Protestant Encounter with Catholicism* (Berkeley, Calif., 1994), 144–145 (quotation on 144).

hood that a community of female nuns and students lived in an institutional household presided over by this mannish woman who usurped the husband and father's rightful role as protector. The defense counsel for the rioters decried the "language of the Lady Superior to the rioters," asserting "that had she addressed them in different terms, it was his firm belief that the Convent would be now standing."[2]

The Ursulines of Charlestown were attacked in part because they did not look and act like women. Their fate on this occasion, though more extreme, resonates with that of the New Orleans Ursulines of 1824. In both instances, the nuns suffered at least partly because they appropriated markers of masculinity: financial independence and assertions of will. They failed to be feminine. More was at work here, however, than affronted masculinity. In nineteenth-century America, nuns challenged the republican gender settlement sealed by Protestant women with the covenant of marriage. The terms of that covenant were most immediately indebted to post-Revolutionary political and social objectives, but they were also deeply indebted to a Protestant construction of religious femininity forged in the Reformation.

When the Protestant Reformation suppressed convents and lay confraternities, it narrowed the acceptable range of action for devout women. Protestant women were left with virtually no opportunities to act outside the realms of family and church over which men presided. The ideal Protestant woman was a wife who obeyed her husband and acceded to his decisions in all earthly matters. In religion she was a congregant, who enjoyed spiritual equality with men but not the privilege of leadership in the institutional life of the church. The spirituality of the New England Puritans valorized feminine qualities of submission and endowed women with a particular kind of status. Yet this recognition of women as models for Christian obedience to God only reinforced unequal earthly power relations.[3]

Reformation theology and doctrine also created symbolic constrictions for Protestant women. The doctrine of transubstantiation was rejected, and the Eucharist could no longer serve as an occasion for the mystical union

2. ["The Charlestown Convent"], *Trial Documents*, 14, 21, 80, quoted in Franchot, *Roads to Rome*, 144–145 (quotation on 145).

3. Amanda Porterfield, *Female Piety in Puritan New England: The Emergence of Religious Humanism* (New York, 1992); Natalie Zemon Davis, "City Women and Religious Change," in Davis, *Society and Culture in Early Modern France: Eight Essays* (Stanford, Calif., 1975), 65–95, remains the classic survey of the Reformation-era gains and losses for Catholic and Protestant women.

of women's bodies with the body of Christ. Women could no longer enact with their own bodies the central mystery of the faith. Protestantism did not supply women with a liturgy that compensated for this loss. Communion ceded its centrality in the worship service to the sermon, an exercise in which women could only participate as passive auditors. The Reformation condemned saintly intercession and suppressed organized Marian devotion. In its place, Martin Luther and successive generations of Protestant divines employed Mary in their sermons to preach the primacy of marriage and motherhood for women. Mary became an example of obedient domesticity to Protestant wives rather than the inspiration for self-directed, apostolic religiosity she was for Catholic nuns.[4]

With a few notable exceptions, the religious activities of pre-Revolutionary American Protestant women were contained within and mediated by institutions headed by men. Some unique personalities, such as Anne Hutchinson and Sarah Osborne, contested those limits, and the Great Awakening afforded evangelical women opportunities to minister and witness in ways usually reserved for men. But these were exceptions to a mainstream in which the boundaries between the private realm of the household and the authority of the sanctuary were enforced. With the exception of the Revolutionary era, when women took advantage of the momentary fluidity in gender roles that is often a product of war, the ideological trend in early America was toward a hardening of the public, visible border between male and female roles in both the religious and civil realms.[5] Protestant American women negotiated the passage to republicanism with a religious identity that supported the importance of marriage and prepared them to find ways to assert economic, social, and political influence from within its boundaries. Post-Revolutionary American elite women enjoyed the benefits that accompanied the rise of companionate marriage, which enjoined symmetry between spouses in terms of educational background

4. Beth Kreitzer, *Reforming Mary: Changing Images of the Virgin Mary in Lutheran Sermons of the Sixteenth Century* (Oxford, 2004), 54, 130, 136.

5. Charles E. Hambrick-Stowe, "The Spritual Pilgrimage of Sarah Osborn (1714–1796)," in Jon Butler and Harry S. Stout, eds., *Religion in American History: A Reader* (New York, 1998), 130–141; Susan Juster, *Disorderly Women: Sexual Politics and Evangelicalism in Revolutionary New England* (Ithaca, N.Y., 1994), 41–43, 108–179; Catherine A. Brekus, *Strangers and Pilgrims: Female Preaching in America, 1740–1845* (Chapel Hill, N.C., 1998), 23–113; Nancy F. Cott, *The Bonds of Womanhood: "Woman's Sphere" in New England, 1780–1835* (New Haven, Conn., 1977); Juster, *Doomsayers: Anglo-American Prophecy in the Age of Revolution* (Philadelphia, 2003), 216–259.

and intellectual and political engagement. But symmetry within the marriage did not translate into equality and individual political and economic agency outside it. Protestant American women were expected to be married and to advance the social and political interests of the middle-class household from their situation within it.

By contrast, Catholic women in postrevolutionary France crafted a different settlement of the terms under which women joined the republican project, one predicated on a construction of religious femininity shaped in the Reformation era. Their accommodation with republicanism was more precarious than the Protestants'. Cultural tradition and social practicalities preserved female religious life and the opportunity it afforded women to act under their own institutional authority. Orders of teaching nuns who had rationalized female education on religious grounds in the seventeenth century were poised to revive their apostolate under a new civic imperative. The virtue of the French republic was to be sustained not only by the wife who exercised critical moral influence over her spouse but also by unmarried nuns.

With the emergence of nation-states in early modern Europe, confessional diversity within states' boundaries proved intolerable, and the divergent femininities of Catholics and Protestants developed in peaceful isolation from one another. In America it was to be different. Maryland's colonial Catholicism provided a quiet counterpoint to American Protestantism, but it lacked the presence of the female apostolic orders that embodied and advanced early modern Catholic religious femininity. The Louisiana Purchase and the influx of Catholic immigrants later in the nineteenth century forced an encounter between Protestant and Catholic womanhood. When the United States acquired Louisiana, the young nation had but two convents of nuns, both located near the nation's capital, close to the Maryland Catholic stronghold. The annexation of the Ursulines of New Orleans marked the beginning of a period of rapid numerical and geographical expansion. Ten other orders of religious women established communities in the United States in the three decades following the Purchase, and they strayed far from the colonial hub of Anglo-American Catholicism. Six of these orders, including the Ursulines, had European origins, and five were indigenous, including the American Sisters of Charity founded by convert Elizabeth Seton in 1809. These new American foundations took up the kind of apostolic work identified with the French tradition exemplified by the Ursulines. Seton's advisers, who were mostly French, suggested that she model her new order on the Filles de la Charité founded by Vincent de Paul in seventeenth-century France. Philippine Duchesne, a Frenchwoman, founded the American branch of the Religious of the Sacred Heart as a teaching order in 1818. By 1845, Catholic religious women had fanned out across America's cities and countryside. They were in major cities, north and south, including New York, Boston, Pittsburgh, Baltimore, Charleston, Savannah, and, of course, New Orleans. More remote places also saw the arrival of communities of vowed women. The Sisters of Loretto served Kentucky when it was still an underpopulated frontier early in the nineteenth century, and the Ursulines founded a convent in Galveston, Texas, in 1845.[6]

The Catholic female religious communities that dotted the antebellum American landscape threatened Protestant political culture most obviously on the matter of gender. They challenged the ideal of domesticity on which it rested by providing women with an alternative to marriage. They also offered a model of female benevolence with institutions that were not only governed by women but operated by women who were themselves self-governing and self-supporting. The nature of these religious women's educational and missionary efforts also posed an invidious threat to male authority at the intersection of race and gender. Even in the slave South — particularly in the slave South — nuns ministered directly to women of color and drew them into the organized life of the church. The Visitation nuns at Georgetown admitted free girls of color to their school, as did the Sisters of Loretto in Kentucky. The founder of the Lorettos, a Belgian missionary priest named Charles Nerinckx, created a special branch of the order for three young black women who took the veil in 1824. Sisters of Our Lady of Mercy in Charleston, South Carolina, operated a school for free women of color intermittently between 1835 and 1848, and the Pittsburgh Sisters of Mercy admitted blacks to their hospital, publicly opposed slavery, and ransomed enslaved individuals. The New Orleans Ursulines supplied teaching

6. Mary Ewens, *The Role of the Nun in Nineteenth Century America* (Salem, N.H., 1984), 32, 45, 58, 61, 64. See also Ewens, "Women in the Convent," in Karen Kennelly, ed., *American Catholic Women: A Historical Exploration* (New York, 1989), 17–47; Barbara Misner, *Highly Respectable and Accomplished Ladies: Catholic Women Religious in America, 1790–1850* (New York, 1988), 203–204; Kathleen Healy, ed., *Sisters of Mercy: Spirituality in America, 1843–1900* (New York, 1992), 15, 130. A community of Dominicans also went to Kentucky in 1822, and missionary groups of Seton's Sisters of Charity went to Kentucky in 1824, Cincinnati in 1829, and Tennessee in 1842. See Mary Electa Boyle, *Mother Seton's Sisters of Charity in Western Pennsylvania* (Greensburg, Pa., 1946), ix; and Misner, *Highly Respectable and Accomplished Ladies*, 39, 40, 41.

nuns and financial support to a school for free girls of color until a community of Sisters of Our Lady of Mount Carmel took charge of it in 1838. The Oblates of Providence in Baltimore and the Sisters of the Holy Family in New Orleans, founded in 1827 and 1836 respectively, were congregations of religious women of African descent likewise dedicated to educating and serving people of color. When nuns intervened to provide people of color, particularly the enslaved, with education, shelter, and sustenance, they usurped the role of the white patriarch and dangerously disturbed the racial order of antebellum America.[7]

The differences between Protestant and Catholic gender prescriptions became plain in the years that followed the Louisiana Purchase and hampered the project of forging a common American identity that could embrace both Protestants and Catholics. The difficulties the Louisiana nuns encountered in the first decades of the nineteenth century present a fully developed episode of opposition to a Catholic institution well before the more familiar outbursts of the antebellum period that have been linked to immigration, class tension, and economic distress. The Ursulines' particular history suggests that the divergent modes of feminine piety born in the Reformation watered the springs of American anti-Catholicism before other forces amplified it and transformed it into Nativism.

The model of Catholic religious femininity exposed Protestant men's unease with women's operating outside male control and their normative expectations of womanly duty within the home. With the establishment of the Episcopal Church Home in 1850 to provide shelter and work for abandoned women and education and practical training for female orphans, the patriarchs of Charleston, South Carolina, attested to the dialectic between Protestant and Catholic femininities. They conceded that the institution

7. Misner, *Highly Respectable and Accomplished Ladies,* 203–204; Cyprian Davis, *The History of Black Catholics in the United States* (New York, 1990), 98; Healy, *Sisters of Mercy,* 29, 318; Stephanie McCurry, *Masters of Small Worlds: Yeoman Households, Gender Relations, and the Political Culture of the Antebellum South Carolina Low Country* (New York, 1995), 208–238; Contract between the Ursuline Community of New Orleans and the Community of the Order of Our Lady of Mount Carmel of New Orleans, Nov. 25, 1840, UCANO. On the Oblate Sisters of Providence, founded in 1827, see Diane Batts Morrow, *Persons of Color and Religious at the Same Time: The Oblate Sisters of Providence, 1828–1860* (Chapel Hill, N.C., 2002). The Sisters of the Holy Family originated as a confraternity in 1836 and received recognition as a religious order in 1852. See Mary Bernard Deggs, *No Cross, No Crown: Black Nuns in Nineteenth-Century New Orleans,* ed. Virginia Meacham Gould and Charles E. Nolan (Bloomington, Ind., 2001).

would need to be operated by single women "sufficiently disengaged from the more urgent claims of natural and social duty" to serve the needy. They also revealed Protestant America's fear of allowing God to replace man as a woman's earthly master when they noted that their female employees would undertake their pious work "without the dangerous entanglement of vows or irrevocable engagement."[8]

Nuns were permanently masterless mistresses, women who would never pass from a period of brief independence as benevolent spinsters into the safe harbor of marriage. They were not welcome in Charleston, but their presence there and elsewhere revealed the potential of women not bound by duty to husband or loyalty to family to abandon the cause of exclusion that marred the polity in antebellum America. America's acquisition of Louisiana in 1803 doubled its territorial expanse even as it led to the restriction of the republican polity's social boundaries. The port of New Orleans and the thriving plantation economy in the Lower Mississippi Valley helped assure the survival of slavery in the post-Purchase nation, and the opening of the West accelerated the exclusion of Indians from the liberties and rights granted to full members of the Republic. People of African descent and Indians fought back, insisting in word and deed on recognition in a nation that rendered them politically voiceless and invisible. Women joined the struggle for equality and inclusion, increasingly dissatisfied with the circuitous route they were obliged to take to exert their intellectual, political, and social wills. Antebellum Protestant women made use of benevolence, education, and reform to chip away at the gender conventions that bound them, but the marital state their confession prescribed and the economic dependence that accompanied it reduced the threat of a significant recalibration of power relations between men and women. The self-supporting antebellum nuns who refused marriage and motherhood to take up the causes of their own choosing in imposing urban compounds and frontier missions were another matter. They openly flaunted the choreography of gender meant to preserve the power and authority of white men. That was a mortal sin in antebellum America, and the nuns' coreligionists endured a penance for it in the magnification of anti-Catholicism it produced.

8. Barbara L. Bellows, *Benevolence among Slaveholders: Assisting the Poor in Charleston, 1670–1860* (Baton Rouge, La., 1993), 168.

APPENDIX 1

CONVENT POPULATION, 1727–1803

TABLE A1. *Roll of Nuns at the New Orleans Ursuline Convent*

Name	Age at Entry	Place of Origin	Year of Entry	Year of Departure or Death
Sr. St. Augustin/ Marie Tranchepain	47	Rouen	1727	1733
+Sr. Ste. Angelique/ Marie-Anne Boulanger	41	Rouen	1727	1766
+Sr. Ste. Marie/ Renée Yviguel	32	Vannes	1727	1763
+Sr. St. Joseph/ St. Marie des Anges/ Cécile Cavalier	30	Elboeuf	1727	1742
+Sr. Ste. Thérèse/ Marguerite de Salaon	28	Ploermel	1727	1733
+Sr. St. Stanislaus/ Marie Madeliene Hachard	23	Rouen	1727	1760
+Sr. Ste. Michel/ Jeanne Marion	?	Ploermel	1727	1727
+Sr. Ste. François Xavier/Madeleine Mahieu	?	Le Havre	1727	1728
+Sr. St. Jean L'Evangeliste/ Marguerite Judde	?	Rouen	1727	1731
+Sr. Anne de St. François, converse	?	?	1727	1728
+Sr. Moelle/ Claude Massy	?	?	1727	1729

+ = Founding member   * = French creole member   § = Cuban member

Name	Age at Entry	Place of Origin	Year of Entry	Year of Departure or Death
+Sr. Ste. Marthe/ Marie-Anne Dain, converse	?	?	1727	1727
Sr. St. Piere/ Marguerite Bernard de St. Martin	57	Caen	1732	1763
Sr. St. André/ Jeanne Melotte	40	Caen	1732	1747
Sr. St. François Xavier/ Charlotte Hebert	34	Bayeux	1732	1762
Sr. St. François de Paule/Marie Threse de Ramarchard	34	Dieppe	1734	1754
Sr. St. Bernard/ Marguerite Antoinette de Ramachard	32	Dieppe	1734	1782
Sr. Ste. Radegonde/ Jeanne de St. Marc	37	St. Paul de Leon	1736	1764
Sr. St. Louis de Gonzague/ Catherine Paule Eulalie Louchard	41	Lisieux	1742	1779
Sr. Ste. Madeleine de Jesus/ Marguerite de Belaire	41	Landerneau	1742	1792
Sr. Ste. Thérèse de Jesus/Jerome Perinne Elizabeth de Belaire	18	Landerneau	1742	1752
Sr. Ste. Marthe/ Marie Turpin, converse	20	Illinois	1749	1761
Sr. St. Jacques/ Marie Thérèse Landelle	35	Nevers	1751	1788

Name	Age at Entry	Place of Origin	Year of Entry	Year of Departure or Death
Sr. St. François Regis/ Marie Madeleine Le Verme	29	Rochelle	1751	1779
Sr. St. Joseph	?	?	1751	1752
*Sr. St. Augustin/ Marie Anne Rilleux	?	New Orleans	1752	1754
Sr. St. Etienne/ Marie des Champs, converse	27	Bayeux	1753	1799
Sr. Ste. Marie des Anges/Françoise Duplesses de Quemenor	34	Morlais	1754	1780
Sr. Ste. Reine	?	Morlais	1754	1772
*Sr. Ste. Ursule/ Jeanne Louise Louchard de Monthion	?	New Orleans?	1754	1756
Sr. Ste. Thérèse de Jesus/ Marie Beaumont	51	Ancenis	1755	1764
Sr. St. Gabriel/ Jeanne de Comoray	33	Ancenis	1755	1768
Sr. Ste. Anne	?	?	1755	1768
Sr. St. Ignace/ Marguerite Perrine DuLiepure	?	LaRochelle	1755	1803
*Sr. St. Antoine/ Marthe Delatre, converse	18	New Orleans	1757	
*Sr. Ste. Monique/ Rose Leblanc, converse	31	New Orleans	1766	1773
*Sr. Ste. Thérèse/ Charlotte de Mouy	21	New Orleans	1766	

Name	Age at Entry	Place of Origin	Year of Entry	Year of Departure or Death
*Sr. Ste. Angele/ Antoinette Caue	20	New Orleans	1770	1782
*Sr. Marie Joseph/ Gertrude Braud (Breaux), converse	?	New Orleans	1770	
*Sr. St. Augustin/ Anne Caue	22	New Orleans	1773	1779
*Sr. Ste. Marie/ Françoise Victoire Olivier de Vezin	17	New Orleans	1774	
*Sr. Ste. Marthe/ Thérèse Lardas, converse	16	New Orleans	1774	1786
*Sr. Ste. Ursule/ Abelle DuFossat	?	New Orleans	1774	1776
*Sr. Ste. Claire/ Louise Françoise Reine	?	New Orleans	1776	1776
§Sr. Ste. Monica/ Antonia María Ramos	28	Havana	1779	1803
§Sr. Ste. Rita/ Antonia María del Santissimo Sacramento del Castillo	?	Havana	1779	1803
*Sr. Ste. Solange/ Adelaide Dusséaux de la Croix	18	New Orleans	1780	1803
*Sr. Ste. Asoye/ Françoise Dusséaux de la Crois	17	New Orleans	1780	1803
§Sr. Ste. Ursule/ María Mercedes Lopez	?	Havana	1780	1788

Name	Age at Entry	Place of Origin	Year of Entry	Year of Departure or Death
*Sr. Ste. Eulalie/ Rosalie Cierra, converse	?	New Orleans	1780	1795
§Sr. St. Augustin/ Perrine Collaze (veuve)	?	Havana	1781	1803
§Sr. St. Michel/ María Josef Mirabal	?	Havana	1781	1803
*Sr. Ste. Justine/ Mlle. Lara	?	New Orleans	1781	1782
§Sr. Ste. Claire/ María Ignacio de Yera	?	Havana	1783	1803
§Sr. St. Raphael/ María Mirabal	?	Havana	1783	1803
§Sr. St. Louis de Gonzague/ Elizabeth Barquez	?	Havana	1783	1803
*Sr. Ste. Angele/ Marguerite Félicité Calder	?	Scotland/ New Orleans	1783	1803
Sr. St. Xavier/ Thérèse Farjon	33	Pont St. Esprit	1786	
Sr. Ste. Félicité/ Françoise Alzas	35	Pont St. Esprit	1786	
Sr. St. André/ Christine Madier	30	Pont St. Esprit	1786	
§Sr. Ste. Ursule/ María Regle Lopez	?	Havana	1791	1803
*Sr. Sr. François de Sales/ Emilie Jourdan	?	New Orleans	1791	
*Sr. Ste. Scholastique/ Rosalie Broutin	26	New Orleans	1792	

Name	Age at Entry	Place of Origin	Year of Entry	Year of Departure or Death
*Sr. Ste. Marthe/ Genevieve Chemite, converse	?	New Orleans	1792	1803
*Sr. Ste. Rosalie/ Marie Bourque, converse	?	New Orleans	1794	1803
§Sr. Ste. Rosa/ María Jesus Sanchez	?	Havana	1794	1803
*Sr. St. Stanislas/ Angela Langeline, converse	?	New Orleans	1798	1803
*Sr. St. Charles/ Marguerite Carriere	27	New Orleans	1799	
Sr. Ste. Madeleine/ Marie Rilleux	?	New Orleans	1799	

Source: "Régistre [des Ursulines de la Nouvelle Orleans]," UCANO.

TABLE A2. *New Orleans Uruline Convent Demographics, 1727–1803*

Year	Average Age	Total French	Total Creole	Total Cuban	Grand Total
1727	33.5	12	0		12
1728	34.3	8	0		8
1729	35.3	7	0		7
1730	36.3	7	0		7
1731	37.3	6	0		6
1732	30.1	9	0		9
1733	40.5	7	0		7
1734	39.6	9	0		9
1735	40.6	9	0		9
1736	41.2	10	0		10
1737	42.2	10	0		10
1738	43.2	10	0		10
1739	44.2	10	0		10
1740	45.2	10	0		10
1741	46.2	10	0		10
1742	43.9	12	0		12
1743	44.9	12	0		12
1744	45.9	12	0		12
1745	46.9	12	0		12
1746	47.9	12	0		12
1747	48.3	11	0		11
1748	49.3	11	0		11
1749	47.8	11	1		12
1750	48.8	11	1		12
1751	43.7	14	1		15
1752	49.8	12	2		14
1753	49.1	13	2		15
1754	48.3	15	2		17
1755	48.0	18	2		20
1756	49.0	18	1		19
1757	48.1	18	2		20
1758	49.1	18	2		20
1759	50.1	18	2		20
1760	50.7	17	2		19
1761	48.5	17	1		18
1762	54.3	16	1		17
1763	51.5	14	1		15

Year	Average Age	Total French	Total Creole	Total Cuban	Grand Total
1764	50.5	12	1		13
1765	51.5	12	1		13
1766	45.1	11	3		14
1767	46.1	11	3		14
1768	47.3	9	3		12
1769	48.3	9	3		12
1770	46.6	9	5		14
1771	47.6	9	5		14
1772	48.6	8	5		13
1773	48.1	8	5		13
1774	44.1	8	8		16
1775	45.1	8	8		16
1776	46.1	8	7		15
1777	47.1	8	7		15
1778	48.1	8	7		15
1779	45.8	6	6	2	14
1780	40.8	5	9	3	17
1781	41.8	5	10	5	20
1782	40.2	4	8	5	17
1783	41.2	4	9	8	21
1784	42.2	4	9	8	21
1785	43.2	4	9	8	21
1786	42.7	7	8	8	23
1787	43.7	7	8	8	23
1788	41.3	6	8	7	21
1789	42.3	6	8	7	21
1790	43.3	6	8	7	21
1791	44.3	6	9	8	23
1792	39.4	5	11	8	24
1793	39.4	5	11	8	24
1794	40.4	5	12	9	26
1795	41.4	5	11	9	25
1796	42.4	5	11	9	25
1797	43.4	5	11	9	25
1798	44.4	5	12	9	26
1799	43.8	4	12	9	25
1800	43.2	4	14	9	27
1801	44.2	4	14	9	27

Year	Average Age	Total French	Total Creole	Total Cuban	Grand Total
1802	45.2	4	14	9	27
1803	47.2	3	8	0	11

Source: "Registre [des Ursulines de la Nouvelle Orleans"], UCANO.

APPENDIX 2

URSULINE SLAVE FAMILIES

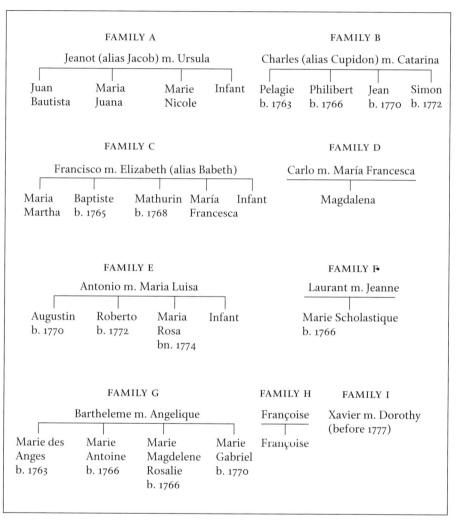

FAMILY A	FAMILY B
Jeanot (alias Jacob) m. Ursula	Charles (alias Cupidon) m. Catarina
Juan Bautista — Maria Juana — Marie Nicole — Infant	Pelagie b. 1763 — Philibert b. 1766 — Jean b. 1770 — Simon b. 1772

FAMILY C	FAMILY D
Francisco m. Elizabeth (alias Babeth)	Carlo m. María Francesca
Maria Martha — Baptiste b. 1765 — Mathurin b. 1768 — María Francesca — Infant	Magdalena

FAMILY E	FAMILY F
Antonio m. Maria Luisa	Laurant m. Jeanne
Augustin b. 1770 — Roberto b. 1772 — Maria Rosa bn. 1774 — Infant	Marie Scholastique b. 1766

FAMILY G	FAMILY H	FAMILY I
Bartheleme m. Angelique	Françoise	Xavier m. Dorothy (before 1777)
Marie des Anges b. 1763 — Marie Antoine b. 1766 — Marie Magdelene Rosalie b. 1766 — Marie Gabriel b. 1770	Françoise	

Note: Baptized is abbreviated as *b.*, and *born,* as *bn.* Most infants born to enslaved parents at the convent were baptized within a year of their birth.
Sources: SLC-B1, SLC-B2, SLC-B3, SLC-B4, SLC-B5, SLC-B6, SLC-B7, SLC-B8, SLC-B10, SLC-B12, SLC-B13, SLC-B15, SLC-F3, SLC-M1, SLC-M2, SLC-M3, SLC-M4, SLC-M5; Sacramental Registers of the Ursuline Convent Chapel, 1835–1853, UCANO; "Délibérations du Conseil," UCANO; "Book of Slaves," UCANO; Notarial Acts, NANO.

FAMILY J

Jacob C (alias Jacques alias Santiago) m. Louise Eulalie

Santiago b. before 1763	Cecelia b. before 1763	Alexis b. 1763	Marie b. 1767	Henri b. 1771	Marie Henriette b. 1774	Marie Regina b. 1779	Honoré b. 1784	Gabriel b. 1788 (free)
m. Luison (free)	m. Louis Leveillé (FAMILY K)	m. Marguerite (FAMILY L)			m. 1794 Louis Gonzague (FAMILY M)			

FAMILY K

Victoire m. Joseph Leveillé (emancipated 1777) m. 1780 Marie Therese Carrière (free)

Louis Leveillé	Noel Carrière (free)	Luis Carrière (free)	Josef Carrière (free)	Mariana Carrière (free)	Susana Carrière (free)
m. Cecelia (FAMILY J)					

FAMILY L

Teresa m. Mathurin

Charles b. 1768	Marguerite b. 1770	Jacinto b. 1775	Estevan b. 1777

m. Domingo

Theresa b. 1785

m. Estevan

Carlos b. 1788

FAMILY M

Charlot m. Marie Therese (emancipated 1777)

Agatha b. before 1763?	Pierre b. 1763	Luis b. 1765	Marie Enriette A b. 1771	Louis Gonzague b. 1772
m. 1785 Rafael (FAMILY N)				m. 1794 Marie Henriette (FAMILY J)

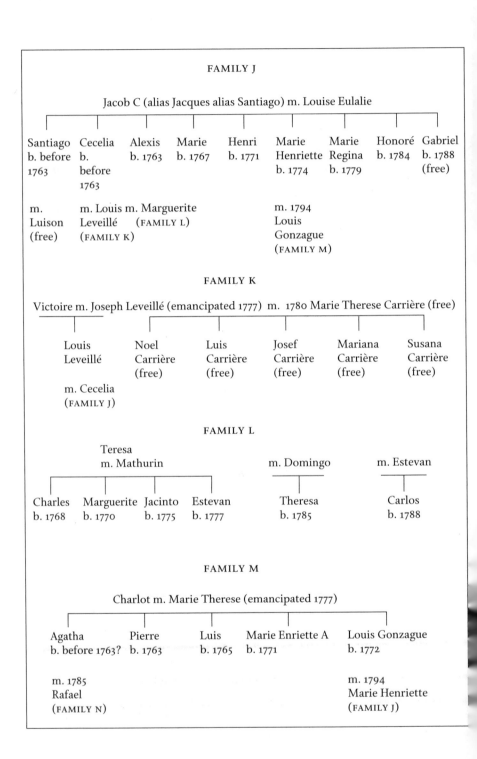

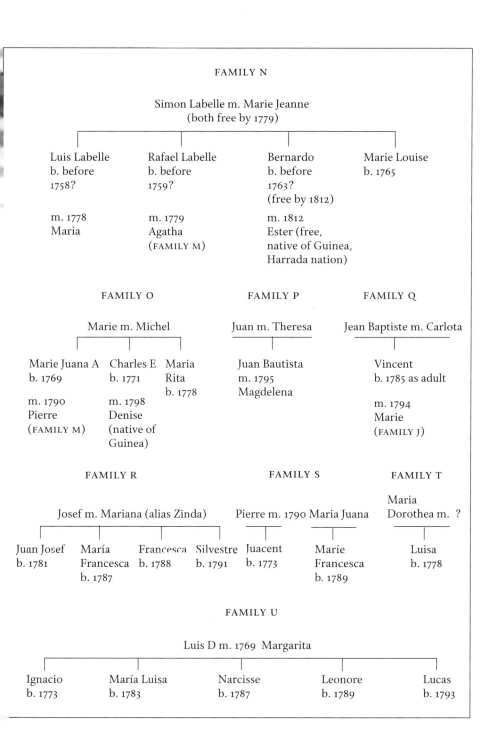

FAMILY N

Simon Labelle m. Marie Jeanne
(both free by 1779)

Luis Labelle	Rafael Labelle	Bernardo	Marie Louise
b. before 1758?	b. before 1759?	b. before 1763? (free by 1812)	b. 1765
m. 1778 Maria	m. 1779 Agatha (FAMILY M)	m. 1812 Ester (free, native of Guinea, Harrada nation)	

FAMILY O

Marie m. Michel

Marie Juana A	Charles E	Maria Rita
b. 1769	b. 1771	b. 1778
m. 1790 Pierre (FAMILY M)	m. 1798 Denise (native of Guinea)	

FAMILY P

Juan m. Theresa

Juan Bautista
m. 1795
Magdelena

FAMILY Q

Jean Baptiste m. Carlota

Vincent
b. 1785 as adult

m. 1794
Marie
(FAMILY J)

FAMILY R

Josef m. Mariana (alias Zinda)

Juan Josef	María Francesca	Francesca	Silvestre
b. 1781	b. 1787	b. 1788	b. 1791

FAMILY S

Pierre m. 1790 Maria Juana

Juacent	Marie Francesca
b. 1773	b. 1789

FAMILY T

Maria
Dorothea m. ?

Luisa
b. 1778

FAMILY U

Luis D m. 1769 Margarita

Ignacio	María Luisa	Narcisse	Leonore	Lucas
b. 1773	b. 1783	b. 1787	b. 1789	b. 1793

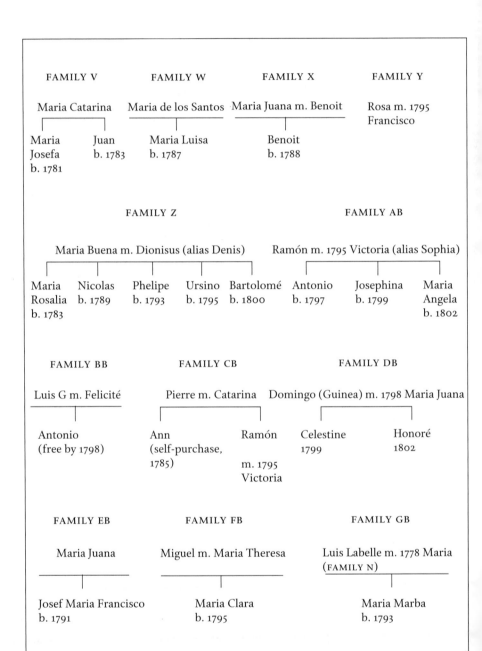

FAMILY V

Maria Catarina

Maria Josefa b. 1781   Juan b. 1783

FAMILY W

Maria de los Santos

Maria Luisa b. 1787

FAMILY X

Maria Juana m. Benoit

Benoit b. 1788

FAMILY Y

Rosa m. 1795 Francisco

FAMILY Z

Maria Buena m. Dionisus (alias Denis)

Maria Rosalia b. 1783   Nicolas b. 1789   Phelipe b. 1793   Ursino b. 1795   Bartolomé b. 1800

FAMILY AB

Ramón m. 1795 Victoria (alias Sophia)

Antonio b. 1797   Josephina b. 1799   Maria Angela b. 1802

FAMILY BB

Luis G m. Felicité

Antonio (free by 1798)

FAMILY CB

Pierre m. Catarina

Ann (self-purchase, 1785)   Ramón m. 1795 Victoria

FAMILY DB

Domingo (Guinea) m. 1798 Maria Juana

Celestine 1799   Honoré 1802

FAMILY EB

Maria Juana

Josef Maria Francisco b. 1791

FAMILY FB

Miguel m. Maria Theresa

Maria Clara b. 1795

FAMILY GB

Luis Labelle m. 1778 Maria (FAMILY N)

Maria Marba b. 1793

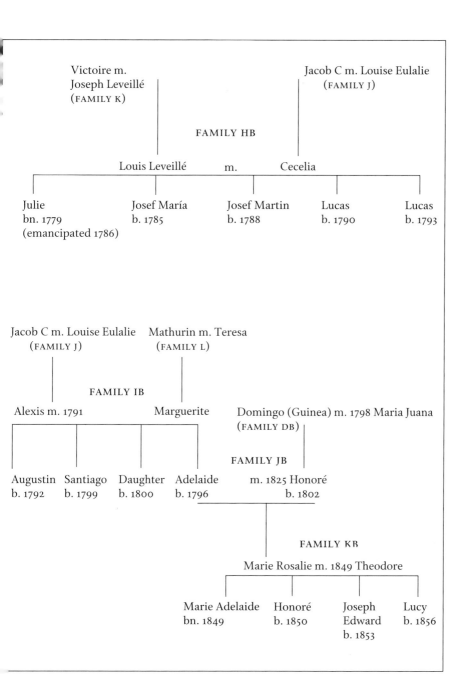

Victoire m.
Joseph Leveillé
(FAMILY K)

Jacob C m. Louise Eulalie
(FAMILY J)

FAMILY HB

Louis Leveillé   m.   Cecelia

Julie	Josef María	Josef Martin	Lucas	Lucas
bn. 1779	b. 1785	b. 1788	b. 1790	b. 1793
(emancipated 1786)				

Jacob C m. Louise Eulalie
(FAMILY J)

Mathurin m. Teresa
(FAMILY L)

FAMILY IB

Alexis m. 1791   Marguerite   Domingo (Guinea) m. 1798 Maria Juana
                                            (FAMILY DB)

FAMILY JB

Augustin	Santiago	Daughter	Adelaide	m. 1825 Honoré
b. 1792	b. 1799	b. 1800	b. 1796	b. 1802

FAMILY KB

Marie Rosalie m. 1849 Theodore

Marie Adelaide	Honoré	Joseph Edward	Lucy
bn. 1849	b. 1850	b. 1853	b. 1856

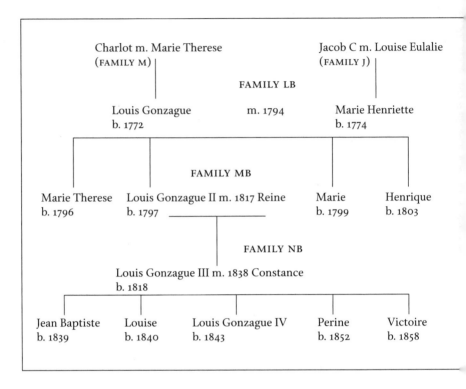

Charlot m. Marie Therese
(FAMILY M)

Jacob C m. Louise Eulalie
(FAMILY J)

FAMILY LB

Louis Gonzague   m. 1794   Marie Henriette
b. 1772   b. 1774

FAMILY MB

Marie Therese   Louis Gonzague II m. 1817 Reine   Marie   Henrique
b. 1796   b. 1797   b. 1799 b. 1803

FAMILY NB

Louis Gonzague III m. 1838 Constance
b. 1818

Jean Baptiste   Louise   Louis Gonzague IV   Perine   Victoire
b. 1839   b. 1840   b. 1843   b. 1852   b. 1858

INDEX

charistic piety, 105–106; practices of, 108–109; descendants of, at Ursuline school, 142–144

Choir nuns, 68–70

Christian doctrine. *See* Catechesis

Cierra, Rosalie, 72

Citizenship, 229–232; exclusion of women from, 233–234

Claiborne, William C. C., 246

Class, 59–64, 66–82, 254–255; at Ursuline convent, 60–61, 73–75, 125, 148–149, 156, 161, 254–255; and Ursuline apostolate, 63–64, 66–82, 150; and colonial officials, 66–67; and frontier conditions, 67; among New Orleans Ursulines, 68–74; conservative observance of, by Ursulines, 129–130, 150–156, 254–255; in Spanish colonial New Orleans, 139, 144, 148–149; and evangelical and radical Protestantism, 150–151, 154; and *Règlemens*, 150–154, 156; in early national New Orleans, 223, 226

Clausura. *See* Cloister

Clergy: disputes among, 16–18, 22

Cloister, 8, 26–28; of Ursulines, 2–3, 24–26, 55, 92, 131; at New Orleans Ursuline convent, 130–131; and Spanish female monasticism, 154; as source of conflict with Spanish colonial clergy, 218

Cluniac reform, 9–10, 12

Code Noir: and conversion of the enslaved, 164; and intermarriage, 165

Colbert, Jean-Baptiste, 163

Commission des secours, 32, 53

Community: female, 3, 60–61, 75, 129, 141–150, 160

Company of the Holy Sacrament, 28

Company of the Indies, 36, 38, 45, 47, 53–55, 64, 66; Ursuline contract with, 53, 55, 171, 201–202, 204–206

Company of the West, 36

Concubinage, 45

Conflict: between French and Spanish colonial nuns, 3, 127, 135–139

Confraternities, 18; and women, 18; Marian and Rosarian, 86. *See also* Children of Mary

Convent economy, 195, 197, 199–204, 207–216; and plantations, 195, 202; in France, 196–200; in New Orleans, 197; and investment strategies, 199, 206–211, 213–215, 240–241; and stipend, 201–202; weakness of, 202–205; and debt, 204–205, 208, 240; and annuities, 207; and slave trading, 207–211; and rental properties, 213–215; comparison of French and colonial, 214–216; and sugar cultivation, 240; and property development, 240–242. *See also* Dowries; Tuition

Convents, history of. *See* Monasticism

Converse nuns, 68, 70–72

Conversion: of Indians, 49–52, 163; of Africans and people of African descent, 80–81, 162, 164; and French Catholicism, 166

Cormoray, Jeanne, 104

Counter-Reformation. *See* Catholic Reformation

Creole nuns, 64, 87, 107, 127–130, 137–139, 211–212

Crozat, Antoine, 36

Dain, Marie-Anne, 70

Delachaise, Jacques, 27, 43–47, 66

Delatre, Antoine, 71

Delatre, Marthe, 71

Delille, Henriette, 192

Demuy, Charlotte, 128, 211

Dépôts de mendicité, 48

Dévots, 26–27, 49

Dieppe Ursulines, 199–200, 214–216

Dimanche, Anne, 78

Disease: in colonial New Orleans, 38, 43, 57; in early national New Orleans, 248–249

Dominic (saint), 10
Dominican movement, 10–11
Dowries, 72; and French convents, 197–201, 217; and New Orleans convent, 201, 211–215
Dreux family, 128
Drouillon, Louis, 77
Dubourg, Louis, 237
Dubreuil, Marianne, 117
Dubreuil, Marie Payen, 76, 117, 143
Duchesne, Philippine, 262
Dues amortissement, 32
Dufossat, Françoise, 128–129
Du Liepure, Marguerite, 137
Du Plessis, Françoise, 104

Echevarría, José de, 211–212
Economy: in early modern France, 26; of Louisiana, 36, 39, 43, 67, 124–125, 135, 202–203, 206, 213, 217, 221, 226–228, 239; sugar, 221, 244–245. *See also* Convent economy; Haitian Revolution
Education: female, 2–3, 18, 19, 22–23, 29; attitudes toward, 9–10, 12; as expression of female piety, 87–88, 92–93
Enslaved Africans, 180–184; transportation of, to Louisiana, 3, 124
Enslaved people: of Ursulines, 168–184, 275–280; population of, 169; family among, 170, 176–179, 193, 275–280; marriage among, 170–176, 182–183; godparenting among, 177–181; naming of, 178–179; creole, 180; African, 180–184; weddings of, 182; Catholic, 184–187; as source of convent income, 189; relations of, with nuns, 190–191; attitudes of, toward nuns, 191–192; occupations of, 209
Externs. *See* Students: day

Fabré, Servan Banville, 80
Farjon, Thérèse, 137

Female Charitable Society (of New Orleans), 249–253
Female Orphan Asylum (of New Orleans). *See* Poydras Orphan Asylum
Femininity: and early modern French Catholicism, 91–92; and Ursulines, 210
Filles de la Charité, 27–29, 33, 36, 44, 48, 53–55, 93, 261
Fontainbleau, Treaty of, 123
Franciscan movement, 10–12
Francis of Assisi, 10
Free people of color, 124–125, 139; as propertyowners, 159
Frontier society, 64, 71–72, 75

Galvez, Bernardo de, 214
Gandry, Marianne, 76
Gender, 5, 120, 226, 257; norms of, 3–5, 12, 83–84, 223, 229; prescriptions of, 4–5, 12–15, 195–196; constructs of, 12–15; and marriage, 196; relationship of, to national identity, 210, 263; comparison of Protestant and Catholic constructions of, 239, 243, 252; divergence of Catholic and Protestant prescriptions of, 259–264; and identity, 263
Girod, Nicholas, 228, 253
Glorious Revolution of 1688, 223
Godparenting: by people of African descent, 177–181, 184–187. *See also* Children of Mary
Gonzague, Louis, III, 192–193
Gray Sisters, 41, 44–46
Great Awakening: and women, 260
Guyart, Marie, 49–51

Hachard, Marie Madeleine, 7, 41, 55, 57, 70, 97, 161
Haitian Revolution: and Louisiana economy, 125, 135, 245; and migration, 246–247; impact of, on New Orleans, 246–247, 250–251

Monroe, James, 222
Mortification, 104–105
Motherhood: spiritual, 29, 89–91, 112, 156–157

Nantes, Edict of, 21, 163
Napoleonic Concordat, 234
Naseau, Marguerite, 27
Natchez Indians. *See* Indians: attack of
New Orleans City Council, 227–228, 253–255
Numeracy: teaching of, by Ursulines, 120
Nuns. *See* Monasticism; Ursuline nuns

Obituary notices, 73, 96–100
Oblates of Providence, 263
Olivier de Vezin, Françoise Victoire, 128, 134, 137
Oratory of Divine Love, 19
O'Reilly, Alexander, 123
Orphans, 26, 48, 57, 64, 71, 75–76, 78, 98–100, 151–153, 203–204, 228, 249, 250, 252–256

Peñalver y Cárdenas, Luis, 106
Pensioners. *See* Students
Piety: history of female, 8–12, 18–21, 84–88; Christian, 16–17; sacramental, 20, 84–86, 107; female French, 21; defined, 84; medieval, 85; corporal, 85–86, 100, 104–105; eucharistic, 85–87, 107; Marian, 88–90, 95, 108–113; active, 91–93, 121–122; and gender relations, 122. *See also* Ursuline piety
Pinckney's Treaty, 221–222
Pommereu, Marie-Augustine de, 94
Population: of Louisiana, 36–39, 67, 74, 123–124, 217–221, 249; of the enslaved, 39, 124, 245; of convent, 64–66, 74, 126, 265–273; of free people of color, 124; of New Orleans, 124, 156
Poverty: in early modern Europe, 16, 26, 37; in France, 26, 37; in New Orleans, 227–228

Poydras Orphan Asylum, 250, 252–256
Prostitution, 37, 45
Protestant Reformation, 4, 16–18; and gender, 259–261; and marriage, 260; and Virgin Mary, 260
Protestant women: in post-Revolutionary America, 236

Quebec Act, 223

Race, 223, 226, 245–247, 251–252; at Ursuline convent, 74, 82, 129–130, 140–141, 150, 161, 255–256; in Spanish colonial Louisiana, 125, 130, 132–134, 139; Spanish construction of, 132–134, 154; French construction of, 133–134; and evangelical and radical Protestantism, 154; Ursuline attitudes toward, 161
Raguet, Gilles Bernard (Abbé), 49–51
Ramachard, Marguerite Antoinette, 97, 207
Ramachard, Marie Thérèse, 97, 104
Ramos, Antonia Maria Peres, 137–139
Rebellion, slave, 134, 245–247
Rebellion of 1768, 123
Reformation. *See* Catholic Reformation; Protestant Reformation
Règlemens des religieuses Ursulines de la Congrégation de Paris (1705), 56–57, 87, 94–96, 150–154, 156, 218
Religious of the Sacred Heart, 262
Renfermement, 26–28, 43
Republicanism: and women, 233–234
Republican motherhood, 196, 234, 236
Rillieux, Marie Anne, 128, 211
Rillieux family, 83, 148–149
Rivard, Antoinette Fourier de Ville-mont, 76

Saint Domingue. *See* Haitian Revolution
Saint Etienne, Sister, 71
Saint Marc, Marie Jeanne de, 207
Salaon, Marguerite, 51–52
Sanchez, Maria Jesus, 137

Sautier, Marie Lepron, 78
Schism of 1805, 230–233, 237, 239
Sedella, Antonio de, 127, 136, 230–231
Seton, Elizabeth, 256, 261
Seven Years' War, 123
Sisters of Charity, 256, 261
Sisters of Loretto, 262
Sisters of Mercy, 262
Sisters of Our Lady of Mount Carmel, 263
Sisters of the Holy Family, 192, 256–257, 263
Slavery: in Spanish colonial Louisiana, 124–125; and Indians, 157; Ursuline attitudes toward, 161–162, 191; and religion, 162
Slaves. *See* Enslaved people
Slave society, 125–126, 221, 239, 245–246, 251–253
Slave trade to Louisiana, 38
Social control, 26–27, 45, 252–253
Social order: in New Orleans, 247–249
Social services: in France, 27–28. *See also* Ursuline nuns; Women religious
Society of Jesus. *See* Jesuits
Soldiers, 43–44
Spanish influence in Louisiana, 123–124
Spanish law, 123
Spirituality: female, 85–88
Students, 54–57, 142–157; African, 54; Indian, 54, 56–57, 64, 74, 81–82; of African descent, 54, 56–57, 64, 74, 81–82, 117, 134–135, 140, 255–257; boarding, 54–57, 74, 81, 134–135, 142–157; day, 55, 74, 150–151, 156–157, 161–162; and eucharistic piety, 106; diversity of, 141–149; French and French creole, 142–144; Spanish creole, 146; Anglophone, 146–148; enslaved, 151, 154–155
Sugar: grown in Louisiana, 125
Superior Council of Louisiana, 123

Teresa of Avila, 17
Tertiaries, 11, 19

Thommelin, Pierre, 77
Tranchepain, Marie, 42–43, 51–55, 57, 201
Trent, Council of, 17–19, 62
Tuition, 196, 199–201, 203, 215–217
Turpin, Marie, 71–72, 211

Ulloa, Antonio de, 123
Ursula, Saint, 62–63, 90–91
Ursuline chapel: and eucharistic piety, 106
Ursuline convent: and 1734 procession, 59–64; and elections, 135–139; physical layout of, 151–154; as site of female community, 151–154, 156–157; as neighborhood anchor, 160; Dauphine Street site of, 242–244
Ursuline education, 15–16, 56–57, 97–98
Ursuline nuns: teaching apostolate of, 2, 48, 52, 54–58, 91–92; relations of, with authorities in New Orleans, 3, 42–43, 58, 205–206, 210–213, 217, 237–238, 241–243; attitudes toward, 3–4, 61; in France, 21–26, 29–33; clerical opposition to, 24; social background of, 25–26, 57, 68–72, 128–129, 197–199; as inculcators of moral virtue, 26–27, 45, 48; relations of, with male authorities, 32–33, 58, 196–198; and New Orleans founders, 41–42, 51–52; in Canada, 49–51; as missionaries, 49–52; attitudes of, toward nursing, 55, 85; occupations of, 57, 70–71, 73; as nurses, 71; temperament of, 71, 73; and race relations, 74, 82, 129–130, 140–141; as allies of clergy, 87, 107, 232–233, 238; Spanish creole, 127, 130, 137–139, 212; French creole, 128–129, 137–139, 211–212; attitudes of, toward race, 157–158; attitudes of, toward slavery, 161, 187–188, 209; and catechesis of Indians, 167–168; and catechesis of Africans, 167–168, 187, 192, 194; and advocacy of marriage among the enslaved, 170–176; and

sale of the enslaved, 171, 173, 175, 187–190, 195, 208–210; and acquisition of the enslaved, 171, 187–188, 202, 207–208; and social control of the enslaved, 172–173, 175, 189–190; and manumission of the enslaved, 188–189, 209; plantations of, 195, 197, 202, 206, 208–209, 240; comparison of, to Anglo-American women, 195–196, 219; as social service providers, 205; in revolutionary France, 233; and sugar cultivation, 240; and support of school for free girls of color, 262–263

Ursuline order: origins of, 19–20; rule of, 25; growth of, in France, 29; decline of, in France, 32–33

Ursuline piety, 56–57, 72–73, 84–85, 87–88, 92–95; and *Règlemens*, 56–57, 87, 94–96, 218; transmission of, to New World, 93–95; eucharistic, 95–96, 105–108; as sustained in New Orleans, 96–97; transformation of, in New Orleans, 96–104; and class relations, 150–151, 154

Ursuline school: as site of female community, 141, 156–157; as agent of assimilation, 144–148

Ursuline spirituality, 62–64, 84–92. *See also* Ursuline piety

Vincent de Paul, 27, 262

Visitation nuns, 262

Vocation: religious, 71; and family strategy, 197–198; of New Orleans nuns, 211

Walsh, Patrick, 231–232, 237–238

Wars of religion: French, 21, 163

Women: as agents of Catholic propagation, 64–65; as allies of clergy, 86–87, 107; as propertyowners, 157–159; as heads of household, 158–159; as majority in New Orleans church, 159–160

Women religious: relations of, with male authority, 3–4, 11, 24–28; growth and decline of, 9–33; as social service providers, 93, 98, 101–103

Yviquel, Rénee, 57, 79, 100, 103, 105